Introduction to
Computer Science Using C++
Third Edition

Knowlton and Hunt

COURSE
TECHNOLOGY
THOMSON LEARNING

Australia • Canada • Mexico • Singapore • Spain • United Kingdom • United States

COURSE
TECHNOLOGY
™
THOMSON LEARNING

Introduction to Computer Science Using C++, Third Edition

by Todd Knowlton and Brad Hunt

Sr. Product Manager:
Dave Lafferty

Marketing Manager:
Kim Wood

Production Editor:
Christine Spillett

Editorial Assistant:
Jodi Dreissig

Print Buyer:
Denise Sandler

Development and Production Management:
Custom Editorial Productions Inc.

Design:
Abby Schulz

Copy Editor:
Nancy Ahr

Cover Image:
Paul Vismara

Compositor:
GEX Publishing Services

Printer:
TransContinental

We've got it all for
C++ Programming!

Our new C++ texts offer hands-on practice with everything needed to master the C++ programming language. These texts cover everything from beginning to advanced topics to meet your programming needs.

■ **NEW! Introduction to Computer Science Using C++, Third Edition,** by Knowlton and Hunt, is a thorough instructional tool designed for an introductory course of 35+ hours-of-instruction. Completely revised and updated, this third edition includes improved coverage of new topics and supports the Advanced Placement® (AP) exam better then ever. This text is suitable as preparation for the AP Exam A. This text is non-software specific and can be flexibly used with any C++ program compiler, including those from Borland®, Microsoft®, Symantec® and others.

0-619-03452-1	Textbook, Hard Case Bound Cover, 480 pages
0-619-03453-X	Textbook, Soft Perfect Bound, 480 pages
0-619-03454-8	Instructor Resource Kit (CD-ROM only; includes manual and ExamView files)
0-619-03455-6	Workbook, 112 pages
0-619-05930-3	Review Pack (Data CD)

■ **NEW! Fundamentals of C++, Introductory Course, Second Edition,** by Lambert and Nance, is designed for the first course in computer science with over 75+ hours-of-instruction. The text provides introduction to the essential features of C++ and emphasizes programming techniques that allow students to solve interesting problems. Correlated to prepare for the AP exam in computer science, Exam A. Programming problems and activities at the end of the chapters allow students to practice the material introduced in the chapter.   Ask about the second course advanced text!

0-538-69558-7	Textbook, Hard Case Bound Cover, 720 pages
0-538-69559-5	Textbook, Soft Perfect Bound Cover, 720 pages
0-538-69560-9	Instructor Resource Kit (CD-ROM only; includes manual and ExamView files)
0-538-69561-7	Workbook
0-619-05933-8	Review Pack (Data CD)

EXTRA PROJECTS!

■ **C++ Programming Projects, Activities Workbook** by CEP, Inc. and Sestak, has over 10 lessons with 50 projects. Also, there are 30 applications exercises and 11 critical thinking projects.   These projects number over 35 hours-of-instruction on the most widely used beginning through advanced features of C++.

0-538-69081-X	Text, Soft Perfect Bound Cover, 272 pages
0-538-69082-8	Electronic Instructor CD-ROM Package, 96 pages

Join Us On the Internet
www.course.com

How to Use This Book

What makes a good programming text? Sound instruction and hands-on skill-building and reinforcement. That is what you will find in *Introduction to Computer Science using C++*. Not only will you find an inviting layout, but also many features to enhance learning.

Objectives —
Objectives are listed at the beginning of each chapter, along with a suggested time for completion of the chapter. This allows you to look ahead to what you will be learning and to pace your work.

SCANS — (Secretary's Commission on Achieving Necessary Skills) — The U.S. Department of Labor has identified the school-to-careers competencies. The eight workplace competencies and foundation skills are identified in exercises where they apply.

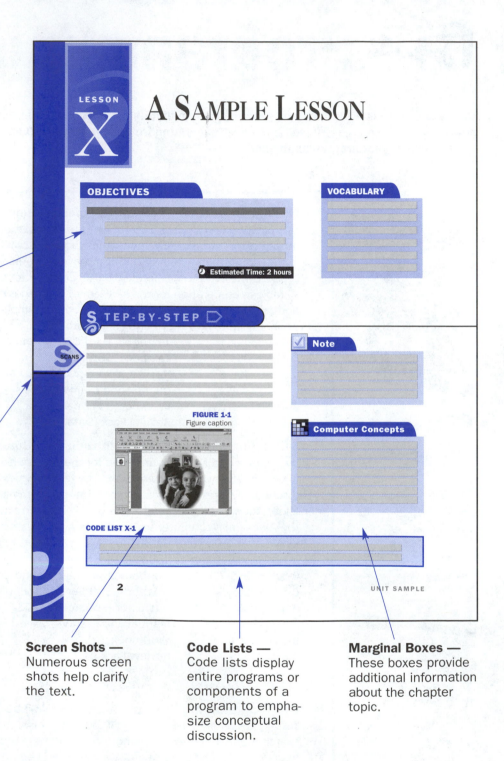

Screen Shots —
Numerous screen shots help clarify the text.

Code Lists —
Code lists display entire programs or components of a program to emphasize conceptual discussion.

Marginal Boxes —
These boxes provide additional information about the chapter topic.

How to Use This Book

Summary — At the end of each chapter, you will find a summary to prepare you to complete the end-of-chapter activities.

Review Questions — Review material at the end of each chapter and each unit enables you to prepare for assessment of the content presented.

Chapter Projects — End-of-chapter hands-on application of what has been learned in the chapter allows you to actually apply the techniques covered.

Critical Thinking Activity — Each chapter gives you an opportunity to apply creative analysis to solve problems.

End-of-Unit Projects — End-of-unit hands-on application of concepts learned in the unit provides opportunity for a comprehensive review.

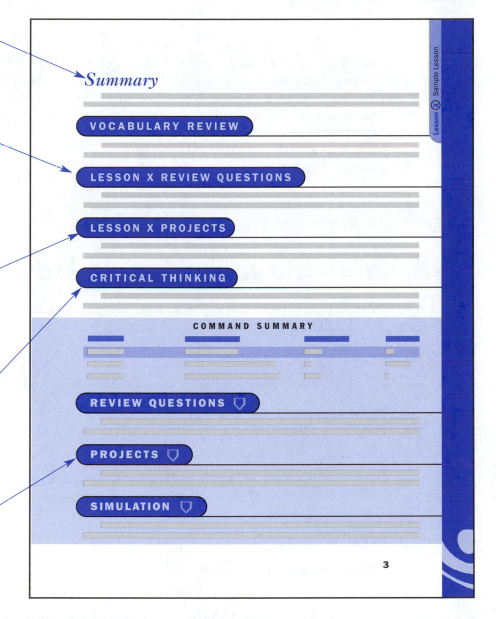

Summary

VOCABULARY REVIEW

LESSON X REVIEW QUESTIONS

LESSON X PROJECTS

CRITICAL THINKING

COMMAND SUMMARY

REVIEW QUESTIONS

PROJECTS

SIMULATION

Lesson X Sample Lesson

3

Internet Activity — Hands-on project that incorporates Internet resources for research and completion.

Case Studies — Case studies reinforce material covered in the units using C++ programs in real-world scenarios.

PREFACE

In writing this third edition of *Introduction to Computer Science Using C++*, Todd Knowlton and Brad Hunt have striven to make this friendly tutorial even friendlier. In the same easy-to-read and clearly written style that has made this book's predecessors successful, the authors have produced an improved and up-to-date presentation of the fundamentals of computer science and the C++ programming language.

This edition introduces object-oriented programming and classes earlier, uses the latest College Board AP classes, and has available an expanded and improved activities workbook by Pat Phillips.

This tutorial takes 60 to 90 hours to complete and is designed for use with most major C++ compilers, including MS-DOS, Windows, and Macintosh compilers. More information about C++ and up-to-date information about this book is available at
http://www.programcpp.com/third

Instructional and Learning Aids

This instructional package is designed to simplify instruction and to enhance learning with the following learning and instructional aids:

The Textbook

- Learning objectives listed at the beginning of each chapter give users an overview of the chapter.

- Step-by-Step exercises immediately follow the presentation of new concepts for hands-on reinforcement.

- Illustrations and code lists explain complex concepts and serve as reference points.

- Five case studies allow students to learn from complete C++ programs and then extend the functionality of those programs. The case studies allow students to see practical programs that make use of the concepts learned in the chapters.

END OF CHAPTER

- Chapter summaries provide quick reviews reinforcing the main points in each chapter.

- True/false and written questions gauge students' understanding of chapter concepts.

- Projects offer minimal instruction so students must apply concepts previously introduced.

- Critical thinking activities stimulate the user to apply analytical and reasoning skills.

END OF UNIT

- Review questions provide a comprehensive overview of unit content and help in preparing for tests.

- Unit applications for reinforcement ask the student to employ all the skills and concepts presented in the unit.

- Internet activities require the student to obtain information from the Internet to complete the activity, reinforcing Internet skills.

PREFACE

In writing this third edition of *Introduction to Computer Science Using C++*, Todd Knowlton and Brad Hunt have striven to make this friendly tutorial even friendlier. In the same easy-to-read and clearly written style that has made this book's predecessors successful, the authors have produced an improved and up-to-date presentation of the fundamentals of computer science and the C++ programming language.

This edition introduces object-oriented programming and classes earlier, uses the latest College Board AP classes, and has available an expanded and improved activities workbook by Pat Phillips.

This tutorial takes 60 to 90 hours to complete and is designed for use with most major C++ compilers, including MS-DOS, Windows, and Macintosh compilers. More information about C++ and up-to-date information about this book is available at

http://www.programcpp.com/third

Instructional and Learning Aids

This instructional package is designed to simplify instruction and to enhance learning with the following learning and instructional aids:

The Textbook

- Learning objectives listed at the beginning of each chapter give users an overview of the chapter.

- Step-by-Step exercises immediately follow the presentation of new concepts for hands-on reinforcement.

- Illustrations and code lists explain complex concepts and serve as reference points.

- Five case studies allow students to learn from complete C++ programs and then extend the functionality of those programs. The case studies allow students to see practical programs that make use of the concepts learned in the chapters.

END OF CHAPTER

- Chapter summaries provide quick reviews reinforcing the main points in each chapter.

- True/false and written questions gauge students' understanding of chapter concepts.

- Projects offer minimal instruction so students must apply concepts previously introduced.

- Critical thinking activities stimulate the user to apply analytical and reasoning skills.

END OF UNIT

- Review questions provide a comprehensive overview of unit content and help in preparing for tests.

- Unit applications for reinforcement ask the student to employ all the skills and concepts presented in the unit.

- Internet activities require the student to obtain information from the Internet to complete the activity, reinforcing Internet skills.

How to Use This Book

Summary — At the end of each chapter, you will find a summary to prepare you to complete the end-of-chapter activities.

Review Questions — Review material at the end of each chapter and each unit enables you to prepare for assessment of the content presented.

Chapter Projects — End-of-chapter hands-on application of what has been learned in the chapter allows you to actually apply the techniques covered.

Critical Thinking Activity — Each chapter gives you an opportunity to apply creative analysis to solve problems.

End-of-Unit Projects — End-of-unit hands-on application of concepts learned in the unit provides opportunity for a comprehensive review.

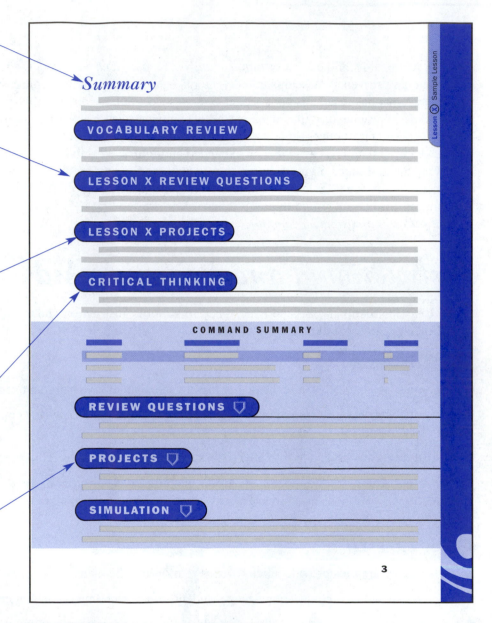

Summary

VOCABULARY REVIEW

LESSON X REVIEW QUESTIONS

LESSON X PROJECTS

CRITICAL THINKING

COMMAND SUMMARY

REVIEW QUESTIONS

PROJECTS

SIMULATION

Lesson X Sample Lesson

3

Internet Activity — Hands-on project that incorporates Internet resources for research and completion.

Case Studies — Case studies reinforce material covered in the units using C++ programs in real-world scenarios.

END OF BOOK

- A rich set of appendices provide additional information, including quick references for the AP classes.

- The glossary is a collection of the key terms from each lesson.

- A comprehensive index supplies quick and easy accessibility to specific parts of the tutorial.

Other Components

- The Activities Workbook provides additional exercises and activities to reinforce each lesson.

- The Instructor Resource Kit package is a CD-ROM that includes features such as guidelines for scheduling, lesson plans, data files necessary to complete the exercises and activities in the lessons, and solutions for exercises, projects, and activities.

- ExamView® testing software allows the instructor to generate printed tests, online exams, and an instructor gradebook.

A Message to Students

This book will introduce you to programming computers using a language called C++. C++ is just one of many computer programming languages in use today. It is, however, one of the most widely used programming languages today. Many of the applications you use every day were written using C++.

Whether your interest is software development, networking, business, art, math, science, agriculture, sales, or almost any other area you can think of, there are great opportunities for men and women who have a passion for technology. Computer programming is just one way that you can be involved with technology.

My co-author, Brad Hunt, and I have both spent time teaching students and working in the computer industry. We believe that what you will learn in the chapters of this book are important programming concepts that will serve you well regardless of the career path you choose. Even if you have no plans to make a career in computing, you will realize benefits from the time you spend studying computer science.

Over the years, I have received e-mail from hundreds of great students and teachers from around the world. I can be reached at todd@knowlton.net. You can also visit my Web site at www.knowlton.net for some links to resources that can help you with your studies and career planning.

Todd Knowlton

Acknowledgments

This book is the result of the work of many people over several years. The authors thank all of the editors, teachers, students, and co-workers who have contributed to the books that have preceded this edition.

The authors also thank Dave Lafferty of Course Technology, Betsy Newberry and Jean Findley of Custom Editorial Productions Inc., and the other hard-working people involved in the editing, reviewing, production, and marketing of this book.

In addition, the authors thank Pat Phillips for producing a great student workbook and Stephen Grassie of Smooth Fusion Digital Media Group for his help tying up loose ends.

Todd Knowlton: I thank my wife Melissa and my girls Kaley and Amy for tolerating my crazy schedule and for being my biggest fans. I also thank all the great folks who I've had the pleasure to know and work with at South-Western Educational Publishing and Course Technology over the years.

Brad Hunt: I would like to thank Todd for giving me a chance to be a part of this project and for teaching me along the way. I would especially like to thank my wife Rebecca for putting up with my schedule and for being patient with me through this process.

TABLE OF CONTENTS

We've got it all for
C++ Programming!

Our new C++ texts offer hands-on practice with everything needed to master the C++ programming language. These texts cover everything from beginning to advanced topics to meet your programming needs.

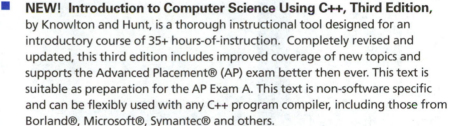

How to Use This Book

What makes a good programming text? Sound instruction and hands-on skill-building and reinforcement. That is what you will find in *Introduction to Computer Science using C++*. Not only will you find an inviting layout, but also many features to enhance learning.

Objectives — Objectives are listed at the beginning of each chapter, along with a suggested time for completion of the chapter. This allows you to look ahead to what you will be learning and to pace your work.

SCANS — (Secretary's Commission on Achieving Necessary Skills) — The U.S. Department of Labor has identified the school-to-careers competencies. The eight workplace competencies and foundation skills are identified in exercises where they apply.

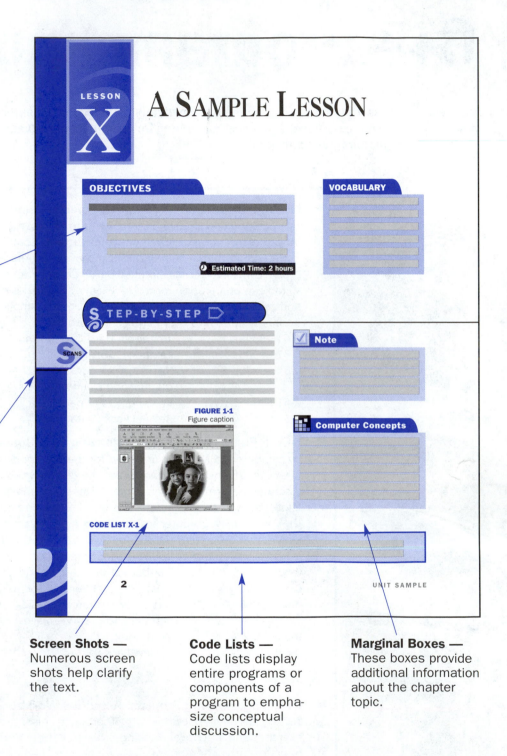

Screen Shots — Numerous screen shots help clarify the text.

Code Lists — Code lists display entire programs or components of a program to emphasize conceptual discussion.

Marginal Boxes — These boxes provide additional information about the chapter topic.

OBJECT-ORIENTED PROGRAMMING AND LINKED LISTS

UNIT 4

COMMON DATA STRUCTURES AND ALGORITHMS

UNIT 5

THE FUNDAMENTALS

CHAPTER 1

THE C++ LANGUAGE

OBJECTIVES

Upon completion of this chapter, you should be able to:

- Describe the various types of programs.
- Describe the role of the operating system.
- Describe how a computer gets instructions.
- Describe the role of a programming language, high- and low-level languages, interpreters, and compilers.
- Describe how to select a programming language.
- Describe the process required to enter, compile, link, and run a C++ program.
- Explain the structure of a C++ program.
- Access the text editor and enter C++ source code.
- Compile, link, and run C++ programs.
- Modify source code.
- Create a stand-alone program.
- Load, compile, and run an existing source code file.

🕐 **Estimated Time: 2 hours**

VOCABULARY

algorithm

assembly language

braces

case sensitive

comments

compiler

compiler directive

executable file

function

graphical user interface (GUI)

header file

high-level language

interpreter

linker

lowercase

low-level language

machine language

main function

object code

object file

operating system

programming language

source code

statement

uppercase

An important part of learning to program in any language is understanding how the software you are creating fits into its world. It is important to understand the various types of programs and how the operating system does its job. It is also important to understand a variety of programming languages and how programming languages differ.

In this chapter, you will learn about the types of programs, the role of the operating system, and the role of a programming language. Specifically, you will learn about C++ and how to write a simple C++ program.

1.1 Introducing Programming Languages

What Is a Computer Program?

Computers are complex machines. They are, however, just machines. Think of a computer as a machine that follows instructions. From the moment a computer is turned on, it begins executing instructions, and it doesn't stop until you turn it off. These instructions are put into a logical sequence to create programs.

When you perform a particular task with your computer, such as use a word processor, a computer program provides the instructions to the computer. Programs such as word processors and games are called *application programs*. Figure 1-1 shows an example of an application program. But even when you are not running a particular application program, the computer is still executing programs.

FIGURE 1-1

Microsoft PhotoDraw is an example of an application program.

When a computer is first turned on, it follows instructions that are embedded in its hardware on chips called *read-only memory* or *ROM*. On some computers, these instructions are called the *BIOS* or *basic input/output system*. The programs in ROM perform very basic operations and help start the computer's operating system.

Operating Systems

The *operating system* is a set of programs that takes charge of fundamental system operations. Application programs rely on the operating system to handle the details. Let's look at some of the things an operating system does.

1. **The operating system manages the hardware resources.** The operating system allocates memory to programs and system operations. It also can allocate processor time in situations where multiple programs are running.

2. **The operating system maintains the system of files.** The operating system organizes programs and files into directories.

3. **The operating system controls input and output operations.** Keyboard input, mouse movements, displaying to the screen, and printing all involve the operating system.

4. **The operating system loads programs and supervises their execution.** When you issue a command to start a program, the operating system loads the program into memory and allows it to begin executing. The operating system regularly interrupts the program so that other programs can run and housekeeping chores such as updating the system date and time can take place.

Some operating systems you may have seen or used are Microsoft Windows, Mac OS, Unix, and MS-DOS.

Many operating systems use graphical user interfaces as a control center from which programs are loaded. A *graphical user interface* is a system that allows the computer user to interact with the computer through pictures. "Graphical user interface" is often abbreviated as GUI, pronounced "gooey."

An example of an operating system with a graphical user interface is Microsoft Windows, shown in Figure 1-2. Modern operating systems such as Microsoft Windows do more than allow you to see your files and launch programs. They allow multiple programs to be run at the same time and provide resources that programs can share. They allow computers to network with each other and the Internet. They also make it easier to learn new programs, because each program has the same look and feel.

FIGURE 1-2

Microsoft Windows is an operating system with a graphical user interface.

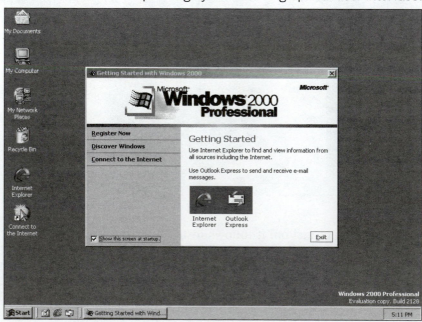

The Computer's Language

The device in the computer that actually processes the instructions being provided by ROM, the operating system, and application programs is the *microprocessor*. Figure 1-3 shows an example of a microprocessor. A microprocessor is designed to "understand" a set of commands called an *instruction set*. Although there are similar instructions among different microprocessors, each model has its own instruction set. Microprocessors can accept and carry out operations that are written in the format of their own unique instruction set only. This is one reason why software written for one kind of computer does not automatically work on another kind of computer.

FIGURE 1-3

The Intel Pentium III processor is an example of a popular microprocessor.

All instructions must be provided to the microprocessor in its native language, called ***machine language***. Machine language is actually a combination of circuits that can be either on or off. The number system commonly used to represent this world of ons and offs is called the *binary number system*. In the binary number system, ones and zeros are used to represent the on and off conditions.

Programming a computer in machine language means programming the combinations of ones and zeros that the microprocessor understands. Writing a program in machine language is difficult because even a simple program requires hundreds or even thousands of microprocessor instructions. Another problem is that the numbers used to represent the instructions are difficult for people to understand. Figure 1-4 shows a short machine language program. Each line is one instruction to the microprocessor.

Computer Concepts

You may have learned that computers use a system of on and off circuits to represent all data and instructions. To learn more about how computers represent data and instructions, and to learn more about the binary number system, read Appendix C.

FIGURE 1-4

Machine language is the language of the microprocessor. This machine language program adds 3 + 2 and stores the result.

```
01010101
10001011  11101100
01001100
01001100
01010110
01010111
10111111  00000011  00000000
10111110  00000010  00000000
10001011  11000111
00000011  11000110
10001001  01000110  11111110
0101111
01011110
10001011  11100101
01011110
11000011
```

Introduction to Programming Languages

Supplying computers with instructions would be extremely difficult if machine language were the only option available to programmers. Fortunately, special languages have been developed that are more easily understood. These special languages, called **programming languages**, provide a way to program computers using instructions that can be understood by computers and people.

Like human languages, programming languages have their own vocabulary and rules of usage. Some programming languages are very technical; others are made to be as similar to English as possible. The programming languages available today allow programming at many levels of complexity.

Assembly Language

The programming language most like machine language is **assembly language**. Assembly language uses letters and numbers to represent machine language instructions (see Figure 1-5). However, assembly language is still difficult for novices to read.

FIGURE 1-5

In assembly language, each microprocessor instruction is assigned a code that makes the program more meaningful to people. It is still difficult, however, for the untrained person to see what the program will do.

Machine Language	Assembly Language
01010101	PUSH BP
10001011 11101100	MOV BP, SP
01001100	DEC SP
01001100	DEC SP
01010110	PUSH SI
01010111	PUSH DI
10111111 00000011 00000000	MOV DI, 0003
10111110 00000010 00000000	MOV SI, 0002
10001011 11000111	MOV AX, DI
00000011 11000110	ADD AX, SI
10001001 01000110 11111110	MOV [BP-02], AX
01011111	POP DI
01011110	POP SI
10001011 11100101	MOV SP, BP
01011110	POP BP
11000011	RET

Assembly language programming is accomplished using an assembler. An *assembler* is a program that reads the codes the programmer has written and assembles a machine language program based on those codes.

Low-Level versus High-Level Languages

Machine language and assembly language are called *low-level languages*. In a low-level language, it is necessary for the programmer to know the instruction set of the microprocessor in order to program the computer. Each instruction in a low-level language corresponds to one or only a few microprocessor instructions. In the program in Figure 1-5, each assembly-language instruction corresponds to one machine-language instruction.

Most programming is done in *high-level languages*. In a high-level language, instructions do not necessarily correspond one-to-one with the instruction set of the microprocessor. One command in a high-level language may represent many microprocessor instructions. Therefore, high-level languages reduce the number of instructions that must be written. A program that might take hours to write in a low-level language can be done in minutes in a high-level language. Programming in a high-level language also reduces the number of errors because the programmer doesn't have to write as many instructions, and the instructions are easier to read. Figure 1-6 shows a program written in four popular high-level languages. Like the machine language and assembly language programs you saw earlier, these high-level programs add the numbers 3 and 2 together.

FIGURE 1-6

The same program can be written in more than one high-level language.

```
BASIC                          Visual Basic
10 I = 3                       Private Sub cmdCalculate_Click()
20 J = 2                          Dim intI, intJ, intK As Integer
30 K = I + J                      intI = 3
                                  intJ = 2
                                  intK = intI + intJ
                               End Sub


Pascal                         C++

program AddIt;                 int main()
                                  {
var                               int i, j, k;
   i, j, k : integer;             i = 3;
                                  j = 2;
begin                             k = i + j;
   i := 3;                        return 0;
   j := 2;                        }
   k := i + j;
end.
```

Another advantage of programs written in a high-level language is that they are easier to move among computers with different microprocessors. For example, the microprocessors in Macintosh computers use an instruction set different from that for microprocessors in most computers running Microsoft Windows. An assembly language program written for a Windows computer will not work on a Macintosh. However, a simple program written in a high-level language can work on both computers with little or no modification.

So why use a low-level language? It depends on what you need to do. The drawback of high-level languages is that they do not always provide a command for everything the programmer wants a program to do. Using assembly language, the programmer can write instructions that enable the computer to do anything the hardware will allow.

Another advantage of low-level languages is that a program written in a low-level language will generally require less memory and run more quickly than the same program written in a high-level language. This is because high-level languages must be translated into machine language before the microprocessor can execute the instructions. The translation is done by another program, and is usually less efficient than the work of a skilled assembly-language programmer. Table 1-1 summarizes the advantages of low- and high-level languages.

TABLE 1-1
Low- and high-level languages

Advantages of Low-Level Languages	Advantages of High-Level Languages
Better use of hardware's capabilities	Require less programming
Require less memory	Fewer programming errors
Run more quickly	Easier to move among computers with different microprocessors
	More easily read

Interpreters and Compilers

Programmers writing in a high-level language enter the program's instructions into a text editor. A *text editor* is similar to a word processor, except the files are saved in a basic text format without the font and formatting codes word processors use. The files saved by text editors are called *text files*. A program in the form of a high-level language is called *source code*.

Programmers must have their high-level programs translated into the machine language the microprocessor understands. The translation may be done by interpreter or compilers. The resulting machine language code is known as *object code*.

INTERPRETERS

An *interpreter* is a program that translates the source code of a high-level language into machine language. An interpreter translates a computer language in a way similar to the way a person might interpret between languages such as English and Spanish. Each instruction is interpreted from the programming language into machine language as the instructions are needed. Interpreters are normally used only with very high-level languages. For example, the versions of BASIC that were included with early computers were interpreted languages.

To run a program written in an interpreted language, you must first load the interpreter into the computer's memory. Then you load the program to be interpreted. The interpreter steps through the program one instruction at a time and translates the instruction into machine language, which is sent to the microprocessor. Every time the program is run, the interpreter must once again translate each instruction.

Because of the need to have the interpreter in memory before the program can be interpreted, interpreted languages are not widely used to write programs that are sold. The buyer of the program would have to have the correct interpreter in order to use the program.

COMPILERS

A *compiler* is another program that translates a high-level language into machine language. A compiler, however, makes the translation once, then saves the machine language so that the instructions do not have to be translated each time the program is run. Programming languages such as Pascal and C++ use compilers rather than interpreters.

Figure 1-7 shows the steps involved in using a compiler. First, the source code is translated using the compiler to a file called an *object file*. An object file, however, is incomplete. A program called a *linker* is used to create an executable program. The linker combines the object file with other machine language necessary to create a program that can run without an interpreter. The linker produces an *executable file* that can be run as many times as desired without having to be translated again.

Although using a compiler involves more steps than using an interpreter, most C++ compilers automate the task and make it easy for the programmer to use. Most compilers allow you to compile and link in a single operation. In fact, most modern compilers are part of a complete programming environment that helps you create source code, compile, link, run, and *debug* your programs. An example of a complete software development environment is Microsoft Visual C++, shown in Figure 1-8.

Programs you use regularly, such as word processors and games, are examples of programs written with a compiler. Compiled programs require less memory than interpreted programs because a compiled program does not require that an interpreter be loaded into memory. Compiled programs also run faster than interpreted programs because the translation has already been done. When a compiled program is run, the program is loaded into memory in the machine language the microprocessor needs.

Choosing and Using a Language

How do you know what programming language to use? The choice of programming language is sometimes a complex decision. In choosing a language, you should consider the needs of the program you are creating. How important is speed? Will the program do anything that may require features that are not available in some of the higher-level languages? Who will maintain the program? Experience is the best preparation for making this decision. That is why most professional programmers have worked with various languages to gain an understanding of the differences that exist among them.

You should not become so accustomed to working in one or two languages that you begin to believe no other languages are necessary. Think of programming languages as tools. Some languages are appropriate for a wide range of tasks; some are appropriate only for specific tasks. The smart programmer knows the available tools and how (and when) to use them.

After a language has been chosen, how do you use a programming language to actually make the computer do something you want it to do? The answer to that question is found in the remaining lessons of this book. Computers operate by following a set of steps, called an **algorithm**. A programming language allows you to provide the computer with algorithms that will produce the results you desire.

FIGURE 1-7
Compiling a program involves a compiler and a linker.

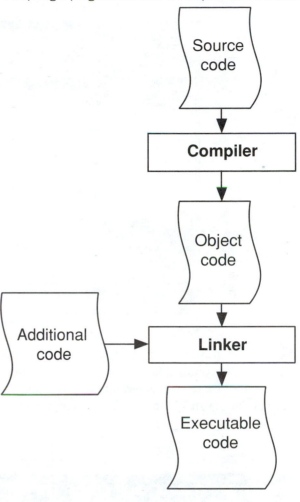

Computer Concepts

Debugging a program refers to correcting programming errors. These errors, known as bugs, can be caused by errors in keying source code, errors in the logic of the program, or other errors.

FIGURE 1-8

Microsoft Visual C++ is one example of a software development environment that includes a compiler.

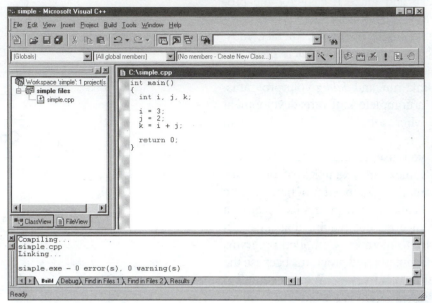

In the next section, you will begin to learn how to assemble the commands and necessary C++ language structures to build a functional computer program. You will also learn about the structure of a C++ program and compile and execute your first C++ program.

Hot Tip

To learn more about algorithms and the programming process, read Appendix D.

SECTION CHECKPOINT

1. What is an application program?

2. List three operations managed by operating systems.

3. What is the device that processes the instructions in a computer?

4. Describe the process involved when using a compiler to program a computer.

5. Why is it important for professional programmers to have worked with various programming languages?

VOCABULARY REVIEW

Define the following terms:

algorithm   high-level language   object code
assembly language   interpreter   object file
compiler   linker   operating system
executable file   low-level language   programming language
graphical user interface (GUI)   machine language   source code

1.2 Entering, Compiling, and Running a C++ Program

Using a C++ Compiler

You learned in the last section that C++ is a compiled language. You also learned that compiling a C++ program is just one step in the process of writing and running a C++ program. C++ source code has to be entered into a text editor, translated by a compiler, and made into an executable program by a linker.

Your task in this section will be to create an actual C++ program on your system. You will first examine the structure of a C++ program. Then you will enter a simple program into the text editor and compile, link, and run the executable file that is created.

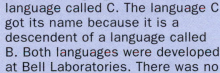

Did You Know?

The C++ language evolved from a language called C. The language C got its name because it is a descendent of a language called B. Both languages were developed at Bell Laboratories. There was no A language. The language B probably got its name because it was based on a language named BCPL.

Various brands of C++ compilers are available. It is important that you learn to use your particular compiler. At the appropriate point in this section, you will be directed to seek information specific to your compiler.

C++ Program Structure

C++ programs have the basic structure illustrated in Figure 1-9. Elements of C++ programs include:

1. **Comments**. *Comments* are remarks that are ignored by the compiler.

2. **Compiler directives**. *Compiler directives* are commands for the compiler, which are needed to effectively compile and run your program.

3. **Main function**. The *main function* is where every C++ program begins.

4. **Braces**. *Braces* are special characters used to mark the beginning and ending of blocks of code.

5. **Statement**. *A statement* is a line of C++ code. Statements end with a semicolon.

FIGURE 1-9
A C++ program has several parts.

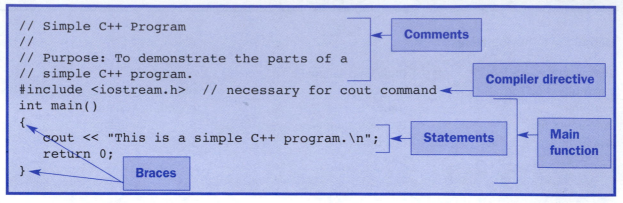

```
// Simple C++ Program
//
// Purpose: To demonstrate the parts of a
// simple C++ program.
#include <iostream.h>  // necessary for cout command
int main()
{
    cout << "This is a simple C++ program.\n";
    return 0;
}
```

Let's examine each part of a C++ program in more detail.

Comments

When writing a program, you may think that you will always remember what you did and why. Most programmers, however, eventually forget. But more important, others may need to make changes in a program you wrote. They probably will be unaware of what you did when you wrote the program. That is why comments are important.

Use comments to:

■ explain the purpose of a program.

■ keep notes regarding changes to the source code.

■ store the names of programmers for future reference.

■ explain the parts of your program.

Computer Concepts

As you will learn later in this course, a C++ program can have other functions in addition to the main function.

Code List 1-1 is an example of a program that is well-documented with comments. The comments at the top of the program assign the program a name, identify its programmer as Jonathan Kleid, and indicate that the purpose of the program is to calculate miles per gallon and price per mile. Within the program, comments help the reader identify what the lines in the program do.

CODE LIST 1-1

```cpp
// Travel Efficiency
// Programmer: Jonathan Kleid
//
// Purpose: Calculates miles per gallon and price per mile when
// given miles traveled, number of gallons used, and gas price.
#include <iostream.h> // necessary for cin and cout commands
int main()
{
  // Variable declarations
  float MilesTraveled;      // stores number of miles
  float GallonsUsed;        // stores number of total gallons used
  float PricePerGallon;     // stores price per gallon
  float PricePerMile;       // stores price per  mile
  float MilesPerGallon;     // stores number of miles per gallon
  // Ask user for input values.
  cout << "How many miles did you travel? ";
  cin  >> MilesTraveled;
  cout << "How many gallons of gas did you use? ";
  cin  >> GallonsUsed;
  cout << "How much did one gallon of gas cost? $";
  cin  >> PricePerGallon;
  // Divide the number of miles by the number of gallons to get MPG.
  MilesPerGallon = MilesTraveled / GallonsUsed;
  // Divide price per gallon by miles per gallon
  // to get price per mile.
  PricePerMile = PricePerGallon / MilesPerGallon;
  // Output miles per gallon and price per mile.
  cout << "You got " << MilesPerGallon << " miles per gallon,\n";
  cout << "and each mile cost $" << PricePerMile << "\n";

  return 0;
}
```

Comments, which are ignored by the compiler, begin with a double slash (//) and may appear anywhere in the program. The comment can take up an entire line or the comment can appear to the right of program statements, as shown in Code List 1-2. Everything to the right of the // is ignored. Therefore, do not include any statements to the right of a comment. Be sure to use the forward-leaning slash (/) rather than the backslash (\) or the compiler will try to translate your comments and an error message will result.

CODE LIST 1-2

```cpp
  float MilesTraveled;      // stores number of miles
  float GallonsUsed;        // stores number of total gallons used
  float PricePerGallon;     // stores price per gallon
  float PricePerMile;       // stores price per mile
  float MilesPerGallon;     // stores number of miles per gallon
```

Compiler Directives

Directives are instructions to the compiler rather than part of the C++ language. The most common compiler directive is the `#include` directive, which instructs the compiler to treat the text file that is enclosed in brackets as if it were keyed into the source code. See Figure 1-10.

FIGURE 1-10

The `#include` compiler directive inserts other code into your program as if it were actually keyed into your program.

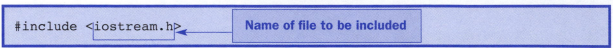

```
#include <iostream.h>          Name of file to be included
```

So why do you need other code included in your source code? The code you are including makes additional commands available to you. For example, the `#include <iostream.h>` directive that you have seen in programs in this chapter makes a set of input and output commands available. These commands make it easy to get input from the user and print to the screen.

The `main` Function

Every C++ program has a `main` function (see Figure 1-9). A *function* is a block of code that carries out a specific task. Although simple programs can be written entirely within the `main` function, C++ programs are typically divided into multiple functions, which are accessed through the `main` function. No matter how many functions you have, the `main` function runs first.

Suppose, for example, that your program needs to calculate the area of a circle. A function could be written to calculate the area of a circle. That function could be used (or "called") wherever the calculation is needed in the program. You will see examples of this sort in a later chapter when you learn to use and create functions.

Did You Know?

Files such as `iostream.h` are called ***header files***. They may be identified by their file extension `.h`. A header file serves as a link between your program code and standard C++ code that is needed to make your program run.

You may have noticed that the word *int* appears before the word `main` in Figure 1-9. The `main` function returns an integer value (a whole number) to the operating system when the program ends. Functions written in C++ often return a value of some kind to the function that called it. The `main` function is "called" by the computer's operating system. The `int` keyword allows the `main` function to return an integer to the operating system. When you learn to work with multiple functions, this will make more sense. For now, it is best to get in the habit of putting *int* before the word `main` when you write your `main` function.

The parentheses that follow the word *main* are required. They tell the compiler that main is a function. All functions have parentheses, although many of them have information inside the parentheses. You will learn more about using functions in a later chapter.

The program ends with a `return 0;` statement. The `return` statement is what actually returns the value to the operating system or calling function. In this case, it returns a value of zero to the operating system.

Braces

Braces are used to mark the beginning and end of blocks of code. Every opening brace must have a closing brace. Notice in Code List 1-3 that the `main` function is enclosed in a set of braces. Providing comments after each closing brace helps to associate it with the appropriate opening brace. Also, aligning the indention of opening and closing braces is a good idea.

CODE LIST 1-3

```
// comments.cpp
// This program prints the common uses for comments
// to the screen.
// Program written by Greg Buxkemper

#include <iostream.h>  // necessary for output statements

int main()
{
   cout << "Use comments to:\n";
   cout << " - explain the purpose of a program.\n";
   cout << " - keep notes regarding changes to the program.\n";
   cout << " - store the names of programmers.\n";
   cout << " - explain the parts of a program.\n";
   return 0;
} // end of main function
```

Statements

Functions contain statements that consist of instructions or commands which make the program work. Each statement in C++ ends with a semicolon.

Semicolons

You must have a semicolon after every statement. The semicolon terminates the statement. In other words, it tells the compiler that the statement is complete. Notice, however, that directives such as `#include` and function declarations such as `int main()` are exempt from being punctuated by semicolons.

C++ and Blank Space

C++ allows for great flexibility in the spacing and layout of the code. Use this feature to make it easier to read the code by indenting and grouping statements as shown in the sample program in Code List 1-1.

Uppercase or Lowercase

In the computer, *A* and *a* are different characters. The capital letters are referred to as ***uppercase***, and small letters are called ***lowercase***.

C++ is known as ***case sensitive*** because it interprets uppercase and lowercase letters differently. For example, to a C++ compiler, the word *cow* is different from the word *Cow*. Be careful to use the same combination of lettering (either uppercase or lowercase) when you enter source code. Whatever capitalization was used when the command was originally named is what must be used. In most cases, you will use lowercase letters in C++ programs. If you key a command in uppercase that is supposed to be lowercase, you will get an error.

From Source Code to Finished Product

The exact process required to enter source code and compile, link, and run will vary depending on the compiler you are using. There are a variety of compilers available for you to use. Additional information about compilers is provided in Appendix I.

Entering Source Code

The first step is to enter your C++ source code into a text file. Most C++ compilers have an integrated development environment that contains a text editor you can use. An integrated programming environment allows you to enter your source code, compile, link, and run while your text editor is on the screen.

Hot Tip

If the compiler you are using is not included in the appendices of this book, check http://www.programcpp.com/basics on the Internet or refer to the documentation that came with your compiler.

STEP-BY-STEP ▷ 1.1

1. Start your text editor with a new, blank file.

2. Enter the C++ source code exactly as it is shown below.

```
// myprog.cpp
// My first C++ Program

#include <iostream.h>

int main()
{
  cout << "My first C++ program.\n";
  return 0;
}
```

3. Save the file as **myprog.cpp** and leave the program on your screen for the next Step-by-Step exercise.

Computer Concepts

The "\n" causes the compiler to move the cursor to the beginning of the next line after printing the output to the screen.

Compiling, Linking, and Running the Program

Most compilers allow you to compile, link, and run with a single command from the integrated environment.

STEP-BY-STEP ▷ 1.2

1. Compile, link, and run the program you entered in Step-by-Step 1.1. If your compiler allows all these operations to be performed with a single command, use that command. If your program fails to compile or link, check to see if you entered the code exactly as shown in Step-by-Step 1.1 and try again.

2. If your program runs successfully, you should see the text *My first C++ program* on your screen, similar to the output shown in Figure 1-11. Otherwise, ask your instructor for help.

3. Leave the source file open for the next Step-by-Step exercise.

FIGURE 1-11

The output of the program should appear on your screen or in a window on your screen.

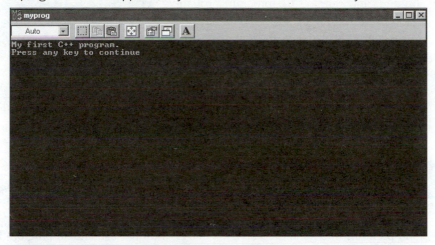

Making Changes and Compiling Again

You can add, change, or delete lines from a program's source code and compile it again. The next time the program is run, the changes will be in effect.

 S TEP-BY-STEP ▷ 1.3

1. Add the following statement to the `main` function, substituting your name in place of *Allison Brackeen*.

```
cout << "By Allison Brackeen\n";
```

Your program should now appear as follows, except your name should be on the new line.

```
// myprog.cpp
// My first C++ program.
#include <iostream.h>
int main()
{
  cout << "My first C++ program.\n";
  cout << "By Allison Brackeen\n;
  return 0;
}
```

2. Compile, link, and run the program again to see the change.

3. Save the source code file and leave it open for the next Step-by-Step exercise.

Computer Concepts

The "Press any key to continue..." message that appears in Figure 1-11 is automatically generated by the Microsoft Visual C++ compiler. If your output window appears and then immediately disappears, check your compiler's documentation for specific information about your compiler.

1 7

Creating a Stand-alone Program

Compiling, linking, and running the program probably created a stand-alone program on disk. The executable file is typically located in the same directory as the source code. A stand-alone program becomes important if you want to pass the program you have created on to another user. By passing on the stand-alone program, the recipient of your program does not have to have a C++ compiler in order to run your program. By distributing a stand-alone program, you also do not have to share your program's source code.

Computer Concepts

When you purchase a computer program in a store, you are purchasing a stand-alone program.

S TEP-BY-STEP ▷ 1.4

1. If a stand-alone program was generated as a result of completing Step-by-Step 1.3, quit the integrated programming environment and run the stand-alone program from the operating system. Otherwise, complete steps 2 through 4 below.

2. Select the option that allows you to compile and link to disk so that a stand-alone executable file is created.

3. Quit the integrated programming environment.

4. Run the executable program from the operating system.

Hot Tip

When you run the stand-alone program, the program is likely to disappear from your screen as soon as the output is printed to the screen. In a later lesson, you will learn how to write code that will cause the program to pause until you are ready for the program to end.

Loading and Compiling an Existing Source File

Often you will load an existing source code file and compile it. Most integrated programming environments have an Open command that can be used to open source files.

S TEP-BY-STEP ▷ 1.5

1. Start your integrated programming environment.

2. Open the source file **travel.cpp**. Your instructor will either provide you with a work disk or give you instructions for accessing the file from the hard disk or network.

3. Compile, link, and run the program.

4. When the program prompts you for data, enter values that seem realistic to you and see what output the program gives.

5. Run the program several times with different values.

6. Close the source file and quit.

Congratulations

Congratulations. You now know the basics of creating and running C++ programs. From here you will simply add to your knowledge to enable you to write more useful programs. If you feel you need more experience with compiling and running C++ programs, repeat this chapter or ask your instructor for additional help. Future exercises require that you know how to compile, link, and run.

SECTION CHECKPOINT

1. What are the five parts of the basic structure of a C++ program identified in this section?

2. What compiler directive inserts source code from another file into your program?

3. What does every C++ statement end with?

4. What purpose do braces serve?

5. What company developed the compiler you are using?

VOCABULARY REVIEW

Define the following terms:

braces	function	main function
case sensitive	header file	statement
comments	lowercase	uppercase
compiler directive		

Summary

In this chapter, you learned:

- Computers are complex machines that follow instructions called programs.

- Application programs are programs that perform tasks for the user.

- Input and output operations and loading of executable files are handled by the operating system. The operating system loads a program and turns over control of the system to the program. When the program ends, the operating system takes control again.

- At the heart of the work a computer does is a device called a microprocessor. The microprocessor responds to commands called machine language.

- High-level programming languages allow programmers to work in a language that people can more easily read. Machine language and assembly language are low-level languages because each instruction in the language corresponds to one or only a few microprocessor instructions. In high-level languages, instructions may represent many microprocessor instructions.

- An interpreter or compiler must translate high-level languages into machine language. An interpreter translates each program step into machine language as the program runs. A compiler translates the program before it is run and saves the machine language as an object file. A linker then creates an executable file from the object file.

- There are many factors to consider when choosing a programming language. Experience will teach you what language is appropriate for a specific task.

- A C++ program has several parts.

- Comments are remarks that are ignored by the compiler. They allow you to include notes and other information in the program's source code.

- Directives are commands for the compiler, rather than part of the C++ language.

- All C++ programs have a `main` function. The `main` function is where the program begins running.

- Braces mark the beginning and end of blocks of code.

- Statements are the lines of code the computer executes. Each statement ends with a semicolon.

- C++ allows you to indent and insert space in any way that you want. You should take advantage of this flexibility to format source code in a way that makes programs more readable.

- C++ is case sensitive, which means that using the wrong capitalization will result in errors.

- Most C++ compilers have an integrated programming environment that contains a text editor for entering source code. The programming environment allows you to enter source code, compile, link, and run while your text editor is on the screen.

CHAPTER 1 REVIEW QUESTIONS

TRUE/FALSE

Circle T if the statement is true or F if the statement is false.

T F **1.** The operating system controls input and output operations of a computer.

T F **2.** A compiler creates a source code file.

T F **3.** The programming language most like machine language is C++.

T F **4.** Programs written in low-level languages usually require less memory than those written in high-level languages.

T F **5.** An interpreter creates an object file that a linker makes into an executable file.

T F **6.** Comments begin with \\.

T F **7.** Compiler directives are not part of the C++ language.

T F **8.** The parentheses after the word *main* indicate to the compiler that it is a function.

T F **9.** Every opening brace must have a closing brace.

T F **10.** It is a good idea to align the opening and closing braces in source code to improve readability.

WRITTEN QUESTIONS

Write a brief answer to the following questions.

1. What does the acronym *ROM* stand for?

2. What is the name of the number system commonly used to represent the state of being on or off?

3. Give an example of a low-level programming language.

4. List three examples of high-level programming languages.

5. List two advantages of a low-level language.

6. Describe one advantage that compiled programs have over interpreted programs.

7. List four uses for comments.

8. What purpose do braces serve?

9. What does the term *case sensitive* mean?

10. What command or commands are used to run a program with your compiler?

CHAPTER 1 PROJECTS

PROJECT 1-1

Make a chart of at least 12 high-level languages. Include a brief description of each language that tells the primary use of the language or its historical significance. If you can find the date the language was created, include that on your chart. Some languages to consider are Ada, ALGOL, BASIC, C, C++, COBOL, FORTRAN, Java, LISP, Logo, Oberon, Pascal, PL/I, Scheme, and Smalltalk.

PROJECT 1-2

Enter the following program but substitute your name and the appropriate information for your compiler. Compile, link, and run. Save the source code as **compinfo.cpp**.

```
// compinfo.cpp
// By Jeremy Wilson
#include <iostream.h>
int main()
{
  cout << "This program was compiled using\n";
  cout << "Colossal C++ version 2.5.\n";
  return 0;
}
```

PROJECT 1-3

Enter the following in Code List 1-3, compile it, link, and run. Save the source code as **comments.ccp**. After you have run the program, close the source file.

PROJECT 1-4

Open the source file **braces.cpp**. Look at the program and observe how the pairs of braces match up. Compile, link, and run the program. After you have run the program, close the source file and quit.

CRITICAL THINKING

ACTIVITY 1-1

Given that the following languages are listed in order from highest level to lowest level, answer the questions that follow.

BASIC, Pascal, C++, assembly language

1. What language would be most appropriate for writing a quick, temporary program with the least effort and shortest code?
   A. BASIC
   B. C++

2. What language would be most appropriate for writing a program that must control the flow of data through a custom-built hardware device?
   A. Pascal
   B. assembly language

ACTIVITY 1-2

Write a program that prints the message of your choice to the screen. Make the message at least four lines long. Save the source code file as **my_msg.cpp**.

ACTIVITY 1-3

Write a program that lists to the screen the name and description of three high-level programming languages. Use three of the languages that you researched in Project 1-1.

CHAPTER 2

VARIABLES AND CONSTANTS

Computer programs process data to provide information. The job of the programmer is to properly organize data for storage and use. Computers store data in many complex arrangements called *data structures*.

Any organized way of storing data in a computer is a data structure. The simplest type of data storage takes place in data structures known as *primitive data structures* or simply *primitives*. These primitive data structures come in two varieties: variables and constants.

A *variable* holds data that can change while the program is running. A *constant* is used to store data that remains the same throughout the program's execution.

2.1 Basics of Using Variables

Understanding Variables

A *variable* is a data structure that holds data that can change while the program is running. C++ has more than a dozen types of variables to store numbers and characters. Many variables are for storing *integers* (whole numbers). You may recall from math courses that an integer is a positive or negative whole number, such as –2, 4, or 5133. Real numbers can be whole numbers or decimals and can be either positive or negative, such as 1.99, –2.5, 3.14159, or 4.

When programming in C++, you must select a type of variable, called a *data type*, that best fits the nature of the data itself.

Computer Concepts

In general, new C++ compilers use 4 bytes for the int type. Older compilers or compilers for older operating systems are more likely to use only 2 bytes for the int type.

Integer Data Types

When you are working with either positive or negative whole numbers, you should use integer data types for your variables. Several integer data types are available in C++ (integer data types can vary by compiler). Selecting which integer data type to use is the next step.

Table 2-1 lists some of the most common integer data types. The table also shows the range of values each type typically holds and the number of bytes of memory required to store a variable of that type. However, these ranges and number of bytes occupied may vary among compilers, especially in regard to the int type.

TABLE 2-1
Common integer data types

Data Type	Minimum Range of Values	Minimum Number of Bytes Occupied
char	–128 to 127	1
unsigned char	0 to 255	1
short	–32,768 to 32,767	2
unsigned short	0 to 65,535	2
int	–2,147,483,648 to 2,147,483,647	4
unsigned int	0 to 4,294,967,295	4
long	–2,147,483,648 to 2,147,483,647	4
unsigned long	0 to 4,294,967,295	4

1. Locate the reference manual or online documentation for your compiler.

2. Search for the sizes of the integer data types used in your compiler. Figure 2-1 shows the information found in the Microsoft online documentation.

3. Record the information specific to your compiler or print the information from your online documentation.

FIGURE 2-1

Your compiler should include information about the size of the integer data types.

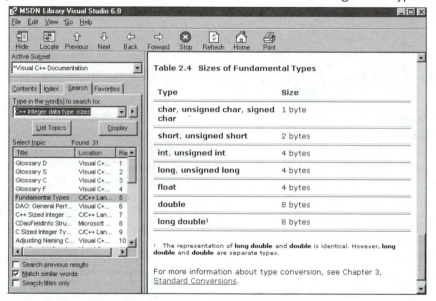

Take a moment to notice the range of values that each type can hold (Table 2-1). For example, any value from –32,768 to 32,767 can be stored in a variable if the short data type is chosen. If you need to store a value outside of that range, you must choose a different data type such as int or long.

An unsigned variable can store only positive numbers. For example, if you were to store the weights of trucks in variables, an unsigned data type might be a good choice. A truck can't weigh less than zero. If you are sure that the integers you are storing cannot be less than zero and will not exceed 65,535, then an unsigned short may be a good choice.

Why would you want to use the short type when the long type has a bigger range? The answer is that you *can* use the int or long types when a short would do, but there is more to consider. Notice the third column of Table 2-1. The variables with the larger ranges require more of the computer's memory. Saving memory used to be much more important than it is today. Computers now have vast amounts of memory. However, conserving space may become more important when lots of data is involved.

In addition, it often takes the computer longer to access data types that require more memory. Also, it is increasingly common for data to be transferred over networks such as the Internet. The smaller the space occupied by data, the faster the data can be delivered. Having all of these data types gives the programmer the ability to use only what is necessary for each variable, decrease memory usage, and increase speed.

Declaring and Naming Variables

Indicating to the compiler what type of variable you want and what you want to call it is called *declaring* the variable.

Declaring Variables

You must declare a variable before you can use it. The C++ statement declaring a variable must include the data type followed by the name you wish to call the variable, and a semicolon. An integer variable named i is declared in Code List 2-1.

CODE LIST 2-1

```
#include <iostream.h>  // necessary for cout command

int main()
{
  int i;    // declare i as an integer
  i = 2;    // initialize i to 2
  cout << i  << '\n';
  return 0;
}
```

Initializing Variables

The compiler assigns a location in memory to a variable when it is declared. However, a value already exists in the space reserved for your variable. A random value could have been stored when the computer was turned on, or the location could retain data from a program that ran earlier. Regardless, the memory location now belongs to your program and you must specify the initial value to be stored in the location. This process is known as initializing.

To *initialize* a variable, you simply assign it a value. In C++, the equal sign (=) is used to assign a value to a variable. In Code List 2-1, the variable i is initialized to the value of 2.

STEP-BY-STEP ▷ 2.2

1. Enter the program shown in Code List 2-1 into a blank editor screen.

2. Save the source code file as **ideclare.cpp**.

3. Compile and run the program. The program should print the number 2 on your screen. If no errors are encountered, leave the program on your screen. If errors are found, check the source code for keyboarding errors and compile again.

4. Change the initialization statement to initialize the value of i to –40 and run again. The number –40 is shown on your screen. Save the source code again and close the program. You may have to close a project or workspace to completely close the current program.

Table 2-2 shows that declaring variables for other data types is just as easy as the example in Code List 2-1. You can also see in Table 2-2 that variable names can be more interesting than just i.

TABLE 2-2
Variables for other data types

Data Type	Example C++ Declaration Statement
short	short temperature;
unsigned short	unsigned short k;
int	int DaysInMonth;
unsigned int	unsigned int Age_in_dog_years;
long	long PopulationChange;
unsigned long	unsigned long j;

Naming Variables

The names of variables in C++ are typically referred to as *identifiers*. When naming variables, use descriptive names and consider how they might help the programmer recall the variable's purpose. For example, a variable that holds a bank balance could be called balance, or the circumference of a circle could be stored in a variable named circumference. The following are rules for creating identifiers.

- Identifiers must start with a letter or an underscore (_). You should, however, avoid using identifiers that begin with underscores because the language's internal identifiers often begin with underscores. By avoiding the use of underscores as the first character, you will ensure that your identifier remains out of conflict with C++'s internal identifiers.

- As long as the first character is a letter, you can use letters, numerals, or underscores in the rest of the identifier.

- Use a name that makes the purpose of the variable clear, but avoid making it unnecessarily long. Most C++ compilers will recognize only the first 31 or 32 characters.

- There can be no spaces in identifiers. A good way to create a multiword identifier is to use an underscore between the words; for example, last_name.

- The following words, called *keywords*, must NOT be used as identifiers because they are part of the C++ language. Your compiler may have additional keywords not listed here.

 Did You Know?

C++ will allow you to declare a variable anywhere in the program as long as the variable is declared before you use it. However, you should get into the habit of declaring all variables at the top of the function. Declaring variables at the top of the function makes for better-organized code, makes the variables easy to locate, and helps you plan for the variables you will need.

 Note

Recall from the previous chapter that C++ is case sensitive. The capitalization you use when the variable is declared must be used each time the variable is accessed. For example, total is not the same identifier as Total.

asm	float	signed
auto	for	sizeof
break	friend	static
case	goto	struct
catch	if	switch
char	inline	template
class	int	this
const	long	throw
continue	new	try
default	operator	typedef
delete	private	union
do	protected	unsigned
double	public	virtual
else	register	void
enum	return	volatile
extern	short	while

Table 2-3 gives examples of illegal identifiers.

TABLE 2-3
Illegal identifiers

Improper C++ Variable Names	Why Illegal
Miles per gallon	Spaces are not allowed
register	register is a keyword
4Sale	Identifiers cannot begin with numerals

S TEP-BY-STEP ▷ 2.3

1. Open the source code file named **ideclare.cpp** that you saved in Step-by-Step 2.2.

2. Save the source code as **intdecl.cpp**.

3. Change the name of the variable `i` to `MyInteger`. Be sure to change the name in every line of code where it appears.

4. Compile and run the program. The output of the program should be unaffected by the change in the variable name.

5. Close the current program.

Declaring Multiple Variables in a Statement

You can declare more than one variable in a single statement as long as all of the variables are of the same type. For example, if your program requires three variables of type int, all three variables could be declared by placing commas between the variables like this:

```
int x, y, z;
```

Characters and the Char Data Type

As you probably know, all data in a computer is represented by numbers, including letters and symbols. Letters and symbols, called **characters**, are assigned a number that the computer uses to represent them. Most computers assign numbers to characters according to the **American Standard Code for Information Interchange (ASCII)**. Table 2-4 shows some of the ASCII (pronounced "ask-e") codes. For a complete ASCII table, see Appendix B.

TABLE 2-4
ASCII codes

Character	Equivalent Decimal Value
$	36
*	42
A	65
B	66
C	67
D	68
a	97
b	98
c	99
d	100

The basic ASCII code is based on 7 bits, which gives 128 characters. About 95 of these are upper and lowercase letters, numbers, and symbols. Some of the characters are used as codes for controlling communication hardware and other devices. Others are invisible characters such as Tab and Return. Most computers extend the ASCII code to 8 bits (a whole byte) to represent 256 characters. The additional 128 characters are used for graphical characters and characters used with foreign languages.

When a computer stores a character, software keeps track of whether the number stored is to be treated as an integer or interpreted as a character. To make it easy, C++ includes a char data type especially for storing characters. The char data type, however, is just an integer. If you use the char data type, the integer you store will be interpreted as a character when you print the character to the screen.

For example, the program shown in Code List 2-2 declares a variable of type char, initializes it, and outputs the character to the screen.

CODE LIST 2-2

```cpp
#include <iostream.h>  // necessary for cout command

int main()
{
  char MyChar;    // declare MyChar as a char

  MyChar = 'A';    // initialize MyChar to 'A'
  cout << MyChar  << '\n';
  return 0;
}
```

STEP-BY-STEP ▷ 2.4

1. Enter the program shown in Code List 2-2 into a blank editor screen.

2. Save the source code file as **chardecl.cpp**.

3. Compile and run the program. The program should print the letter *A* on your screen. If no errors are encountered, leave the program on your screen. If errors are found, check the source code for keyboarding errors and compile again.

4. Change the initialization statement to initialize the value of `MyChar` to 'B' and run again. The letter *B* is shown on your screen. Save the source code again and close the program.

Each variable of the char data type can hold only one character. In order to store words or sentences, you must string characters together. A group of characters put together to make a word or phrase is called a *string*. You will learn more about characters and strings in a later chapter.

SECTION CHECKPOINT

1. What is another term for *integer*?

2. What integer data type has a range of –128 to 127?

3. What must identifiers begin with?

4. What is placed between variable names in order to declare multiple variables in a statement?

5. How many characters can a variable of type char hold?

VOCABULARY REVIEW

Define the following terms:

American Standard Code for Information Interchange (ASCII)	data type	integer
	declaring	keyword
	identifier	string
characters	initialize	variable

2.2 Floating Point Variables, Boolean Variables, and Constants

Floating-Point Data Types

Integer variables are inappropriate for certain types of data. For example, tasks as common as working with money call for using *floating-point numbers*. In other words, the task requires fractional numbers or numbers that include a decimal point. Just as there is more than one integer data type, there is more than one data type for floating-point variables.

Table 2-5 lists the three floating-point data types and their range of values. The ranges of floating-point data types are more complicated than the range of integers. Selecting an appropriate floating-point type is based upon both the range of values and the required decimal precision.

TABLE 2-5
Floating-point data types

Data Type	Appropriate Range Of Values	Digits Of Precision	Number Of Bytes Occupied
float	3.4×10^{-38} to 3.4×10^{38}	7	4
double	1.7×10^{-308} to 1.7×10^{308}	15	8
long double	3.4×10^{-4932} to 1.1×10^{4932}	19	10

When you are choosing a floating-point data type, first look to see how many digits of precision are necessary to store the value you need to store. For example, to store π as 3.1415926535897 requires 14 digits of precision, so you should use the double type. You should also verify that your value will fit within the range of values the type supports. But unless you are dealing with very large or very small numbers, the range is not usually as important an issue as the precision.

 Note

The information in Table 2-5 may vary among compilers. Check your compiler's manual for exact data type ranges and bytes occupied for both integers and floating-point numbers.

Let's look at some examples of values and what data types would be appropriate for the values:

- Dollar amounts in the range $–99,999.99 to $99,999.99 can be handled with a variable of type float. A variable of type double can store dollar amounts in the range $–9,999,999,999,999.99 to $9,999,999,999,999.99.

- The number 5.98×10^{24} kg, which happens to be the mass of the Earth, can be stored in a variable of type float because the number is within the range of values and requires only three digits of precision.

Assigning a floating-point value to a variable works the way you probably expect, except when you need to use ***exponential notation***. You may have used exponential notation and called it scientific notation. In exponential notation, very large or very small numbers are represented with a fractional part (called the *mantissa*) and an exponent. Use an *e* to signify exponential notation. Just place an *e* in the number to separate the mantissa from the exponent. Following are some examples of statements that initialize floating-point variables.

```
x = 2.5;
ElectronGFactor = 1.0011596567;
Radius_of_Earth = 6.378164e6;    // radius of Earth at equator
Mass_of_Electron = 9.109e-31;    // 9.109 x 10-31 kilograms
```

Code List 2-3 shows a program that declares and initializes three floating-point variables.

```
// floatdec.cpp
// Example of floating-point variable declaration.

#include <iostream.h>

int main()
{
  float x;
  double Radius_of_Earth, Mass_of_Electron;
  x = 2.5;
  Radius_of_Earth = 6.378164e6;
  Mass_of_Electron = 9.109e-31;

  cout << x << '\n';
  cout << Radius_of_Earth << '\n';
  cout << Mass_of_Electron << '\n';
  return 0;
}
```

STEP-BY-STEP ▷ 2.5

1. Enter the program shown in Code List 2-3.

2. Save the source code as **floatdec.cpp**.

3. Compile and run the program. The three values should appear, as shown in Figure 2-2.

4. When the program runs successfully, save and close the program.

 Note

The format in which the floating-point values appear on your screen may differ from Figure 2-2, depending on the compiler you are using.

FIGURE 2-2

The program prints three floating-point values to the screen.

THE FUNDAMENTALS

Boolean Variables

A *Boolean variable* is a variable that can have only two possible values. One of the values represents true (or some other form of the affirmative), and the other value represents false (or some other form of the negative). Boolean variables are very useful in programming to store information such as whether an answer is yes or no, whether a report has been printed or not, or whether a device is currently on or off.

Some C++ compilers do not support a Boolean variable. Others have a data type bool, which can be used to declare Boolean variables. If your compiler does not support the bool data type, you can use the `bool.h` header file on your work disk to make the feature available in your programs. Your instructor can help you access this header file. Later in this course, you will use the bool data type and examine the header file that makes it work.

Constants

In C++, a *constant* holds data that remains the same as the program runs. Constants allow you to give a name to a value that is used several times in a program so that the value can be more easily used. For example, if you use the value of π (3.14159) several times in your program, you can assign the value 3.14159 to the name PI. Then, each time you need the value 3.14159, you need only use the name PI.

Constants are defined in a manner that is similar to the way you define a variable. You still must select a data type and give the constant a name. But you also tell the compiler that the data is a constant using the `const` keyword and assign a value all in the same statement.

The following statement declares PI as a constant.

```
const double PI = 3.14159;
```

Any valid identifier name can be used to name a constant. The same rules apply as with variables. Traditionally, uppercase letters have been used when naming constants. Lowercase letters are generally used with variable names. Therefore, uppercase letters help distinguish constants from variables. Some C++ programmers think lowercase letters should be used for constants as well as variables. In this book, we will use uppercase letters for constants because it will help you quickly identify constants in programs. Just be aware that you may see programs elsewhere that use lowercase letters for constants.

Code List 2-4 shows a complete program that uses a constant for PI. Notice that the identifier PI is used in the line that calculates the circumference of the circle. Because PI is a constant, you don't have to be concerned about the value of PI changing while the program runs. The double data type is used for at least two reasons. By using the larger data type, the floating-point values have more digits of accuracy. In addition, some compilers will give a warning if you use a constant of type float because of concern about losing digits of accuracy.

```
// circle.cpp
// Example of using a constant.

#include <iostream.h>

int main()
{
  const double PI = 3.14159;     // declare PI as a constant
  double circumference, radius;

  // Ask user for the radius of a circle
  cout << "What is the radius of the circle? ";
  cin  >> radius;

  circumference = 2 * PI * radius;  // calculate circumference

  // Output the circle's circumference
  cout << "The circle's circumference is ";
  cout << circumference << '\n';
  return 0;
}
```

STEP-BY-STEP ▷ 2.6

1. Enter the program shown in Code List 2-4. Save the source code as **circle.cpp**.

2. Compile and run the program. Enter 4 as the radius of the circle. The program will return 25.1327 as the circumference. The number of digits displayed after the decimal point may vary.

3. An error message is generated if you add the following line at the end of the program because you cannot change the value of a constant while the program is running. Add the line before the return line at the end of the program.

```
PI = 2.5;
```

4. Compile the program again to see the error generated.

5. Delete the line causing the error and compile the program again.

6. Save and close the program.

Computer Concepts

C++ error messages are often not very helpful to beginning programmers. For example, when you attempted to reassign a value to the constant PI, you may have received an error such as "l-value specifies const object," which may not tell you much. If you get an error message that does not make sense and you cannot detect your error, try using the help system or your compiler's documentation to get a clearer explanation of the error.

The compiler prohibits the assignment of another value to a constant after the declaration statement. If you fail to initialize the constant in the declaration statement, however, whatever value is in the memory location remains assigned to the constant throughout the execution of the program.

A good reason to use constants in a large program is that it gives you the ability to easily change the value of the constant in one place in the program. For example, suppose you have a program that needs the sales tax rate in several places. If you declare a constant named TAX_RATE, when the tax rate changes you have to change the constant only where it is declared. Every place in the program that uses the TAX_RATE constant will use the new value.

SECTION CHECKPOINT

1. What category of data type is used to store fractional values?

2. Which floating-point data type has the most digits of precision?

3. What type of variable has only two possible values?

4. Why are uppercase letters often used to name constants?

5. When is the value of a constant set?

VOCABULARY REVIEW

Define the following terms:

Boolean variable   exponential notation   floating-point number
constant

Summary

In this chapter, you learned:

- Computers store data in many complex arrangements called data structures.

- Most data is stored in either variables or constants. Variables hold data that can change while the program is running. Constants are used to store data that remains the same throughout the program's execution.

- Integer data types are selected based on the range of values you need to store. Some integer data types are unsigned, meaning they can store only positive numbers.

- Variables must be declared before they are used. Variables should also be initialized to clear any random values that may be in the memory location. When a variable is declared, it must be given a legal name called an identifier.

- Characters are stored in the computer as numbers. The char data type can store one character of data.

- Floating-point data types are selected based on the range of values and the required precision.

- Boolean variables are variables that can have only two possible values: true or false.

- Constants are declared in a way similar to variables. The const keyword tells the compiler that the data is a constant. The constant must be assigned a value in the declaration statement.

CHAPTER 2 REVIEW QUESTIONS

TRUE/FALSE

Circle T if the statement is true or F if the statement is false.

T F **1.** An integer is a number with digits after the decimal point.

T F **2.** The unsigned char data type has a range of values of 0 to 255.

T F **3.** Each char variable can store one character.

T F **4.** Variables must be declared before they are used.

T F **5.** Identifiers must start with a letter or a numeral.

T F **6.** Underscores are not allowed to be a part of an identifier.

T F **7.** Variables must be initialized because they have an indeterminate value when declared.

T F   8.   A constant is data that remains the same as the program runs.

T F   9.   Constants do not have data types.

T F   10.   Constants must be named with uppercase characters.

WRITTEN QUESTIONS

Write a brief answer to the following questions.

1. Why is it important to use data types that store your data efficiently?

2. Which floating-point data type occupies the greatest number of bytes?

3. What is a string?

4. What are words called that cannot be used as identifiers because they are part of the C++ language?

5. Why can't "first name" be used as an identifier?

6. What character is used to assign a value to a variable?

7. What is a constant?

8. What keyword is used to declare a constant in C++?

9. When is it appropriate to use constants?

10. Give an example of a program that might use a constant.

CHAPTER 2 PROJECTS

PROJECT 2-1

Write code statements for each of the following.

1. Write a statement to declare an integer named `age` as an unsigned short.

2. Write a statement that declares four int data type variables `i`, `j`, `k`, and `l` in a single statement.

3. Write a constant declaration statement to create a constant for the number of feet in a mile (5,280).

4. Write a statement that declares a variable of type double named `MyDouble`.

5. Write a statement that assigns the value 9.999 to the variable `MyDouble`.

1. Enter, compile, and run the following program. Save the source code file as **datatype.cpp**.

```cpp
// datatype.cpp
// Examples of variable declaration and
// initialization.

#include <iostream.h>

int main()
{
   // declare a constant for the square root of two
   const double SQUARE_ROOT_OF_TWO = 1.414214;
   int i;                  // declare i as an integer
   long j;                 // j as a long integer
   unsigned long k;        // k as an unsigned long integer
   float n;                // n as a floating point number

   i = 3;                  // initialize i to 3
   j = -2048111;           // j to -2,048,111
   k = 4000000001;         // k to 4,000,000,001
   n = 1.887;              // n to 1.887

   // output constant and variables to screen
   cout << SQUARE_ROOT_OF_TWO << '\n';
   cout << i << '\n';
   cout << j << '\n';
   cout << k << '\n';
   cout << n << '\n';
   return 0;
}
```

2. Add declarations using appropriate identifiers for the following values. Declare e, the speed of light, and the speed of sound as constants. Initialize the variables. Use any identifier you want for those values that give you no indication as to their purpose.

    100   e (2.7182818)

    –100   Speed of light (3.00 _ 10^8 m/s)

    –40,000   Speed of sound (340.292 m/s)

    40,000

3. Print the new values to the screen.

4. Save, compile, and run. Correct any errors you have made.

5. Close the program.

CRITICAL THINKING

ACTIVITY 2-1

1. Write a program that declares two constants (A and B).

2. Initialize A = 1 and B = 2.2.

3. Declare an int named C and a float named D.

4. Initialize C = A and D = B.

5. Write statements to print C and D to the screen.

6. Save the source code as **abcddec.cpp**.

7. Compile and run. Correct any errors you have made.

8. Close the program.

MATH OPERATIONS

OBJECTIVES

Upon completion of this chapter, you should be able to:

- Use the assignment and arithmetic operators.
- Use operators in output statements.
- Explain the problem with division by zero.
- Increment and decrement variables.
- Explain the order of operations.
- Properly mix data types in calculations.
- Avoid overflow and underflow in calculations.
- Explain floating-point rounding errors.

🕐 **Estimated Time: 3 hours**

VOCABULARY

++ operator

-- operator

arithmetic operators

assignment operator

decrementing

"E" notation

expression

incrementing

modulus operator

order of operations

overflow

promotion

quotient

remainder

truncate

typecast operator

typecasting

underflow

Math operations are central to almost every type of computer program. Even word processors, which seem to deal strictly with words and characters, involve many math operations behind the scenes.

In this chapter you will learn about the fundamental mathematical operators, and unique operations such as incrementing and decrementing variables. You will also learn about the important concept of the order of operations, and how to properly mix data types in your calculations.

3.1 The Fundamental Operators

Assignment Operator

You have already used the assignment operator (=) to initialize variables, so you already know most of what there is to know about the assignment operator. The *assignment operator* changes the value of the variable to the left of the operator. Consider the following statement:

```
i = 25;
```

The statement i = 25; changes the value of variable i to 25, regardless of what it was before the statement.

STEP-BY-STEP ▷ 3.1

1. Turn on your computer and access the C++ compiler's text editor. Enter the program in Code List 3-1 and save your source code file as **iassign.cpp**.

2. Compile and run the program. Notice the difference between the value of i when it is displayed after the first output statement and after the second.

3. Close the program.

 Hot Tip

When the instructions in this book direct you to close a program, close the entire project or workspace to prepare the compiler to work with another source code file.

CODE LIST 3-1

```cpp
#include <iostream.h> // necessary for cout command

int main()
{
  int i;        // declare i as an integer
  i = 10000;    // assign the value 10000 to i
  cout << i << '\n';
  i = 25;       // assign the value 25 to i
  cout << i << '\n';
  return 0;
}
```

Recall from Chapter 2 that you can declare more than one variable in a single statement. For example, instead of:

```cpp
int i;
int j;
int k;
```

you can use:

```
int i,j,k;
```

You can use a similar shortcut when initializing multiple variables. If you have more than one variable that you want to initialize to the same value, you can use a statement such as:

```
i = j = k = 25;
```

S TEP-BY-STEP ▷ 3.2

1. Enter the program in Code List 3-2 and save your source code file as **multinit.cpp**.

2. Compile and run the program. The program's output is:

```
10
10
10
```

3. Close the program.

Hot Tip

You may want to create a source code file that consists of the #include statement, int main(), and the opening and closing braces and use it as a starting point every time you need to create a new source code file. Just open the template file and save it under a new name before compiling.

CODE LIST 3-2

```
#include <iostream.h> // necessary for cout command

int main()
{
   int i,j,k;          // declare i,j, and k as integers

   i = j = k = 10;   // initialize all of the variables to 10
   cout << i << '\n';
   cout << j << '\n';
   cout << k << '\n';
   return 0;
}
```

Variables may also be declared and initialized in a single statement. For example, both of the following are valid C++ statements.

```
int i = 2;
float n = 4.5;
```

Arithmetic Operators

A specific set of *arithmetic operators* is used to perform calculations in C++. These arithmetic operators, shown in Table 3-1, may be somewhat familiar to you. Addition and subtraction are performed with the familiar + and - operators. Multiplication uses an asterisk (*), and division uses a forward slash (/). C++ also uses what is known as a modulus operator (%) to determine the integer remainder of division. A more detailed discussion of the modulus operator is presented later in this chapter.

TABLE 3-1
Arithmetic operators

Symbol	Operation	Example	Read as...
+	Addition	3 + 8	three plus eight
-	Subtraction	7 - 2	seven minus two
*	Multiplication	4 * 9	four times nine
/	Division	6 / 2	six divided by two
%	Modulus	7 % 3	seven modulo three

Using Arithmetic Operators

The arithmetic operators are used with two operands, as in the examples in Table 3-1. The exception to this is the minus symbol, which can be used to change the sign of an operand. Arithmetic operators are most often used on the right side of an assignment operator, as shown in the examples in Table 3-2. The portion of the statement on the right side of the assignment operator is called an *expression*.

TABLE 3-2

Statement	Result
cost = price + tax;	cost is assigned the value of price plus tax
owed = total - discount;	owed is assigned the value of total minus discount
area = l * w;	area is assigned the value of l times w
one_eighth = 1 / 8;	one_eighth is assigned the value of 1 divided by 8
r = 5 % 2;	r is assigned the integer remainder of 5 divided by 2 by using the modulus operator
x = -y;	x is assigned the value of –y

The assignment operator (=) functions differently in C++ from the way the equal sign functions in algebra. Consider the following statement:

```
x = x + 10;
```

4 5

This statement is invalid for use in algebra because the equal sign is the symbol around which both sides of an equation are balanced. The left side equals the right side. But your C++ compiler looks at the statement differently. The expression on the right side of the equal sign is evaluated, and the result is stored in the variable to the left of the equal sign. In the statement, the value of x is increased by 10.

S TEP-BY-STEP ▷ 3.3

1. Retrieve the file named **assign.cpp**. The program shown in Code List 3-3 appears.

2. Look at the source code and try to predict the program's output.

3. Run the program and see if you were correct in your prediction.

4. Close the program.

CODE LIST 3-3

```cpp
// assign.cpp

#include <iostream.h>

int main()
{
 int i = 2;
 int j = 3;
 int k = 4;
 int l;
 float a = 0.5;
 float b = 3.0;
 float c;

 l = i + 2;
 cout << l << '\n';

 l = l - j;
 cout << l << '\n';

 l = i * j * k;
 cout << l << '\n';

 l = k / i;
 cout << l << '\n';
```

```
c = b * a;
cout << c << '\n';

c = b / a;
cout << c << '\n';

return 0;
}
```

More About Modulus

The *modulus operator*, which may be used only for integer division, returns the remainder rather than the result of the division. As shown in Figure 3-1, integer division is similar to the way you divide manually.

When integer division is performed, any fractional part that may be in the answer is lost when the result is stored into the integer variable. The modulus operator allows you to obtain the fractional part of the result as an integer remainder.

Consider the program in Code List 3-4. The user is prompted for two integers. Notice the program calculates the *quotient* using the division operator (/) and the *remainder* using the modulus operator (%).

FIGURE 3-1

The division operator and the modulus operator return the quotient and the remainder.

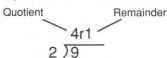

CODE LIST 3-4

```
// remain.cpp

#include <iostream.h> // necessary for cin and cout commands

int main()
{
   int dividend, divisor, quotient, remainder;

   // Get the dividend and divisor from the user.
   cout << "Enter the dividend ";
   cin >> dividend;
   cout << "Enter the divisor ";
   cin >> divisor;

   // Calculate the quotient and remainder
   quotient = dividend / divisor;
   remainder = dividend % divisor;

   // Output the quotient and remainder
   cout << "The quotient is " << quotient;
   cout << " with a remainder of " << remainder << '\n';
   return 0;
}
```

1. Enter the program from Code List 3-4. Save the source file as **remain.cpp**.

2. Run the program several times using values that will produce different remainders. On paper, record the inputs you used and the quotients and remainders produced.

3. Leave the source file open for the next Step-by-Step exercise.

Using Operators in Output Statements

The program in Code List 3-4 required four variables and nine program statements. The program in Code List 3-5 accomplishes the same output with only two variables and seven statements. Notice in Code List 3-5 that the calculations are performed in the output statements. Rather than storing the results of the expressions in variables, the program sends the results to the screen as part of the output.

CODE LIST 3-5

```cpp
// remain2.cpp

#include <iostream.h> // necessary for cin and cout commands

int main()
{
  int dividend, divisor;

  // Get the dividend and divisor from the user.
  cout << "Enter the dividend ";
  cin >> dividend;
  cout << "Enter the divisor ";
  cin >> divisor;

  // Output the quotient and remainder
  cout << "The quotient is " << dividend/divisor;
  cout << " with a remainder of " << dividend % divisor << '\n';
  return 0;
}
```

Avoid including the calculations in the output statements if you need to store the quotient or remainder and use them again in the program. But in situations like this, it is perfectly fine to use operators in the output statement.

STEP-BY-STEP ▷ 3.5

1. Modify the program on your screen to match Code List 3-5. Verify that you have changed each line that needs modification and removed the lines that are no longer necessary. Save the source file as **remain2.cpp**. Compile it and run it.

2. Test the program using the data you recorded on paper in Step-by-Step 3.4 to make sure you are still getting the same results.

3. Leave the source file open for the next Step-by-Step exercise.

Dividing by Zero

In mathematics, division by zero is without a practical purpose. The same is true with computers. In fact, division by zero always generates some type of error.

STEP-BY-STEP ▷ 3.6

1. Run the program on your screen again. Enter zero for the divisor and see what error message is generated.

2. Close the program.

Most programs that have the potential of creating or allowing a division by zero include code that checks for this condition before the division occurs.

SECTION CHECKPOINT

1. In the statement i = j; which variable has its value changed?

2. What symbol is used to represent the division operation?

3. What operator returns the remainder of division?

4. When a calculation is performed in an output statement, where does the result of the calculation appear?

5. What happens when a statement attempts to perform a division by zero?

Define the following terms:

arithmetic operators   expression   quotient
assignment operator   modulus operator   remainder

3.2 Counting by One and the Order of Operations

Counting by One

Adding or subtracting 1 from a variable is very common in programs. Adding 1 to a variable is called *incrementing* and subtracting 1 from a variable is called *decrementing*. For example, you increment or decrement a variable when a program must execute a section of code a specified number of times or when you need to count the number of times a process has been repeated.

Did You Know?

The ++ operator is also part of the C programming language, which was the language from which C++ evolved. Can you guess where the name C++ came from? The ++ operator was made part of the new language's name to suggest that the C language had been incremented.

The ++ and -- Operators

C++ provides operators for incrementing and decrementing. In C++, you can increment an integer variable using the **++ *operator***, and decrement using the **-- *operator***, as shown in Table 3-3.

TABLE 3-3
Incrementing and decrementing

Statement	Equivalent to...
counter++;	counter = counter + 1;
counter- -;	counter = counter - 1;

STEP-BY-STEP ▷ 3.7

1. Retrieve the file **inc_dec.cpp**. The program shown in Code List 3-6 appears.

2. Compile and run the program.

3. Examine the output and leave the source code file open for the next Step-by-Step exercise.

 Computer Concepts

Earlier in this chapter you learned that spacing does not matter in math operations. The only time you must be careful with spacing is when using the minus sign to change the sign of a variable or number. For example, x = y – –z; is perfectly fine. The sign of the value in the variable z is changed and then it is subtracted from y. If you failed to include the space before the –z, you would have created a problem because two minus signs together (––) are interpreted as the decrement operator.

CODE LIST 3-6

```cpp
// inc_dec.cpp

#include <iostream.h>

int main()
{
  int j;    // declare j as int

  j = 1;    // initialize j to 1
  cout << "j = " << j << '\n';
  j++;        // increment j
  cout << "j = " << j << '\n';
  j--;        // decrement j
  cout << "j = " << j << '\n';

  return 0;
}
```

Variations of Increment and Decrement

At first glance, the ++ and -- operators seem very simple. But there are two ways each of these operators can be used. The operators can be placed either before or after the variable. The location of the operators affects the way they work.

Used in a statement by themselves, the ++ and -- operators can be placed before or after the variable. For example, the following statements both increment whatever value is in j.

```
j++;
++j;
```

The difference in where you place the operator becomes important if you use the ++ or -- operator in a more complex expression, or if you use the operators in an output statement. First let's look at how the placement of the operators affects the following statement. Assume that j holds a value of 10.

```
k = j++;
```

In this case, k is assigned the value of the variable j before j is incremented. Therefore, the value of 10 is assigned to k rather than the new value of j, which is 11. If the placement of the ++ operator is changed to precede the variable j (for example k = ++j;), then k is assigned the value of j after j is incremented to 11.

S T E P - B Y - S T E P ▷ 3.8

1. Add a statement to the file named **inc_dec.cpp** that declares k as a variable of type int.

2. Add the following lines to the program on your screen before the closing brace.

```
k = j++;
cout << "k = " << k << '\n';
cout << "j = " << j << '\n';
k = ++j;
cout << "k = " << k << '\n';
cout << "j = " << j << '\n';
```

3. Save the new source code file as **inc_dec2.cpp**.

4. Compile and run the program to see the new output. Remember, you may have to close the current project or workspace to compile and run **inc_dec2.cpp**.

5. Close the program.

Order of Operations

Y ou may recall the rules related to the order in which operations are performed from your math classes. These rules are called the ***order of operations***. The C++ compiler uses a similar set of rules for its calculations. Calculations are processed in the following order:

1. Minus sign used to change sign (-)

2. Multiplication and division (* / %)

3. Addition and subtraction (+ -)

C++ lets you use parentheses to override the order of operations. For example, consider the two statements in Figure 3-2.

FIGURE 3-2

Parentheses can be used to override the order of operations.

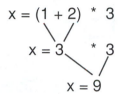

 Hot Tip

To see a complete table of the order of operators, see Appendix E.

S TEP-BY-STEP ▷ 3.9

1. Retrieve the file named **order.cpp**. The program in Code List 3-7 appears.

2. Look at the source code and try to predict the program's output.

3. Run the program and see if your prediction is correct.

4. Close the program.

CODE LIST 3-7

```
// order.cpp

#include <iostream.h>

int main()
{
 int answer;

 answer = 1 + 2 * 2 + 3;
 cout << answer << '\n';

 answer = (1 + 2) * (2 + 3);
 cout << answer << '\n';

 answer = 1 + 2 * (2 + 3);
 cout << answer << '\n';
```

```
answer = (1 + 2) * 2 + 3;
   cout << answer << '\n';

   return 0;
}
```

SECTION CHECKPOINT

1. When might incrementing or decrementing be used?

2. What operator will subtract 1 from a variable?

3. In the statement a = b++; is a assigned the value of b before or after the variable b is incremented?

4. What happens first in the order of operations?

5. What can you use to override the order of operations?

VOCABULARY REVIEW

Define the following terms:

++ operator   decrementing   order of operations
-- operator   incrementing

3.3 How Data Types Affect Calculations

Mixing Data Types

C++ allows you to mix data types in calculations (for example, dividing a float value of 125.25 by an integer such as 5). Many programming languages do not allow the mixing of data types because it can lead to errors if you don't understand the proper way to deal with mixed data types and the consequences of mixing them.

You learned in Chapter 2 that each data type is able to hold a specific range of values. When performing calculations, the capacity of your variables must be kept in mind. It is possible for the result of an expression to be too large or too small for a given data type.

C++ can automatically handle the mixing of data types (called *promotion*), or you can direct the compiler on how to handle the data (called *typecasting*).

Promotion

Consider the program in Code List 3-8. The variable `number_of_people` is an integer. The other variables involved in the calculation are floating-point numbers. Before you mix data types, you should understand the way the compiler is going to process the variables.

CODE LIST 3-8

```
// share.cpp

#include <iostream.h>

int main()
{
  int number_of_people;   // declare number_of_people as an integer
  float money;            // declare money as a float
  float share;            // declare share as a float

  cout << "How many people need a share of the money? ";
  cin >> number_of_people;
  cout << "How much money is available to share among the people? ";
  cin >> money;

  share = money / number_of_people;

  cout << "Give each person $" << share << '\n';

  return 0;
}
```

In cases of mixed data types, the compiler makes adjustments so as to produce the most accurate answer. In the program in Code List 3-8, for example, the integer value (`number_of_people`) is temporarily converted to a float so that the fractional part of the variable `money` can be used in the calculation. This is called **promotion**. The variable called `number_of_people` is not actually changed. Internally, the computer treats the data as if it were stored in a float. But after the calculation, the variable is still an integer.

The reason that data types must match when a calculation is performed is because of the way that the microprocessor handles calculations. The values involved in the calculation must be of the same number of bytes and same format to ensure correct results. By converting all values in the calculation to the data type with the most precision before performing the calculation, the most accurate results are guaranteed.

1. Retrieve the file named **share.cpp**. The program from Code List 3-8 appears in your editor.

2. Compile and run the program and observe how the mixed data types function.

3. Close the program.

Promotion of the data type can occur only while an expression is being evaluated. Consider the program in Code List 3-9.

CODE LIST 3-9

```cpp
// losedata.cpp

#include <iostream.h>

int main()
{
  int answer, i;
  float x;

  i = 3;
  x = 0.5;
  answer = x * i;

  cout << answer << '\n';
  return 0;
}
```

The variable `i` is promoted to a float when the expression is calculated, which gives the result 1.5. But then the result is stored in the integer variable `answer`. You are unable to store a floating-point number in space reserved for an integer variable. The floating-point number is *truncated*, which means the digits after the decimal point are dropped. The number in `answer` is 1, which is not correct in this case.

 Computer Concepts

Truncation is the equivalent of chopping off everything to the right of the decimal point. When a number is truncated, 1.00001 becomes 1 and 1.999999 also becomes 1.

1. Retrieve the file **losedata.cpp**. The program in Code List 3-9 appears.

2. Compile the program. You may get a warning that points out the loss of data that will occur when the program is run.

3. Run the program and verify that the result is truncated.

4. Close the program.

Typecasting

Even though C++ handles the mixing of data types fairly well, unexpected results can occur. To give the programmer more control over the results when data types are mixed, C++ allows you to explicitly change one data type to another using operators called *typecast operators*. Using a typecast operator is usually referred to as *typecasting*.

Consider the program you ran in Step-by-Step 3.10 (**share.cpp**), shown again in Code List 3-10. The calculated value in the variable share is of type float. If you are interested only in round dollar amounts, you can force the compiler to interpret the variable money as an integer data type by typecasting.

CODE LIST 3-10

```
// share.cpp

#include <iostream.h>

int main()
{
  int number_of_people;   // declare number_of_people as an integer
  float money;            // declare money as a float
  float share;            // declare share as a float

  cout << "How many people need a share of the money? ";
  cin >> number_of_people;
  cout << "How much money is available to share among the people? ";
  cin >> money;

  share = money / number_of_people;

  cout << "Give each person $" << share << '\n';

  return 0;
}
```

To typecast a variable, simply supply the name of the data type you want to use to interpret the variable, followed by the variable placed in parentheses. The following statement, for example, typecasts the variable `diameter` to a float.

```
C = PI * float(diameter);
```

In cases where the data type to which you want to typecast is more than one word (for example, long double), place both the data type and the variable in parentheses as shown in the following example.

```
C = PI * (long double)(diameter);
```

STEP-BY-STEP ▷ 3.12

1. Retrieve the file **share.cpp** again.

2. Change the type of `share` to int.

3. Change the calculation statement to read as shown in Code List 3-11.

4. Compile and run the program again.

5. Save the source code file and close it.

CODE LIST 3-11

```
share = int (money) / number_of_people;
```

There are a number of ways to accomplish what was done in Step-by-Step 3.12. The purpose of the exercise is to show you how to use the typecast operator in case you ever need it.

Overflow

Overflow is the condition where a value becomes too large for its data type. The program in Code List 3-12 shows a simple example of overflow. The expression `j = i + 2000;` results in a value of 34000, which is too large for the short data type.

CODE LIST 3-12

```
// overflow.cpp

#include <iostream.h>

int main()
{
  short i,j;

  i = 32000;
```

CODE LIST 3-12 (continued)

```
    j = i + 2000; // The result (34000) overflows the short int type
    cout << j << '\n';
    return 0;
}
```

S TEP-BY-STEP ▷ 3.13

1. Retrieve the file **overflow.cpp**. The program shown in Code List 3-12 appears.

2. Compile and run to see the result of the overflow.

3. Change the data type from short to long. Compile and run again. This time the result should not overflow.

4. Save and close the program.

Underflow

Underflow is similar to overflow. Underflow occurs with floating-point numbers when a number is too small for the data type. For example, the number 1.5×10^{-144} is too small to fit in a standard float variable. It is such a small number that the float data type considers it to be zero.

S TEP-BY-STEP ▷ 3.14

1. Enter the program shown in Code List 3-13. Save the source code as **unflow.cpp**.

2. Compile and run the program to see that the small value underflows the variable. You may get a compiler warning because of the potential for underflow.

3. Change the data type of x to double and run again. The value can now be successfully stored in the variable.

4. Change the data type of x back to float and run again. The value again underflows.

5. Save and close the program.

CODE LIST 3-13

```
// unflow.cpp

#include <iostream.h>

int main()
{
    float x;
x = 1.5e-144;
```

```
  cout << x << '\n';
   return 0;
}
```

Floating-Point Rounding Errors

Using floating-point numbers can produce incorrect results if you fail to take the precision of floating-point data types into account.

In Chapter 2, you assigned floating-point values to variables using statements such as the one following.

```
Mass_of_Electron = 9.109e-31;    // 9.109 x 10-31 kilograms
```

The form of exponential notation used in this statement is called **"E" notation**. "E" notation makes it possible to represent very large and very small floating-point numbers. For example, the number 3.5×10^{20} can be represented as 3.5e20 in your program.

You must keep the precision of your data type in mind when working with numbers in "E" notation. Look at the program in Code List 3-14.

CODE LIST 3-14

```
// floaterr.cpp

#include <iostream.h>  // necessary for cout command

int main()
{
 float x,y;

 x = 3.9e10 + 500.0;
 y = x - 3.9e10;

 cout << y << '\n';
 return 0;
}
```

At first glance, the two calculation statements appear simple enough. The first statement adds 3.9×10^{10} and 500. The second one subtracts the 3.9×10^{10}, which should leave the 500. The result assigned to y, however, is not 500. Actual values vary depending on the compiler, but the result is incorrect whatever the case.

The reason is that the float type is not precise enough for the addition of the number 500 to be included in its digits of precision. If you converted 3.9×10^{10} to standard notation, the value would be represented as 39,000,000,000. Adding 500 to that number would result in 39,000,000,500. In exponential notation, that is $3.90000005 \times 10^{10}$.

In science you may have worked with the concept of *significant digits*. The concept of significant digits states that the accuracy of the result of a calculation is only as good as the accuracy of your least accurate value. The accuracy of floating-point values in a computer must be treated in a similar way.

Because the float type is precise to only about 7 digits, the 5 gets lost after the string of zeros and is too insignificant to have ever been properly added to such a large number.

However, the double data type is accurate to about 15 digits, which is more than enough to properly include the addition of the 500 to the 39 billion.

S TEP-BY-STEP ▷ 3.15

1. Enter, compile, and run the program in Code List 3-14. See that the result in the variable `y` is not 500.

2. Change the data type of `x` and `y` to double and run again. The increased precision of the double data type should result in the correct value in `y`.

3. Save the source code file as **floaterr.cpp** and close the source code file.

SECTION CHECKPOINT

1. After a calculation in which a variable of type float is promoted to another type, what data type does the variable retain?

2. If a calculation results in the value 4.9, and that value is assigned to a variable of type short, what value will the variable of type short contain after the assignment is complete?

3. Write a statement that changes the contents of a variable named radius to type float, multiplies it by 2.5, and assigns the result to a variable named A.

4. If an integer becomes too large for its data type, what condition is said to have occurred?

5. How would you write -3.1×10^{-6} in "E" notation?

VOCABULARY REVIEW

Define the following terms:

"E" notation	truncate	typecasting
overflow	typecast operator	underflow
promotion		

Summary

In this chapter, you learned:

- The assignment operator (=) changes the value of the variable to the left of the operator to the result of the expression to the right of the operator.

- You can initialize multiple variables to the same value in a single statement.

- The arithmetic operators are used to create expressions.

- The modulus operator (%) returns the remainder of integer division.

- Expressions can be placed in output statements.

- Dividing by zero generates an error in C++.

- Spaces can be placed around all operators but are not required in most cases.

- The ++ and -- operators increment and decrement arithmetic variables respectively.

- The placement of the ++ and -- operators becomes important when the operators are used as part of a larger expression or in an output statement.

- C++ calculations follow an order of operations.

- C++ allows data types to be mixed in calculations.

- When C++ is allowed to handle mixed data types automatically, variables are promoted to other types.

- You can explicitly change data types using typecasting.

- When the digits after the decimal point are dropped from a value, it is said to have been truncated.

- Overflow is a condition where an integer becomes too large for its data type.

- Underflow occurs when a floating-point number is so small that a data type interprets it as zero.

- Floating-point rounding errors can occur if you are not aware of the data types used in calculations.

CHAPTER 3 REVIEW QUESTIONS

TRUE/FALSE

Circle T if the statement is true or F if the statement is false.

T F **1.** Variables can be declared and initialized in the same statement.

T F **2.** The * operator performs multiplication.

T F **3.** The modulus operator is the @ sign.

T F **4.** C++ allows you to divide by zero.

T F **5.** Subtracting one from a variable is called incrementing.

T F 6. The ++ operator can appear before or after a variable.

T F 7. Addition and subtraction are performed before multiplication and division.

T F 8. Promotion permanently changes the data type of a variable.

T F 9. Underflow occurs when a number is too small for a variable.

T F 10. Floating-point precision can affect calculations.

WRITTEN QUESTIONS

Write a brief answer to the following questions.

1. When using the assignment operator, on which side of the operator must you place the variable getting the new value?

2. What symbol is used to represent the subtraction operation?

3. What does the modulus operator do?

4. When is it not a good idea to perform calculations in output statements?

5. Explain the difference between the following two statements. `k=j++;  k=++j;`

6. What is the term that means the numbers to the right of the decimal point are removed?

7. When a variable of type int is multiplied by a variable of type float, which variable is promoted?

8. What operator is used to explicitly change one data type to another?

9. What floating-point data type is the most likely to have difficulty with underflow?

10. How would you write 6.9×10^8 in "E" notation?

CHAPTER 3 PROJECTS

PROJECT 3-1

1. Write a program that declares an integer named up_down and initializes it to 3.

2. Have the program print the value of up_down to the screen.

3. Have the program increment the variable and print the value to the screen.

4. Add statements to the program to decrement the variable and print the value to the screen again.

5. Save the source code as **updown.cpp**, compile it, and run it.

6. Close the program.

PROJECT 3-2

1. Retrieve the file named **salestax.cpp**. The file is a complete program with the exception of one line of code.

2. Under the comment line that reads "Calculate sales tax due," enter a line of code that will calculate the amount of tax due. To calculate the tax due you must divide the tax rate by 100 and then multiply that value by the cost of the item.

3. Save the modified source code and run the program.

4. Test the program several times before closing it.

PROJECT 3-3

Write a program that evaluates the following expressions and prints the different values that result from the varied placement of the parentheses. Store the result in a float variable to allow for fractional values. Save the source code file as **paren.cpp**.

```
2 + 6 / 3 + 1 * 6 - 7
(2 + 6) / (3 + 1) * 6 - 7
(2 + 6) / (3 + 1) * (6 - 7)
```

PROJECT 3-4

The volume of a box is calculated using the formula $V = abc$, where a, b, and c are the lengths of the box's sides. Write a program that calculates the volume of a box based on the input of the length of three sides by the user. Use the code from **salestax.cpp** as an example of using cin to get the input. Save the source code file as **volbox.cpp**. Compile, run, and test the program.

PROJECT 3-5

1. Enter and compile the following program. Save the source code as **datatest.cpp**.

```
// datatest.cpp

#include <iostream.h>

int main()
{
```

```
    short x;

    cout << "Enter a value: ";
    cin >> x;

    cout << "The value you entered is: ";
    cout << x << '\n';
    return 0;
}
```

2. Run the program repeatedly. Enter increasing large values until you create an overflow. Try the following values: 290, 1000, 30000, 35000, 70000.

3. Refer to the documentation you gathered about your compiler in Step-by-Step 2.1 in Chapter 2. Test the limits of the short data type to see if the overflow occurs where expected.

4. Leave the program open for the next project.

PROJECT 3-6

1. Change the data type of x in **datatest.cpp** to int.

2. Using the information you have about the range of a variable of type int, run the program several times to test the limits of the int data type. Test the range of the positive and negative ends.

3. Change the data type of x to unsigned int.

4. Test the range of x by running the program several times. Test the largest positive value and verify that the data type will not hold negative values.

5. Leave the program open for the next project.

PROJECT 3-7

1. Change the data type of x in **datatest.cpp** to float.

2. Run the program repeatedly. Use the following values for input and record the output on paper. *Note*: The format of the output will vary among compilers.

   3.14159
   2.9e38
   2.9e39
   5.1e-38
   5.1e-39
   0.0000000005

3. Close the program.

ACTIVITY 3-1

Suppose you have a group of people that needs to be transported on buses and vans. You can charter a bus only if you can fill it. Each bus holds 50 people. You must provide vans for the 49 or fewer people who will be left over after you charter buses. Write a program that accepts a number of people and determines how many buses must be chartered and reports the number of people left over that must be placed on vans. *Hint*: Use the modulus operator to determine the number of people left over.

ACTIVITY 3-2

Write a program similar to the **datatest.cpp** program you wrote in Projects 3-5 through 3-7. Name the source code file **floattst.cpp**. The program should declare a variable of each floating-point data type (x, y, and z). Have the program prompt the user for three values and output the values back to the screen. Run the program repeatedly. Each time you run the program, use the same value in all three variables and compare the three outputs.

Some values to try are:

3.4e38
3.4e100
1.7e308
1.7e309
4.6e1000
1.1e4932
1.1e4933

STRINGS AND SCREEN I/O

OBJECTIVES

Upon completion of this chapter, you should be able to:

■ Define strings and literals.

■ Explain classes and objects.

■ Use the string class to store strings in your programs.

■ Perform basic string operations.

■ Use cin and cout.

■ Use special characters.

■ Format output.

■ Accept characters and strings as input.

🕑 **Estimated Time: 3 hours**

VOCABULARY

concatenation

console I/O

containment

dot operator

extraction operator

field width

input stream

insertion operator

instance

I/O manipulators

literals

message

method

new line character

object-oriented programming

special character

stream

string class

string object

In Chapter 2, you learned about the character data type and that a group of characters put together to create text is called a *string*. Strings are one of the most useful kinds of data in a program. Strings help programs communicate with the user and allow computers to process data other than numbers. For example, when you prompt the user with a statement such as "Enter the cow's weight:" you are using a string. Or when you ask the user to enter the cow's name, the name the user enters is a string.

In this chapter, you will learn about using strings in C++. In particular, you will learn how to use elements called string objects to store strings. You will also learn how to input text into your programs and how to print text that has been stored in strings.

4.1 Strings and the String Class

Introduction to Strings and Literals

C++ does not have a data type specifically for strings. Many C++ programmers work with strings by manually manipulating groups of characters, called *character arrays*. Working with character arrays requires a thorough understanding of how the C++ language deals with strings. Character arrays provide programmers with considerable flexibility. However, as you will learn in this chapter, C++ also allows you to hide the details of the character array using a special set of code and data called a string class. In this chapter, you will learn a little about strings, and then use a string class for your own programs.

Recall that when you have worked with numeric values, some of the values are keyed directly into the source code and some values are calculated or are entered by the user. Values that are keyed directly into the source code are often called *hard-coded* values. Values or strings that are hard coded into the source code are called **literals**. A hard-coded numeric value is called a *numeric literal*. A string of text that is hard coded is called a *string literal*.

A single character can also be hard coded. A *character literal* appears in single quotes. A string literal appears in double quotes. Code List 4-1 shows examples of literals.

CODE LIST 4-1

```
x = 6.3;         // 6.3 is a numeric literal
cout << "Hello"; // "Hello" is a string literal
MyChar = 'A';    // 'A' is a character literal
```

Obviously, literals do not change when the program runs. However, when a literal is used to initialize a variable, the value in the variable can change.

Just as you have used numeric literals when working with numeric data types and variables, you will use string literals and character literals when working with strings and characters.

Introduction to Classes and Objects

You may have heard that C++ is an *object-oriented programming language.* **Object-oriented programming (OOP)** is a way of programming that treats parts of a computer program as objects that are similar to real-world objects. The best way to understand object-oriented programming is to consider an example.

In the chapters you have completed in this book, you have used floating-point data types such as double to store data. You have also used the addition operator to add values together. The double data type and the addition operator are part of the C++ language. You don't have to know how they work. All you have to know is how to use them. When a line of code like the following is executed, the addition takes place and the result is stored. But you don't have to know exactly how the addition is achieved or exactly how the data is stored. Those details have been taken care of for you.

```
x = x + 4.2;
```

As you learned in Chapter 1, the purpose of a high-level language is to hide the details and make programming a more rapid and dependable process. In that chapter, you saw how a simple statement is translated into many machine-language instructions.

Object-oriented programming takes the concept of a high-level language to a new level by allowing programmers to create their own operations and even data types, while hiding the details in a way similar to the built-in features of the language. For example, you learned earlier in this chapter that C++ has no built-in string data type. The object-oriented features of C++, however, allow you (or better yet, someone else) to create a string data type for you to use. And just as for the double data type, you will not have to know how the string data type works. You will just have to know how to use it.

When working with OOP, it is important to understand some basic object-oriented programming terms. To learn these terms, let's stick with the example of the object-oriented string data type. An object-oriented string data type is referred to as a *string class*. A string class is actually a definition used to create a *string object*.

The distinction between a *class* and an *object* is important. Think of a class as a generic definition from which an object is created. In the real world, dog would be an example of a class, while Rover would be an object based on the dog class. An object is said to be an *instance* of a class. Therefore, Rover is an instance of the dog class. Or, in programming terms, a string object is an instance of a string class. In order to store an actual string, a programmer creates a string object using a string class.

This will all make more sense once you have used a class yourself. In the Step-by-Step exercises ahead, you will use a string class that is provided with this textbook to store strings.

Using the String Class

Using the string class is a little more complicated than using the built-in data types. However, once you have mastered a few simple tasks, you will see how easy using the string class really is.

Preparing to Use the String Class

To use the string class, you must include a header file in your source code, in this case apstring.h. The string class used in this book is the string class provided by the College Board for Advanced Placement Computer Science. The class consists of two files: **apstring.h** and **apstring.cpp**. Your compiler must also be set up properly to compile a program that uses the string class. Specific instructions for some of the more commonly used compilers are provided in appendices at the end of this book.

To give the string class a try with your compiler, let's compile and run a program that uses the string class.

 Hot Tip

If your compiler does not have the bool data type, you will receive an error message when you compile **apstring.cpp**. See the special instructions in Appendix F.

STEP-BY-STEP 4.1

1. Open **apstring.cpp** and **stringex.cpp** into a project in your compiler. The file **apstring.h** must also be available to your compiler.

2. Compile and run the program. The program creates a string object, assigns the string

"Hello World!" to the string object, and prints the string to the screen.

3. Leave the project open for the next Step-by-Step exercise.

Declaring a String Object

Now that you have successfully compiled and run a program that uses the string class, we can look at the features offered by the string class.

When you declare a string object, you can create an empty string object or you can initialize the object with a string. As the code in Code List 4-2 shows, the process of declaring a string object is similar to declaring other data.

CODE LIST 4-2

```
apstring MyString1;              // declaring an empty string object
apstring MyString2("ABCDEF"); // initializing while declaring
```

Assigning Strings to String Objects

You can assign strings to string objects in one of three ways:

1. You can assign the contents of one string object to another string object.

2. You can assign a string literal to a string object.

3. You can assign a character literal to a string object.

Code List 4-3 shows an example of each of the three ways to assign a string to a string object.

 Did You Know?

The string class uses an array of characters that can adjust its length as the program runs. Therefore, when you declare a string object, declaring a size is not necessary. When you assign a string to the object, the length is adjusted to properly contain the string. There is no official limitation on the length of a string in a string object. A string object can easily hold thousands of characters.

CODE LIST 4-3

```
MyString1 = MyString2;
MyString1 = "string literal";
MyString1 = 'A';
```

Printing the Contents of a String Object to the Screen

You can use cout to display the contents of a string object. The following statement shows a typical line of code that outputs the contents of a string class.

```
cout << MyString1 << '\n';
```

1. Modify the source code of **stringex.cpp** to match the program in Code List 4-4.

2. Save the source code. Compile and run the program. The program stores two strings using separate objects.

3. Leave the program open for the next Step-by-Step exercise.

CODE LIST 4-4

```
// stringex.cpp

#include <iostream.h>
#include "apstring.h"

int main()
{
  apstring MyString1;
  apstring MyString2("ABCDEFGHIJKLMNOPQRSTUVWXYZ");

  MyString1 = "Hello World!";

  cout << MyString1 << '\n';
  cout << MyString2 << '\n';

  return 0;
}
```

Step-by-Step 4.2 is an example of how more than one object can be created from the same class. A program can include as many string objects as necessary. The name of the object is used to distinguish among them.

String Operations

Programs that use strings often need to perform a variety of operations on the strings they have stored. For example, to properly center a string, you may need to know the number of characters in the string. You may also need to add strings together.

One of the reasons objects are especially useful is that

Computer Concepts

The #include statements you have been using have placed the filename being included in angle brackets (<>). These are pre-compiled libraries that are stored in a special directory when the compiler is installed. When you include apstring.h, you place it in double quotes to tell the compiler that it is not pre-compiled and to look for it in the current directory.

they do more than hold data. Objects also perform operations on the data they hold. A string object is no exception. In fact, as you will see, a string object is a great example of an object that holds data and performs operations on that data.

Messages

One of the important concepts behind the use of objects is the idea of ***containment*** (or *encapsulation*). These terms refer to the way an object hides the details of how data are stored and how operations work. The data, and the code required to work with that data, are contained or encapsulated within the object itself. To make the object do what we want it to do, we send the object a ***message***.

For example, when you want to know the length of the string stored in a string object, you send the object a message that asks the object to report the string's length. How it calculates the length of the string doesn't matter. We just want an accurate answer. It is the object's job to provide that answer.

Obtaining the Length of a String

The message used to obtain the length of a string is simply *length*. The following statement shows an example of the code required to send the length message to a string object.

```
l = MyString2.length();
```

Let's look at the statement piece by piece. First, `l` is an integer variable that will store the length that the object reports. The assignment operator (=) assigns the value returned by the string object to the variable `l`. `MyString2` is the name of the string object to which we want to send the message. The period that follows the name of the object is called the ***dot operator*** (or *class-member operator*). The dot operator separates the name of the object from the message, in this case `length`.

The code inside the object that performs the length operation is called a ***method***. Therefore, when you are sending the length message you could say that you are using the string class' length method.

S TEP-BY-STEP ▷ 4.3

1. Modify the source code of **stringex.cpp** to match the program in Code List 4-5. See if you can predict the output of the program.

2. Save the source code. Compile and run the program to see if your prediction was correct.

3. Leave the program open for the next Step-by-Step exercise.

```
// stringex.cpp

#include <iostream.h>
#include "apstring.h"

int main()
{
  int len1, len2;
  apstring MyString1;
  apstring MyString2("ABCDEFGHIJKLMNOPQRSTUVWXYZ");


  MyString1 = "Hello World!";

  len1 = MyString1.length();
  len2 = MyString2.length();

  cout << MyString1 << '\n';
  cout << "Length = " << len1 << '\n';
  cout << MyString2 << '\n';
  cout << "Length = " << len2 << '\n';


  return 0;
}
```

String Concatenation

Concatenation is a big word that describes the operation of adding one string onto the end of another string. Suppose, for example, that you have one string object holding a first name and another string object holding a last name. To get both strings together in one string object, you need to concatenate the last name onto the first name. Actually, you would first concatenate a space onto the end of the first name to insert a space between the first and last names.

The string class includes the ability to perform concatenation. To make the concatenation process the most flexible, the string class offers two operators for performing concatenation. The most intuitive operator to use is the + operator. The + operator can be used to add two string objects together or to add a character literal before or after an existing string. The class also allows use of a compound operator, which we will look at in a moment.

Consider the statements in Code List 4-6. The statements build a new string in MyString1 using the + operator to perform concatenations. The statement adds a space to MyString1 before adding the second string object. Therefore, the resulting string has a space between the first and last names.

```
MyString1 = "Tracy";
MyString2 = "Stewart";

MyString1 = MyString1 + ' ' + MyString2;

cout << MyString1 << '\n';
```

The other allowable form of string concatenation makes use of an operator called a *compound operator*. The operator is +=. The += operator is specifically intended to provide a shorthand method for adding a value to an existing variable or object. For example, x += 1 is equivalent to x = x + 1. Table 4-1 provides some additional examples.

TABLE 4-1
Concatenation examples

Shorthand Method	Long Method
j += 7;	j = j + 7;
k += n;	k = k + n;

To concatenate strings using the compound operator, use statements like the examples in Table 4-2.

TABLE 4-2
Concatenation statements

Statement	Description
MyString1 += MyString2;	Add MyString2 to the end of MyString1
MyString1 += "string literal";	Add a string literal to the end of MyString1
MyString1 += Ch;	Add a character to the end of MyString1
MyString1 += 'A';	Add a character literal to the end of MyString1

The decision of whether to use the + or += operator is determined on a case-by-case basis. If your code needs to simply add a string object, a string literal, or a character to an existing string object, then the compound operator may be the best choice. The + operator, however, can accomplish anything the compound operator can do.

STEP-BY-STEP ▷ 4.4

1. Add the code in Code List 4-6 to the end of the program on your screen (before the `return 0;`). Can you predict the output of the concatenated string?

2. Compile and run the program to see the result of the concatenation.

3. Close the program.

SECTION CHECKPOINT

1. What kind of literal appears in single quotes?

2. Explain the distinction between a class and an object.

3. Explain the concept of encapsulation.

4. What is the method used to determine the length of a string in a string object?

5. What is the compound operator used to concatenate strings?

VOCABULARY REVIEW

Define the following terms:

concatenation	literals	object-oriented programming
containment	message	string class
dot operator	method	string object
instance		

4.2 Input and Output Using cin and cout

We have treated cin and cout (pronounced "see-in" and "see-out") as commands up to this point. You may be surprised, however, to learn that the << and >> symbols actually represent the action. Consider the following simple statements.

```
cout << j;
cin >> i;
```

The << and >> symbols are operators, as + and * are operators. The << symbol is the output operator, and >> is the input operator. As you know, the variable to the right of the << or >> operator is what is being input or output. So what are cout and cin? They are actually objects. The cout object is the destination of the output, and the cin object is the source of the input.

 Warning

The `#include <iostream.h>` directive is required to use streams.

Streams

The cin and cout objects are known as streams. When you think of a stream, you probably think of water flowing from one place to another. In C++, a *stream* is data flowing from one place to another. You should think of C++ streams as channels that exist to provide an easy way to get data to and from devices. The stream that brings data from your keyboard is cin, and the stream that takes data to your screen is cout.

Some beginning programmers find it difficult to remember when to use << and when to use >>. There is a method you can use to help you remember. The symbols in the input and output operators point in the direction that the data is flowing. For example, in the statement `cout << j;`, the data is flowing from the variable `j` to the destination of the output (`cout`). When you use the input operator (as in `cin >> i;`), the data flows from the source of the input (`cin`) to the variable `i`.

For example, your monitor (screen) is a device. You don't have to understand exactly how output gets to the screen. You just have to know that the cout object is the stream that leads to your screen. When you use the output operator to place something in the cout stream, your screen is the destination.

Using Console I/O

The term *console I/O* refers to using the screen and keyboard for input and output (I/O is an abbreviation of input/output). In other words, the standard use of cin and cout is console I/O. Let's look at some examples of console I/O to make sure you understand the role of each part of the statements.

Figure 4-1 illustrates the general form of the << operator. The << operator indicates to the compiler that the statement is producing output. The destination of the output is the standard output device (the screen). The output can be any valid C++ expression.

FIGURE 4-1
The << operator is used for output.

Output stream

Output expression

```
cout << expression;
```

Extraction operator

The examples in Code List 4-7 show how the output can be a string literal, a variable, or a mathematical expression. The figure also shows that more than one item can be output in a single statement by using multiple output operators.

CODE LIST 4-7

```
cout << "This string literal will appear on the screen. \n";
cout << distance;
cout << length_of_room * width_of_room;
cout << "The room is " << area << " square feet.\n";
```

Figure 4-2 illustrates the general form of the >> operator. The >> operator tells the compiler that the statement is requesting input. The source of the input is the standard input device (the keyboard). The destination of the input must be a variable or variables.

FIGURE 4-2

The >> operator is used for input.

Variable receiving input

Input stream

cin >> variable;

Insertion operator

Note

Remember, << is an operator. Therefore, you can use it many times in the same output expression, just as you can use a mathematical operator multiple times in the same expression. For example, the statement n = 2 + 4 + 5 uses the addition operator twice. In the same way, the output operator can appear more than once in a statement.

S TEP-BY-STEP ▷ 4.5

1. Load, compile, and run **basicio.cpp** to review the basic use of input and output operators.

2. Close the program.

New Line and Other Special Characters

You have been including '\n' in output statements without a good explanation of what '\n' does. It is an important part of formatting output because it causes the cursor to return to the next line of the screen. The \n character is one of the special characters available in C++.

What Is \n?

The \n character is called the ***new line character*** or the *end-of-line character*. Use it in any output statement that completes a line. The new line character has the same effect in an output statement as pressing the Return or Enter key in a word processor.

The \n character must appear in double quotes if it is used in conjunction with other characters or may be used with single quotes if it appears alone. See the examples in Code List 4-8.

CODE LIST 4-8

```
cout << i << '\n';  // single quotes because it is a single character
cout << "String\n"; // double quotes because it is part of a string
```

Special Characters

The end-of-line character is called a ***special character***. Although \n appears as two characters in the source code, the compiler interprets it as one character. The backslash (\) tells the compiler that a special character is being formed. The reason for this system is because there is no single keyboard character available to represent the end-of-line character.

Table 4-3 shows other special characters available for use in output statements. The first one generates a tab character. The others are used to print characters to the screen that would otherwise be unprintable because they have other meanings to the compiler. For example, because the backslash is used by the compiler to signify a special character, you must use a special character to print a back-slash. There are also special characters for printing single and double quote marks.

Hot Tip

The \n character can be enclosed in double quotes, even when it appears alone. The compiler will treat the character as a string because it is in double quotes. The statement will, however, produce the same result.

TABLE 4-3
Special characters used in output statements

Character Sequence	Result
\t	Generates a tab character to move the cursor to the next tab stop.
\\	Prints a backslash (\).
\'	Prints a single quote mark (').
\"	Prints a double quote mark (").

Using endl

There is an alternative to \n that you may find easier to enter and more readable. You can enter endl in the place of '\n'. For example, the two statements in Code List 4-9 are functionally identical.

CODE LIST 4-9

```
cout << i << '\n';
cout << i << endl;
```

You can use endl in place of the character '\n', but do not use endl as part of a larger string. Think of endl as a constant that holds the value '\n'. If used in a statement such as cout << "String endl";, the endl will be considered as part of the string, and no end-of-line char-acter will be included. To use endl with string literals, use a statement like the following.

```
cout << "How now brown cow." << endl;
```

STEP-BY-STEP ▷ 4.6

1. Enter the program shown in Code List 4-10. Save the source code as **specchar.cpp**.

2. Compile and run the program. The output window should appear similar to Figure 4-3.

THE FUNDAMENTALS

3. Compare the output on your screen to the statements in the source code to see that you understand the way the output was achieved.

4. Add the numbers 5 and 6 to the line of tab-separated numerals. Be sure to include the tab character in between the numbers.

5. Run the program again to verify that your modifications worked.

6. Add a statement before the first cout statement that prints your name to the screen in double quote marks. For example, "Dale Lee".

7. Run the program again.

8. When you have the program producing the correct output, close the program.

FIGURE 4-3

The special characters allow you to print characters to the screen that you otherwise would not be able to display.

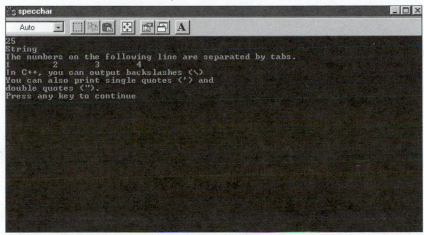

CODE LIST 4-10

```
// specchar.cpp
// Example of new line and special characters

#include <iostream.h>

int main()
{
  int i;

  i = 25;
  cout << i << '\n';  // single quotes because it is a single character
  cout << "String\n"; // double quotes because it is part of a string

  cout << "The numbers on the following line are separated by tabs.\n";
  cout << "1 \t 2 \t 3 \t 4 \n";
```

```
      // The following lines use endl
      cout << "In C++, you can output backslashes (\\)" << endl;
      cout << "You can also print single quotes (\') and" << endl;
      cout << "double quotes (\")." << endl;

      return 0;
}
```

Using setf and unsetf

The cout object has format options that can be changed. To change these options, you send a message to the object using setf and unsetf. Table 4-4 lists the options that can be used.

Hot Tip

The exact result of the format options may vary slightly among compilers.

TABLE 4-4
Cout format options

Option	Description
left	Left-justifies the output
right	Right-justifies the output
showpoint	Displays decimal point and trailing zeros for all floating-point numbers, even if the decimal places are not needed
uppercase	Displays the "e" in "E" notation as "E" rather than "e"
showpos	Displays a leading plus sign before positive values
scientific	Displays floating-point numbers in scientific ("E") notation
fixed	Displays floating-point numbers in normal notation

Now, examine how the format option *right* (indicating that the output is to be right justified) is used in the following expanded format statement.

```
cout.setf(ios::right);
```

THE FUNDAMENTALS

You will learn more about how to use statements like the preceding one later. What is important now is that you understand that the word *right* is the format option and the setf method is what changes the option in the cout object.

You can remove the options by replacing setf with unsetf, as in the following example.

Did You Know?

If neither the scientific nor fixed option is set, most compilers decide the method to display floating-point numbers based on whether the number can be displayed more efficiently in scientific or fixed notation.

```
cout.unsetf(ios::scientific);
```

STEP-BY-STEP ▷ 4.7

1. Enter the program in Code List 4-11 and save the source code file as **coutsetf.cpp**.

2. Run the program to see how the format options change the output. Your compiler's

results may vary slightly from the predictions made in the program's comments.

3. Close the program.

CODE LIST 4-11

```
// coutsetf.cpp

#include <iostream.h>

int main()
{
  float x = 24.0;

  cout << x << endl;           // displays 24

  cout.setf(ios::showpoint);
  cout << x << endl;           // displays 24.0000

  cout.setf(ios::showpos);
  cout << x << endl;           // displays +24.0000

  cout.setf(ios::scientific);
  cout << x << endl;           // displays +2.400000e+001

  cout.setf(ios::uppercase);
  cout << x << endl;           // displays +2.400000E+001

  cout.unsetf(ios::showpoint);
  cout << x << endl;           // displays +2.400000E+001
```

```
    cout.unsetf(ios::showpos);
    cout << x << endl;              // displays 2.400000E+001

    cout.unsetf(ios::uppercase);
    cout << x << endl;              // displays 2.400000e+001

    cout.unsetf(ios::scientific);
    cout << x << endl;              // displays 24

    return 0;
}
```

Using the I/O Manipulators

Another set of format options available in C++ is the *I/O manipulators*. The most common of these are setprecision and setw. They may be placed directly in the output statement.

Using setprecision

When used in conjunction with the fixed format option, the setprecision I/O manipulator sets the number of digits that are to appear to the right of the decimal point. This is very convenient when printing amounts where a specific number of digits is important—for example, when printing dollars and cents.

Look at the example in Code List 4-12. First the fixed format option is set. Then in the output statement, the desired precision is set. The setprecision manipulator sets the number of digits displayed to the number provided in the parentheses. The setprecision manipulator affects all floating-point numbers that follow it in the statement. It also affects any floating-point numbers output to the cout stream until setprecision is called again to set another precision.

Computer Concepts

If you do not set the fixed option before using setprecision, the results will vary, depending on your compiler. Some compilers will set the number of digits to the right of the decimal point anyway. Others will set the overall number of digits on both sides of the decimal point. To be safe, you should set the fixed option.

CODE LIST 4-12

```
    cout.setf(ios::fixed);
    cout << setprecision(2) << price << '\n';
```

STEP-BY-STEP ▷ 4.8

1. Retrieve the source code file named **iomanip.cpp**. The program shown in Code List 4-13 appears. Notice that the program uses two new line characters in a row to cause the output to skip a line.

2. Compile and run the program to see the difference that the formatting makes.

3. Change the line that includes the setprecision I/O manipulator to match Code List 4-14. The new line includes text to print a dollar sign as part of the output. Notice that the dollar sign appears in single quotes because it is a single character.

4. Run the program again to see the dollar sign display.

5. Leave the program open for the next Step-by-Step exercise.

Hot Tip

In order to use I/O manipulators, you must use the directive `#include <iomanip.h>` to include the necessary code to make the manipulators available.

CODE LIST 4-13

```
// iomanip.cpp

#include <iostream.h>
#include <iomanip.h>

int main()
{
  double cost = 34.99;
  double total;

  total = cost + (cost * 0.07875);  // add tax to cost to get total

  // Display total without formatting
  cout << "Total with no formatting:\n";
  cout << total << "\n\n"; // use two new line characters to skip line

  // Display total with fixed precision
  cout << "Total with formatting:\n";
  cout.setf(ios::fixed);
  cout << setprecision(2) << total << "\n\n";

  return 0;
}
```

CODE LIST 4-14

```
  cout << setprecision(2) << '$' << total << "\n\n";
```

Using setw

The setw manipulator can be used to change the number of spaces the compiler uses when it displays a number. The amount of space used to display a number is called the *field width*. You can use setw to set a minimum field width or use it to format numbers.

For example, if i = 254, j = 44, and k = 6, the statement cout << i << j << k << '\n'; produces the output 254446 because only the space necessary to output the numbers is used. The following statement, however, adds spaces to the left of each number to give formatted output.

```
cout << setw(10) << i << setw(10) << j << setw(10) << k << endl;
```

The output of the previous statement appears as follows.

```
       254        44         6
```

The best way to see the difference is to try it yourself in the next Step-by-Step exercise.

STEP-BY-STEP ▷ 4.9

1. Add the declarations in Code List 4-15 to the top of the program on your screen.

2. Add the code in Code List 4-16 before the `return` statement at the end of the program.

3. Compile and run to see how the setw manipulators affect the output of the integers.

4. Save and close the program.

CODE LIST 4-15

```
int i = 1499;
int j = 618;
int k = 2;
```

CODE LIST 4-16

```
// Output with no field widths
cout << "Output of i, j, and k with no field widths specified:\n";
cout << i << j << k << "\n\n";

// Output with field widths set
cout << "Output of i, j, and k with field widths specified:\n";
cout << setw(10) << i << setw(10) << j << setw(10) << k << "\n\n";
```

Inputting Characters

The >> operator can be used to input characters. If the user enters more than one character, only the first character will be stored in the variable.

STEP-BY-STEP ▷ 4.10

1. Retrieve the source code file named **inchar.cpp**. The program shown in Code List 4-17 appears.

2. Run the program to see how inputting a character works. Run the program multiple times.

Try entering a variety of characters and more than one character at a time.

3. Close the program.

CODE LIST 4-17

```cpp
// inchar.cpp

#include <iostream.h>

int main()
{
  char c;

  cout << "Enter a single character: ";
  cin >> c;
  cout << "You entered " << c << '\n';
  return 0;
}
```

Inputting Strings

In the previous section, you assigned strings to string objects at the time of declaration and later, using the assignment operator. You may have been thinking, "How do I enter a string provided by the user into a string object?" As you might have guessed, the string object has a method for doing just that. It is called getline.

 Did You Know?

When you enter a number such as 4 into a character variable, the character '4' is stored rather than the integer 4. Therefore, you perform mathematical operations on numbers when they are stored as characters.

Consider the following statement. The getline method is used somewhat differently than the other object methods you have used. When you use getline, the parentheses specify the input stream object and the string object you wish to input the string into.

```
getline(cin, MyString);
```

When you use getline, you can use it just like the previous statement. Just change `MyString` to the name of your string object.

STEP-BY-STEP ▷ 4.11

1. Retrieve the source code file named **instring.cpp**. The program shown in Code List 4-18 appears.

2. Compile and run the program. As an object is supposed to do, the string object hides the details of the operation, making getline easy to use.

3. Leave the program open for the next Step-by-Step exercise.

CODE LIST 4-18

```cpp
// instring.cpp

#include <iostream.h>
#include "apstring.h"

int main()
{
  apstring FirstName;
  apstring LastName;

  cout << "Enter your first name: ";
  getline(cin, FirstName);

  cout << "Enter your last name: ";
  getline(cin, LastName);

  cout << "Your name is " << FirstName << " " << LastName << ".\n";

  return 0;
}
```

Flushing the Input Stream

The cin object is often referred to as the *input stream*. Think of the input stream as a line at a checkout stand. Characters are lined up in the input stream as keys are pressed on the keyboard. Each character, however, must wait its turn to be processed. Therefore, if a prompt for input does not use every character in the input stream, the remaining characters wait in the input stream for the next prompt.

Using statements such as `cin >> x;` for inputting numbers and getline for inputting strings works well—until you try to use them together. The problem arises because after you have input a number using a statement like the previous one, the new line character that is generated when you press Enter stays in the input stream. That character stays in the stream until the program requests something else from the stream. In other words, statements such as `cin >> x;` do not clean up after themselves very well.

This is not a problem if the next input from the user is another number, because C++ will ignore that new line character that is still waiting in the stream and wait for a number to come down the stream. When the next input is a string, however, you have a problem. The problem arises because the getline method is looking for any sequence of characters ending in a new line character. If a new line character, or any other characters for that matter, are waiting in the input stream, that's what you get in your string.

Let's see the problem firsthand.

STEP-BY-STEP ▷ 4.12

1. Retrieve the source code file named **flush.cpp.** The program asks for a numeric value and then asks for a string.

2. Compile and run the program. Enter **12** for the quantity and press **Enter**. Notice that the program rushes to the end without stopping to ask for the description.

The new line character left over from the input of the integer was accepted as input by the getline method.

3. Leave the program open for the next Step-by-Step exercise.

To remedy this problem, you must remove the extra characters from the input stream before the getline method is executed. This operation is called flushing the input stream. To flush the input stream, insert the following line after the statement where the number was input.

```
cin.ignore(80, '\n');
```

The `80` tells the program to ignore the next 80 characters in the stream. The `'\n'` tells the function to stop ignoring characters when it gets to a new line character. You could use a number smaller than 80 in most cases. The function will usually stop ignoring after only a few characters, because it will find a new line character. Most programmers use 80 to play it safe.

Code List 4-19 shows the **flush.cpp** program with the addition of the flush statement.

```
// flush.cpp

#include <iostream.h>
#include "apstring.h"

int main()
{
  int quantity;
  apstring desc;

  cout << "Enter the quantity desired: ";
  cin >> quantity;
  cin.ignore(80, '\n'); // Flush the input stream

  cout << "Enter the description of the item: ";
  getline(cin, desc);

  cout << "You requested " << quantity << " of item described as \n";
  cout << desc << ".\n";

  return 0;
}
```

It is a good idea to flush the input stream after all numeric input statements in programs where strings are also used.

S TEP-BY-STEP ▷ 4.13

1. Add the line required to flush the input stream. Use Code List 4-19 as a reference.

2. Compile and run the program again. The prompt for description now works properly.

3. Close the program.

Using Descriptive Prompts

When writing programs that interact with the user, be sure to output prompts that clearly explain the input the program is requesting. For example, if prompting the user for his or her name, use a descriptive prompt like the following.

```
Please enter your last name:
```

If prompting for a telephone number or some other formatted data, you may want to use the prompt to give an example.

```
Please enter your phone number using the format (555) 555-5555:
```

The more descriptive and clear your prompts, the more likely the user is to enter the information in the form your program is expecting.

Clearing the Screen and Printing a Hard Copy

Now that you have learned more about screen I/O, you may be interested in learning how to clear the screen or print to a printer. The techniques required to clear the screen and print to a printer vary, depending on the compiler and operating system you are using. Your compiler may have a function available for clearing the screen, or you may have to use another technique. Modern operating systems sometimes require special programming in order to send output to a printer. You may wish to send output to a text file on disk and then use a text editor to print the contents of the file.

SECTION CHECKPOINT

1. What is the name of the standard output stream object?

2. What is the special character used to print a backslash?

3. What format option displays floating-point numbers in "E" notation?

4. What two pieces of information must be provided when using getline?

5. Why is it important to use descriptive prompts when prompting for data?

VOCABULARY REVIEW

Define the following terms:

console I/O	input stream	new line character
extraction operator	insertion operator	special character
field width	I/O manipulators	stream

Summary

In this chapter, you learned:

- Strings allow computers to process text as well as numbers.

- Hard-coded numeric values are called numeric literals. Hard-coded text is called a string literal.

- Object-oriented programming is a way of programming that treats parts of a computer program as objects that are similar to real-world objects.

- A class is a definition used to create an object. An object is said to be an instance of a class.

- Compiling a program that uses classes requires special setup.

- When declaring a string object, you can declare an empty object or initialize the object with a string.

- You can assign one string to another, a string literal to a string object, or a character literal to string object.

- You can use cout to display the contents of a string object.

- Objects hold data and the operations you can perform on that data.

- To make an object perform an operation on itself, you send the object a message.

- The length method is used to determine the length of a string stored in a string object.

- Concatenation is the operation of adding one string onto the end of another string.

- The << and >> symbols are actually operators. The cin and cout keywords are actually objects.

- The cin and cout objects are streams. A stream is data flowing from one place to another.

- The cin object brings data from the standard input device. The cout object takes data to the standard output device.

- Console I/O refers to using the screen and keyboard for input and output.

- The \n character is a special character called the new line character or end-of-line character.

- There are special characters for printing characters such as tab, the backslash, and quotes.

- You can use endl in place of the character '\n'.

- The cout object has format options that can be changed with the setf and unsetf methods.

- The setprecision I/O manipulator is used to set the number of digits that will appear to the right of the decimal point.

- The setw I/O manipulator is used to set a field width for numbers that are output to the screen.

- The >> operator can be used to input characters.

- To input strings, use the getline method of the string class.

- When a program includes numeric and string input, it is necessary to flush the input stream after each numeric entry to remove characters left in the input stream.

- Programs should use prompts that clearly explain the input that the program is requesting.

- The process for clearing the screen and printing a hard copy varies among compilers and operating systems.

CHAPTER 4 REVIEW QUESTIONS

TRUE/FALSE

Circle T if the statement is true or F if the statement is false.

T F 1. C++ has a built-in data type specifically for strings.

T F 2. A hard-coded string of text is called a string literal.

T F 3. A class is said to be an instance of an object.

T F 4. A string object adjusts its length as necessary as the program runs.

T F 5. Concatenation refers to the process of disposing of a string object when you are done with it.

T F 6. The cin stream reads from the standard output device.

T F 7. The new line character is represented as \1.

T F 8. The forcepoint format option displays decimal point and trailing zeros for all floating-point numbers, even if the decimal places are not needed.

T F 9. The >> operator can be used to input characters.

T F 10. The getline method is part of the string object.

WRITTEN QUESTIONS

Write a brief answer to the following questions.

1. What are the names of the two files that make up the string class?

2. Write a statement that declares a string object named `FirstName` and initializes the string object with your first name.

3. Write a statement that assigns the contents of a string object named `NewName` to a string object named `MyName`.

4. Write a statement that displays the contents of the string object named `MyName` to the screen.

5. Write a statement that assigns the length of the string named `MyName` to an integer variable named `len`.

6. What is another name for the input operator (>>)?

7. What is another name for the output operator (<<)?

8. What is the alternative to entering \n to generate a new line character?

9. What I/O manipulator sets the number of digits to be displayed after the decimal point?

10. Write the statement used to flush the input stream.

CHAPTER 4 PROJECTS

PROJECT 4-1

1. Write a program that declares two string objects named `FavoriteColor` and `FavoritePlace`. Initialize `FavoriteColor` with the name of your favorite color at the time the object is declared. Leave `FavoritePlace` empty.

2. Use the assignment operator to assign the name of your favorite place to visit to the `FavoritePlace` object.

3. Write statements to produce output similar to the following lines. The statements should use the contents of your string objects to fill in the blanks.

   My favorite color is _____.

   My favorite place to visit is _____.

4. Save the source code as **favorite.cpp**, compile, and run the program.

5. Close the program.

PROJECT 4-2

1. Write a program that declares a string object named `MyString`. Leave the object empty.

2. Use the assignment operator to assign the character 'A' to the string object.

3. Print the contents of the string to the screen.

4. Concatenate the character 'B' to the end of the string.

5. Print the contents of the string to the screen.

6. Print the length of the string to the screen using a statement like the following.

```
cout << MyString.length() << '\n';
```

7. Concatenate the string "CDEFG" to the end of the string.

8. Print the contents of the string to the screen.

9. Print the length of the string to the screen again.

10. Save the source code as **abc.cpp**, compile, and run the program.

11. Close the program.

PROJECT 4-3

Write a program that asks the user for three floating-point numbers. Print the numbers back to the screen with a precision of one decimal point. Use a field width for the output that places the three numbers across the screen as in the following example. Save the source code as **float3.cpp**.

```
123.4      33.2      1.9
```

PROJECT 4-4

Write a program that asks the user for a name, address, city, state, ZIP code, and phone number and stores each in appropriate string objects. Use descriptive prompts for each input. After the strings are stored, print the information back to the screen in the following order. Save the source code as **address.cpp**.

Name
Address
City, State ZIP Code
Phone Number

PROJECT 4-5

Write a program that prompts the user for the names of three colors and stores the responses in three string objects. Use descriptive prompts for each input. After the strings are stored, print the information back to the screen on one line, separated by tabs. Save the source code as **tabs.cpp**.

ACTIVITY 4-1

1. Write a program that declares a string object named `spacer` and initializes the object to hold nine blank spaces.

2. Declare a string object named `ruler`.

3. Use concatenation to build a string that matches the following string. The first character in the string should be a zero (0) and the last character should be a three (3). There should be nine spaces between each numeral. *Hint*: You can use multiple concatenation statements.

```
0         1         2         3
```

4. Print the concatenated string to the screen.

5. Report the length of the concatenated string to the screen.

6. Name the source code file **spacer.cpp**.

ACTIVITY 4-2

Write a program that uses the special characters to print the following line of code to the screen. The code should appear on the screen exactly as shown below, including backslashes, single quotes, and double quotes. Save the source code as **special.cpp**.

```
cout << "The answer is: " << Answer << '\n';
```

ACTIVITY 4-3

Write a program that asks the user for two floating-point numbers. The program should multiply the numbers together and print the product to the screen. Next, ask the user how many digits to display to the right of the decimal point and print the product again with the new precision. Save the source code as **setprec.cpp**.

The Fundamentals

REVIEW QUESTIONS

MATCHING

Write the letter of the description from Column 2 that best matches the term or phrase in Column 1.

Column 1	Column 2
____ 1. algorithm	**A.** Data flowing from one place to another
____ 2. compiler	**B.** Stores data that remains the same throughout a program's execution
____ 3. executable file	**C.** Adding one string to another
____ 4. interpreter	**D.** A program in the form of a high-level language
____ 5. linker	**E.** Takes data from a stream
____ 6. object code	**F.** Tells an object what to do
____ 7. source code	**G.** A set of sequential instructions that are followed to solve a problem
____ 8. identifier	**H.** The machine language code produced by a compiler
____ 9. Boolean variable	**I.** A program that translates a high-level language into machine language, then saves the machine language
____ 10. decrementing	**J.** The definition for an object
____ 11. constant	**K.** Subtracting one
____ 12. expression	**L.** A math statement made up of terms and operators
____ 13. incrementing	**M.** The process of assigning a value to a variable

95

____ **14.** initializing

____ **15.** overflow

____ **16.** variable

____ **17.** class

____ **18.** concatenation

____ **19.** extraction operator

____ **20.** insertion operator

____ **21.** literal

____ **22.** message

____ **23.** new line character

____ **24.** object

____ **25.** stream

N. Stores data that can change while the program runs

O. A variable that can have only two possible values: true or false

P. An instance of a class

Q. A program that links object files created by a compiler into an executable program

R. Names given to variables and constants

S. Adding one

T. A program that translates a high-level language into machine language but does not save the machine language

U. Puts data into a stream

V. The output of a linker

W. Causes the cursor to move to the next line of text

X. Hard-coded data

Y. The condition where a value becomes too large for its data type

WRITTEN QUESTIONS

Write a brief answer to the following questions.

1. What is the purpose of the binary number system?

2. What kinds of programs are usually found in a computer's ROM?

3. Why does a program written in a low-level language typically require less memory?

4. Is Pascal a high- or low-level language?

5. What term refers to correcting programming errors?

6. What character or characters tell the compiler that the text to follow is a comment?

7. What character is used to end a C++ statement?

8. What is the file extension typically used to signify a header file?

9. When a C++ program is executed, what function is run first?

10. List three data types that can store floating-point values.

11. What happens if you attempt to use a variable that has not been declared?

12. What is the operator symbol that performs multiplication?

13. What is the purpose of the modulus operator?

14. What is the operator that increments a variable?

15. In the order of operations, which is performed first, multiplication or addition?

16. What is the term that describes the feature where C++ automatically changes a data type of a value in order to perform a calculation?

17. Which floating-point data type has the greatest chance of having a problem with precision?

18. Which comes first, a class or an object?

19. What happens if you assign a string to an object and that string is longer than the existing object's length?

20. When working with objects, what is the purpose of a message?

21. Where does the cout stream lead?

22. What are two ways to represent a new line character in source code?

23. In source code, what character generates a tab?

24. What option displays the decimal point and trailing zeros for all floating-point numbers, even if the decimal places are not needed?

25. When is it necessary to flush the input stream?

PROJECT 1-1

In the spaces below, write the names of the parts of the C++ program shown in Figure U1-1.

FIGURE U1-1

```
// Simple C++ Program    ←――――― A

#include <iostream.h>    ←――――― B

int main()          ←――――― C

{
 cout << "Hello World!\n";   E
 return 0;
}  ←――――― D
```

A._____

B._____

C._____

D._____

E._____

PROJECT 1-2

1. Write a statement that declares a variable named salary of type float.

2. Write a statement to assign the value 42,000.00 to the variable named `salary`.

3. Write a statement that stores the remainder of dividing the variable `i` by `j` in a variable named `k`.

4. Write a statement that declares a constant named `SALES_TAX` of type double with the value 0.075.

5. Write a statement that calculates the sales tax for an item. Assign the cost of the item (use 19.99) to a variable named `item_cost`. Use the `SALES_TAX` constant you declared above as the tax rate. Store the result in a variable named `tax_due`. You do not have to declare types.

6. Write a statement that increments a variable `m` using the increment operator.

7. Write a statement that decrements a variable `n` using the decrement operator.

8. What will the value of `j` be after the following statement is executed?
   ```
   j = 3 + 4 / 2 + 5 * 2 - 3;
   ```

9. What will the value of `j` be after the following statement is executed?
   ```
   j = (3 + 4) / (2 + 5) * 2 - 3;
   ```

10. Suppose that you have a program in which `x` is experiencing overflow. Rewrite the following declaration statement to minimize the chance of an overflow when a value is assigned to `x`.
    ```
    short x;
    ```

PROJECT 1-3

In this application, you will create a program that calculates the area of an ellipse. The area of an ellipse is found by multiplying the length of the ellipse by the width of the ellipse and then multiplying by PI, as shown in the following statement.

Area of Ellipse = Length $\times$ Width $\times$ 3.14159

Write a program to calculate the area of an ellipse following these steps:

1. Begin a new source code file. Name the file **ellipse.cpp**.

2. Declare three variables named `width`, `length`, and `area`. Use an appropriate floating-point data type.

3. Enter the following lines to prompt the user for input.

```
cout << "Enter the width of the ellipse: ";
cin >> width;

cout << "Enter the length of the ellipse: ";
cin >> length;
```

4. Write a statement to calculate the area of the ellipse based on the formula above.

5. Enter the following statement to output the result of your calculation.

```
cout << "\nArea of ellipse: " << area << '\n';
```

6. Complete the program and save the source code.

7. Compile and run the program.

8. Enter 3.5 as the width and 7.0 as the length. The result should be approximately 76.969.

9. Try some other values before closing the program.

PROJECT 1-4

1. Write a statement that declares a string object named `City` and initializes it with the name of your city.

2. Write a statement that changes the string stored in `City` to *Grand Rapids*.

3. Write a statement that prints the content of the `City` string object to the screen.

4. Write a statement that assigns the length of the `City` string object to an integer named `CityLength`.

5. Write statements necessary to append a comma and *Michigan* to the `City` string.

6. Write a statement that gets a number from the keyboard and stores it in a variable `i`.

7. Write a statement that prints the letters A, B, and C to the screen, separated by tabs.

8. Write a statement that uses setf to display a leading plus sign before positive values.

9. Write the statements necessary to output the variable `cost` with two decimal places.

10. Write a statement that inputs a line of text into a string object named `address`.

PROJECT 1-5

1. Open **instring.cpp**.

2. Add a declaration for a string object named `FullName`.

3. Add a statement that assigns `FirstName`, a space, and `LastName` to the `FullName` object.

4. Modify the current output statement to output the `FullName` object instead of outputting first and last name separately.

PROJECT 1-6

Write a program that asks the user for the diameter of a circle and returns the circumference of the circle. First, store the user's input (diameter) in a floating point variable. Next, the program should calculate PI * diameter using a declared constant for PI of 3.14159. Output the result of PI * diameter in normal notation with a precision of four digits to the right of the decimal point. Save the source code file as **circumfr.cpp**.

PROJECT 1-7

Write a program that takes in the name, opening value, closing value, and number of shares owned of a publicly-traded stock. Have the program print the stock name, opening value, closing value, and the amount of value gained or lost that day in one formatted line. Save the source code file as **stocks.cpp**.

INTERNET ACTIVITIES

INTERNET ACTIVITY 1-1

In this Internet activity, you will use the Internet to learn more about your microprocessor and your compiler.

1. Open your Web browser.

2. Go to the following Web address.

   http://www.programcpp.com/third

3. On the home page, click the link called **Internet Activities**.

4. On the Internet Activities page, click the **Unit 1 Internet Activity** link.

5. Click the **Microprocessors** link. Links to the Web pages of major microprocessor companies appear. Determine if the manufacturer of your microprocessor appears in the list.

6. If the manufacturer of your microprocessor appears in the list, visit the site by clicking the appropriate link. Otherwise, search the Internet for the manufacturer of your microprocessor.

7. While on the Web site of the microprocessor manufacturer, list the latest microprocessors released by the company or print Web pages that list the microprocessors they have available.

8. Return to the Unit 1 Internet Activities page.

9. Click the **Compilers** link. Links to the Web pages of major compiler developers appear. Determine if your compiler appears on the list.

10. If the developer of your C++ compiler appears in the list, visit their site by clicking the appropriate link. Otherwise, search the Internet for the developer of your compiler.

11. While on the Web site of the compiler developer, list the latest compilers released by the company or print Web pages that list the compilers they have available.

12. Close your Web browser when finished.

INTERNET ACTIVITY 1-2

Boolean variables are named in honor of George Boole, an English mathematician who lived in the 1800s. Boole created a system called Boolean algebra, which is a study of operations using variables with the values true and false. In this Internet activity, you will use the Internet to learn more about George Boole and Boolean algebra.

1. Open your Web browser.

2. Go to the following Web address.

   http://www.programcpp.com/third

3. On the home page, click the link called **Internet Activities**.

4. On the Internet Activities page, click the **Unit 1** link.

5. Read the information presented there about Boole and Boolean algebra. Follow the links provided there.

6. When you have read the information and visited the sites, answer the written questions on the Unit 1 Internet Activity Web page.

INTERNET ACTIVITY 1-3

In this Internet activity, you will use the Internet to find a conversion factor on which to base a program.

1. Open your Web browser.

2. Go to the following Web address.

   http://www.programcpp.com/third

3. On the home page, click the link called **Internet Activities**.

4. On the Internet Activities page, click the **Unit 3** link.

5. Follow the links provided to find conversion factors for converting among different units of measurement.

6. Select one of these conversion factors and write a program that prompts the user to the measurement in the initial units. The program should convert the measurement to the new unit of measure.

7. Apply proper formatting and set the precision of the output.

8. Save the source code as **convert.cpp**.

AIRLINE FLIGHT ANALYSIS

🕐 **Estimated Time: 1 hour**

Overview

In this case study, you will examine a program that analyzes the cost of an airline flight. The program asks for the number of passengers on the flight, the length of the flight, and the average ticket price. The program then calculates and outputs several values, including the time required for the flight, the cost of the flight, total fares collected from ticket sales, and the profit for the flight.

Obviously, there is much more to take into consideration when calculating the profit an airline makes on a specific flight. The program, however, demonstrates many of the topics covered in the first unit.

Let's begin by loading, compiling, and running the program. Then we'll analyze the source code.

STEP-BY-STEP ▷ CSI.1

1. Retrieve the source code file **airline.cpp**. The program makes use of the string class. Therefore, you need to set up your project or workspace to use the string class the way you did in Chapter 4.

2. Compile and run the program. The program is configured for the Boeing 747-400 jet.

3. Enter 300 for the number of passengers, 2500 for the length of the flight, and 349.25 as the average ticket price.

4. Leave the source code file open.

Analyzing the Program

The complete source code for the program appears in Code List CSI-1. Spend a few minutes looking over the complete source code before reading the analysis that follows.

```
// Airline Flight Cost Analysis

#include <iostream.h>   // necessary for input/output
#include <iomanip.h>    // necessary for setprecision manipulator
#include "apstring.h"   // necessary for string object

// main function
int main ()
{
 // Specifications for a Boeing 747-400
 // Source: The World Almanac and Book of Facts 1995
 apstring plane_name("Boeing 747-400");
 int const plane_speed = 533;
 int const number_of_seats = 398;
 int const max_flight_length = 4331;
 int const cost_per_hour = 6939;

 int num_pass;              // number of passengers on the plane
 float num_miles;           // flight distance
 float avg_ticket_price;    // average ticket price for flight
 float flight_cost;         // cost for the flight
 float cost_per_pass;       // cost per passenger
 float total_fares;         // total fares collected for the flight
 float profit;              // profit for the flight
 float hours;               // length of flight in hours

 cout << "\nAIRLINE FLIGHT ANALYSIS\n";
 cout << "Airplane name: " << plane_name << endl;
 cout << "Enter the number of passengers on the flight (maximum "
     << number_of_seats << "): ";
 cin >> num_pass;
 cout << "Enter the distance (in miles) of the flight (maximum "
     << max_flight_length << "): ";
 cin >> num_miles;
 cout << "Enter the average ticket price: ";
 cin >> avg_ticket_price;

 hours = num_miles / plane_speed;  // calculate flight time
 flight_cost = hours * cost_per_hour; // calculate cost of flight
 cost_per_pass = flight_cost / num_pass; // cost per passenger
 total_fares = num_pass * avg_ticket_price; // calculate total fares
 profit = total_fares - flight_cost; // calculate flight profit

 cout.setf(ios::showpoint);  // force decimal point to be displayed
 cout.setf(ios::fixed);      // prevent scientific notation
 cout << "\nAnalysis for " << plane_name << endl;
 cout << "\nThe flight will take approximately " << setprecision(2)
     << hours << " hours.\n";
 cout << "The cost of the flight will be $" << flight_cost
     << ", with a \n";
```

(continued)

CODE LIST CSI-1 (continued)

```
cout << "cost per passenger of $" << cost_per_pass << ".\n";
cout << "The total fares collected from ticket sales is $"
    << total_fares << ",\n";
cout << "resulting in a profit of $" << profit << ".\n";
return 0;
}
```

The program begins with three compiler directives that include `iostream.h`, `iomanip.h`, and `apstring.h`. The first two are necessary to make the input and output functions available. The `apstring.h` include is necessary to use the string class.

Next, the `main` function begins. The remainder of the program is contained in the `main` function. Notice that the `#include` directives must appear before the `main` function.

The first set of statements in the `main` function (shown again in Code List CSI-2) define the specifications for a particular aircraft. Currently, the values are based on a particular model of the Boeing 747. The name of the aircraft is stored in a string object. The other values are stored in constants. These values will be used in calculations later in the program.

CODE LIST CSI-2

```
// Specifications for a Boeing 747-400
// Source: The World Almanac and Book of Facts 1995
apstring plane_name("Boeing 747-400");
int const plane_speed = 533;
int const number_of_seats = 398;
int const max_flight_length = 4331;
int const cost_per_hour = 6939;
```

The next step is to declare variables (see Code List CSI-3). The variable that holds the number of passengers on the flight is declared as an integer; the others are floating-point variables. All the constants and variables could have been declared as floating-point types to avoid the mixing of data types. Here, we will use integers where appropriate and allow the integer data types to be promoted during calculation.

CODE LIST CSI-3

```
int num_pass;            // number of passengers on the plane
float num_miles;         // flight distance
float avg_ticket_price;  // average ticket price for flight
float flight_cost;       // cost for the flight
float cost_per_pass;     // cost per passenger
float total_fares;       // total fares collected for the flight
float profit;            // profit for the flight
float hours;             // length of flight in hours
```

You should always clarify the use for each variable using comments, as was done in the declarations in Code List CSI-3.

The next group of statements (shown in Code List CSI-4) gets the required input from the user. Remember, \n or endl can be used to force the cursor to the next line of the screen. To give the user more information about the range of possible input, the number of seats and maximum flight length for the particular aircraft are part of the prompt for the input.

CODE LIST CSI-4

```
cout << "\nAIRLINE FLIGHT ANALYSIS\n";
cout << "Airplane name: " << plane_name << endl;
cout << "Enter the number of passengers on the flight (maximum "
     << number_of_seats << "): ";
cin >> num_pass;
cout << "Enter the distance (in miles) of the flight (maximum "
     << max_flight_length << "): ";
cin >> num_miles;
cout << "Enter the average ticket price: ";
cin >> avg_ticket_price;
```

After the input is gathered, the calculations must be performed. First, the time required for the flight is calculated using the following statement.

```
hours = num_miles / plane_speed;  // calculate flight time
```

The constant plane_speed is an integer, but num_miles and hours are both floating-point variables. Therefore, plane_speed is promoted to a floating-point type for the calculation, and the result, also a floating-point value, is stored in hours.

A similar promotion of an integer type occurs in the other calculations that follow. In each case, the result is a floating-point value. As shown in the statements in Code List CSI-5, the cost of the flight is calculated by multiplying the time required by the cost of operating the aircraft for an hour. That flight cost is divided by the number of passengers to get a cost per passenger. The total number of dollars collected from ticket sales is estimated by multiplying the average ticket price by the number of passengers. Finally, the projected profit for the flight is calculated by subtracting the cost of the flight from the dollars collected from ticket sales.

CODE LIST CSI-5

```
flight_cost = hours * cost_per_hour; // calculate cost of flight
cost_per_pass = flight_cost / num_pass; // cost per passenger
total_fares = num_pass * avg_ticket_price; // calculate total fares
profit = total_fares - flight_cost; // calculate flight profit
```

The only task remaining is printing the output to the screen. The statements shown in Code List CSI-6 format the output in paragraph form. The first two statements are necessary to have the numbers appear in the desired format. The showpoint format option causes the decimal point to be displayed, even if a non-fractional value is being printed. The fixed option prevents numbers from appearing in scientific or "E" notation. In the fourth statement, the setprecision manipulator is used to specify that only two digits should be displayed to the right of the decimal point.

CODE LIST CSI-6

```
cout.setf(ios::showpoint);  // force decimal point to be displayed
cout.setf(ios::fixed);      // prevent scientific notation
cout << "\nAnalysis for " << plane_name << endl;
cout << "\nThe flight will take approximately " << setprecision(2)
     << hours << " hours.\n";
cout << "The cost of the flight will be $" << flight_cost
     << ", with a \n";
cout << "cost per passenger of $" << cost_per_pass << ".\n";
cout << "The total fares collected from ticket sales is $"
     << total_fares << ",\n";
cout << "resulting in a profit of $" << profit << ".\n";
```

Modifying the Program

As an additional exercise, modify the program to analyze another aircraft. Choose one of the four airplanes in the following table.

Aircraft	Seats	Speed	Flight Length	Cost per Hour
L-1011	288	496	1498	4564
DC-10-10	281	492	1493	4261
B737-500	113	408	532	1594
F-100	97	366	409	1681
Source: The World Almanac and Book of Facts 1995.				

When you run the program with specifications from an airplane other than the 747-400, notice how the input prompts change to provide you with the allowable range of values.

PROGRAM STRUCTURE

UNIT 2

Estimated Time for Unit 2: 6 hours

DECISION MAKING

When you make a decision, your brain goes through a process of comparisons. For example, when you shop for clothes you compare the prices with those you previously paid. You compare the quality to other clothes you have seen or owned. You probably compare the clothes to what other people are wearing or what is in style. You might even compare the purchase of clothes to other possible uses for your available money.

Although your brain's method of decision making is much more complex than what a computer is capable of, decision making in computers is also based on comparing data. In this chapter, you will learn to use the basic tools of computer decision making. You will also learn how to use the structures of the C++ language that allow programs to make decisions.

5.1 Building Blocks of Decision Making

Decision Making in Programs

Almost every program that is useful or user-friendly involves decision making. Although some algorithms progress sequentially from the first to the last instruction, most algorithms branch out into more than one path. At the point where the branching takes place, a decision must be made as to which path to take.

It often helps to illustrate the flow of a program with a special drawing called a *flowchart*. A flowchart maps the decisions a program is to make and the path down which each decision leads. The flowchart in Figure 5-1 is part of an algorithm in which the program is preparing to output a document to the printer. The user enters the number of copies he or she wants to print. To make sure the number is valid, the program verifies that the number of copies is not less than zero. If the user enters a negative number, a message is printed and the user is asked to reenter the value. If the user's input passes the test, the program simply goes on to the next step.

Did You Know?

Each shape used in a flowchart has a special meaning. The shapes are connected with arrows that show the direction of the flow of the program. Rectangles represent processing or action. Diamonds represent a decision. Parallelograms like those in Figure 5-1 represent input or output.

FIGURE 5-1

The decision-making part of this flowchart prevents the program from proceeding with invalid data.

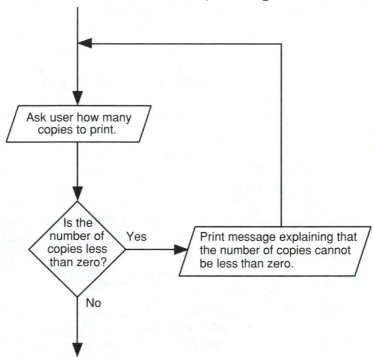

Decisions may also have to be made based on the wishes of the user. The flowchart in Figure 5-2 shows how the response to a question changes the path the program takes. If the user wants instructions printed on the screen, the program displays the instructions. Otherwise, that part of the program is bypassed.

FIGURE 5-2

The path a program takes may be dictated by the user.

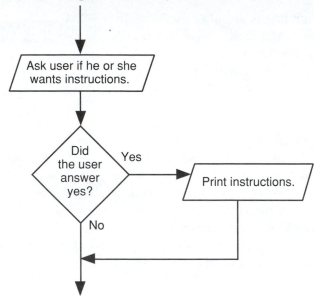

The examples in Figures 5-1 and 5-2 show two common needs for decisions in programs. There are many other instances in which decisions must be made. As you do more and more programming, you will use decision making in countless situations.

Representing True and False in C++

The way computers make decisions is very primitive. Even though computers make decisions in a way similar to the way the human brain does, computers don't have intuition or "gut" feelings. Decision making in a computer is based on performing simple comparisons. The microprocessor compares two values and "decides" if they are equivalent. Clever programming and the fact that computers can do millions of comparisons per second sometimes make computers appear to be "smart."

In Chapter 2 you learned about the Boolean data type, which provides a convenient way to store true and false values. Internally, however, true and false are represented as numbers. When the computer makes a comparison, the comparison results in a value of either zero or one. If the resulting value is zero, it means the comparison proved false. If the result is one, the comparison proved true. So in C++, the Boolean value of false is represented by the integer 0 and true is represented by the integer 1.

Computer Concepts

Fuzzy logic is a system that allows more than simply true or false. Fuzzy logic allows for some gray area. For example, instead of simply having a 0 for false and a 1 for true, fuzzy logic might allow a 0.9 as a way of saying "it's probably true."

Relational Operators

To make comparisons, C++ provides a set of *relational operators*, shown in Table 5-1. They are similar to the symbols you have used in math when working with equations and inequalities.

TABLE 5-1
Relational operators

Operator	Meaning	Example
==	equal to	i == 1
>	greater than	i > 2
<	less than	i < 0
>=	greater than or equal to	i >= 6
<=	less than or equal to	i <= 10
!=	not equal to	i != 12

The relational operators are used to create expressions like the examples in Table 5-1. The result of the expression is one (true) if the data meets the requirements of the comparison. Otherwise, the result of the expression is zero (false). For example, the result of 2 > 1 is one (true), and the result of 2 < 1 is zero (false).

The program in Code List 5-1 demonstrates how expressions are made from relational operators. The result of the expressions is to be displayed as either a one or zero.

Warning

Do not confuse the relational operator (==) with the assignment operator (=). Use == for comparisons and = for assignments.

CODE LIST 5-1

```cpp
// relate.cpp

#include <iostream.h>

int main()
{
  int i = 2;
  int j = 3;
  bool true_false;

  cout << (i == 2) << endl; // displays a 1 (true)
  cout << (i == 1) << endl; // displays a 0 (false)
  cout << (j > i) << endl;
  cout << (j < i) << endl;  // Can you predict
  cout << (j <= 3) << endl; // the output of
```

```
   cout << (j >= i) << endl; // these statements?
   cout << (j != i) << endl;

   true_false = (j < 4); // the result can be stored
                         // to a Boolean variable
   cout << true_false << endl;
   return 0;
}
```

S TEP-BY-STEP ▷ 5.1

1. Enter the program from Code List 5-1 into a blank editor screen. Save the source code file as **relate.cpp**. Can you predict its output?

2. Compile, link, and run the program.

3. After you have analyzed the output, close the program.

Logical Operators

Sometimes it takes more than two comparisons to obtain the desired result. For example, if you want to test to see if an integer is in the range 1 to 10, you must do two comparisons. In order for the integer to fall within the range, it must be greater than 0 *and* less than 11.

C++ provides three *logical operators*. Table 5-2 shows the three logical operators and their meaning.

 Note

The key used to enter the two vertical lines of the or operator (||) is usually located near the Enter or Return key. It is usually on the same key with the backslash (\).

TABLE 5-2
Logical operators

Operator	Meaning	Example
&&	and	(j == 1 && k == 2)
||	or	(j == 1 || k == 2)
!	not	result = !(j == 1 && k == 2)

Figure 5-3 shows three diagrams called *truth tables*. They will help you understand the result of comparisons with the logical operators and, or, and not.

FIGURE 5-3
Truth tables illustrate the results of logical operators.

AND			OR			NOT	
A	B	A && B	A	B	A || B	A	!A
false (0)	false (0)	false (0)	false (0)	false (0)	false (0)	false (0)	true (1)
false (0)	true (1)	false (0)	false (0)	true (1)	true (1)	true (1)	false (0)
true (1)	false (0)	false (0)	true (1)	false (0)	true (1)		
true (1)	true (1)	true (1)	true (1)	true (1)	true (1)		

Consider the following C++ statement.

```
in_range = (i > 0 && i < 11);
```

The variable `in_range` is assigned the value 1 if the value of `i` falls into the defined range, and 0 if the value of `i` does not fall into the defined range.

The not operator (!) turns true to false and false to true. For example, suppose you have a program that catalogs old movies. Your program uses an integer variable named `InColor` that has the value 0 if the movie was filmed in black and white and the value 1 if the movie was filmed in color. In the following statement, the variable `Black_and_White` is set to 1 (true) if the movie is not in color. Therefore, if the movie is in color, `Black_and_White` is set to 0 (false).

```
Black_and_White = !InColor;
```

STEP-BY-STEP ▷ 5.2

1. Retrieve the source code file named **logical.cpp**. The program shown in Code List 5-2 appears. Look closely at the statements that include the logical operators.

2. Compile and run the program to see the output.

3. After you have analyzed the output, close the source code file.

```
// logical.cpp

#include<iostream.h>
int main()
{
  int i = 2;
  int j = 3;
  bool true_false;

  true_false = (i < 3 && j > 3);
  cout << "The result of (i < 3 && j > 3) is "
   << true_false << '\n';

  true_false = (i < 3 && j >= 3);
  cout << "The result of (i < 3 && j >= 3) is "
   << true_false << '\n';

  cout << "The result of (i == 1 || i == 2) is "
       << (i == 1 || i == 2) << '\n';

  true_false = (j < 4);
  cout << "The result of (j < 4) is "
   << true_false << '\n';

  true_false = !true_false;
  cout << "The result of !true_false is "
   << !true_false << '\n';

  return 0;
}
```

Combining More than Two Comparisons

You can use logical operators to combine more than two comparisons. Consider the following statement that decides whether it is okay for a person to ride a roller coaster.

```
ok_to_ride = (height_in_inches > 45 && !back_trouble
            && !heart_trouble);
```

In this statement, `back_trouble` and `heart_trouble` hold the value 0 or 1 depending on whether the person being considered has the problem. For example, if the person has back trouble, the value of `back_trouble` is set to 1. The not operator (!) is used because it is okay to ride if the person does not have back trouble and does not have heart trouble. The entire statement says that it is okay to ride if the person's height is greater than 45 inches and the person has no back trouble and no heart trouble.

Order of Logical Operations

You can mix logical operators in statements as long as you understand the order in which the logical operators will be applied. The not operator (!) is applied first, then the and operator (&&), and finally the or operator (||). Consider the following statement.

```
dog_acceptable = (white || black && friendly);
```

This example illustrates why it is important to know the order in which logical operators are applied. At first glance it may appear that this statement would consider a dog to be acceptable if the dog is either white or black and also friendly. But in reality, the statement considers a white dog that wants to chew your leg off to be an acceptable dog. Why? Because the and operator is evaluated first and then the result of the and operation is used for the or operation. The statement can be corrected with the following additional parentheses.

```
dog_acceptable = ((white || black) && friendly);
```

C++ evaluates operations in parentheses first just as in arithmetic statements. The program in Code List 5-3 demonstrates the difference that the parentheses make. Also notice that the Boolean variables white and black are initialized using the true and false keywords. These keywords provide a more readable way to assign one and zero to the Boolean variables.

CODE LIST 5-3

```cpp
// logical2.cpp

#include<iostream.h>

int main()
{
 bool white, black, friendly, acceptable;

 white = true;      // dog is white
 black = false;     // dog is not black
 friendly = false;  // dog is not friendly

 // The following statement produces incorrect results due to the
 // order of operations.
 acceptable = (white || black && friendly);
 cout << acceptable << endl;

 // The parentheses in the following statement overrides the
 // order of operations and the statement produces the correct result.
 acceptable = ((white || black) && friendly);
 cout << acceptable << endl;

 return 0;
}
```

1. Open **logical2.cpp**. The program shown in Code List 5-3 appears.

2. Compile, link, and run the program to see the effect of the parentheses.

3. Close the source code file.

Short-Circuit Evaluation

Suppose you have decided you want to go to a particular concert. You can only go, however, if two conditions can be met: You must get tickets and you must get off work the night of the concert. Before you check whether you can get off work, you discover that the concert is sold out and you cannot get a ticket. There is no longer a need to check whether you can get off work because you don't have a ticket anyway.

C++ has a feature called ***short-circuit evaluation*** that allows the same kind of determinations in your program. For example, in an expression such as `in_range = (i > 0 && i < 11);`, the program first checks to see if `i` is greater than 0. If it is not, there is no need to check any further because regardless of whether `i` is less than 11, `in_range` will be false. So the program sets `in_range` to false and goes to the next statement without evaluating the right side of the &&.

Short-circuiting also occurs with the or (||) operator. In the case of the or operator, the expression is short-circuited if the left side of the || is true because the expression will be true regardless of the right side of the ||.

 Computer Concepts

Compilers often have an option to disable short-circuit evaluation.

SECTION CHECKPOINT

1. What does a flowchart illustrate?

2. What relational operator performs the greater than or equal to operation?

3. What are the three logical operators?

4. What do you call the tables that show the combination of results of logical operators?

5. What condition would make the following statement use short-circuit evaluation?

```
z = (x > 10 && x < 100);
```

VOCABULARY REVIEW

Define the following terms:

flowchart   logical operators   short-circuit evaluation
fuzzy logic   relational operators   truth tables

5.2 Selection Structures

Introduction to Selection Structures

Programs consist of statements that solve a problem or perform a task. Up to this point, you have been creating programs with sequence structures. *Sequence structures* execute statements one after another without changing the flow of the program. Other structures, such as the ones that make decisions, *do* change the flow of the program. The structures that make decisions in C++ programs are called *selection structures*. When a decision is made in a program, a selection structure controls the flow of the program based on the decision. In this section, you will learn how to use selection structures to make decisions in your programs. The three selection structures available in C++ are the if structure, the if/else structure, and the switch structure.

Using if

Many programming languages include an *if structure*. Although the syntax varies among programming languages, the if keyword is usually part of every language. If you have used the if keyword in other programming languages, you should have little difficulty using it in C++. The if structure is one of the easiest and most useful parts of C++.

The expression that makes the decision is called the *control expression*. Look at the code segment in Code List 5-4. First the control expression (i == 3) is evaluated. If the result is true, the code in the braces that follow the if statement is executed. If the result is false, the code in the braces is skipped.

 Warning

Remember to be careful of confusing the == operator with the = (assignment) operator. Entering if (i = 3) will cause i to be assigned the value 3, and the code in the braces that follow will be executed regardless of what the value of i was before the if structure.

CODE LIST 5-4

```
if (i == 3)
  {
    cout << "The value of i is 3\n";
  }
```

You can place more than one line between the braces, as shown in Code List 5-5.

CODE LIST 5-5

```
if (YesNo == 'Y')
  {
    cout << "Enter the title: ";
    getline(cin, title);
  }
```

Figure 5-4 shows the flowchart for an if structure. The if structure is sometimes called a ***one-way selection structure*** because the decision is whether to go "one way" or just bypass the code in the if structure.

FIGURE 5-4

The if structure is sometimes called a one-way selection structure.

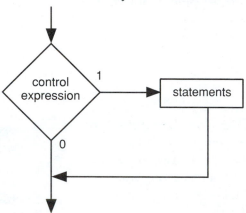

Analyze the program in Code List 5-6. The program declares a string object and an unsigned long integer. The user is asked for the name of his or her city or town and for the population of the city or town. The if structure compares the population to a value that would indicate whether the city is among the 100 largest U.S. cities. If the city is one of the 100 largest U.S. cities, the program prints a message saying so.

```
// city.cpp

#include <iostream.h>
#include "oostring.h"

int main()
{
 oostring city_name;
 unsigned long population;

 cout << "What is the name of your city or town? ";
 getline(cin, city_name);

 cout << "What is the population of the city or town? ";
 cin >> population;
 cin.ignore(80,'\n');

 if (population >= 185086)
 {
   cout << "According to estimated population figures, "
 << city_name << endl
 << "is one of the 100 largest U.S. cities.\n";
 }

 return 0;
}
```

S TEP-BY-STEP ▷ 5.4

1. Open **city.cpp**. The program from Code List 5-6 appears without the if structure.

2. Add the if structure shown in Code List 5-6 to the program. Enter the code carefully.

3. Compile, link, and run the program. Enter your city or town to test the program.

4. If your city or town is not one of the 100 largest cities, or if you do not know your city or town's population, enter Albuquerque, a city in New Mexico with a population of about 420,000. *Warning*: Do not enter the comma when entering populations.

5. Leave the source code file open for the next Step-by-Step exercise.

Using if/else

The ***if/else structure*** is sometimes called a ***two-way selection structure***. Using if/else, one block of code is executed if the control expression is true and another block is executed if the control expression is false. Consider the code fragment in Code List 5-7.

CODE LIST 5-7

```
if (i < 0)
   {cout << "The number is negative.\n";}
else
   {cout << "The number is zero or positive.\n";}
```

The else portion of the structure is executed if the control expression is false. Figure 5-5 shows a flowchart for a two-way selection structure.

FIGURE 5-5

The if/else structure is a two-way selection structure.

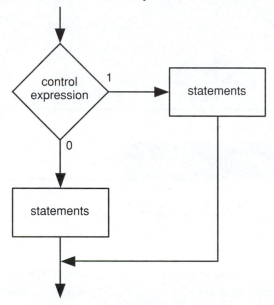

The code shown in Code List 5-8 adds an else clause to the if structure in the program in Step-by-Step 5.4. Output is improved by providing information on whether the city's population qualifies it as one of the 100 largest U.S. cities. If the population is 185,086 or more, the first output statement is executed; otherwise the second output statement is executed. In every case, one or the other output statement is executed.

Computer Concepts

Many programmers make the mistake of using > or < when they really need >= or <=. In the code segment in Code List 5-8, using > rather than >= would cause Glendale, California, the 100th largest city, to be excluded because its population is 185086, not greater than 185087.

CODE LIST 5-8

```
if (population >= 185086)
  {
    cout << "According to estimated population figures, "
         << city_name << endl
         << "is one of the 100 largest U.S. cities.\n";
  }
else
  {
    cout << "According to estimated population figures, "
         << city_name << endl
         << "is not one of the 100 largest U.S. cities.\n";
  }
```

STEP-BY-STEP ▷ 5.5

1. Add the else clause shown in Code List 5-8 to the if structure in the program on your screen. Save the new program as **cityelse.cpp**.

2. Compile, link, and run the program.

3. Enter the city of Gary, Indiana (population 108,469). The program reports that Gary is not one of the 100 largest cities in the United States.

4. Run the program again using Lubbock, Texas (population 190,974). Lubbock is among the 100 largest U.S. cities.

5. Close the program.

Nested if Structures

You can place if structures within other if structures. When an if or if/else structure is placed within another if or if/else structure, the structures are said to be *nested*. The flowchart in Figure 5-6 decides whether a student is exempt from a final exam based on grade average and days absent.

FIGURE 5-6
This flowchart can be programmed using nested if structures.

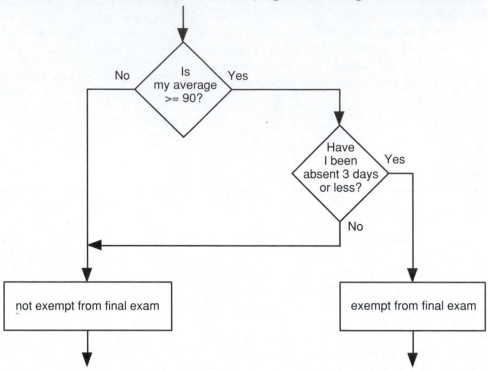

To be exempt from the final, a student must have a 90 average or better and cannot have missed more than three days of class. The algorithm first determines if the student's average is greater than or equal to 90. If the result is false, the student must take the final exam. If the result is true, the number of days absent is checked to determine if the other exemption requirement is met. Code List 5-9 shows the algorithm as a C++ code segment.

CODE LIST 5-9

```
exempt_from_final = false;

if (my_average >= 90)
  {                                  // if your average is 90 or better
    if (my_days_absent <= 3)         // and you have missed three days
    { exempt_from_final = true; }    // or less, you are exempt.
  }
```

The code in Code List 5-9 is written to initially assume that the student is not exempt from the final exam. If the requirements are met, as determined by the nested if structures, the exemption will be granted.

Algorithms involving nested if structures can get more complicated than the one in Code List 5-9. Figure 5-7 shows the flowchart from Figure 5-6 expanded to include another way to be exempted from the final exam. In this expanded algorithm, students can also be exempted if they have an 80 or higher average, as long as they have missed no more than one day of class.

FIGURE 5-7

This algorithm provides two paths to exemption from the final exam.

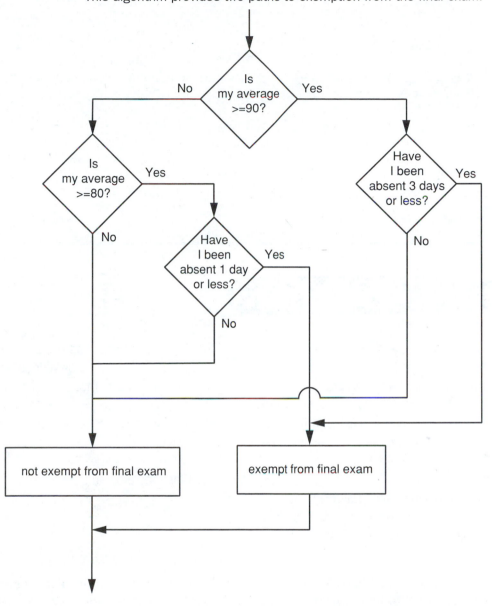

As you can probably imagine, programming the algorithm in Figure 5-7 will require careful construction and nesting of if and if/else structures. Code List 5-10 shows you how it is done.

Computer Concepts

Earlier you learned that it is a good idea to always use braces with if structures. Code List 5-10 illustrates another reason why you should do so. Without the braces, the compiler may assume that the else clause goes with the nested if structure rather than the first if.

```
    exempt_from_final = false;

    if (my_average >= 90)
       {                                  // If your average is 90 or better
        if (my_days_absent <= 3)          // and you have missed three days
        { exempt_from_final = true; }     // or less, you are exempt.
       }
    else  // if you don't have a 90+ average, you still have a chance
       { if (my_average >= 80)
         {                                // If your average is 80 or better
          if (my_days_absent <= 1)        // and you have missed one day or
            { exempt_from_final = true; } // less, you are exempt.
         }
       }
```

S TEP-BY-STEP ▷ 5.6

1. Open **final.cpp**.

2. Compile, link, and run the program.

3. Enter 90 as your grade average and 3 as your days absent. The program reports that you are exempt from the final exam.

4. Run the program again. Enter 88 as your grade average and 1 as your days absent. You are still exempt.

5. Run the program again. Enter 89 as your grade average and 2 as your days absent. The program reports that you must take the final.

6. Run the program again using values of your own choice.

7. Close the program.

Code List 5-11 shows a simple program that includes a nested if structure. The program asks the user to input the amount of money he or she wishes to deposit in order to open a new checking account. Based on the value provided by the user, the program recommends a type of account.

```
// deposit.cpp

#include <iostream.h>

int main()
{
  float amount_to_deposit;

  cout << "How much do you want to deposit to open the account? ";
```

CODE LIST 5-11 (continued)

```
    cin  >> amount_to_deposit;

    if(amount_to_deposit < 1000.00 )
     {
      if(amount_to_deposit < 100.00 )
       { cout << "You should consider the EconoCheck account.\n"; }
      else
       { cout << "You should consider the FreeCheck account.\n"; }
     }
    else
     { cout << "You should consider an interest-bearing account.\n"; }
    return 0;
  }
```

S TEP-BY-STEP ▷ 5.7

1. Open **deposit.cpp**. The program in Code List 5-11 appears.

2. Compile, link, and run the program. Run the program several times using values that are

less than $100, between $100 and $1000, and greater than $1000.

3. Close the program.

The switch Structure

You have studied one-way (if) and two-way (if-else) selection structures. C++ has another method of handling multiple options known as the *switch structure*. The switch structure has many uses but may be used most often when working with menus. A *menu* is a set of options presented to the user of a program. Code List 5-12 displays a menu of choices and asks the user to enter a number that corresponds to one of the choices. Then a case statement is used to handle each of the options.

CODE LIST 5-12

```
    cout << "How do you want the order shipped?\n";
    cout << "1 - Ground\n";
    cout << "2 - 2-day air\n";
    cout << "3 - Overnight air\n";
    cout << "Enter the number of the shipping method you want: ";
    cin >> shipping_method;
```

127

```
switch(shipping_method)
 {
   case 1:
     shipping_cost = 5.00;
     break;
   case 2:
     shipping_cost = 7.50;
     break;
   case 3:
     shipping_cost = 10.00;
     break;
   default:
     shipping_cost = 0.00;
     break;

 }
```

Let's analyze the switch structure in Code List 5-12. It begins with the keyword `switch`, followed by the control expression (the variable `shipping_method`) to be compared in the structure. Within the braces of the structure are a series of `case` keywords. Each one provides the code that is to be executed in the event that `shipping_method` matches the value that follows `case`. The `default` keyword tells the compiler that if nothing else matches, execute the statements that follow.

Note

In C++, only integer or character types may be used as control expressions in switch statements.

The `break` keyword, which appears at the end of each case segment, causes the flow of logic to jump to the first executable statement after the switch structure.

STEP-BY-STEP ▷ 5.8

1. Open **shipping.cpp**. The program includes the segment from Code List 5-12.

2. Compile, link, and run the program. Choose shipping method 2. The cost of shipping by second-day air appears.

3. Add a fourth shipping option called `Carrier Pigeon` to the menu.

4. Add the following code to the switch structure, before the `default` keyword.

```
case 4:
  shipping_cost = 99.99;
  break;
```

5. Compile, link, and run to test your addition to the options.

6. Save the source code and close.

Nested if/else structures could be used in the place of the switch structure. But the switch structure is easier to use and a programmer is less prone to making errors that are related to braces and indentions. Remember, however, that an integer or character data type is required in the control expression of a switch structure. Nested ifs must be used if you are comparing floating-point values.

When using character types in a switch structure, enclose the characters in single quotes like any other character literal. The code segment in Code List 5-13 is an example of using character literals in a switch structure.

CODE LIST 5-13

```
switch(character_entered)
  {
    case 'A':
      cout << "The character entered was A, as in albatross.\n";
      break;
    case 'B':
      cout << "The character entered was B, as in butterfly.\n";
      break;
    default:
      cout << "Illegal entry\n";
      break;
  }
```

STEP-BY-STEP ▷ 5.9

1. Open **chswitch.cpp**. The program includes the segment from Code List 5-13.

2. Compile, link, and run the program. Enter **A** as input. The appropriate output is generated.

3. Run the program again. Enter **B** as input. The second case is executed.

4. Run the program again. Enter **C** as input. The input is reported to be illegal.

5. Close the program.

 Computer Concepts

C++ allows you to place your case statements in any order. You can, however, increase the speed of your program by placing the more common choices at the top of the switch structure and less common ones toward the bottom. The reason is that the computer makes the comparisons in the order they appear in the switch structure. The sooner a match is found, the sooner the computer can move on to other processing.

SECTION CHECKPOINT

1. What selection structure is classified as a one-way selection structure?

2. What selection structure is classified as a two-way selection structure?

3. What term describes an if structure within another if structure?

4. What data types can be used as control expressions in switch statements?

5. What structure is often used when working with menus?

VOCABULARY REVIEW

Define the following terms:

control expression	menu	sequence structures
if structure	one-way selection structure	switch structure
if/else structure	selection structures	two-way selection structure

Summary

In this chapter, you learned:

- Computers make decisions by comparing data.

- A flowchart is an illustration that helps show the flow of a program.

- In C++, true is represented by 1 and false is represented by 0.

- Relational operators are used to create expressions that result in a value of 1 or 0.

- Logical operators can combine relational expressions.

- Parentheses can be used to control the order in which logical expressions are evaluated.

- Short-circuit evaluation allows the evaluation of a logical expression to be stopped early if the ultimate result of the expression is already determined.

- Selection structures are how C++ programs make decisions.

- The if structure is a one-way selection structure. When a control expression in an if statement is evaluated to be true, the statements associated with the structure are executed.

- The if/else structure is a two-way selection structure. If the control expression in the if statement evaluates to true, one block of statements is executed; otherwise another block is executed.

- It is possible to nest if structures and if/else structures.

- The switch structure is a multi-way selection structure that executes one of many sets of statements depending on the value of the control expression. The control expression must evaluate to an integer or character value.

TRUE/FALSE

Circle T if the statement is true or F if the statement is false.

T F 1. Decision making in computers is based on comparing data.

T F 2. The result of an expression that includes relational operators is either true or false.

T F 3. The not operator turns a result to false regardless of its previous value.

T F 4. Parentheses can be used to change the order of logical operations.

T F 5. Compilers often have an option to disable short-circuit evaluation.

T F 6. Selection structures execute statements one after another without changing the flow of the program.

T F 7. The expression that makes the decision in an if structure is called a control expression.

T F 8. The = operator and the == operator are interchangeable.

T F 9. Placing if structures within if structures is called stacking if structures.

T F 10. The operation of a switch structure can be replaced by if/else structures.

WRITTEN QUESTIONS

Write a brief answer to the following questions.

1. What flowchart symbol represents a decision?

2. What is the value that represents the boolean condition *false*?

3. What is the relational operator that performs the "not equal to" operation?

4. Why is the order of logical operations important?

5. In the order of logical operations, what operator is applied first?

6. What are the three selection structures available in C++?

7. When are the braces in an if structure not necessary?

8. When is the else portion of an if/else structure executed?

9. What keyword in a switch structure tells the compiler what statements to execute if none of the options match?

10. What does the break keyword in a switch structure do?

CHAPTER 5 PROJECTS

PROJECT 5-1

In the blanks beside the statements in the following program, write a T or F to indicate the result of the expression. Fill in the answers beginning with the first statement and follow the program in the order in which the statements would be executed in a running program.

```
int main()
{
 int i = 4;
 int j = 3;
 bool true_false;

 true_false = (j < 4);                               _____

 true_false = (j < 3);                               _____

 true_false = (j < i);                               _____

 true_false = (i < 4);                               _____

 true_false = (j <= 4);                              _____

 true_false = (4 > 4);                               _____

 true_false = (i != j);                              _____

 true_false = (i == j || i < 100);                   _____

 true_false = (i == j && i < 100);                   _____

 true_false = (i < j || true_false && j >= 3);       _____

 true_false = (!(i > 2 && j == 4));                  _____

 true_false = !1;                                    _____

 return 0;
}
```

PROJECT 5-2

1. Retrieve the file named **truth.cpp**.

2. Compile, link, and run the program. The program displays a truth table for the and operation.

3. Duplicate the code that displays the and truth table and modify it to display an or truth table.

4. Save and close the program.

PROJECT 5-3

1. Write an if structure that prints the word *complete* to the screen if the variable named `percent_complete` is equal to 100.

2. Write an if structure that assigns the value 100 to the variable named `percent_complete` if the character in the variable named `Done` equals *Y*.

3. Write an if/else structure that prints the word *complete* to the screen if the variable named `percent_complete` is equal to 100 and prints the phrase *not complete* to the screen otherwise.

PROJECT 5-4

Write a program that uses the if/else structure in Code List 9-4 to report whether an integer entered by the user is positive or negative. Save the source code file as **sign.cpp**.

PROJECT 5-5

Rewrite **final.cpp** so that it begins with the assumption that the student is exempt and makes comparisons to see if the student must take the test. Save the revised source code as **final2.cpp**.

PROJECT 5-6

1. Open **lengths.cpp** and analyze the source code.

2. Compile and link the program. *Note*: The program requires the string class.

3. Run the program several times and try different conversions and values.

4. Add a conversion for miles to the program. Use 0.00018939 for the conversion factor.

5. Test the program to see that your addition is working properly.

PROJECT 5-7

1. Obtain the exchange rates for at least three foreign currencies. Currency exchange rates can be found in most newspapers or on the Internet at the Web sites of major banks and financial services companies. You can also call a local bank to obtain the information you need.

2. Write a program similar to **lengths.cpp** that asks the user for an amount of money in dollars and then prompts the user to select the currency into which the dollars are to be converted.

3. Save the program as **currency.cpp**.

CRITICAL THINKING

ACTIVITY 5-1

Modify the **truth.cpp** program from Project 5B to also display a truth table for the not operation. Use Figure 5-3 as a reference.

ACTIVITY 5-2

Write a program that asks for an integer and reports whether the number is even or odd. *Hint*: Use if/else and the modulus operator. Save the source code file as **evenodd.cpp**.

LOOPS

OBJECTIVES

Upon completion of this chapter, you should be able to:

■ Describe the purpose of loops.

■ Use for loops.

■ Use while loops.

■ Use do while loops.

■ Use the break and continue statements.

■ Nest loops.

⏱ **Estimated Time: 2 hours**

VOCABULARY

do while loop

for loop

infinite loop

iteration

iteration structures

loop

nested loop

parameters

while loop

You have probably noticed that much of the work a computer does is repeated many times. For example, a computer can print a personalized letter to each person in a database. The basic operation of printing the letter repeats for each person in the database. When a program repeats a group of statements a given number of times, the repetition is accomplished using a *loop*.

In Chapter 5, you learned about sequence structures and selection structures. In this chapter, you will learn about another category of structures: *iteration structures*. Loops are iteration structures. Each "loop" or pass through a group of statements is called an *iteration*. A condition specified in the program controls the number of iterations performed. For example, a loop may iterate until a specific variable reaches the value 100.

6.1 for Loops

The for Loop

The *for loop* repeats one or more statements a specified number of times. A for loop is difficult to read the first time you see one. Like an if statement, the for loop uses parentheses. In the parentheses are three items called *parameters*, which are needed to make a for loop work. Each parameter in a for loop is an expression. Figure 6-1 shows the format of a for loop.

FIGURE 6-1

A for loop repeats one or more statements a specified number of times.

```
for (initializing expression; control expression; step expression)
  { statements to execute }
```

Look at the program in Code List 6-1. The variable i is used as a counter. The counter variable is used in all three expressions of the for loop. The first parameter, called the *initializing expression*, initializes the counter variable. The second parameter is the expression that will end the loop, called the *control expression*. As long as the control expression is true, the loop continues to iterate. The third parameter is the step expression. It changes the counter variable, usually by adding to it.

 Computer Concepts

As with if structures, you are not required to use braces in for loops when there is only one statement in the loop.

CODE LIST 6-1

```cpp
// forloop.cpp

#include <iostream.h>

int main()
{
 int i; // counter variable
 for(i = 1; i <= 3; i++)
    { cout << i << endl; }
 return 0;
}
```

In Code List 6-1, the statements in the for loop will repeat three times. The variable i is declared as an integer. In the for statement, i is initialized to 1. The control expression tests to see if the value of i is still less than or equal to 3. The control expression is tested *before* the statements in the loop are executed. When i exceeds 3, the loop will end. The step expression increments i by one each time the loop iterates.

 Important

Placing a semicolon after the closing parenthesis of a for loop will prevent any lines from being iterated.

S TEP-BY-STEP ▷ 6.1

1. Key the program from Code List 6-1 into a blank editor screen.

2. Save the source code file as **forloop.cpp**.

3. Compile and run the program. The program counts to three.

4. Close the source file.

Counting Backward and Other Tricks

A counter variable can also count backward by having the step expression decrement the value rather than increment it. The program in Code List 6-2 counts backward from 10 to 1. The counter is initialized to 10. With each iteration, the decrement operator subtracts one from the counter.

CODE LIST 6-2

```
// backward.cpp

#include <iostream.h>

int main()
{
  int i; // counter variable
  for(i = 10; i >= 0; i--)
    { cout << i << endl; }
  cout << "End of loop.\n";
  return 0;
}
```

STEP-BY-STEP ▷ 6.2

1. Enter the program in Code List 6-2 into a blank editor screen.

2. Save the source file as **backward.cpp**.

3. Compile and run the program. Figure 6-2 shows the output you should see.

4. Close the source code file.

FIGURE 6-2
A for loop can decrement the counter variable.

The output prints numbers from 10 to 0 because i is being decremented in the step expression. The phrase *End of loop.* is printed only once because the loop ends with the semicolon that follows the first cout statement.

The counter variable can do more than step by one. In the program in Code List 6-3, the counter variable is doubled each time the loop iterates.

CODE LIST 6-3

```
// dblstep.cpp

#include <iostream.h>

int main()
{
 int i;   // counter variable
 for(i = 1; i <= 100; i = i + i)
   { cout << i << endl; }
 return 0;
}
```

S TEP-BY-STEP ▷ 6.3

1. Enter the program from Code List 6-3 into a blank editor screen.

2. Save the source file as **dblstep.cpp**. Can you predict the program's output?

3. Compile and run the program to see if your prediction was right.

4. Close the program.

The for statement gives you a lot of flexibility. As you have already seen, the step expression can increment, decrement, or count in other ways. Some additional examples of for statements are shown in Table 6-1.

TABLE 6-1
Examples of for statements

for Statement	Count Progression
for (i = 2; i <= 10; i = i + 2)	2, 4, 6, 8, 10
for (i = 1; i < 10; i = i + 2)	1, 3, 5, 7, 9
for (i = 10; i <= 50; i = i + 10)	10, 20, 30, 40, 50

Using a Statement Block in a for Loop

If you need to include more than one statement in the loop, place all the statements that are to be part of the loop in the braces. The statements in the braces will be repeated each time the loop iterates. The statements that follow the braces are not part of the loop.

In Code List 6-4, an output statement as been added inside the loop of the **backward.cpp** program. The phrase *Inside Loop* will appear with each iteration of the loop.

CODE LIST 6-4

```
// backward.cpp

#include <iostream.h>

int main()
{
  int i; // counter variable
  for(i = 10; i >= 0; i—)
  {
  cout << i << endl;
  cout << "Inside Loop\n";
  }
  cout << "End of loop.\n";
  return 0;
}
```

STEP-BY-STEP ▷ 6.4

1. Open **backward.cpp** (the file you saved in Step-by-Step 6.2) and edit the source code to match the Code List 6-4.

2. Compile and run the program to see that the phrase *Inside Loop* prints on every line. The

second cout statement is now part of the loop because it is within the braces.

3. Close the source file without saving changes.

SECTION CHECKPOINT

1. A loop is what type of structure?

2. What type of loop repeats one or more statements a specified number of times?

3. What is the first parameter provided in a for loop statement?

4. How can a for loop be made to count backward?

5. What do you need to do to include more than one statement in a loop?

Define the following terms:

for loop iteration structures parameters
iteration loop

6.2 while Loops

A *while loop* is similar to a for loop. Actually, while loops are sometimes easier to use than for loops and are better suited for many loops. With a for loop, the parameters in the parentheses control the number of times the loop iterates, and the statements in the loop structure are just along for the ride. In a while loop, something inside the loop triggers the loop to stop.

For example, a while loop may be written to ask a user to input a series of numbers until the number 0 is entered. The loop would repeat until the number 0 is entered.

There are two kinds of while loops: the standard while loop and the do while loop. The difference between the two is where the control expression is tested. Let's begin with the standard while loop.

The while Loop

The while loop repeats a statement or group of statements as long as a control expression is true. Unlike a for loop, a while loop does not use a counter variable. The control expression in a while loop can be any valid expression. The program in Code List 6-5 uses a while loop to repeatedly divide a number by 2 until the number is less than or equal to 1.

CODE LIST 6-5

```
// while1.cpp

#include <iostream.h>

int main()
{
 float num;

 cout << "Please enter the number to divide: ";
 cin >> num;
 while (num > 1.0)
   {
    cout << num << endl;
    num = num / 2;
   }
 return 0;
}
```

In a while loop, the control expression is tested before the statements in the loop begin. Figure 6-3 shows a flow chart of the program in Code List 6-5. If the number provided by the user is less than or equal to 1, the statements in the loop are never executed.

FIGURE 6-3

A while loop tests the control expression before the loop begins.

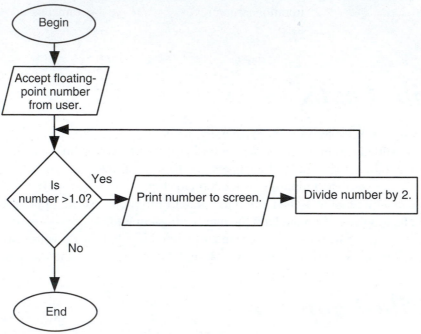

STEP-BY-STEP ▷ 6.5

1. Enter the program shown in Code List 6-5 into a blank editor screen.

2. Save the source file as **while1.cpp.**

3. Compile and run the program. Run the program several times. Try the following numbers as input: 8, 21, 8650, 1, 2.1, 0.5.

4. Close the program.

> **Important**
>
> As with the for loop, placing a semicolon after the closing parenthesis of a while loop will prevent any lines from being iterated.

In order for a while loop to come to an end, the statements in the loop must change a variable used in the control expression. The result of the control expression must be false for a loop to stop. Otherwise, iterations continue indefinitely in what is called an *infinite loop*. In the program you compiled in Step-By-Step 6.5, the statement num = num / 2; divides the number by 2 each time the loop repeats. Even if the user enters a large value, the loop will eventually end when the number becomes less than 1.

A while loop can be used to replace any for loop. So why have a for loop in the language? Because sometimes a for loop offers a better solution. Figure 6-4 shows two programs that produce the same output. The program using the for loop is better in this case because the counter variable is initialized, tested, and incremented in the same statement. In a while loop, a counter variable must be initialized and incremented in separate statements.

FIGURE 6-4

Although both of these programs produce the same output, the for loop gives a more efficient solution.

```
#include <iostream.h>

int main()
{
  int j;
  for(j = 1; j <= 3; j++)
    { cout << j << endl; }
  return 0;
}
```

```
#include <iostream.h>

int main()
{
  int j;
  j = 1;
  while(j <= 3)
    {
      cout << j << endl;
      j++;
    }
  return 0;
}
```

The do while Loop

The last iteration structure in C++ is the *do while loop*. A do while loop repeats a statement or group of statements as long as a control expression is true at the end of the loop. Because the control expression is tested at the end of the loop, a do while loop is executed at least one time. Code List 6-6 shows an example of a do while loop.

CODE LIST 6-6

```
// dowhile.cpp

#include <iostream.h>

int main()
{
  double num, squared;
  do
    {
      cout << "Enter a number (Enter 0 to quit): ";
      cin >> num;
      squared = num * num;
      cout << num << " squared is " << squared << endl;
    }
  while (num != 0);
  return 0;
}
```

143

To help illustrate the difference between a while and a do while loop, compare the two flow charts in Figure 6-5. Use a while loop when you need to test the control expression before the loop is executed the first time. Use a do while loop when the statements in the loop need to be executed at least once.

FIGURE 6-5

The difference between a while loop and a do while loop is where the control expression is tested.

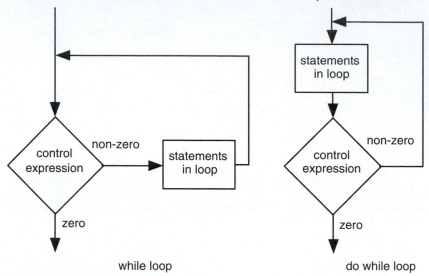

while loop   do while loop

S TEP-BY-STEP ▷ 6.6

1. Enter the program from Code List 6-6 into a blank editor screen.

2. Save the source file as **dowhile.cpp**.

3. Compile and run the program. Enter several numbers greater than 0 to cause the loop to repeat. Enter 0 to end the program.

4. Leave the program open for the next Step-By-Step exercise.

Stopping in the Middle of a Loop

The keyword break, also utilized with switch statements, can be used to end a loop before the conditions of the control expression are met. Once a break terminates a loop, the execution begins with the first statement following the loop. In the program you ran in Step-By-Step 6.6, entering 0 caused the program to end. But the program squares 0 before it ends, even though the step is unnecessary. The program in Code List 6-7 uses a break statement to correct the problem.

CODE LIST 6-7

```
// dowhile.cpp

#include <iostream.h>

int main()
{
 double num, squared;
 do
   {
    cout << "Enter a number (Enter 0 to quit): ";
    cin >> num;
    if (num == 0.0) // break out of loop if
      { break; }        // number entered is zero.
    squared = num * num;
    cout << num << " squared is " << squared << endl;
   }
 while (1); // Create an infinite loop and allow the
            // break statement to end the loop.
 return 0;
}
```

In the program in Code List 6-7, the value entered by the user is tested with an if statement as soon as it is input. If the value is 0, the break statement is executed to end the loop. If the value is any number other than 0, the loop continues.

The while loop's control expression can remain num ! = 0 without affecting the function of the program. In this case, however, the break statement will stop the loop before the control expression is reached. Therefore, the control expression can be changed to 1 to create an infinite loop. The 1 creates an infinite loop because the loop continues to iterate as long as the control expression is true, which is represented by the value 1. The loop will repeat until the break statement is executed.

STEP-BY-STEP 6.7

1. Modify the program on your screen to match Code List 6-7.

2. Save the source file.

3. Compile and run the program. Enter several numbers greater than 0 to cause the loop to repeat. Enter 0 to end the program. Notice that the program now ends without squaring the zero.

4. Close the program.

Computer Concepts

You should allow the control expression to end an iteration structure whenever practical. Whenever you are tempted to use a break statement to exit a loop, make sure that using the break statement is the best way to end the loop.

The continue statement is another way to stop a loop from completing each statement. But instead of continuing with the first statement after the loop, the continue statement skips the remainder of a loop and starts the next iteration of the loop. Code List 6-8 shows an example of how the continue statement can be used to cause a for loop to skip an iteration.

CODE LIST 6-8

```
// continue.cpp

#include <iostream.h>

int main()
{
 int i;
 for(i = 1; i <= 10; i++)
  {
    if (i == 5)
    { continue; }
    cout << i << endl;
  }
 return 0;
}
```

The continue statement in Code List 6-8 causes the statements in the for loop to be skipped when the counter variable is 5. The continue statement also can be used in while and do while statements.

STEP-BY-STEP ▷ 6.8

1. Open **continue.cpp**. The program shown in Code List 6-8 appears.

2. Compile and run the program. Notice that the number 5 does not appear in the output because of the continue statement.

3. Close the program.

Nesting Loops

You have already learned how to nest if structures. Loops can also be nested. In fact, loops within loops are very common. You must, however, trace the steps of the program carefully to understand how **nested loops** behave. The program in Code List 6-9 provides output that will give you insight into the behavior of nested loops.

CODE LIST 6-9

```
// nestloop.cpp

#include <iostream.h>

int main()
{
 int i,j;
 cout << "BEGIN\n";
 for(i = 1; i <= 3; i++)
  {
    cout << " Outer loop: i = " << i << endl;
    for(j = 1; j <= 4; j++)
      { cout << "      Inner loop: j = " << j << endl;}
  }
 cout << "END\n";
 return 0;
}
```

The important thing to realize is that the inner for loop (the one that uses j) will complete its count from 1 to 4 every time the outer for loop (the one that uses i) iterates. That is why in the output, for every loop the outer loop makes, the inner loop starts over.

STEP-BY-STEP ▷ 6.9

1. Open **nestloop.cpp**.

2. Compile and run the program.

3. Close the source file.

Hot Tip

If you know how to use your compiler's debugger, step through the program to trace the flow of logic.

Nesting may also be used with while loops and do while loops, or in combinations of loops. In the upcoming Unit Review, you will run a program that nests a do while loop in a for loop.

SECTION CHECKPOINT

1. Where is the control expression tested in a while loop?

2. Where is the control expression tested in a do while loop?

3. In what type of loop are the statements in the loop always executed at least once?

4. What keyword can be used to end a loop before the conditions of the control expression are met?

5. What types of loops can be nested?

VOCABULARY REVIEW

Define the following terms:

do while loop   nested loop   while loop
infinite loop

Summary

In this chapter, you learned:

- A loop is used to cause a program to repeat a group of statements a given number of times.

- Loops are iteration structures.

- Each loop through a group of statements is called an iteration.

- A for loop repeats one or more statements a specified number of times.

- A for loop uses three parameters to control the loop.

- A for loop can count backward by having the step expression decrement the value rather than increment it. The step expression can also count by values other than one.

- Braces group the statements in a loop.

- A while loop repeats a statement or group of statements as long as a control expression is true. The control expression is tested at the top of the loop.

- A do while loop repeats a statement or group of statements as long as a control expression is true at the end of the loop.

- The break keyword ends a loop before the conditions in the control expression are met.

- The continue keyword skips the remainder of the statements in the loop and continues with the next iteration of the loop.

- Loops may be nested to have loops inside loops.

CHAPTER 6 REVIEW QUESTIONS

TRUE/FALSE

Circle T if the statement is true or F if the statement is false.

T F **1.** A loop is a sequence structure.

T F **2.** A for loop repeats a group of statements a specified number of times.

T F **3.** The items in the parentheses of a for loop are called parameters.

T F **4.** Counting backward in a for loop is accomplished by the initializing expression.

T F **5.** In a while loop, the control expression is tested at the end of the loop.

T F **6.** In order for a while loop to come to an end, the statements in the loop must change a variable used in the control expression.

T F **7.** The statements in a while loop are always executed at least once.

T F   8. A do while loop allows the program to do other things while the statements in the loop repeat.

T F   9. The `break` keyword ends a loop before the conditions of the control expression are met.

T F   10. Only for loops may be nested in programs.

WRITTEN QUESTIONS

Write a brief answer to the following questions.

1. What is each "loop" or pass through a group of statements in a loop called?

2. What are the three expressions in the parentheses of a for loop?

3. Describe the purpose of the counter variable in a for loop.

4. What is the count progression of the following for loop?

```
for (j = 5; j <= 40; j = j + 5)
```

5. What is wrong with the following while loop?

```
while (num > 1.0);
  {
   cout << num << endl;
   num = num - 2.0;
  }
```

6. What term describes a loop that loops indefinitely?

7. Explain the difference between a while loop and a do while loop.

8. What is the result of using a control expression of 1 in a do while loop?

9. What effect does the continue statement have on a loop?

10. In the following code, what message will be printed to the screen the most times, "Red" or "Blue"?

```
for(j = 1; j <= 3; j++)
  {
   cout << "Red\n";
   for(k = 1; k <= 3; k++)
      { cout << "Blue\n"; }
  }
```

CHAPTER 6 PROJECTS

PROJECT 6-1

Write a program that uses a for loop to print the odd numbers from 1 to 21. Save the source code file as **oddloop.cpp**.

PROJECT 6-2

Write a program that implements the flow chart in Figure 6-6. Save the source code file as **sumitup.cpp**.

FIGURE 6-6

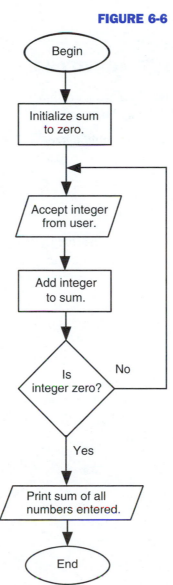

PROJECT 6-3

Write a program that prints the numbers 1 to 20, but skips the numbers 3, 11, and 16. Save the source code file as **skipthem.cpp**.

CRITICAL THINKING

ACTIVITY 6-1

Write a program that uses nested loops to produce the following output. Save the source code file as **abbb.cpp**.
A1B1B2B3A2B1B2B3

ACTIVITY 6-2

Write a program that asks the user for a series of integers one at a time. When the user enters the integer 0, the program displays the following information:

■ the number of integers in the series (not including zero)

■ the average of the integers

■ the largest integer in the series

■ the smallest integer in the series

■ the difference between the largest and smallest integer in the series

Save the source file as **ints.cpp**.

FUNCTIONS

OBJECTIVES

Upon completion of this chapter, you should be able to:

- Build structured programs that are divided into functions.

- Describe the flow of execution in a program with multiple functions.

- Describe what is meant by the phrase "scope of variable."

- Pass data to functions.

- Get values from functions using `return`.

- Describe and use library functions.

- Use common math functions.

- Use character manipulation functions.

⏱ **Estimated Time: 3 hours**

VOCABULARY

argument

automatic variable

bottom-up design

external variable

global variable

header file

library functions

local variable

parameter

pass

passing by reference

passing by value

prototype

scope

top-down design

Up to now you have written programs with only a main function. In Chapter 1 you learned that programs are often divided into more than one function. Programs are divided so that each function performs a specific task. In this chapter, you will learn how to create functions, how to get data into and out of functions, and how to use the pre-written functions that are included with your compiler.

7.1 Building Programs with Functions

How to Build Programs with Functions

Examine the source code in Code List 7-1. The program consists of one function, `main()`. You may have difficulty, however, quickly determining what the program accomplishes.

```cpp
// series.cpp

#include <iostream.h>

int main()
{
 int choice;   // variable for user input
 int i;        // variable for loops and output

 do  // loop until a valid choice is entered
  {
    cout << "Which series do you wish to display?\n";
    cout << "1 - Odd numbers from 1 to 30\n";
    cout << "2 - Even numbers from 1 to 30\n";
    cout << "3 - All numbers from 1 to 30\n";
    cin >> choice;  // get choice from user
    if ((choice < 1) || (choice > 3))  // if invalid entry, give message
     {
       cout << "Choice must be 1, 2, or 3\n";
     }
  } while ((choice < 1) || (choice > 3));

  switch (choice)
    {
      case 1:
        for (i = 1; i <= 30; i = i + 2)
        cout << i << ' ';
        cout << endl;
        break;
      case 2:
        for (i = 2; i <= 30; i = i + 2)
        cout << i << ' ';
        cout << endl;
        break;
      case 3:
        for (i = 1; i <= 30; i++)
        cout << i << ' ';
        cout << endl;
        break;
    }
  return 0;
}
```

When the program is run, the user is prompted from a menu to choose to view a series of numbers. Depending upon the user's choice, the program displays a series of odd numbers, even numbers, or all integers from 1 to 30.

Let's run the program to see its output.

1. Retrieve the source file **series.cpp**.

2. Compile and run the program to see the program's output.

3. Close the source code file.

The program you just executed could have been better built using more than one function. The diagram in Figure 7-1, known as a Visual Table of Contents (VTOC), illustrates the point. The lines represent connections between functions. Each function can be accessed by the function above it as long as a line connects them.

FIGURE 7-1
A diagram that shows the functions of a program is sometimes called a Visual Table of Contents.

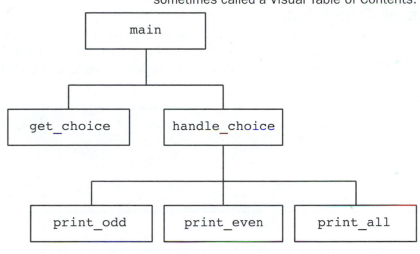

In this case, the `main` function "calls" the `get_choice` function to ask the user to choose the series to display. Next, the `handle_choice` function is called to direct the program flow to one of the three functions under it—one for each series. The source code for Figure 7-1 is presented in the next section.

Guidelines for Building a Program with Functions

Using functions helps the programmer develop programs that can be easily coded, debugged, and maintained. Keep the following guidelines in mind when building programs of more than one function.

1. **Organization**. A large program is easier to read and modify if it is logically organized into functions. It is easier to work with a program in parts, rather than one large chunk. A well-organized program, consisting of multiple functions, is easier to read and debug. Once a single function is tested and performs properly, you can set it aside and concentrate on problem areas.

2. **Autonomy**. Programs should be designed so that they consist mainly of stand-alone functions or modules. Each function is autonomous, meaning the function does not depend on data or code outside the function any more than necessary.

3. **Encapsulation**. The term *encapsulation* refers to enclosing the details of a function within the function itself, so that those details do not have to be known in order to use the function.

4. **Reusability**. Because functions typically perform a single and well-defined task, they may be reused in the same program or even in other programs.

Functions may be written for any purpose. For example, you could create a function that converts Fahrenheit temperatures to Celsius or a function that gets input from the user. A function can also be a go-between for other parts of the program, as illustrated in the `handle_choice` function of Figure 7-1.

There are two popular methods of designing programs. The first method, called ***top-down design***, begins with the functions at the top of the VTOC and works toward the functions at the bottom of the VTOC. In other words, the general organization and flow of the program is decided before the details are coded.

Bottom-up design involves beginning with the bottom of the VTOC and working your way up. Some programmers prefer to work out the details of how the program will perform specific tasks and then bring the details together to create the overall organization and flow.

Whether you use top-down or bottom-up design, it is important to take an organized approach to writing a multifunction program.

The Syntax of Functions

With each program you have written, you have created a `main` function. You can use a similar syntax to create other functions. But before we look at other functions, let's take another look at the `main` function. The `main` function in the programs shown in this book have looked like the one in Code List 7-2.

CODE LIST 7-2

```
int main()
{
 // body of program
 return 0;
}
```

When the program reaches the `return 0;` statement, the value zero is returned to the operating system. This value tells the operating system that the program ended normally. The value returned is a standard integer because we specified an int data type when the `main` function was declared.

There are times when a function has no reason to return a value. To prevent a value from being returned, the `void` keyword is used in place of a data type. You may have seen programs with a `main` function like the one in Code List 7-3.

CODE LIST 7-3

```
void main()
{
 // body of program
}
```

In a void function, no value is returned; therefore, no `return` statement is included. Newer operating systems are more likely to take advantage of the value returned by the `main` function. Therefore, you should get into the habit of creating `main` functions that return a zero when they terminate normally. The void `main` functions are used less frequently now than in the past.

As mentioned earlier, creating other functions in C++ programs is similar to creating the `main` function. Code List 7-4 shows a simple function that prints a message to the screen.

CODE LIST 7-4

```
void print_title()
 {
  cout << "Soccer Tournament Scheduler Program\n";
  cout << "By Ben and Conrad McCue\n";
 }
```

The name of the function is `print_title`. The `void` keyword indicates that no value is returned. The parentheses after the name let the compiler know that `print_title` is a function. The statements between the braces are executed when the function `print_title` is "called." The `main` function in Code List 7-5 includes an example of a call to the `print_title` function.

CODE LIST 7-5

```
int main()
 {
  print_title(); // call to print_title

  // insert the rest of the program here

  return 0;
 }
```

Function Prototypes

There is one more thing you have to do to make your own functions work. At the top of your program, you must tell the compiler that your function exists. You do this by creating a *prototype*. Basically, a prototype defines the function for the compiler. Code List 7-6 shows the functions from Code Lists 7-4 and 7-5 assembled into a working program, including the required function prototype.

CODE LIST 7-6

```
// 1stfunct.cpp

#include <iostream.h>

void print_title();  // prototype for print_title function

int main()
 {
  print_title(); // call to print_title

  // insert the rest of the program here

  return 0;
```

```
    } // end of main function

    // Function to print program title to the screen.
    void print_title()
     {
       cout << "Soccer Tournament Scheduler Program\n";
       cout << "By Ben and Conrad McCue\n";
     } // end of print_title
```

The function prototype is identical to the first line of the function itself. There is, however, a semicolon at the end of the prototype.

To understand why a function prototype is necessary, consider the way a compiler works. A program is compiled one line at a time. As the compiler works its way down the program, it interprets the source code it reads and compiles that source code into machine code. The function prototypes at the top of the program inform the compiler that later in the source code it will find references to a custom-made function.

For example, in Code List 7-6, the function prototype for print_title tells the compiler to be expecting a call to a function named print_title. It also tells the compiler important information such as the fact that print_title is a void function. So when the main function makes the call to print_title, the compiler knows what print_title is and whether print_title is being called correctly. The compiler is content to wait for the bottom of the program before learning what the print_title function actually does.

Computer Concepts

The compiler itself does not care whether it finds an actual function to match the prototype at the top of the program. It is the linker's job to link all the pieces together and find the functions referred to in a prototype. Often, a function prototype exists in C++ source code and the actual function is in another file or in a pre-compiled library. For example, when you include iostream.h in your programs, you are basically including function prototypes for the iostream features. The linker takes care of linking your program to those actual functions.

STEP-BY-STEP 7.2

1. Carefully enter the program in Code List 7-6 into a blank editor screen. Save the program as **1stfunct.cpp**.

2. Compile, link, and run the program. The main function calls the print_title function and prints the message to the screen.

3. Leave the program open for the next Step-by-Step exercise.

Functions and Program Flow

In Step-by-Step 7.1, the `main` function began executing when the program was run. The first statement in the `main` function called the `print_title` function. The call caused execution to jump to the `print_title` function. When a function is called, the computer executes the statements in the function beginning with the first statement. When the end of the function is reached, program execution resumes with the statement that follows the call to the function.

Suppose you are washing a car and you hear the phone ring. You leave the car for a moment and answer the phone. When you complete the phone call, you return to the car and begin washing where you left off. That's basically how the flow of a program works. Programs execute one statement at a time. Functions are just another way of controlling the flow of a program to make the program more efficient and better organized.

Figure 7-2 shows the sequence of execution in a simple three-function example.

FIGURE 7-2

The numbers next to the statements show the order of execution.

```
      int main ()
      {  ◄───────────────────────   Program Begins
(1)   print_title(); // call to print_title
      // insert the rest of the program here

(4)   print_goodbye();

      return 0;
(6) } // end of main function  ◄──────   Program Ends


      // Function to print program title to the screen.
      void print_title()
      }
(2)   cout << "Soccer Tournament Scheduler Program\n";
(3)   cout << "By Ben and Conrad McCue\n";
      } // end of print_title

      // Function to print closing message
      void print_goodbye()
      {
(5)   cout << "Thank you for using the Soccer Tournament Scheduler.\n";
      { // end of print_goodbye
```

The program begins with the first statement of the `main` function (1), which is a call to the `print_title` function. The flow of logic goes to the `print_title` function, which includes two statements (2 and 3), and they are executed next. When the last statement (3) in the `print_title` function is executed, the flow of logic returns to the statement (4) that follows the previous function call in `main()`. The statement in the `print_goodbye` function (5) is then executed. The flow of logic then returns to `main()` where the program ends (6).

 Hot Tip

Notice that a function's prototype is just like the first line of the function, except for the semicolon. An error will result if you forget to include the semicolon at the end of a prototype.

```cpp
// 1stfunct.cpp

#include <iostream.h>

void print_title();    // prototype for print_title function
void print_goodbye(); // prototype for print_goodbye function

 int main()
 {
  print_title(); // call to print_title

  // insert the rest of the program here

  print_goodbye();

  return 0;
 } // end of main function


// Function to print program title to the screen.
 void print_title()
 {
   cout << "Soccer Tournament Scheduler Program\n";
   cout << "By Ben and Conrad McCue\n";
 } // end of print_title


// Function to print closing message
 void print_goodbye()
 {
   cout << "Thank you for using the Soccer Tournament Scheduler.\n";
 } // end of print_goodbye
```

S TEP-BY-STEP ▷ 7.3

1. Modify **1stfunct.cpp** to match the program shown in Code List 7-7. Don't forget to add the new function prototype.

2. Compile, link, and run the program.

3. When you have run the program successfully, close the program.

Scope of Variables

When building a program that consists of functions, you must be concerned with how data is made available to the functions. In this section, you will learn about the accessibility of variables in functions and how to get data to and from functions.

As programs get larger, it is important to keep tight control over variables to prevent errors in your programs. One of the ways to do this is to make the data in variables accessible only in the areas where that data is needed. When data is needed in another part of the program, it is better to send that data and that data only to the part of the program that needs it.

You have been working primarily with programs that have only one function: `main()`. Within `main()`, you declared variables. These variables, however, would be inaccessible outside of `main()`. The "availability" of a variable is known as its *scope*. While this may sound difficult, in C++ the scope of variables is easy to understand.

> **✓ Note**
>
> Local variables are sometimes called **automatic variables** and global variables are sometimes called **external variables**.

Variables in C++ can either be local or global. A *local variable* is declared within a function and is accessible only within that function. A *global variable* is declared before the `main` function. Global variables are accessible by any function.

Consider the program in Code List 7-8. One variable (`i`) is declared before the `main` function, making it a global variable. Because `j` and `k` are declared in the `main` function, they are local to the `main` function. Therefore, `j` and `k` cannot be used outside of the `main` function. Within the function named `myfunction`, the variable `l` is declared. It, too, is local and accessible only within `myfunction`. After the last statement in `myfunction` is executed, the variable `l` is gone from memory.

CODE LIST 7-8

```
// scope.cpp

#include <iostream.h>

int i = 3;      // global variable

void myfunction();

int main()
 {
   int j,k; // variables local to the main function
            // j and k are not accessible outside of the main function
   j = 2;
   k = i + j;
   cout << "j = " << j << " and k = " << k << '\n';
   cout << "i = " << i << " before the call to myfunction.\n";
   myfunction(); // call to myfunction
   cout << "i = " << i << " after the call to myfunction.\n";
   return 0;
 }

void myfunction()
 {
   int l;    // local variable
   l = ++i; // the variable i is accessible because i is global
            // the variable i is changed globally
   cout << "l = " << l << '\n';
   cout << "The variable l is lost as soon as myfunction exits.\n";
 }
```

Because the variable i is accessible from the entire program, changes made to i while in myfunction will be made to the global variable. Therefore, those changes will still be in effect when the program returns to the main function.

If a statement were added to myfunction that attempted to access the variable k, located in main, an error would result. The variable k is accessible only from within the main function. In a similar manner, the variable l is inaccessible outside of myfunction because it is local to myfunction.

STEP-BY-STEP ▷ 7.4

1. Open **scope.cpp**. The program from Code List 7-8 appears on your screen.

2. Compile and run the program as it appears. Study the source code to get clear in your mind where each variable is available.

3. Enter the following statement at the end of myfunction.

```
k = i + j;
```

4. Compile the program to see the errors the new statement generates. Your compiler will probably generate an error telling you that the variables j and k are not defined. The error is generated because j and k are available only in the main function.

5. Delete the erring statement and close the program.

Why have local variables if they are inaccessible to other parts of the program? One reason is that they exist only while the function is executing and memory is released when the function terminates. If a variable is needed only within a particular function, you save memory by creating and disposing of the variable within the function.

Using local variables could limit the number of errors that occur in a program. If all variables were global, an error made in a variable and used by various functions could cause multiple errors. However, if you use local variables, any errors are limited to the function in which the variable is declared.

Use local variables whenever possible. Even a large program should have very few global variables. Using local variables keeps a tighter control over your program's data, resulting in fewer bugs and programs that are easier to maintain.

You may be wondering how data can get to other functions if everything is local. As you will learn in the next section, when a function is created, you can choose what data you want to send to the function.

SECTION CHECKPOINT

1. What is an advantage of dividing a program into multiple functions?

2. What is the name of the diagram that shows the functions that make up a program?

3. What term refers to enclosing the details of a function within the function itself, so that the details do not have to be known in order to use the function?

4. What does a function prototype do?

5. What is meant by the scope of a variable?

VOCABULARY REVIEW

Define the following terms:

automatic variable

global variable

scope

bottom-up design

local variable

top-down design

external variable

prototype

7.2 Passing Data

Getting Data to and from Functions

You have learned that the parentheses following a function's name let the compiler know that it is a function. The parentheses can serve another purpose as well. That is, parentheses can be used to **pass** data to a function and in some cases to return data from a function.

When a function is called, the data in the parentheses (called the **argument**) is passed into the receiving function. There are two ways to pass data to functions: **passing by value** and **passing by reference**.

Computer Concepts

Getting data to and from functions is called *passing data*. Programmers talk about passing data to a function and the function passing a value back.

Passing by Value

When you pass a variable to a function by value, a copy of the value in the variable is given to the function for it to use. If the variable is changed within the function, the original copy of the variable in the calling function remains the same. Code List 7-9 is an example of a function that accepts data using the passing by value technique.

CODE LIST 7-9

```
void print_true_or_false(bool True_False)
 {
  if True_False        // If True_False is true,
   {                   // display the word TRUE.
    cout << "TRUE\n";
   }
  else                 // If True_False is false,
   {                   // display the word FALSE.
    cout << "FALSE\n";
   }
 }
```

A value comes into the function through the parentheses, and the copy of the value will be placed in the variable `True_False`. The variable `True_False` is called a **parameter**.

163

When you write a call to a function, you can put any variable or literal in the parentheses to be passed to the function as long as the data types do not conflict. For example, the statements in Code List 7-10 are all legal calls to the print_true_or_false function.

CODE LIST 7-10

```
print_true_or_false(complete);          // passes a variable
print_true_or_false(true);              // passes a literal
print_true_or_false(j == 3 && k == 2);  // passes the result
                                        // of an expression
```

The program in Code List 7-11 illustrates how a value passed to the function named print_value does not pass back to the main function. Notice that the print_value function uses a variable named j, even though the main function passes a variable named i. The data types must match, but the names are often different.

CODE LIST 7-11

```
// passval.cpp

#include <iostream.h>

void print_value(int j);   // function prototype

int main()
 {
  int i = 2;
  cout << "The value before the function is " << i << endl;
  print_value(i);
  cout << "The value after the function exits is " << i << endl;
  return 0;
 }

void print_value(int j)
 {
  cout << "The value passed to the function is " << j << endl;
  j = j * 2; // the value in the variable i is doubled
  cout << "The value at the end of the function is " << j << endl;
 }
```

STEP-BY-STEP ▷ 7.5

1. Enter the program shown in Code List 7-11. Save the source code as **passval.cpp**.

2. Compile and run the program to see that the value passed to the print_value function is not passed back to the main function.

3. Leave the source code file open for the next Step-by-Step exercise.

Passing by Reference

Functions that pass variables by reference will pass any changes you make to the variables back to the calling function. For example, suppose you need a function that gets input from the user. The function in Code List 7-12 uses passing by reference to get two values from the user and pass them back through parentheses.

CODE LIST 7-12

```
void get_values(float &income, float &expense)
 {
  cout << "Enter this month's income amount: $";
  cin >> income;
  cout << "Enter this month's expense amount: $";
  cin >> expense;
 }
```

To pass a variable by reference, simply precede the variable name with an ampersand (&) in the function definition. But even though it is easy to pass by reference, you should do so sparingly. You should write functions that pass variables by value whenever possible because passing variables by value is safer. When you pass a variable by value, you know it cannot be changed by the function you call. When you pass a variable by reference, a programming error in the function could cause a problem throughout the program.

As a general rule, you should use passing by reference only when data needs to be passed back to the calling function. In the preceding example, the data entered by the user must be passed back to the calling function.

The program you ran in the last exercise passed a variable by value. Let's modify the program to make it pass the variable by reference.

Did You Know?

Many people use the terms *argument* and *parameter* interchangeably, but there is a difference. An argument is a value or expression passed to a function through the parentheses when a function is called. A parameter is the variable that receives the value or any other identifier in the parentheses of the function declaration. In other words, an argument is passed to a function, but once in the function, the argument is a parameter.

S TEP-BY-STEP ▷ 7.6

1. Add an ampersand (&) before the identifier j in both the prototype and the function declaration. Save the source code as **passref.cpp**.

2. Compile and run the program again to see the difference passing by reference makes.

3. Close the source code file.

Returning Values Using Return

As you learned earlier in this chapter, unless a function is declared with the keyword void, the function will return a value. In the case of the main function, it returns a value to the operating system. Other functions, however, return a value to the calling function. The value to be returned is specified using the return statement.

The function in Code List 7-13 is an example of a function that returns a value of type double. The temperature in Celsius is passed into the function by value and the temperature in Fahrenheit is returned using the `return` statement.

CODE LIST 7-13

```
double celsius_to_fahrenheit(double celsius)
 {
  double fahr;  // local variable for calculation
  fahr = celsius * (9.0/5.0) + 32.0;
  return(fahr);
 }
```

Any function that is not declared as void should include a `return` statement. The value or expression in the `return` statement is that which is returned to the calling function. In the `celsius_to_fahrenheit` function, the value stored in `fahr` is returned to the calling function.

The program in Code List 7-14 shows how you can use this function. The statement `fahrenheit = celsius_to_fahrenheit(celsius);` calls the `celsius_to_fahrenheit` function and passes the value in the variable `celsius` to the function. The function returns the temperature in Fahrenheit degrees, and the calling statement assigns the Fahrenheit temperature to the variable `fahrenheit`.

CODE LIST 7-14

```
// ctof.cpp

#include <iostream.h>

int main()
 {
  double fahrenheit;
  double celsius = 22.5;

  fahrenheit = celsius_to_fahrenheit(celsius);

  cout << celsius << " C = " << fahrenheit << " F\n";
  return 0;
 }
```

The `celsius_to_fahrenheit` function could be rewritten as shown in Code List 7-15 to include only one statement and return the same result. Any valid expression can appear in the parentheses of the `return` statement. In this case, performing the calculation in the `return` statement eliminates the local variable `fahr`.

Computer Concepts

You can use any data type when declaring a function.

CODE LIST 7-15

CODE LIST 7-15

```
double celsius_to_fahrenheit(double celsius)
{
  return(celsius * (9.0/5.0) + 32.0);
}
```

When using the `return` statement, keep the following important points in mind.

1. The `return` statement does not require that the value being returned be placed in parentheses. You may, however, want to get into the habit of placing variables and expressions in parentheses to make the code more readable.

2. A function can return only one value using `return`. Use passing by reference to return multiple values from a function.

3. When a `return` statement is encountered, the function will exit and return the value specified, even if other program lines exist below the `return`.

4. A function can have more than one `return` statement to help simplify an algorithm. For example, a `return` statement could be in an if structure allowing a function to return early if a certain condition is met.

5. The calling function is not required to use or even to capture the value returned from a function it calls.

STEP-BY-STEP ▷ 7.7

1. Open **ctof.cpp**. The complete Celsius to Fahrenheit program appears.

2. Compile, link, and run the program.

3. Leave the program open for the next Step-by-Step exercise.

One additional important note: When the last line of a function is reached, or when a `return()` statement is executed, the function ends and the program returns to the calling function and begins executing statements from where it left. Do not end functions with a call back to the original function or the function will not terminate properly. Continually calling functions without returning from them will eventually cause the program to crash.

If you call the `main` function at the end of a function you wrote, the `main` function will begin with the first statement, rather than beginning with the statement following the call to your function.

More About Function Prototypes

A function prototype consists of the function's return type, name, and argument list. In this lesson, the function prototypes specified the parameter names in the argument list. However, this is not necessary as long as the type is specified. For example, the prototype for the `celsius_to_fahrenheit` function could be written as:

```
double celsius_to_fahrenheit(double);
```

The prototype for the `get_values` function could be written as:

```
void get_values(float &, float &);
```

1. Change the function prototype in **ctof.cpp** to specify the data type only, as shown in the previous examples.

2. Compile, link, and run the program. The program still functions normally. After you have seen it work, close the program.

Dividing the Series Program into Functions

Now that you have practiced creating functions and moving data to and from them, let's take another look at the program from Step-by-Step 7.5. In the previous section, you studied a VTOC of the program divided into functions. That VTOC appears again in Figure 7-3.

FIGURE 7-3

This Visual Table of Contents shows the series program divided into functions.

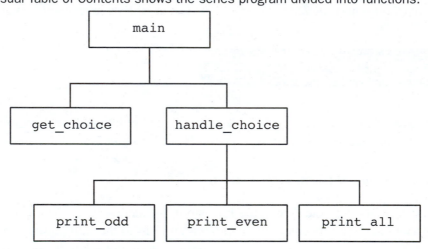

1. Retrieve the source code file **series2.cpp**. Analyze the source code to see that the program is divided into functions.

2. Compile and run the program to see that it has the same result as the single-function version you ran in Step-by-Step 7.5.

3. Close the program.

SECTION CHECKPOINT

1. What happens when a variable is passed by value?

2. What happens when a variable is passed by reference?

3. How many values can be returned by a return statement?

4. Can a function have more than one return statement?

5. What are the three parts of a function prototype?

VOCABULARY REVIEW

Define the following terms:

argument	pass	passing by value
parameter	passing by reference	

7.3 Using Library Functions

Using Library Functions

C++ compilers include pre-written, ready-to-use functions to make programming easier. The number and type of functions available to you will vary depending on your compiler. The functions that come with your compiler are called *library functions*. This section shows you how to use some of the more common library functions.

Library functions are just like functions you create and may be used in the same way. The difference is that the source code for library functions does not appear in your program. The prototypes for library functions are provided to your program using the #include compiler directive.

Let's examine a common C++ library function, pow(), which is used to raise a value (x) by a designated power (y). The pow() function prototype is as follows.

```
double pow(double x, double y);
```

The function pow receives two values or expressions of type double and returns the result as a double. The following is an example of a call to the pow function.

```
z = pow(x, y); // z equals x raised to the y power
```

In order to use the pow function, you must include the math.h header file using the compiler directive below. A **header file** is a text file that provides the prototypes of a group of library functions. The linker uses the information in the header file to properly link your program with the function you want to use.

```
#include <math.h>
```

The program in Code List 7-16 is a simple example of the use of the pow function.

CODE LIST 7-16

```
// power.cpp

#include <iostream.h>
#include <math.h>

int main()
  {
    double base;
    double exponent;
    double answer;

    cout << "Enter the base: ";      // Prompt user for base
    cin >> base;
    cout << "Enter the exponent: "; // Prompt user for exponent
    cin >> exponent;

    answer = pow(base, exponent);    // Calculate answer

    cout << "The answer is " << answer << endl;

    return 0;
  }
```

STEP-BY-STEP ▷ 7.10

1. Enter the program in Code List 7-16 into a blank editor screen. Save the program as **power.cpp**.

2. Compile, run, and test your program.

3. Close the program.

Popular Math Functions

Many C++ compilers provide basic math functions, such as the one you used to calculate x^y. Table 7-1 describes some basic math functions and shows their prototypes and their purpose.

> ✅ **Note**
>
> All of the functions in Table 7-1 require that math.h be included in the calling program.

TABLE 7-1
Basic math functions

Function	Prototype	Description
abs	`int abs(int x);`	Returns the absolute value of an integer
labs	`long int labs(long int x);`	Returns the absolute value of a long integer
fabs	`double fabs(double x);`	Returns the absolute value of a floating-point number
ceil	`double ceil(double x);`	Rounds up to a whole number
floor	`double floor(double x);`	Rounds down to a whole number
hypot	`double hypot(double a,` `double b);`	Calculates the hypotenuse (c) of a right triangle where $c^2 = a^2 + b2$
pow	`double pow(double x,` `double y);`	Calculates x to the power of y
pow10	`double pow10(int x);`	Calculates 10 to the power of x
sqrt	`double sqrt(double x);`	Calculates the positive square root of x

STEP-BY-STEP ▷ 7.11

1. Open **math.cpp** and analyze the source code to see the usage of the `ceil` and `floor` functions.

2. Compile and run the program. Be sure to enter a value with a fractional part, such as 2.4.

3. Add the following line to the program, below the other output statements.

4. Save, compile, and run the program again. Run the program multiple times, entering both positive and negative numbers.

5. Close the program.

```
cout << "The absolute value of " << x << " is " << fabs(x) << endl;
```

 Note

In addition to the math functions covered in this section, C++ compilers also include many trigonometric and logarithmic library functions.

Functions for Working with Characters

C++ compilers also include many functions for analyzing and changing characters. The header file ctype.h must be included for a calling program to use the functions listed in Table 7-2. The conditional functions in the table return a non-zero integer if the condition is true and zero if the condition is false.

TABLE 7-2
Character functions

Function	Prototype	Description
isupper	int isupper(int c);	Determines if a character is uppercase
islower	int islower(int c);	Determines if a character is lowercase
isalpha	int isalpha(int c);	Determines if a character is a letter (a–z, A–Z)
isdigit	int isdigit(int c);	Determines if a character is a digit (0 – 9)
toupper	int toupper(int c);	Converts a character to uppercase
tolower	int tolower(int c);	Converts a character to lowercase

The program in Code List 7-17 demonstrates the use of the isalpha, isupper, and isdigit functions. The program asks for a character and then reports to the user whether the character is uppercase or lowercase. If the user enters a numeral, the program detects and reports that as well. Finally, the program detects and reports if the character is neither a letter nor a number.

CODE LIST 7-17

```cpp
// charfun.cpp

#include <iostream.h>
#include <ctype.h>

int main()
{
  char c;

  cout <<"Enter a character\n";
  cin >> c;

  if(isalpha(c))
    {
     if(isupper(c))
        { cout << c <<" is an uppercase letter\n";}
     else
        { cout << c <<" is a lowercase letter\n";}
    }
```

CODE LIST 7-17 (continued)

```
if(isdigit(c))
  { cout << c <<" is a number\n";}

if(!(isdigit(c)||isalpha(c)))
  {cout << c <<" is neither a letter nor a number\n";}

return 0;
}
```

S TEP-BY-STEP ▷ 7.12

1. Open **charfun.cpp**. The program in Code List 7-17 appears, without the three if structures.

2. Enter the missing if structures using Code List 7-17 as a reference.

3. Save, compile, and run the program. Run it several times, trying uppercase and lowercase letters, numbers, and symbols.

4. Close the program.

SECTION CHECKPOINT

1. What do you call the functions that come with the compiler?

2. What compiler directive is used to provide the prototypes for the functions that come with the compiler?

3. What function returns the absolute value of an integer?

4. Write a statement that prints the square root of the value stored in x to the screen.

5. What function determines whether a character is uppercase?

VOCABULARY REVIEW

Define the following terms:

header file   library functions

Summary

In this chapter, you learned:

- Designing a program that consists of functions results in code that is better organized, reusable, and easier to debug.

- The syntax of functions you create is very similar to that of the `main` function. The parentheses after the function name tell the compiler that you are defining a function.

- You must create a prototype for your functions to let the compiler know your function exists. Prototypes are placed at the top of the program.

- A local variable is created within a function and is accessible only from within that function. A global variable is declared outside of all functions and is accessible from any function.

- Getting data to and from functions is called passing data.

- Data can be passed to functions by value or by reference.

- When possible, you should pass by value. Passing by value passes a copy of the data, and the original data cannot be changed from within the function.

- Data passed by reference brings back changes made to it within a function.

- A value can be passed to the calling function using `return`.

- A void function does not return a value.

- In a function prototype, you are required to provide only the data types of the parameters.

- Library functions are functions that come with the compiler.

- A header file provides the prototypes for library functions.

- C++ includes common math functions and functions for working with characters.

CHAPTER 7 REVIEW QUESTIONS

TRUE/FALSE

Circle T if the statement is true or F if the statement is false.

T F   **1.** When a program jumps from one function to another, we say that the first function *called* the second.

T F   **2.** Dividing a program into functions can improve the organization of a program.

T F 3. A drawback to dividing a program into functions is that it makes it more difficult to debug.

T F 4. In a top-down design, the `main` function is written first.

T F 5. Passing by value gives the function a copy of the passed variable.

T F 6. An @ symbol signifies a variable is to be passed by reference.

T F 7. You should pass data by reference whenever possible.

T F 8. Any function that is not void should include a `return` statement.

T F 9. Any valid expression can appear in the parentheses of a `return` statement.

T F 10. The source code for a library function appears in your program.

WRITTEN QUESTIONS

Write a brief answer to the following questions.

1. What does VTOC stand for?

2. List two guidelines that you can use to decide what code is a good candidate for being made into a function.

3. Briefly describe top-down and bottom-up design.

4. Why is a `return` statement unnecessary in a void function?

5. Suppose a program includes a function with the following prototype. Write the line of code necessary to call the function.

```
void print_message();
```

6. Describe one advantage of using local variables.

7. Where must a variable be declared in order for it to be local?

8. Where must a variable be declared in order for it to be global?

9. What header file is required to use the `pow` function?

10. What function returns the absolute value of a floating-point number?

PROJECT 7-1

1. Open **gascheck.cpp**. An incomplete program appears. To complete the program, you will add two functions and an if structure that calls the new functions.

2. Add a void function called `print_warning` that warns the program has calculated that the user will run out of gas before the next available gas station. Don't forget to add the necessary function prototype.

3. Add a void function called `print_okay` that tells the user he or she will make it to the next gas station. Don't forget to add the necessary function prototype.

4. Add an if/else structure to the `main` function that calls `print_warning` if `fuel_miles` is less than `miles_remaining`. Otherwise, `print_okay` should be called.

5. Save and run the program.

6. Close the program.

PROJECT 7-2

Write a program that asks the user for an integer. The program should call one of three functions, based on the value entered. If the value is negative, call a function that prints a message indicating the value is negative. Create similar functions to call when the value is zero and positive. Save the source code as **valtest.cpp**.

PROJECT 7-3

Write a program source code template that you can use as a starting point for programs you create in the future. Include comments at the top that give your name and provide places for you to fill in the date and description of the program. Set aside a place for `#include` directives, prototypes, constants, and global variables. Create an empty `main` function. Save the source code file as **newprog.cpp** and close the file.

PROJECT 7-4

1. Open the version of **ctof.cpp** that you saved in Step-by-Step 7.8.

2. Add the following function to the program.

```
double get_celsius()
  {
    double celsius_in;

    cout << "Enter the temperature in Celsius: ";
    cin >> celsius_in;
    return celsius_in;
  }
```

3. Add the appropriate function prototype for the new function.

4. Add the following line to the main function, immediately following the variable declarations.

```
celsius = get_celsius();
```

5. Change the declaration of the variable celsius to remove the initialization.

6. Save, compile, and run the program.

PROJECT 7-5

Write a program that uses the sqrt function to calculate the circumference of a circle, given its area. Use the formula $2\sqrt{\pi} * area$. Save the program as **circ.cpp** and close the source code when you have completed the exercise.

PROJECT 7-6

Write a program that prompts the user for a single character that must be either an uppercase or lowercase letter. The program should use a do while loop to repeat the prompt if the character entered is not a letter. Once the user has entered a letter, the program should change the case of the letter. If the letter was entered as uppercase, the program should change the character to lowercase and vice versa. The changed letter should be output, along with the original character entered by the user. *Hint*: The syntax for converting a character's case is shown in the following example.

```
c = tolower(c);
```

Save the source code as **charchng.cpp**.

PROJECT 7-7

Modify **series2.cpp** so that the call to `get_choice` and `handle_choice` are in a do while loop. Add an item to the menu numbered 0 (zero) that exits the program. Have the loop continually redisplay the menu until zero is chosen. *Note*: Make sure you change the do while loop in the `get_choice` function so that zero is a valid input. Save the source code as **series3.cpp**.

CRITICAL THINKING

ACTIVITY 7-1

Write a program that meets the following requirements. Save the program as **scopex.cpp**. The program should:

1. Declare a global integer variable named `x` and initialize it to zero.

2. Declare a local integer variable within `main` named `y`.

3. From within `main`, prompt the user for a value for `y`.

4. Include a loop that calls a function named `incx` `y` number of times.

5. Include the function `incx` to increment the value of `x` by one.

6. Print the value of `x` after each iteration of the loop.

ACTIVITY 7-2

Modify the `get_celsius` function in the program you saved in Project 7-4 to use passing by reference to return the temperature to the `main` function.

Program Structure

REVIEW QUESTIONS

MATCHING

Write the letter of the description from Column 2 that best matches the term or phrase in Column 1.

Column 1	Column 2
___ 1. bottom-up design	**A.** A variable accessible only within a function
___ 2. do while loop	**B.** The classification of structures that execute statements one after another without changing the flow
___ 3. flowchart	**C.** Operators used to make comparisons
___ 4. for loop	**D.** The classification of structures that make decisions
___ 5. global variable	**E.** The availability of a variable
___ 6. header file	**F.** A method of passing that allows the passed variable to be changed by the receiving function
___ 7. iteration structures	**G.** Selects one of many paths of execution
___ 8. library function	**H.** Designing functions at the bottom of the VTOC first
___ 9. local variable	**I.** Designing functions at the top of the VTOC first
___ 10. logical operators	**J.** The classification of structures that repeat statements
___ 11. passing by reference	**K.** A method of passing that sends a copy to the receiving function
___ 12. passing by value	**L.** Defines a function for the compiler
___ 13. prototype	**M.** A variable accessible to any function
___ 14. relational operators	**N.** A loop that repeats a specified number of times
___ 15. scope	**O.** Provides function prototypes for functions that exist outside your program
___ 16. selection structures	**P.** A loop that tests the control expression at the top of the loop

_____ **17.** sequence structures   **Q.** A drawing that helps illustrate the flow of a program

_____ **18.** switch structure   **R.** Operators used to combine comparisons

_____ **19.** top-down design   **S.** Functions that come with the compiler

_____ **20.** while loop   **T.** A loop that tests the control expression at the end of the loop

WRITTEN QUESTIONS

Write a brief answer to the following questions.

1. On what is decision making in computers based?

2. Describe the shape and purpose of two flowchart symbols.

3. Internally, what is used to represent true and false?

4. What are the three logical operators?

5. What is the name of the expression that makes the decision in an if structure?

6. What is the purpose of the == operator?

7. Give an example of a two-way selection structure.

8. What term describes placing if structures or loops inside other if structures or loops?

9. What kind of loop always executes the statements in the loop at least once before reaching the control expression?

10. What keyword causes a loop to stop and continue with the next iteration?

11. What effect does dividing a program into functions have on the ease of debugging and why?

12. In a top-down design, what function is written first?

13. When the last line in a function is executed, what line is executed next?

14. What kind of variable is sometimes called an automatic variable?

15. What is the scope of a variable declared within the `main` function?

16. Where are global variables declared?

17. What symbol signifies that a variable is to be passed by reference?

18. When a function is called, what term is used to describe the items in the parentheses?

19. What method of passing data should be used whenever possible?

20. What function rounds a decimal value up to the next whole number?

PROJECTS

PROJECT 2-1

1. Write a statement that declares a Boolean variable named `t_f`.

2. Write a statement that determines if `k` is equal to 4 and assigns the result to `t_f`.

3. Write a statement that determines if `k` is greater than `m` and prints the result of the comparison to the screen. Include an end-of-line character in the output statement.

4. Write a statement that assigns the value `true` to a Boolean variable named `in_range` if `k` is 4, 5, or 6. You do not have to declare the variables.

5. Write an if structure that prints the message "The number is in range." to the screen if `in_range` is true.

6. Write an if/else structure that assigns `true` to the Boolean variable named `CanAfford` if the value in the variable `Price` is twenty dollars or less. Otherwise, the structure should set `CanAfford` to `false`.

7. Complete the following switch structure. Add a case that prints the message "The character entered was C, as in cow." when C is entered. Also enter a default case that prints the message "Illegal entry" if no other case applies.

```
switch(character_entered)
  {
    case 'A':
      cout << "The character entered was A, as in albatross.\n";
      break;
    case 'B':
      cout << "The character entered was B, as in butterfly.\n";
      break;
```

8. Write a for loop that produces the count progression 4, 8, 12, 16, 20. The counter should be printed to the screen on each iteration.

9. Write a while loop that repeats a number of statements until a counter variable becomes less than 10. The counter variable should be initialized before the loop as 100. Each iteration of the loop should divide the counter by 3 and then print the value of the counter variable.

10. Write a do while loop that asks the user to enter a number in the range of 1 to 10 and repeats until the user enters a valid number.

PROJECT 2-2

Write a program that determines your weight on another planet. The program should ask for the user's weight on Earth, then present a menu of the other planets in our solar system. The user should choose one of the planets from the menu and use a switch statement to calculate the weight on the chosen planet. Use the following conversion factors for the other planets. Save the program as **planets.cpp**.

Planet	Multiply by	Planet	Multiply by
Mercury	0.37	Saturn	1.15
Venus	0.88	Uranus	1.15
Mars	0.38	Neptune	1.12
Jupiter	2.64	Pluto	0.04

PROJECT 2-3

Modify the **planets.cpp** program from Project 2-2 to ask for the user's weight once and then repeatedly ask the user to choose a planet for which to calculate the weight until the user enters a menu selection directing the program to exit.

PROJECT 2-4

In Chapter 6, you added a break statement to the do while loop in the program named **dowhile.cpp** to cause the loop to end if the user entered zero. Modify that program to use an if structure instead of the break keyword. The program should use an if structure to test the value of num. The statements that square num and print the output should execute only if num is not zero. Save the new version of this program as **ifskip.cpp**.

PROJECT 2-5

Write a program that asks the user to think of a number between 1 and 100, then attempts to guess the number. The program should make an initial guess of 50. The program should then ask the user if 50 is the number the user has in mind, or if 50 is too high or too low. Based on the response given by the user, the program should make another guess. Your program must continue to guess until the correct number is reached. The program should report the number of guesses it made in order to guess the number. Save the source file as **hi-lo.cpp**.

PROJECT 2-6

Given the following prototypes and instructions, write the statement necessary to call the function.

1. Use the `floor` function to round down the value in x and store the result in y. The prototype appears below.

```
double floor(double x);
```

2. Use the `pow` function to calculate 4 raised to the power of 7 and store the value in a variable called `four_to_the_seventh`. The prototype appears below.

```
double pow(double x, double y); // raises x to the y
```

3. Use the `abs` function to return the absolute value of the integer named `amount` and store it in the same variable.

```
int abs(int x);
```

4. Use the `toupper` function to change the character stored in the variable `MyChar` to uppercase.

```
int toupper(int c);
```

5. Use the `islower` function in an if structure that executes the statement you wrote in number 4 above if the character stored in `MyChar` is lowercase.

```
int islower(int c);
```

PROJECT 2-7

Modify the program you wrote in Project 2-3 (**planets.cpp**) that determines your weight on another planet. Divide the program into three functions. The `main` function should call a function that prompts the user for his or her weight on Earth and return the value using the `return` statement. The menu should remain in the `main` function. However, the user's selection should be passed to a function that uses the switch statement to calculate the user's weight on the chosen planet and print the results. *Note*: You may have to use passing by reference.

PROJECT 2-8

Use the template you created in Project 7-3 in Chapter 7 as a starting point to write a program that will function as a point-of-sale system at a rodeo snack bar. The snack bar sells only six different items: a sandwich, chips, pickle, brownie, regular drink, and a large drink. All items are subject to sales tax. Set prices for the products.

The program should repeatedly display the following menu until the sale is totaled. The program should keep a running total of the amount of the sale based on costs that you place in constants for each of the food items. The running total should be displayed somewhere on the screen each time the menu is displayed again.

S - Sandwich
C - Chips
B - Brownie
R - Regular drink
L - Large drink
X - Cancel sale and start over
T - Total the sale

If the sale is canceled, clear your running total and display the menu again. When the sale is totaled, calculate the sales tax based on your local tax rate (use 6% if you have no sales tax in your area). Print the final total due on the screen.

You can use your own functions to design a solution to the problem. You are required to use a function to calculate the sales tax. Other use of functions is up to you. Save the source code as **rodeo.cpp**.

PROJECT 2-9

Steel measuring tapes vary in length slightly depending on the temperature. When they are manufactured, they are standardized for 20° Celsius (68° Fahrenheit). As the temperature varies above or below 20° C, the tape becomes slightly inaccurate, which must be taken into consideration. The following formula will produce a length correction given the length measured by the tape and the temperature in Celsius. (T = temperature, L = measured length)

C = 0.0000116 * (T - 20) * L

The adjusted length can be calculated using the following formula.

new length = L + C

Write a program that asks the user for a measured length and temperature in Celsius and outputs an adjusted length using the given formulas. The program should include a function that accepts the measured length and temperature and returns the adjusted length. Save the source code as **adjlen.cpp**.

Source of formulas: *Elementary Surveying*, Seventh Edition, Brinker & Wolf, Harper & Row, 1984.

INTERNET ACTIVITIES

INTERNET ACTIVITY 2-1

1. Open **reps.cpp**.

2. Study the program carefully before you run it. The program asks the user for the number of U.S. Representatives in his or her state. A for loop is used to ask the user to identify the party of each representative. The do while loop is used to repeat the prompt if the user enters an invalid party choice.

3. Compile and run the program. Enter some invalid data to cause the nested loop to iterate. If you have trouble understanding the program, study the source code and run it again.

4. Open your Web browser and go to **http://www.programcpp.com/third**.

5. On the home page, click the link called **Internet Activities** and then go to the **Unit 2** link.

6. On that page, you will find a link to a Web page that will allow you to search for your state's U.S. Representatives. Gather the information for your state.

7. Run the program again using the actual data for your state.

8. Modify the program to calculate the percentage of your state's representatives that belong to each party.

9. Run and test the program with the data from your state.

10. Save and close the program.

INTERNET ACTIVITY 2-2

1. Open the program you wrote in Project 1-7 (from The Fundamentals Unit Review) called **stocks.cpp**.

2. Modify the program to include a function named `Calculate_Value` that calculates the change in value based on the opening price, closing price, and number of shares.

3. Open your Web browser and go to **http://www.programcpp.com/third**.

4. One the home page, click the link called **Internet Activities** and then go to the **Unit 2** link. On that page, you will find links to sites that provide stock price information.

5. Use values of real stocks to test your program. Some suggested stocks are listed on the Unit 2 Web page.

CASE STUDY II

COMPOUND INTEREST

Estimated Time: 1 hour

Overview

Although there are many approaches to writing programs, many programmers develop programs by performing the following steps. These steps are called the programming process.

1. Define the problem.

2. Develop an algorithm.

3. Code the program.

4. Test and debug the program.

5. Document and maintain the program.

Note

Appendix D describes the programming process in detail.

In this case study, you will follow the steps of the programming process to develop a program that calculates the growth of money using compound interest. When money is placed in an interest-bearing account, the bank adds the interest earned at a regular interval, often monthly. Each month, you earn interest on a larger amount of money because you are also earning interest on the interest you earned in previous months.

Defining the Problem

We'll begin by defining the problem. As input, the program will ask for several pieces of data.

1. The amount of money placed in the savings account.

2. The interest rate the money will earn in the account.

3. The year that the money is placed in the account.

4. The month that the money is placed in the account.

5. The number of months the money is to remain in the account.

The output will be a table that shows the month and year and the amount of money to which the account has grown by that month.

Developing an Algorithm

The flow of the program is fairly simple. First, it must ask the user for the needed values. Then the program will use a loop as it calculates the new principal amount for each month. The flowchart in Figure CSII-1 illustrates the flow of logic necessary for the program.

FIGURE CSII-1
A flowchart helps a programmer
visualize the flow of logic in a program.

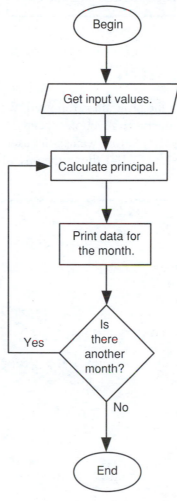

The next step is to develop a Visual Table of Contents (VTOC) to decide what functions must be written. Functions need to be written that get the input from the user, calculate the new account balance, and print a line of the table, as shown in the VTOC in Figure CSII-2.

A Visual Table of Contents shows the functions of the program.

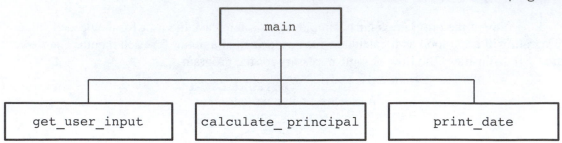

Coding the Program

A top-down approach to coding the program is followed. We begin by writing the main function, and then write the functions on which the main function depends. As our flowchart showed, the program must first ask the user to input values. But before we ask the user for those values, there must be variables in which to store the data. Code List CSII-1 shows the main function.

CODE LIST CSII-1

```cpp
// main function
int main()
{
  double principal, interest_rate;
  int first_year, first_month,
      total_months, month_count,
      current_year, current_month;
  oostring Wait;   // used in "Press Enter to Continue" input

  get_user_input(principal, interest_rate, first_year,
                 first_month, total_months);

  current_year = first_year;
  current_month = first_month;

  cout.setf(ios::fixed);      // prevent exponential notation
  for (month_count = 0; month_count < total_months; month_count++)
   {
    print_date(current_year, current_month);
    cout << "$" << setprecision(2) << principal << '\n';
    calculate_principal(principal, interest_rate);
    if (current_month < 12)
     {                    // If not yet December, increment month
      current_month++;
     }
    else             // else stop output until Enter is pressed,
     {               // set month back to January, and increment year
      cout << "\nPress Enter to Continue...\n";
      getline(cin, Wait);
```

CODE LIST CSII-1 (continued)

```cpp
        current_month = 1;
        current_year++;
      }
    }
    return 0;
}
```

After the variables are declared, the `main` function calls `get_user_input` to get the necessary values from the user. Once those values are returned to the `main` function, `current_year` and `current_month` are initialized to the initial values entered by the user.

Next, the fixed format option is set to ensure that the output does not appear in exponential notation. The fixed option also allows the `setprecision` to set the number of decimal places to the right of the decimal point. Now we're ready for the loop that prints the output.

We'll use a for loop to print the table because we know the number of times we need to iterate. The for loop uses a loop counter variable named `month_count`.

The first statement in the loop calls a function named `print_date`, which prints the name of the month followed by the year. The principal is then printed on the same line of the screen. Next, the `calculate_principal` function takes the principal and interest rate and returns a new principal amount for the next month. The principal will grow with each iteration of the loop.

The remainder of the loop is an if structure used to increment the month and, when necessary, the year. Each time the year is incremented, the output pauses to allow the user time to read the output.

STEP-BY-STEP ▷ CSII.1

1. Enter the following lines into a blank editor screen. You can replace Jonathan's name with your own.

```cpp
// compound.cpp
// By Jonathan Kleid
// Calculates future value of an amount of money placed in an interest-
// bearing account over time.

#include <iostream.h>
#include <iomanip.h>
#include "oostring.h"

// function prototypes
void get_user_input(double &principal, double &interest_rate,
                    int &first_year, int &first_month,
                    int &total_months);
void calculate_principal(double &principal, double interest_rate);
void print_date(int year, int month);
```

2. Add the `main` function at the bottom of the source code file.

3. Save the source code file as **compound.cpp** and leave it open for the next Step-by-Step exercise.

Now that we have analyzed the `main` function, let's look at the functions required to finish the program. The `get_user_input` function (shown in Code List CSII-2) receives variables by reference, prompts the user for values for the variables, and returns the values to the `main` function. The function uses do while loops to repeat prompts until valid values are input.

CODE LIST CSII-2

```cpp
// Function that gets the input values from the user.
void get_user_input(double &principal, double &interest_rate,
                    int &first_year, int &first_month,
                    int &total_months)

  cout << "Enter the starting principal: ";
  cin  >> principal;
  cin.ignore(80,'\n');
  cout << "Enter the current interest rate (Ex. 0.09 for 9%): ";
  cin  >> interest_rate;
  cin.ignore(80,'\n');
  do
   {
     cout << "Enter the first year: ";
     cin  >> first_year;
     cin.ignore(80,'\n');
     if ((first_year < 1900) || (first_year > 2050))
      {
       cout << "Invalid year.\n";
      }
   } while((first_year < 1900) || (first_year > 2050));

  do
   {
     cout << "Enter the first month (1 for Jan., 2 for Feb., etc...): ";
     cin  >> first_month;
     cin.ignore(80,'\n');
     if ((first_month < 1) || (first_month > 12))
      {
        cout << "Invalid month.\n";
      }
   } while((first_month < 1) || (first_month > 12));

  cout << "Enter the total number of months: ";
  cin  >> total_months;
  cin.ignore(80,'\n');
}
```

STEP-BY-STEP ▷ CSII.2

1. Add the `get_user_input` function to the source code on your screen.

2. Leave the source code file open for the next Step-by-Step exercise.

The `print_date` function (shown in Code List CSII-3) is primarily a switch structure that prints the name of the month based on the month number that is passed to the function. The year and month are passed by value because there is no need to return the values to the `main` function. After the switch structure prints the month, a statement prints the year.

CODE LIST CSII-3

```cpp
// Function that prints the month and year to the screen.
void print_date(int year, int month)
{
  switch(month)
   {
     case 1:
        cout << "Jan";
        break;
     case 2:
        cout << "Feb";
        break;
     case 3:
        cout << "Mar";
        break;
     case 4:
        cout << "Apr";
        break;
     case 5:
        cout << "May";
        break;
     case 6:
        cout << "Jun";
        break;
     case 7:
        cout << "Jul";
        break;
     case 8:
        cout << "Aug";
        break;
     case 9:
        cout << "Sep";
        break;
     case 10:
        cout << "Oct";
        break;
     case 11:
        cout << "Nov";
```

191

```
        break;
    case 12:
        cout << "Dec";
        break;
    }
  cout << " " << year << ": ";
}
```

The final function required for the program is a simple function (shown in Code List CSII-4) that calculates the new principal amount. The variable `principal` is passed by reference because the new principal amount must be passed back to the `main` function. The interest rate is passed by value because there is no need to pass it back to the `main` function.

CODE LIST CSII-4

```
// Function that adds the interest earned and calculates the
// new principal amount.

void calculate_principal(double &principal, double interest_rate)
{
  principal = principal + (principal * (interest_rate / 12));
}
```

STEP-BY-STEP ▷ CSII.3

1. Enter the `print_date` and `calculate_principal` functions.

2. Save the source code file and leave it open for the next Step-by-Step exercise.

Testing and Debugging

Once the code for a program has been entered, the program must be tested and debugged before it can be used and distributed as a reliable program.

STEP-BY-STEP ▷ CSII.4

1. Issue the command to compile the program. If errors occur during the compilation, check your source code for syntax errors or other typographical errors.

2. When the program compiles and runs successfully, test it with the following input.
Starting Principal: 1000.00
Interest Rate: 0.08
Year: 2002
Month: 4 (April)
Number of months: 12

3. Calculating by hand, we have determined that the given input should produce the following output. Compare the program's output to these values to see if the program is working correctly.
Apr 2002: $1000.00
May 2002: $1006.67

Jun 2002: $1013.38
Jul 2002: $1020.13
Aug 2002: $1026.93
Sep 2002: $1033.70
Oct 2002: $1040.67
Nov 2002: $1047.61
Dec 2002: $1054.59
Jan 2003: $1061.63
Feb 2003: $1068.70
Mar 2003: $1075.83

4. When the program functions properly, save the source code and close the program.

Documenting and Maintaining

The final step is to write documentation and maintain the program. Some of the lines in the program already contain comments. The analysis in this case study is similar to the external documentation written for some programs.

The user documentation for a program such as this should explain how the program expects the input to be entered. For example, the user should be shown the proper format for entering each of the required inputs.

STEP-BY-STEP ▷ CSII.5

1. Write user documentation for the program. Begin with a paragraph describing the purpose of the program.

2. Next, describe the necessary inputs and explain the formats required for each.

3. If you entered the documentation in a text editor or word processor, print it.

Modifying the Program

As an additional exercise, modify the program to display the interest earned each month, in addition to the new principal. You may also want to change the program so that a yearly total of interest earned is printed.

ARRAYS AND FILES

UNIT 3

chapter 8   3 hrs.

Data File Basics

chapter 9   3 hrs.

Arrays

Estimated Time for Unit 3: 6 hours

DATA FILE BASICS

Many useful programs collect all input from the keyboard and print all output to the screen. However, the ability to input data from a disk file and send output to a disk file opens the door to many more possibilities. A program that organizes names and addresses, for example, must store the data somewhere other than RAM. Otherwise, the data is lost when the program ends.

In this chapter, you will learn about sequential-access and random-access data files. You will learn how to open and close a sequential-access file, how to write data to a file, how to read data from a file, and how to add data to the end of an existing file. You will also learn how to detect the end of a file and how to use multiple files at the same time.

8.1 File Concepts

Understanding Data Files

Data files are not difficult to understand. Storing data in a file simply involves taking data from your computer's RAM and copying it to a disk. Retrieving data from a file is just the opposite. Data stored on disk is copied into variables or other data structures in RAM.

Why Use Data Files?

Recall that your computer's memory (RAM) holds data only as long as the computer is on. Furthermore, data in RAM is lost as soon as your program ends. Disks and other forms of secondary storage hold data even after the computer is turned off. Therefore, any data that your program needs again should be stored on disk so that it can be reloaded into the program.

For example, suppose you have a program that prints mailing addresses on labels and envelopes. Unless a data file is used to store the addresses, the user must enter the data from the keyboard every time the program runs.

Another reason to use data files is the greater amount of space available on a disk as compared to RAM. In the example of the program that prints addresses, a data file can store hundreds or even thousands of addresses—many times the number that could fit in RAM.

Sequential-Access vs. Random-Access Files

There are two types of data files: sequential access and random access. The difference between the two is in how they access the data stored in them.

SEQUENTIAL-ACCESS DATA FILES

A *sequential-access file* works like an audiocassette tape. When you place a cassette tape in a stereo, you must fast forward or rewind to get to a specific song. You must move through the songs sequentially until you reach the one you want to hear. Data stored in a sequential-access data file is placed one after the other like songs on a cassette tape. To retrieve specific data from a sequential-access data file, you must start at the beginning of the file and search for the data or records you want while moving through the file.

Sequential-access files are the most widely used type of data files. Word processors save documents in sequential-access files. Spreadsheets, graphic files, and some databases are stored as sequential-access files.

A sequential-access file can contain data of mixed types and sizes. For example, a word processor file may begin with general information about the document, followed by the text of the document itself. Codes that control formatting may be mixed in with the document's text. The programmers who developed the word processor program place data in the file using their own rules. When the program loads the document from disk, those same rules are followed in order to correctly interpret the data file.

Figure 8-1 represents a sequential-access file storing a list of names. Notice that the names vary in length. To find the fourth name in the list (Beau Chenoweth), the three names that precede it must be read first.

FIGURE 8-1

A sequential-access file requires that data be read from the beginning of the file each time it is accessed.

Shelley Neff	James MacCloskey	Kim Fan	Beau Chenoweth	Sarah Boyd	Britney Sooter

RANDOM-ACCESS DATA FILES

A *random-access file* works like an audio compact disc (CD). With the touch of a button, you can immediately access any song on the CD. You can play the songs on a CD in any order, regardless of the order in which they appear. A random-access data file allows to you to move directly to any data in the file.

Random-access files are most often used to store databases. A database with a large number of records is more efficiently managed with a random-access file because you can move quickly to any desired record in the database.

The secret to a random-access file is that data is written to the file in blocks (records) of equal size. In reality, the file appears on the disk as a sequential-access file. Because the file is made up of equal-sized blocks, a program can predict how far to move forward from the beginning of the file in order to get to the desired data.

Figure 8-2 represents a random-access file. Regardless of the length of the name, the same amount of disk space is occupied by the data. While the random-access file allows almost instant access to any data in the file, the disadvantage is that random-access files often occupy more disk space than sequential-access files.

Computer Concepts

Many modern operating systems include a file manager or their own set of file-handling functions that make it easier for programmers to create complex and full-featured data files.

FIGURE 8-2

A random-access file allows any record in the file to be accessed directly.

Shelley Neff	James MacCloskey	Kim Fan	Beau Chenowe

In this book, you will write programs that use only sequential-access data files. However, the concept of random-access files is important.

SECTION CHECKPOINT

1. List three reasons to use data files.

2. What are the two types of data files?

3. List some types of files stored as sequential-access files.

4. Describe an advantage of using random-access data files.

5. Describe a disadvantage of using random-access data files.

VOCABULARY REVIEW

Define the following terms:

random-access file
sequential-access file

8.2 Using Sequential-Access Files

Opening and Closing Files

Using a sequential-access file requires that you complete a few simple (but important) steps. First, the file must be opened. Data can then be stored or retrieved from the file. Finally, the file must be closed.

A file is a container for data. Whether you think of a file as a drawer, a folder, or a box, the concept of opening and closing the file makes sense. Before you can put something in a file or take something out, the file must be opened. When you have finished accessing the file, it must be closed.

In a paper filing system, a folder or drawer left open may result in the loss of important information. Closing a computer file may be even more important. A data file left open by a program can be destroyed if a power failure occurs or if a program crash occurs. A closed data file is almost always protected from such occurrences.

Declaring a File Stream

You have been using streams to get data from the keyboard and to the screen. Getting data to and from files also involves streams called *file streams*. The cin and cout streams are already set up for you. You must, however, declare the stream objects you will use to access files. When declaring a file stream, you select a stream type and a name for the stream.

Note

The ofstream and ifstream classes are made available by including the header file named **fstream.h**.

How you declare a file stream varies depending on how you intend to use the file. If you will be storing data to the file (called *writing*), you declare a file stream of type ofstream as shown in the following statement.

```
ofstream outfile;  // Declare a file stream for writing to file.
```

If you will be getting data from a file (called *reading*), you declare a file stream of type ifstream as shown in the following statement.

```
ifstream infile;  // Declare a file stream for reading a file.
```

To help you remember the file stream types, understand that ofstream is short for "output file stream" and ifstream is short for "input file stream."

You can use any valid identifier for file streams. The preceding examples used the names outfile and infile because they describe the purpose of the stream. In some situations, you may want to use a name that describes the data in the file, such as customers_in or high_scores.

After you have declared a stream object, the next step is to open the file.

Opening a File

When you *open* a file, a physical disk file is associated with the file stream you declared. You must provide the name of the file you want to open, and you must specify whether you want to put data in the file (write) or get data from the file (read). Consider the statements in Code List 8-1.

Note

If you need to work with more than one file at a time, you can declare more than one file stream and assign each file stream to a different file on the disk.

```
ofstream high_scores;  // Declare a file stream for writing to file.
high_scores.open("SCORES.DAT", ios::out); // Create the output file.
```

The previous statements declare a file stream named `high_scores` and open a file on disk with the filename **scores.dat**. After the filename, you must specify the way you want to access the file, called *stream operation modes*. There are several modes available, most of which you will learn about as you need them. For now, you need to know only two: `ios::out` and `ios::in`. Use `ios::out` when creating an output file and `ios::in` when opening a file for input. Your compiler may not require that you specify the stream operation mode when using these basic modes. It is a good idea, however, to specify the mode in all cases.

Note

Compilers differ slightly in the way they handle file operations. The way files are opened can vary among compilers as well. If you have trouble with the exercises in this lesson, consult your compiler's documentation.

If a file named **scores.dat** already exists in the same location, the existing file will be replaced with the new one. If no such file exists, one is created and made ready for data.

Let's look at another example. The statements in Code List 8-2 will open a file named **mydata.dat** for input using a file stream named `infile`.

CODE LIST 8-2

```
ifstream infile;  // Declare a file stream for reading a file.
infile.open("MYDATA.DAT", ios::in); // Open the file for input.
```

Because opening a file associates a file stream with an actual file on your computer, the filename you provide must be a legal filename for your operating system.

Closing a File

After a file has been opened, you can begin writing to it or reading from it (depending on the stream operation mode). When you complete your work with the file, you must *close* it. The following statement closes the file pointed to by the file stream named `infile`.

Hot Tip

You must be careful when opening a file for output. You will receive no warning if a file of the same name as that you are opening already exists. Many times you will want the existing file to be erased, but if not, it is up to you to use filenames that will not harm other data.

```
infile.close(); // Close the input file.
```

The statement format is the same whether you are closing an input or output file.

Writing Data to Files

Writing data to a sequential-access data file employs the insertion operator (<<) that you use when printing data to the screen. Instead of using the output operator to direct data to the standard output device (cout), you direct the data to the file stream. For example, the program listed in Code List 8-3 prompts the user for his or her name and age, opens a file for output, and writes the data to the output file.

CODE LIST 8-3

```cpp
// filewrit.cpp

#include <iostream.h>
#include <fstream.h>  // necessary for file I/O
#include "apstring.h" // necessary for string object

int main()
{
 apstring user_name;
 int age;
 ofstream outfile; // Declare file stream named outfile.

 cout << "Enter your name: "; // Get name from user.
 getline(cin, user_name);
 cout << "Enter your age: ";   // Get age from user.
 cin >> age;

 outfile.open("NAME_AGE.DAT",ios::out);  // Open file for output.

 if (outfile)  // If no error occurs while opening file
  {           // write the data to the file.
   outfile << user_name << endl;   // Write the name to the file.
   outfile << age << endl;         // Write the age to the file.
   outfile.close();  // Close the output file.
  }
 else          // If error occurred, display message.
  {
   cout << "An error occurred while opening the file.\n";
  }
 return 0;
}
```

Notice the user is prompted to provide input in a manner similar to previous programs with which you have worked. Next, the statement `if (outfile)` appears. This code is the functional equivalent of `if (outfile != 0)`. Thus, if an error results in the attempt to open the file, the file stream (`outfile`) is assigned the value of 0.

 Hot Tip

By this time you are sending output to cout by habit. When outputting to a file, make sure you use the file stream name in place of cout.

A number of conditions can cause an error to occur as a file is opened. The disk could be protected so that new data cannot be written to it. If you are attempting to open a file on a floppy disk, there is always the possibility that the disk is in the wrong drive. Because a disk drive is a hardware device, there may also be mechanical problems. Whatever the case, you must check to be sure that the file was opened successfully before sending data to the file.

Note

In most compilers, the `#include <fstream.h>` directive makes the use of `iostream.h` unnecessary because `fstream.h` contains everything `iostream.h` has and more. In this chapter we include both for compatibility.

STEP-BY-STEP ▷ 8.1

1. Enter the program shown in Code List 8-3. Save the source code as **filewrit.cpp**.

2. Compile and run the program. *Note:* You will need to add the **apstring.cpp** file to the project and have the **apstring.h** file in the same folder with **filewrit.cpp**.

3. Enter your name and age at the prompts. The program creates the **name_age.dat** file in the same folder.

4. When the program ends, open **name_age.dat** using your compiler's text editor. The data you entered is in readable form in the file.

5. Close your program and **name_age.dat**.

When writing to files using the technique of Step-by-Step 8.1, the output file receives data in text form in the same way output sent to cout appears on the screen. The output must be separated with spaces or end-of-line characters or the data will run together in the file. The reason you write data to a file is so that it can be read in again later. Therefore, you must separate data with spaces or end-of-line characters when you write it to a text file.

The program in Code List 8-4 uses a loop to ask the user for a series of numbers. Each number the user enters is stored in a file named **floats.dat**. When the user enters a zero, the program ends.

CODE LIST 8-4

```
// loopwrit.cpp

#include <iostream.h>
#include <fstream.h>  // necessary for file I/O

int main()
{
 float x;            // variable for user input
 ofstream outfile; // Declare file stream named outfile.

 outfile.open("FLOATS.DAT",ios::out);  // Open file for output.

 if (outfile)
  {
```

CODE LIST 8-4 (continued)

```
    cout << "Enter a series of floating-point numbers.\n"
        << "Enter a zero to end the series.\n";
    do    // Repeat the loop until user enters zero.
     {
      cin >> x;                  // Get number from user.
      outfile << x << endl;   // Write the number to the file.
     } while (x != 0.0);
   }
  else
   {
    cout << "Error opening file.\n";
   }
  outfile.close();   // Close the output file.
  return 0;
 }
```

S TEP-BY-STEP ▷ 8.2

1. Enter the program shown in Code List 8-4. Save the source code as **loopwrit.cpp**.

2. Compile and run the program. Enter five or six floating-point numbers and then be sure to end by entering a zero.

3. When the program ends, open **floats.dat** using your compiler's text editor. The numbers you entered are in readable form in the file.

4. Close **floats.dat** and **loopwrit.cpp**.

Reading Data from Files

The main reason data is written to a file is so that it can later be read and used again. In other cases, your program may read a data file created by another program.

As you learned earlier in this chapter, before you can read data from a file you must open the file for input using a file stream. The statements in Code List 8-5 are an example of declaring an input file stream and opening a file named **mydata.dat** for input.

CODE LIST 8-5

```
ifstream infile;  // Declare a file stream for reading a file.
infile.open("MYDATA.DAT", ios::in); // Open the file for input.
```

Once the file is open, you can read the data using methods familiar to you. However, reading from a data file can be more complicated than getting input from the keyboard. In this chapter you will learn two methods of reading from data files. Other methods can be used, but these methods should give the desired results without too much complication.

Reading Numeric Data

When reading strictly numeric data, you can use the extraction operator (>>) as if you were getting input from the keyboard. Instead of using cin as the input stream, use your file stream name. The program in Code List 8-6 reads the numbers you wrote to disk in Step-by-Step 8.2, prints the numbers to the screen, and calculates the sum and average of the numbers.

 Warning

When you open a file using `ios::in`, the file must already exist. Some compilers will create an empty file and give unpredictable results. Other compilers may give an error message.

CODE LIST 8-6

```cpp
// numread.cpp

#include <fstream.h>
#include <iostream.h>
#include <iomanip.h>

int main()
{
 float x, sum;
 int count;
 ifstream infile; // Declare file stream named infile.

 infile.open("FLOATS.DAT",ios::in);  // Open file for input.

 sum = 0.0;
 count = 0;

 if (infile)  // If no error occurred while opening file
  {           // input the data from the file.
  cout.setf(ios::fixed);
  cout << "The numbers in the data file are as follows:\n"
       << setprecision(1);

  do  // Read numbers until 0.0 is encountered.
   {
     infile >> x;        // Get number from file.
     cout << x << endl;  // Print number to screen.
     sum = sum + x;      // Add number to sum.
     count++;            // Increment count of how many numbers read.
   } while(x != 0.0);

   // Output sum and average.
   cout << "The sum of the numbers is " << sum << endl;
   cout << "The average of the numbers (excluding zero) is "
        << sum / (count - 1) << endl;
  }
```

CODE LIST 8-6 (continued)

```
else            // If error occurred, display message.
 {
  cout << "An error occurred while opening the file.\n";
 }
infile.close();  // Close the output file.
return 0;
}
```

STEP-BY-STEP 8.3

1. Retrieve the file **numread.cpp**. The program shown in Code List 8-6 appears.

2. Make sure the **floats.dat** file is in the same directory with **numread.cpp**.

3. Compile and run the program. The numbers you entered in Step-by-Step 8.2 should appear, along with the sum and the average of the values.

4. Close the source code file.

SECTION CHECKPOINT

1. What are the two ways that you can declare a filestream?

2. What happens if you open a file for output that already exists?

3. Why is it important to add the `endl` character at the end of each line when you are writing to a file?

4. What do you have to keep in mind when opening a file with `ios::in`?

5. What operator can you use to read in exclusively numeric data?

VOCABULARY REVIEW

Define the following terms:

close   open   stream operation modes
file streams

8.3 Sequential File Techniques

You now know how to write and read sequential-access data files. In this section, you will learn techniques that will help you work more efficiently with files. You will learn how to add data to the end of a file, detect the end of a file, and use multiple data files at the same time.

Adding Data to the End of a File

One of the limitations of sequential-access files is that most changes require that you rewrite the file. For example, to insert data somewhere in a file, the entire file must be rewritten. You can, however, add data to the end of a file without rewriting the file. Adding data to the end of an existing file is called *appending*. To append data to an existing file, open the file using the `ios::app` stream operation mode, as shown in the following statement.

```
outfile.open("MYDATA.DAT",ios::app);  // Open file for appending.
```

The program in Code List 8-7 opens the **name_age.dat** data file and allows you to add more names and ages to the file. The only difference between the program in Code List 8-7 and the program you ran in Step-by-Step 8.1 is the stream operation mode in the line that opens the file.

Note

If the file you open for appending does not exist, the operating system creates one just as if you had opened it using `ios::out` mode.

CODE LIST 8-7

```cpp
// fileapp.cpp


#include <iostream.h>
#include <fstream.h>  // necessary for file I/O
#include "apstring.h" // necessary for string object

int main()
{
 apstring user_name;
 int age;
 ofstream outfile; // declares file stream named outfile

 cout << "Enter your name: "; // get name from user
 getline(cin, user_name);
 cout << "Enter your age: ";  // get age from user
 cin >> age;

 outfile.open("NAME_AGE.DAT",ios::app);  // open file for appending

 if (outfile)  // If no error occurs while opening file
  {           // write the data to the file.
   outfile << user_name << endl;   // write the name to the file
   outfile << age << endl;         // write the age to the file
   outfile.close();  // close the output file
  }
```

CODE LIST 8-7 (continued)

```
    else            // If error occurred, display message.
     {
       cout << "An error occurred while opening the file.\n";
     }
     return 0;
}
```

STEP-BY-STEP ▷ 8.4

1. Open the program **fileapp.cpp**. The program in Code List 8-7 appears, except that the statement that opens the file for output has not yet been changed to append data.

2. Run the program with the `ios::out` stream operation mode. *Note:* You will need to add the **apstring.cpp** file to the project and have the **apstring.h** file in the same folder with **fileapp.cpp**.

3. Enter your name and age as input.

4. Open the output file (**name_age.dat**) to see that the file's only contents are what you just entered. Close **name_age.dat**.

5. Run the program again. This time enter Ben Conrad for the name and 16 for the age.

6. Open **name_age.dat** again to see that your name and age have been replaced in the file. Close **name_age.dat**.

7. Change the statement that opens the file for output from

```
outfile.open("NAME_AGE.DAT",ios::out);  // Open file for output.
```

to

```
outfile.open("NAME_AGE.DAT",ios::app);  // Open file for appending.
```

8. Run the program again. This time enter your name and age again.

9. Open **name_age.dat** again to see that Ben Conrad's name and age have not been replaced by yours. Because the file was opened for appending, your name and age were added to the end of the file.

10. Close **name_age.dat**.

11. Close the program.

Detecting the End of a File

Often the length of a file is unknown to the programmer. In Step-by-Step 8.3, the series of numbers you read into your program ended with a zero. Because you knew the data ended with a zero, you knew when to stop reading. In other cases, however, you may not have a value in the file that signals the end of the file. In those cases, there are other techniques for detecting the end of the file.

When reading strings from a file, the getline method returns a value of true as long as it finds valid data to read. If the end of the file is reached, the getline method will return a value of false. Therefore, a loop like the one in Code List 8-8 will read all of the lines in a data file and stop reading when the end of the file is reached.

CODE LIST 8-8

```
while(getline(infile,instring))
  {
      cout << instring << endl;
  }
```

STEP-BY-STEP ▷ 8.5

1. Open the program **str_end.cpp**. The program includes a loop like the one in Code List 8-8.

2. If the file named **strings.dat** is not already in the same directory as **str_end.cpp**, copy it there now. You will also need to add the **apstring.cpp** file to the project and have the **apstring.h** file in the same folder with **str_end.cpp**.

3. Compile and run **str_end.cpp**. The contents of the **strings.dat** file are read from the file and printed to the screen.

4. Close the program.

When reading numeric values, you must detect whether the operation has failed, indicating that the end of the file has been reached. Code List 8-9 shows a loop that reads numbers into the variable x until the operation fails. Also notice that the line which prints the value to the screen is in an if structure that prevents the value of x from being printed if the input operation failed.

CODE LIST 8-9

```
  do  // Read numbers until the end of file is encountered.
  {
    infile >> x;          // Get number from file.
     if(!infile.fail())   // If the end of file is not
     {                     // reached...
      cout << x << endl;  // Print number to screen.
     }
  } while(!infile.fail());
```

The `fail` function does not detect when the last line in the file is read. Instead, it detects when the program attempts to read past the end of the file. The results of reading past the end of the file vary, but in most cases the last number in the file is read again. The if structure prevents the last value in the file from being printed twice.

The `fail` function returns the value of true if an attempt has been made to read past the end of the file. To use the `fail` function, use the name of the file stream, a period, and `fail()`, as shown in Code List 8-9.

S TEP-BY-STEP ▷ 8.6

1. Open the program **num_end.cpp**. The program includes a loop like the one in Code List 8-9. The program is a modified version of **numread.cpp** that does not require the last number in the file to be zero. Instead, it detects the end of the file.

2. If the file named **nums.dat** is not already in the same directory as **num_end.cpp**, copy it there now.

3. Open **nums.dat** to see that it contains four floating-point numbers and that the list does not end in zero.

4. Compile and run **num_end.cpp**. The program operates like **numread.cpp**.

5. Close the program.

 Note

The `fail` function detects a variety of file errors, not just the end of a file. Some compilers support an `eof` function that can be used in place of `fail` to find the end of a file. The `eof` function, however, can have unpredictable results. The `fail` function is recommended because in the event of any error, attempting to read from the file should be discontinued.

Using Multiple Files

As mentioned earlier, you can have more than one file open at a time. Just declare and use a separate file stream for each file. Why would you want more than one file open at a time? There are many reasons. Let's look at two of them.

Suppose you need to add some data to the middle of a file. Since you cannot insert data in a file, you must read the data from the original file and write it to a new file. At the position where the new data is to be inserted, you write the data to the new file and then continue writing the rest of the data from the original file.

Large database programs, called relational database systems, use multiple database files. For example, a program for an animal clinic might use one database file to store information about the owners of pets and another file to store information about the pets themselves. The database of pets would include a field that linked the pet to its owner in the other database file. The term relational database comes from the fact that multiple database files are related or linked by certain fields.

Another example of when more than one file may be necessary is when performing a conversion process on a file. Suppose you need to convert all lowercase alphabetic characters in a file to uppercase letters. The program in Code List 8-10 reads the text in one file one character at a time, converts where necessary, and writes the converted characters to another file.

```
#include<fstream.h>  // necessary for file I/O
#include<iostream.h>

int main()
{
 char ch;             // Declare character variable used for input.
 ifstream infile;     // Declare file pointer for input file.
 ofstream outfile;    // Declare file pointer for output file.

 infile.open("LOWER.TXT",ios::in);    // Open file for input.
 outfile.open("UPPER.TXT",ios::out); // Open file for output.

 if ((!infile) || (!outfile))  // If file error on either file,
  {                            // print message and stop program.
    cout << "Error opening file.\n";
    return 0;
  }

 infile.unsetf(ios::skipws); // prevents spaces from being skipped

 while (!infile.eof())  // Loop while not the end of the file.
  {
    infile >> ch;        // Get character from file.
    if (!infile.eof())
     {
       if ((ch > 96) && (ch < 123))  // if character is lowercase a-z,
        {                            // subtract 32 to make uppercase.
          ch = ch - 32;
        }
       outfile << ch;    // Write character to output file.
     }
  } // end of while loop

 infile.close();  // Close the input file.
 outfile.close(); // Close the output file.
 return 0;
}
```

To convert the lowercase characters to uppercase, the ASCII value of the character is tested to see if it falls within the range of 97 to 122, which are the ASCII values of the lowercase letters. If the character falls within that range, the value in the character variable is reduced by 32, which converts it to the uppercase equivalent of the letter. This works because the uppercase letters have ASCII values from 65 to 90, which is 32 less than 97 to 122. To see the ASCII values in a table, refer to Appendix B.

Note: The code segment `if ((ch > 96) && (ch < 123))` could be rewritten as `if ((ch > 'a') && (ch < 'z'))`

The statement `infile.unsetf(ios::skipws);` is probably new to you. Without this statement, the `infile >> ch;` statement will not read the spaces, tabs, or end-of-line characters. By default, white space (spaces, tabs, and end-of-line characters) is ignored when reading from a file. The `skipws` (which is short for *skip white space*) setting allows you to override the default.

The statement `infile.unsetf(ios::skipws);` is necessary in this program because the spaces, tabs, and end-of-file characters that are in the input file must be included in the output file. If the white space is skipped when the input file is read, the white space will not appear in the converted file.

Computer Concepts

When using multiple files in a program, open files only as you need them and close them as soon as possible to avoid data loss in the event of power failure or program crash.

STEP-BY-STEP ▷ 8.7

1. Open **convert.cpp**. The program in Code List 8-10 appears.

2. Create a text file that includes a variety of characters, both uppercase and lowercase. Save the file as ASCII text and name it **lower.txt**. Make sure the file is in the current directory or supply the path in the statement that opens the file.

3. Compile and run the program. The program produces no output on the screen.

4. Open **upper.txt** to see that all lowercase letters have been converted to uppercase.

5. Close **convert.cpp**, **upper.txt**, and **lower.txt**.

SECTION CHECKPOINT

1. What stream operation mode is used when adding data to the end of an existing file?

2. Write a code segment that prints the message END OF FILE REACHED if the file pointer named `infile` has reached the end of the file.

3. What happens if a file that you open for appending does not exist?

4. What is the purpose of the `fail` function?

5. What statement prevents spaces in a file from being skipped?

VOCABULARY REVIEW

Define the following terms:

appending

Summary

In this chapter, you learned:

- Data files allow for the storage of data prior to a program's ending and the computer's being turned off. Data files also allow for more data storage than can fit in RAM.

- A sequential-access file is like an audiocassette tape. Data must be written to and read from the file sequentially.

- A random-access file is like a compact disc. Any record can be accessed directly.

- The first step to using a file is declaring a file stream. Some file streams are for writing data and some are for reading data.

- After a file stream has been declared, the next step is to open the file. Opening a file associates the file stream with a physical data file.

- After data is written or read, the file must be closed.

- The insertion operator (<<) is used to write to a data file.

- When reading numeric data, use the extraction operator. When reading string data or when reading from a file with both string and numeric data, read the data into string objects.

- Adding data to the end of an existing file is called appending.

- The getline method detects the end of the file when reading strings from a file. The fail function detects the end of a file when reading numbers.

- You can use more than one file at a time by declaring multiple file streams.

CHAPTER 8 REVIEW QUESTIONS

TRUE/FALSE

Circle T if the statement is true or F if the statement is false.

T   F   1. A computer's RAM can generally hold much more data than will fit in a data file.

T   F   2. To retrieve data from a sequential-access data file, you must start reading at the beginning of the file.

T   F   3. Any file stream can be used for both input and output.

T   F   4. Opening a file associates a physical disk file with a file stream.

T   F   5. The statement that closes a disk file must include the filename.

T   F   6. When a file contains a mixture of numeric and string data, all of the data should be read into string objects.

T F 7. The `ios::app` stream operation mode is used when adding data to the end of an existing file.

T F 8. The getline method returns a value of false if the end of the file is not yet reached.

T F 9. The `fail` function detects the end of a file and other file errors.

T F 10. Working with two files simultaneously requires two file streams.

WRITTEN QUESTIONS

Write a brief answer to the following questions.

1. List a type of file stored as a random-access file.

2. What type of data file is the most widely used?

3. What is the danger of leaving a file open?

4. What happens if you open an existing file for output using `ios::out`?

5. Describe a condition that could cause an error when opening a file.

6. How can you test to see if an error occurred while opening a file?

7. Why are end-of-line characters included when data is written to a file?

8. What term describes adding data to the end of an existing file?

9. When does the `fail` function return a value of true?

10. Give an example of a situation where more than one file may need to be opened at once.

CHAPTER 8 PROJECTS

PROJECT 8-1

Write a program that asks the user's name, address, city, state, and ZIP code. The program should then save the data to a data file. Save the source code as **addrfile.cpp**. (*Note:* You will need to add the **apstring.cpp** file to the project and have the **apstring.h** file in the same folder.)

PROJECT 8-2

Modify the program written in Project 8-1 so that it appends a name and address to the data file every time the program is run, rather than rewriting the output file. Run the program several times to append several names and addresses to the output file.

PROJECT 8-3

Write a program that reads the data saved in Project 8-2 and prints the data to the screen. Save the source code as **nameprnt.cpp**.

CRITICAL THINKING

ACTIVITY 8-1

Write a program that prompts the user for his or her full name. The program should check the first character of each name to make sure it appears in uppercase, making conversion where necessary. For example, if the user enters *jessica hope baldwin*, the program should output Jessica Hope Baldwin. Save the program as **namecaps.cpp**.

ARRAYS

OBJECTIVES

Upon completion of this chapter, you should be able to:

- Describe what arrays are and how they are used.
- Declare a vector object.
- Index elements in a vector.
- Explain why arrays are needed.
- Work with vectors and use vector features.
- Use parallel vectors.
- Declare a matrix object.
- Work with matrices and use matrix features.

⏱ **Estimated Time: 2 hours**

VOCABULARY

array

elements

matrix

parallel vectors

subscript

template class

vector

Programs commonly need to store lists and tables of numbers and other types of data. Most programming languages support some kind of structure for storing lists and tables of values. In C++, the best way to store lists and tables is to use object-oriented techniques. In this chapter, you will use object-oriented classes to store and work with lists and tables.

9.1 Arrays and Vectors

Understanding Arrays

An *array* is a list of variables or other data structures that are accessed using a single identifier. For example, suppose you need to store a list of five integers. You could declare five integer variables using a statement such as the following.

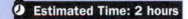

```
int a, b, c, d, e;
```

There is nothing to stop you from declaring five separate variables and managing the list of integers that way. However, writing code to manage the five variables as a list becomes difficult. In an array, an entire list is accessed using a single identifier. You then use a number to access a specific item in the array. In this chapter, you will use two classes of object-oriented arrays (the *vector* and the matrix) to implement arrays.

Arrays are useful in a variety of situations. Suppose you need to store exam grades for an entire class of students. Rather than have a separate variable for each student's grade, you can declare an array (or vector) that can hold the exam grades for all students in the class. Each student's grade will occupy a position in the list. So, for example, you can retrieve the third student's grade by taking the third grade from the array.

Declaring a Vector Object

Declaring a vector object is similar to declaring a string object. A string object, in fact, is basically an array of characters. You could think of a string object as a vector of characters that has some special methods included for dealing with text.

A vector object, however, is more generic. While a string object is always an array of characters, a vector object can be an array of any data type. Thus when you declare a vector object, you must specify a data type. The following statement is an example of the simplest form of vector declaration.

```
apvector <int> MyVector;
```

In this statement, `apvector` is the name of the class and `MyVector` is the name of the particular vector object you are declaring. In between you place the data type in angle brackets. You must supply a data type when declaring a vector or the program will fail to compile.

Template Classes

The vector class is an example of a template class. A *template class* is designed to customize the data type at the time the program is compiled. When you write a program that declares an object from a template class, the data type you specify in the code is applied to the class when the program is compiled. The resulting object will include the data type specified when you declared the object.

Three Ways to Declare

Like a string object, a vector object can change its length as necessary. For this reason, it is not absolutely necessary that you determine in advance the length of the vector. However, if you know the required length of the vector, it is a good idea to specify the length when the object is declared. The vector class also includes a feature that allows you to initialize each item (called *elements*) with a value at the time the object is declared.

Let's look at the three ways to declare a vector object.

EMPTY VECTORS

A vector that does not have a specified length is called an empty vector. To declare an empty vector, just specify the data type and identifier, as shown in the following example.

```
apvector <float> MyValues;
```

SPECIFYING THE NUMBER OF ELEMENTS

To declare a vector object of a specific length, specify the number of elements the vector should contain, as shown in the following example.

```
apvector <float> MyValues(100); // a vector with 100 elements
```

INITIALIZING THE VECTOR

To declare a vector object of a specific length and initialize the elements at the same time, specify a value along with the number of elements, as shown in the following example.

```
apvector <float> MyValues(100,0); // a vector with 100 elements
                                  // initialized to 0
```

Compiling a Program Using the Vector Class

Compiling a program using the vector class is actually easier than using the string class. Because the vector class is a template class, the entire class is contained in the file **apvector.h**. All you have to do to successfully compile and use the vector class is include the **apvector.h** file and have that file available in the same directory as your program or in some other directory where the compiler will look for the file. The line required to include the **apvector.h** file is as follows:

```
#include "apvector.h"
```

The program shown in Code List 9-1 declares three vectors. The first (Vector1) is an empty vector, Vector2 is a ten-element uninitialized vector, and Vector3 is a ten-element vector with each element initialized to zero.

CODE LIST 9-1

```
// vectorex.cpp

#include <iostream.h>
#include "apvector.h"

int main()
{
  apvector <int> Vector1;
  apvector <int> Vector2(10);
  apvector <int> Vector3(10,0);

  return 0;
}
```

1. Enter the program in Code List 9-1 into a blank editor screen.

2. Save the source code as **vectorex.cpp**.

3. Copy the **apvector.h** file from your data files to the folder where **vectorex.cpp** is saved or to your compiler's Include directory.

4. Compile and run the program. There will be no visible output from the program. Leave the program open for the next Step-by-Step exercise.

Indexing Elements in a Vector

Once you have created a vector, it is easy to put data into the vector and pull data from it. To set an element of the vector, indicate the element to which you want to assign a value using square brackets. For example, the following code assigns the value 2.5 to the third element of the vector named MyValues. The value in the square brackets is called a *subscript*.

```
MyValues[2] = 2.5;
```

You may think that this line of code has an error. Are you wondering why using a subscript of 2 causes the third element to be accessed? What you are seeing is a feature of C++ that beginning students often find confusing. In C++ vectors, the subscript refers to the position of an element from the beginning of the list. The vector assumes that the starting point for the list is the first element. The first element is zero spaces from the beginning. The remaining elements are offset by one space. Therefore, the third element is two spaces from the beginning.

When you want to retrieve a value stored in the vector, you use a statement like the following one. The same offset numbering system applies when you are retrieving data. Thus the following statement copies the value in the third element of the vector to the variable named value.

```
value = MyValues[2];
```

STEP-BY-STEP ▷ 9.2

1. Add the following lines to **vectorex.cpp** below the declarations.

```
Vector2[0] = 1;
Vector2[1] = 2;

cout << Vector2[0] << endl;
cout << Vector2[1] << endl;
cout << Vector3[0] << endl;
```

2. Compile and run the program. Analyze the output to see that the values were stored in the vectors. The zero value in Vector3 is a result of the value specified when the vector was declared.

3. Add a line to the program to output the value in the third element of `vector2`. Compile and run to see the value that appears in the element by default because the vector was not initialized when it was declared.

4. Save and close the program.

When Are Arrays Needed?

Why would you want to store an array of integers or floating-point numbers? Actually, you will find lots of uses for arrays of data. Let's look at some examples.

Suppose you want to write a program that stores the high temperature for every day of the month and then calculates an average. You can use a 31-element vector, such as the following, to store the high temperature for every day of any given month.

Note

When you use a vector to store data such as the ten highest scores of a game, the scores will be lost when the program ends. To keep the scores for the next time the game is run, you would have to save the scores to disk and then reload them into a vector when the game restarts. In the next section, you will learn how to save data to files.

```
apvector <int> daily_temp(31,0);
```

The elements of this vector are accessed using subscripts 0 to 30. Remember that the first element is accessed with the subscript 0 and the 31st element is accessed using the subscript 30.

Let's look at another example. Suppose you have written a computer game and you want to display the ten highest scores between games. The following vector declaration will hold the scores. The statement declares a ten-element array of unsigned long integers.

```
apvector <unsigned long> score(10);
```

Using Loops to Work with Vectors

Let's consider the previous vector example that stores the high temperatures for a series of days. It would be very convenient to prompt the user for values for the vector using a for loop. Code List 9-2 shows a for loop that prompts the user for temperatures for the vector. The loop's index variable is used to index the vector, resulting in very efficient code.

CODE LIST 9-2

```
// The following loop gets the high temperatures from the user for as
// many days as the user specified in num_values.
for(index = 0; index <= (num_values - 1); index++)
{
    cout << "Enter the high temperature for day " << index + 1 << ": ";
    cin >> daily_temp[index];  // input value into array
}
```

Inside the loop are two statements. The first is an output statement that lets the user know what day's temperature is being entered. Notice that the code adds 1 to the index to account for the difference between the index required for the vector and the day number expected by the user. The second statement gets the temperature using a cin statement and places it in the vector by indexing the vector with the index variable.

A loop can also be used to efficiently output the values in a vector. Code List 9-3 shows the code required to output the values from the `daily_temp` vector.

CODE LIST 9-3

```
// Print the values in the array to the screen.
cout << " array contains high temperatures for " << num_values
    << "days.\n";
cout << "The values are as follows.\n";
for(index = 0; index <= (num_values - 1); index++)
{
  cout << "Day " << index + 1 << ": " << daily_temp[index] << endl;
  total = total + daily_temp[index]; // update total for averaging
}
```

Notice that only one statement is required for outputting the values. However, while the program is going to the trouble of looping through the entire list of values, we add one line of code to calculate a total of all the temperatures. This total will be used to calculate an average high temperature. Although you cannot see it from these segments of code, the total variable was initialized to zero when it was declared.

Calculating the average temperature requires only one line of code, as shown in Code List 9-4. Because the `total` and `num_values` variables are integers, we use typecasting to allow a floating-point result to be achieved. The `average_high` variable has been declared as a double.

CODE LIST 9-4

```
// Calculate average by typecasting total and num_values to doubles
// before dividing and assigning the result to average_high.
average_high = double(total) / double(num_values);
```

S TEP-BY-STEP ▷ 9.3

1. Retrieve the source code file named **hightemp.cpp**. The program that appears includes the code you have just analyzed. If necessary, copy the **apvector.h** file to the same folder that contains **hightemp.cpp**.

2. Study the code on your screen to see how the entire program works.

3. Compile and run the program.

4. Test the program by providing five temperatures as input.

220

5. Run the program again. When prompted for the number of days for which you have data, enter a value less than 1 or greater than 31. The program should prompt you to enter a valid value. Enter a valid value and complete the session with the program.

6. Close the program.

Other Vector Features

Earlier in the chapter you learned that the vector class and the string class are similar. Like a string object, a vector object can report its length. Because a vector is a more generic data structure than a string, you can manually resize a vector. In addition, you can assign an entire vector to another vector object.

Obtaining the Length of a Vector

The length method is used to determine the length of a vector. You may need to know the length of a vector for a variety of reasons. For example, suppose you want to write a loop to print all the values in a vector. By obtaining the length, you can determine how many times the loop must iterate. The following code shows how to determine the number of elements in a vector.

```
num_elements = MyVector.length();
```

Resizing a Vector

You can specify a new size for a vector using the resize method. The resize method can make a vector longer or shorter. If you lengthen a vector, the elements added to the vector will be uninitialized. If you shorten a vector, the data in the elements at the end of the vector will be lost. The following code will resize the MyVector vector to a new length of 50 elements.

```
MyVector.resize(50);
```

Assigning One Vector to Another

Assigning the contents of one vector to another is easy. A statement such as the following is all that is necessary.

```
MyVector1 = MyVector2;
```

The vector that is receiving the contents of the other vector is resized, and all its existing data is lost. Assigning a vector in this manner is a good way to make a copy of a vector before performing some process on the data.

1. Retrieve the source code file named **vectorex.cpp** that you saved in Step-by-Step 9.2. Either open the project you were using in that exercise or create a new project that successfully compiles the vector class.

2. Add the following lines of code to the end of the program, before the `return` statement.

```
cout << "Vector3 is " << Vector3.length()
    << " elements in length.\n";
Vector3.resize(5);
cout << "Vector3 was resized to " << Vector3.length()
    << " elements in length.\n";
```

3. Compile and run the program again. Notice the length of the vector before and after the resize method is called.

4. Add the following lines of code to the end of the program, before the `return` statement.

```
cout << "Vector1 is " << Vector1.length()
    << " elements in length.\n";
Vector1 = Vector2;
cout << "Vector1 is now " << Vector1.length()
    << " elements in length.\n";
```

5. Compile and run the program again. Notice that assigning the contents of `Vector2` to `Vector1` changed the length of `Vector1` to match the length of `Vector2`. `Vector1` is now an exact copy of `Vector2`.

6. Save and close the program.

SECTION CHECKPOINT

1. Give an example of a set of data that might be stored in an array.

2. What is unique about a template class?

3. Write a line of code that declares a vector named `Grades` that contains 12 elements of the type float and initialize them all to 50.

4. What subscript do you use to index the first element of a vector?

5. For what reason might you need to know the length of a vector?

Define the following terms:

array   subscript   vector
elements   template class

9.2 Parallel Vectors

Often, a one-dimensional array is all you need to handle your program's data. Some applications, however, require data to be stored in a two-dimensional form, such as a table. A spreadsheet program is a good example of a program that stores data in columns and rows in a tabular format.

There are two ways to store data in tables. You can use more than one vector in parallel or you can use a class specifically designed for two-dimensional storage.

Using Parallel Vectors

Suppose you need to store the data in Table 9-1 in a data structure. Because of the tabular organization of the data, you can use what are called *parallel vectors* to store the data.

TABLE 9-1

GOLD RESERVES OF SELECTED COUNTRIES* (in millions of fine troy ounces)				
Year	United States	Japan	Germany	United Kingdom
1980	264.32	24.23	95.18	18.84
1981	264.11	24.23	95.18	19.03
1982	264.03	24.23	95.18	19.01
1983	263.39	24.23	95.18	19.01
1984	262.79	24.23	95.18	19.03
1985	262.65	24.33	95.18	19.03
1986	262.04	24.23	95.18	19.01
1987	262.38	24.23	95.18	19.01
1988	261.87	24.23	95.18	19.00
1989	261.93	24.23	95.18	18.99

* Source: *The World Almanac and Book of Facts, 1995.*

Using parallel vectors, each country's data is stored in a separate vector with subscripts 0–9. The vectors are called parallel because the same subscript can access any country's data for a given year. For example, the subscript 0 accesses the first element of any of the vectors, which is the 1980 data. One index variable can index all the vectors to give the data for the chosen year. The code in Code List 9-5 shows how a simple for loop can print the table to the screen using the same index variable for each vector.

CODE LIST 9-5

```
// Loop that prints the table to the screen
for (index=0;index<=9;index++)
{
  cout << 1980+index << "       " << setw(10) << us[index] << setw(10)
       << japan[index] << setw(10) << germany[index] << setw(10)
       << uk[index] << endl;
}
```

In order to write a program that stores the data from Table 9-1 into a set of parallel vectors, you will need to declare the parallel vectors and then load the elements of the vectors with the data from the table. While you could assign a value to each element of each vector individually by hard-coding the values into your program, a better method is to load the values from a data file and use loops to insert the values into the appropriate elements of the vectors. In the Step-By-Step exercise that follows, you will see an example of a program that does just that.

STEP-BY-STEP ▷ 9.5

1. Open the text files **us.dat**, **germany.dat**, **uk.dat**, and **japan.dat** in your text editor. Compare the values in the text files with the data in Table 9-1 to see that all the values are there.

2. Close all the text files. Do not save any changes that may have been made to the files.

3. Retrieve the file **gold.cpp**. Using what you learned about data files in the previous chapter, analyze the code to see how the vectors are loaded with data from the file.

4. Compile and run the program to see the data printed from the parallel vectors.

5. Close the program.

Parallel vectors can consist of different data types. The data in Table 9-2, for example, shows the times attained by a runner in each of six events.

TABLE 9-2

Chapter 9   Arrays

Distance (in meters)	Time (in seconds)
50	7.39
100	13.44
200	27.67
400	69.82
800	160.68
1000	230.13

The data in Table 9-2 can be stored in two parallel vectors. The distance can be stored in a vector of ints, and the time can be stored in a parallel vector of floats.

STEP-BY-STEP ▷ 9.6

1. Retrieve the file **running.cpp**. Analyze the code to see how the vectors are loaded with data using loops and prompts to the user.

2. Compile and run the program. The program will ask how many races you would like to enter. Enter **6** and then enter the data shown in Table 9-2. When the last of the data is entered, the program will print a results table,

showing that the data was indeed stored in the parallel vectors.

3. Look over the code one more time to ensure that you understand how the vectors were loaded and how the program created the results table.

4. Close the program.

SECTION CHECKPOINT

1. Why are parallel vectors called "parallel"?

2. What is a quick way to load values into a vector?

3. Write a for loop that would display the contents of Table 9-2 using parallel vectors.

Define the following terms:

parallel vectors

9.3 The Matrix Class

You have discovered by now that there is more than one way to represent the same data in a computer. Part of what makes a good programmer is the ability to choose an efficient method of storing and processing data. While parallel vectors are ideal for many applications, another common data structure is the multi-dimensional array. Using a multi-dimensional array, a single identifier (or variable name) can access values in a table or even more complex arrangements.

Two-Dimensional Arrays

The two-dimensional array is the most common type of multi-dimensional array. A two-dimensional array can be visualized as a table or spreadsheet with rows and columns. The table of shipping rates shown in Figure 9-1 can be implemented using a two-dimensional array. What makes the table a good candidate for a two-dimensional array is the fact that all the values can be easily managed from a single identifier, and all the values can be stored with the same data type. All elements of a two-dimensional array must be the same data type. In this chapter, we will use a class called a *matrix* class to create two-dimensional arrays.

FIGURE 9-1

The rates in this table are a good candidate for a two-dimensional array in the form of a matrix object.

SHIPPING RATES								
Weight (up to)	Shipping Zones							
	1	2	3	4	5	6	7	8
5 lbs.	2.65	2.75	2.87	3.06	2.65	3.35	4.73	6.13
10 lbs.	3.05	3.18	3.35	3.84	4.60	5.58	7.68	9.33
15 lbs.	3.25	3.40	3.63	4.24	5.08	6.13	8.46	10.38
20 lbs.	4.10	4.28	4.59	5.34	6.20	7.39	9.93	11.85
25 lbs	4.65	4.95	5.35	6.23	7.25	8.66	11.55	13.58
30 lbs	5.25	5.49	5.99	6.90	8.03	9.69	12.69	15.49

When the table of shipping rates is placed in a matrix (named **ship_rate**, for example), the rows and columns of the table become subscripts of the matrix, as shown in Figure 9-2. For example, `ship_rate[2][3]` points to the value at the intersection of the third row and fourth column (4.24). Because matrix subscripts begin at zero, the third row is identified with subscript 2, and the fourth column is identified with subscript 3.

FIGURE 9-2

In a two-dimensional array, the subscripts relate to rows and columns.

Shipping Zones

ship_rate		0	1	2	3	4	5	6	7
	0	2.65	2.75	2.87	3.06	2.65	3.35	4.73	6.13
W	1	3.05	3.18	3.35	3.84	4.60	5.58	7.68	9.33
e i	2	3.25	3.40	3.63	4.24	5.08	6.13	8.46	10.38
g h	3	4.10	4.28	4.59	5.34	6.20	7.39	9.93	11.85
t	4	4.65	4.95	5.35	6.23	7.25	8.66	11.55	13.58
	5	5.25	5.49	5.99	6.90	8.03	9.69	12.69	15.49

Declaring a Matrix

A matrix is actually very similar to a vector. The basic operations you learned for vectors will apply in some form to the matrix. Think of a matrix as a vector of vectors, because that is really what it is.

As with vectors, a matrix can be declared in three ways. You can declare a matrix of zero rows and zero columns, you can declare a matrix of a specific size, or you can declare a matrix of a specific size and initialize each element to a specified value. Code List 9-6 shows an example of each way to declare a matrix.

Note

To use the matrix class, the `apmatrix.h` header must be included in your code.

CODE LIST 9-6

```
// Declare a matrix of type float with size 0 x 0.
apmatrix <float> MyMatrix;

// Declare a matrix of type double with 4 rows and 3 columns.
apmatrix <double> MyDoubleMatrix(4,3);

// Declare a matrix of type int with 3 rows and 2 columns
// initialized with the value 0.
apmatrix <int> MyIntMatrix(3,2,0);
```

Using a Matrix Object

Declaring a matrix is straightforward. The two dimensions, however, make using the matrix more challenging than using a vector object. Loading data in a two-dimensional array is typically done from a data file. Nested loops can be used to load the rows and columns with data.

In the next Step-By-Step exercise, you will open, analyze, and run a program that implements the shipping rate table from Figure 9-1. The program will declare a matrix, load it with data from a file, and then allow the user to enter a weight and a shipping zone. Using the weight and zone, the program will look up the appropriate shipping rate and report it to the user.

Code List 9-7 shows the `main` function from the program you will run in Step-by-Step 9.7. The program declares a matrix to hold the table, then calls a function to load the table with data. If no error occurs loading the table, functions are called to get the weight and zone from the user.

CODE LIST 9-7

```
apmatrix <double> ship_rate(6,8,0); //declare the matrix here so that
                                     //it has global scope

// main function
int main()
 {
  double weight;           // weight of package
  int weight_category;     // weight category in table
  int zone;                // zone of package's destination
  int ErrCode;             // error detection for loading file


  ErrCode = load_table(); // call function to load table with rates

  if(ErrCode)
  {
    cout << "File error. Terminating program.\n";
  }
  else
  {
    weight = get_weight();  // call function to get package weight
    zone = get_zone();      // call function to get shipping zone number

    // Subtract one from the zone number so the number will
    // correspond to the subscript of the array.
    zone--;

    // Divide by 5 and truncate to get subscript for the array.
    weight_category = int(weight / 5.0);
```

CODE LIST 9-7 (continued)

```
    cout.setf(ios::showpoint);
    cout.setf(ios::fixed);
    cout << "The cost of shipping the package is $" << setprecision(2)
        << ship_rate[weight_category][zone] << '\n';
  }
  return 0;
}
```

The functions `get_weight` and `get_zone` return the weight in pounds and the zone number of the package's destination. Before looking up the shipping cost in the table, the zone must be decremented so that the zone numbers 1 through 8 will correspond with the matrix subscripts 0 through 7.

Because the shipping rate changes every five pounds, we are able to get the subscript for the table row by dividing the weight by 5 and allowing the fractional part to be truncated. Any weight under five pounds becomes 0; a weight over five pounds, but less than ten, becomes 1; and so on. The result of the division is typecast as an integer to truncate the fractional part, leaving an integer that can be used as a subscript to access the array.

Note

Recall that truncation means that digits to the right of the decimal point are removed.

STEP-BY-STEP 9.7

1. Open the text file **rates.dat** in your text editor. Compare the values in the text file with the data in Figure 9-1 to see that all the values are there.

2. Close the **rates.dat** file. Do not save any changes that may have been made to the file.

3. Retrieve the file **shiprate.cpp**. Analyze the code to see that the `main` function that appears in Code List 9-7 is the `main` function for this program. Study the remainder of the code to see how the matrix is loaded with data from a file. Also look at the `get_weight` and `get_zone` functions to see how they verify that the user has entered correct data.

4. Compile and run the program. The program will ask for a weight and a zone. Enter **9.5** for the weight and **4** for the shipping zone. The program should report that the cost to ship the item is 3.84.

5. Run the program again. This time enter a weight of 30 or more or a shipping zone outside the range of 1 to 8 to see how the program reacts. Then enter valid data and verify the result with the table in Figure 9-1.

6. Close the program.

1. What is a two-dimensional array?

2. To use the matrix class, which header must be included in your code?

3. What is different concerning data types in two-dimensional arrays (matrices) and parallel vectors?

4. Write a line of code that declares a matrix of type long with 7 rows and 6 columns initialized with a value of 345.

5. What type of loops are especially useful when loading values into a matrix?

VOCABULARY REVIEW

Define the following terms:

matrix

Summary

In this chapter, you learned:

- An array is a list of variables or other data structures that are accessed using a single identifier.

- A vector object is an object-oriented array.

- The vector class is a template class, so you are allowed to declare a data type for the vector before the class is compiled.

- You can declare an empty vector, a vector of a particular size, or an initialized vector of a particular size.

- You must include the **apvector.h** file in order for the vector class to compile.

- Individual elements in a vector are accessed using a number called a subscript.

- Loops provide a convenient way to process the data in vectors.

- Other vector features include obtaining the length of a vector, manually resizing a vector, and assigning the contents of one vector to another.

- Parallel vectors are separate vectors that are indexed with the same variable in order to create columns of data. Parallel vectors do not have to be of the same data type.

- A matrix is a two-dimensional array. The subscripts of a matrix relate to rows and columns.

CHAPTER 9 REVIEW QUESTIONS

TRUE/FALSE

Circle T if the statement is true or F if the statement is false.

T F 1. An array is a list in which each element is accessed using a different identifier.

T F 2. A vector is an object-oriented array.

T F 3. The string class is more generic that the vector class.

T F 4. When you declare a vector object, you must specify a data type.

T F 5. There are three ways to declare a vector.

T F 6. If you attempt to manually store data in an empty vector, the vector will resize to accommodate the data.

T F 7. A vector of ten elements is indexed using the subscripts 1 to 10.

T F 8. Parallel vectors are well suited for two-dimensional storage.

T F   9. Elements of a matrix can be made up of two or more data types.

T F   10. A matrix is really a vector of vectors.

WRITTEN QUESTIONS

Write a brief answer to the following questions.

1. Why is an array more convenient to use than individual variables when storing a list?

2. From what field of study does the term *vector* come?

3. Why is the vector class written as a template class?

4. What information must be provided when declaring an empty vector?

5. What information must be provided when declaring a vector of a specified length with each element initialized to a specific value?

6. What subscript range is used to index the vector declared by the following statement?

   ```
   apvector <int> j(100);
   ```

7. When one vector's contents are assigned to another vector object, what happens to the length and existing contents of the vector receiving the contents of the other vector?

8. What are the two types of data structures discussed in this chapter that can be used to hold two-dimensional data?

9. Could the **gold.cpp** program be rewritten using a matrix? Why or why not?

10. Based on the examples in this chapter, explain why data stored in parallel vectors can have different data types while data stored in a matrix cannot.

CHAPTER 9 PROJECTS

PROJECT 9-1

Write the code required for the following.

1. Write a statement that declares an empty vector of type long named `LongVector`.

2. Write a statement that declares a vector named `n` of type float with ten uninitialized elements.

3. Write a statement that declares a vector named `z` of type int with 100 elements initialized to 0.

4. Write a loop that will print the values in a 20-element vector named `quantity` to the screen.

5. Write a loop that will initialize the values in a 100-element vector of type double named x with the loop's index value. For example, the element at subscript 0 should have the value 0 and the element at subscript 11 should have the value 11.

PROJECT 9-2

Modify **hightemp.cpp** so that it reports the coolest and warmest days in the vector to the screen.

PROJECT 9-3

Write a program that declares a vector of ten floating-point values. Have the program prompt the user for each of the ten floating-point values and store them into the vector. The program should then report how many of the values entered are larger than the value in the first element of the vector. For example, if the values entered are 5.2, 6.1, 2.8, 8.9, 3.3, 2.0, 9.7, 1.4, 7.3, and 5.5, the program should report that five of the values in the vector are larger than the value in the first element. Save the source code as **floatvec.cpp**.

PROJECT 9-4

Modify the **gold.cpp** program to include a loop that creates a table that shows the amount of change in the gold reserves in the years 1981 through 1989. For example, the 1981 values should show how much the gold reserves increased or decreased from 1980. Show decreased reserves with negative numbers. Save the new program as **goldchng.cpp**.

PROJECT 9-5

Write a program that uses parallel vectors to store the ages and heights of a group of children. Use one vector for age and another for height. In a way similar to **running.cpp**, the program should prompt the user for the number of children in the group and then ask for each child's age in years and height in inches. After all the data is loaded into the vectors, the program should print the data back to the screen in the form of a table and report the average age and average height of the group. Save the source code as **kidsize.cpp**.

PROJECT 9-6

Look at the AP Matrix Class Quick Reference in Appendix J. Using the information found in that reference, write a program that performs the following tasks.

1. Declare a matrix of type int named M1 with 15 rows and 14 columns, initialized with a 1 in each element.

2. Declare a matrix of type int named M2 without specifying a size.

3. Use the `numrows` function to determine the number of rows in matrix M1. Print the number of rows to the screen.

4. Use the `numrows` function to determine the number of rows in matrix M2. Print the number of rows to the screen.

5. Use the `numcols` function to determine the number of columns in matrix M1. Print the number of columns to the screen.

6. Resize M1 to 8 rows and 4 columns.

7. Use the `numcols` function to determine the number of columns in matrix M1. Print the number of columns of the resized matrix to the screen.

8. Store the value 100 in first row of the first column of matrix M1.

9. Assign the contents of matrix M1 to the empty matrix M2.

10. Use the `numrows` function to determine the number of rows now in matrix M2. Print the number of rows to the screen.

11. Print the value in the first row of the first column of matrix M2. It should now match the value in the same element of M1.

Save the program as **m1m2.cpp**.

CRITICAL THINKING

ACTIVITY 9-1

Write a program that declares a 16-element vector of type double named x. The program should use a loop to initialize each element with the square root of the subscript. For example, the element at subscript 9 (the tenth element) should be initialized with the square root of 9, which is 3. The program should then include a second loop that prints the contents of the vector. The output should appear like the following example. Use three digits of accuracy to the right of the decimal point. Save the program as **sqroot.cpp**.

```
The square root of 0 is 0.000
The square root of 1 is 1.000
The square root of 2 is 1.414
The square root of 3 is 1.732
The square root of 4 is 2.000
The square root of 5 is 2.236
The square root of 6 is 2.449
The square root of 7 is 2.646
The square root of 8 is 2.828
The square root of 9 is 3.000
The square root of 10 is 3.162
The square root of 11 is 3.317
The square root of 12 is 3.464
The square root of 13 is 3.606
The square root of 14 is 3.742
The square root of 15 is 3.873
```

ACTIVITY 9-2

Write a program that declares a matrix with four rows and four columns and uses a loop to initialize the matrix in the pattern below. Name the program **pattern.cpp**. Hint: Study the pattern of the numbers in the following matrix to discover a simple way to initialize the array.

0	0	0	0
0	1	2	3
0	2	4	6
0	3	6	9

Arrays and Files

REVIEW QUESTIONS

MATCHING

Write the letter of the description from Column 2 that best matches the term or phrase in Column 1.

Column 1

____ **1.** appending

____ **2.** array

____ **3.** element

____ **4.** matrix

____ **5.** file streams

____ **6.** parallel vectors

____ **7.** vector

____ **8.** subscript

____ **9.** close

____ **10.** template class

____ **11.** open

____ **12.** random access file

____ **13.** sequential access file

____ **14.** stream operation modes

Column 2

A. the final step of using a data file

B. a two-dimensional array of any data type

C. a file in which all data is stored in a specified order

D. a list of data structures accessed with a single identifier

E. the first step of using a data file

F. a file in which data may be accessed in any order

G. the mode in which one can access data in a file

H. objects that provide a connection to a data file

I. adding data to the end of a file

J. a class designed to have the data type customized when compiled

K. a data structure in an array

L. two or more vectors that are indexed with the same variable

M. a number that allows you to access a specific element in an array

N. a one-dimensional array of any data type

WRITTEN QUESTIONS

Write a brief answer to the following questions.

1. What might happen if a programmer forgets to check to see if an error occurred while opening a file?

2. An analogy can be made between sequential files, random access files, compact discs, and audio-cassette tapes. Form the analogy and explain it.

3. If you needed to store two related variables such as age, measured in years, and height, measured to the nearest quarter inch, would you use parallel vectors or a matrix? Why?

4. Can one file stream be used to read in data and write data at the same time? Why or why not?

5. In a sequential-access file, where must you begin reading?

6. What are the three ways to declare a vector?

7. What subscripts are used to index a three-element vector?

8. What happens to the data in a vector if you manually shorten the vector?

9. What stream operation mode is used when adding data to the end of an existing file?

10. What is the major difference between a matrix and a vector?

PROJECTS ⬦

PROJECT 3-1

1. Write the code statement necessary to make the vector class available to your program.

2. Write the code necessary to declare a 50-element vector of type int, initialized to one, named `IntVect`.

3. Write the code necessary to determine the number of elements in `IntVect` and store that value in a variable named `NumElements`.

4. Write the code necessary to declare a file stream named outstream to be used for writing to a file.

5. Write the code necessary to close the file attached to the outstream file stream.

PROJECT 3-2

Write a program named **postage.cpp** that declares two vectors of six elements each of type double. One vector should be named `weight` and one should be named `rate`. The program should use a loop to prompt the user for a weight in ounces and a postage rate for that weight and store the values in parallel elements of the vectors. After the six weights and rates have been gathered and stored in the vectors, a loop should print a table of the weights and rates to the screen. You can use any data you wish to test the program. A suggested data set follows.

Weight	Rate
1.0	0.33
2.0	0.55
3.0	0.77
4.0	0.99
5.0	1.21
6.0	1.43

PROJECT 3-3

Modify the **rodeo.cpp** program that you saved in Project 2-8 to save each transaction to a data file. The program should open a file stream to a data file and write the information as the order is taken, in a format similar to the following.

```
Sandwich 1.25
Chips 0.50
Large Drink 1.00
Sub Total 2.75
Total 2.92
```

PROJECT 3-4

In this project, you are to write a program that loads the letters of the alphabet and the numerals 0 through 9 into a 6 × 6 matrix as shown in the following figure. After your program loads the data into the matrix, it is to display the matrix to the screen and prompt you for a row and a column number. The program will then report the character located at the specified position in the matrix. Use the numbered steps that follow to guide you through the application.

1. Open a new source code file and name it **secret.cpp.**

2. Write a program that performs each of the following functions:
   A. Declare a matrix of 6 rows and 6 columns.
   B. Open the data file named **alpha.dat** and load the matrix with the characters in the data file as shown in the figure.
   C. Display the matrix to the screen to show that the characters were successfully loaded into the matrix in the same order as the figure illustrates.
   D. Have the program prompt the user for a row number (0–5) and then a column number (0–5).
   E. Display the character found at the intersection of the row and column the user entered.

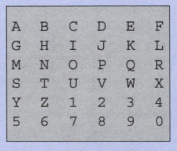

3. Compile and run the program. Verify that the matrix printed does appear as shown in the figure.

4. Test the program by entering 4 for the row and 1 for the column. The response should be the letter Z.

5. Now modify the program to have it load the data file **scramble.dat** instead of **alpha.dat**. The format of **scramble.dat** is the same, and all the characters are present. In **scramble.dat**, however, the characters have been shuffled.

6. Run the program again. See that the characters are not scrambled.

7. Now that the letters are scrambled, what letters do you find at the following locations?
   A. (0,0)
   B. (3,1)
   C. (5,4)
   D. (5,0)
   E. (2,0)
   F. (3,2)

8. Save and close the program.

INTERNET ACTIVITIES

ACTIVITY 3-1

1. Open your Web browser.

2. In your Web browser, go to the following address.

   http://www.programcpp.com/third

3. One the home page, click the link called **Internet Activities**, and then go to the **Unit 3** link. On that page, you will find information about the Fibonacci Series.

4. Write a C++ program called **fseries.cpp** that will load and then display the first 25 numbers in the Fibonacci Series. Find the most efficient way to load the numbers into a vector and then display them on the screen.

MILEAGE LOOK-UP TABLE

 Estimated Time: 1 hour

Overview

The look-up table is a widely used data structure that can be implemented using a two-dimensional array or matrix. An example of how a look-up table can be used is to determine the amount of deduction from an employee's paycheck. The amount of gross pay, along with the number of dependents the employee claims, are used to look up a deduction amount in a table. Even microprocessors sometimes use look-up tables to help them perform some operations more quickly.

In this case study, you will analyze a program that uses a matrix as a look-up table of mileage between major cities. The program will ask for two cities as input and provide output of the number of miles between the cities.

Building the Look-Up Table

The look-up table is the heart of this case study's program. The program will store each possible output value in a matrix. Instead of calculating the distance between two cities, the program will look up the distance in a table (the matrix). Figure CSIII-1 shows the look-up table required for our program.

FIGURE CSIII-1

This look-up table will be implemented in the program as a matrix.

	Atlanta	Boston	Chicago	Cincinnati	Dallas	Denver	Detroit	Los Angeles	New York	Seattle
Atlanta	0	1037	674	440	795	1398	699	2182	841	2618
Boston	1037	0	963	840	1748	1949	695	2979	206	2976
Chicago	674	963	0	287	917	996	266	2054	802	2013
Cincinnati	440	840	287	0	920	1164	259	2179	647	2300
Dallas	795	1748	917	920	0	781	1143	1387	1552	2078
Denver	1398	1949	996	1164	781	0	1253	1059	1771	1307
Detroit	699	695	266	259	1143	1253	0	2311	637	2279
Los Angeles	2182	2979	2054	2179	1387	1059	2311	0	2786	1131
New York	841	206	802	647	1552	1771	637	2786	0	2815
Seattle	2618	2976	2013	2300	2078	1307	2279	1131	2815	0

To keep the problem manageable, ten cities have been selected for the look-up table. To find the mileage between two of the cities, locate the row of your originating city and the column of your destination. The intersection of that row and column gives the road mileage between the cities.

Implementing the Look-Up Table

In our program, the look-up table must be implemented as a matrix. We will declare the matrix and then initialize it later in the program with values from a data file. The following statement declares the matrix and initializes the 10×10 matrix to 0.

```
apmatrix <int> cities(10,10,0);
```

The Completed Program

Code List CSIII-1 is a listing of the entire completed program. Let's compile and run the program, and then analyze it piece by piece.

CODE LIST CSIII-1

```cpp
// mileage.cpp

#include <iostream.h>    // necessary for input/output
#include <fstream.h>     // necessary for file input/output
#include "apmatrix.h"    // necessary for matrix class

// function prototypes
void get_cities(int &originating_city, int &destination_city);

// main function
int main()
{
  // integer matrix declared for the look-up table
  apmatrix <int> cities(10,10,0);

  int originating_city;  // Holds the choice of the starting point
  int destination_city;  // Holds the choice of the ending point
  int row_counter;       // Used to count rows in loops
  int column_counter;    // Used to count columns in loops
  char answer;           // Used for ending or not ending the loop
  ifstream input_file;   // Holds file pointer for input file


  input_file.open("mileage.dat",ios::in); //open file for input
  for(row_counter = 0 ; row_counter < 10 ; row_counter++)
  { // iterate through input file to get data for each row
    for(column_counter = 0 ; column_counter < 10 ; column_counter++)
    { // iterate through input file to get data for each column
      input_file >> cities[row_counter][column_counter];
    }
```

```
}
input_file.close();  // close the input file

 do
   { // iterate until user chooses not to continue

     // call get_cities function to get input from the user
     get_cities(originating_city, destination_city);

     originating_city—; // decrement the number of the originating and
     destination_city—; // destination cities for use in the array

     // index array using the decremented city numbers and print mileage
     cout << "\nMileage = " << cities[originating_city][destination_city]
         << endl;

     // ask user if he/she wants to repeat look-up
     cout << "\nContinue? [Y]es [N]o: ";
     cin >> answer;
      // loop as long as user answers y or Y
   } while ((answer == 'y') || (answer == 'Y')); // end of do loop
   return 0;
} // end main function

// function that gets the input from the user
void get_cities(int &originating_city, int &destination_city)
{
  cout << "\nOriginating City     Destination City\n";
  cout << "----------------     ----------------\n";
  cout << " 1 Atlanta           1 Atlanta\n";
  cout << " 2 Boston            2 Boston\n";    // Table of starting
  cout << " 3 Chicago           3 Chicago\n";   // and ending points
  cout << " 4 Cincinnati        4 Cincinnati\n";
  cout << " 5 Dallas            5 Dallas\n";
  cout << " 6 Denver            6 Denver\n";
  cout << " 7 Detroit           7 Detroit\n";
  cout << " 8 Los Angeles       8 Los Angeles\n";
  cout << " 9 New York          9 New York\n";
  cout << "10 Seattle          10 Seattle\n";

  cout << "\nOriginating City [1-10]: ";
  cin >> originating_city;

  cout << "\nDestination City [1-10]: ";
  cin >> destination_city;
} // end of get_cities function
```

S TEP-BY-STEP ▷ CS III.1

1. Open **mileage.cpp.** The program in Code List CSIII-1 appears on your screen.

2. Compile and run the program. In order for the program to compile and run, **apmatrix.h**, **apmatrix.cpp**, and **mileage.dat** must be present in the same folder. Run the program with several combinations of cities.

3. Enter the same city number for both the originating and the destination city. The mileage should be reported as 0.

4. Exit the program and leave the source code file open.

The program begins with a comment that identifies the program, followed by the compiler directives necessary for console input and output, file input and output, and the matrix class definition. The program consists of only two functions (main and get_cities), so only the get_cities function requires a prototype.

Next, the main function begins. As usual, the main function begins with variable declarations, as shown again in Code List CSIII-2. In addition to the matrix discussed earlier, two variables that hold the numbers of the originating and destination cities are declared. Two other variables are declared that are used as counters in the for loops that load the values from the data file into the matrix. Another variable is declared that is used to store the user's response to a question of whether to continue. Finally, a file pointer is declared so that a data file can be used.

CODE LIST CSIII-2

```
// integer matrix declared for the look-up table
apmatrix <int> cities(10,10,0);

int originating_city; // Holds the choice of the starting point
int destination_city; // Holds the choice of the ending point
int row_counter;      // Used to count rows in loops
int column_counter;   // Used to count columns in loops
char answer;          // Used for ending or not ending the loop
ifstream input_file;  // Holds file pointer for input file
```

Following the variable declaration, the program opens the data file **mileage.dat**, which contains the data needed to initialize the matrix (see Code List CSIII-3). Two nested for loops initialize the matrix. The first loop iterates through all of the rows in the matrix, while the second loop is responsible for initializing each column in the current row with a value from the data file. When each position in the matrix has been initialized, the data file is closed.

```
input_file.open("mileage.dat",ios::in); //open file for input
 for(row_counter = 0 ; row_counter < 10 ; row_counter++)
 { // iterate through input file to get data for each row
   for(column_counter = 0 ; column_counter < 10 ; column_counter++)
   { // iterate through input file to get data for each column
     input_file >> cities[row_counter][column_counter];
   }
 }
 input_file.close();  // close the input file
```

After the matrix is initialized, the `main` function enters the loop shown in Code List CSIII-4. The loop calls the `get_cities` function to get the originating and destination cities from the user. The variables `originating_city` and `destination_city` are passed by reference to allow the user's input to be passed back to the `main` function.

CODE LIST CSIII-4

```
do
 { // iterate until user chooses not to continue

   // call get_cities function to get input from the user
   get_cities(originating_city, destination_city);

   originating_city--; // decrement the number of the originating and
   destination_city--; // destination cities for use in the array

   // index array using the decremented city numbers and print mileage
   cout << "\nMileage = " << cities[originating_city][destination_city]
       << endl;

   // ask user if he/she wants to repeat look-up
   cout << "\nContinue? [Y]es [N]o: ";
   cin >> answer;
    // loop as long as user answers y or Y
  } while ((answer == 'y') || (answer == 'Y')); // end of do loop
```

The values returned for the cities are in the range of 1 to 10. Recall, however, that array and matrix subscripts in C++ begin with zero. Therefore, the look-up table is indexed using the values 0 to 9. To adjust for the difference, the statements shown again in Code List CSIII-5 subtract 1 from the values in the variables to prepare them to index the matrix.

CODE LIST CSIII-5

```
originating_city--; // Decrement the number of the originating and
destination_city--; // destination cities for use in the array
```

Now that the city numbers have been adjusted to properly index the matrix, a single statement, shown in Code List CSIII-6, is used to look up the value and output the result.

CODE LIST CSIII-6

```
    // index array using the decremented city numbers and print mileage
    cout << "\nMileage = " << cities[originating_city][destination_city]
        << endl;
```

Finally, the `main` function asks the user if he or she wants to repeat the look-up process. The control expression of the do while loop tests the user's response to determine whether the loop should repeat or exit.

The `get_cities` function, shown in Code List CSIII-7, is very straightforward. First, a table of cities is displayed to give the user the options. Next, the user is asked for the originating city and, finally, the destination city. The ampersands (&) in the function declaration cause the parameters to be passed by reference, so the values entered by the user can be returned to the `main` function.

CODE LIST CSIII-7

```
    // function that gets the input from the user
    void get_cities(int &originating_city, int &destination_city)
    {
      cout << "\nOriginating City      Destination City\n";
      cout << "----------------      ----------------\n";
      cout << " 1 Atlanta            1 Atlanta\n";
      cout << " 2 Boston             2 Boston\n";    // Table of starting
      cout << " 3 Chicago            3 Chicago\n";   // and ending points
      cout << " 4 Cincinnati         4 Cincinnati\n";
      cout << " 5 Dallas             5 Dallas\n";
      cout << " 6 Denver             6 Denver\n";
      cout << " 7 Detroit            7 Detroit\n";
      cout << " 8 Los Angeles        8 Los Angeles\n";
      cout << " 9 New York           9 New York\n";
      cout << "10 Seattle           10 Seattle\n";

      cout << "\nOriginating City [1-10]: ";
      cin >> originating_city;

      cout << "\nDestination City [1-10]: ";
      cin >> destination_city;
    } // end of get_cities function
```

Modifying the Program

As an additional exercise, modify the program to include Memphis, Tennessee. Table CSIII-1 shows the road mileage between Memphis and the other ten cities.

Atlanta	371	Denver	1040
Boston	1296	Detroit	713
Chicago	530	Los Angeles	1817
Cincinnati	468	New York	1100
Dallas	452	Seattle	2290

Finally, modify the program to check the validity of the values entered by the user. *Hint*: Use a do while loop to continually call the get_cities function until valid input is received.

OBJECT-ORIENTED PROGRAMMING AND LINKED LISTS

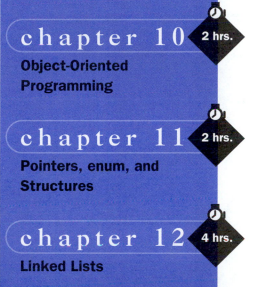
247

OBJECT-ORIENTED PROGRAMMING

OBJECTIVES

Upon completion of this chapter, you should be able to:

■ Compare and contrast procedural programming and object-oriented programming.

■ Describe the concepts of reusability, containment, and inheritance.

■ Use a simple class.

■ Design and implement a simple class.

⏱ **Estimated Time: 2 hours**

VOCABULARY

constructors

containment

encapsulation

has-a relationship

information hiding

inheritance

is-a relationship

member functions

members

object-oriented paradigm

object-oriented programming

paradigm

procedural paradigm

reusability

scope-resolution operator

This chapter is not your first exposure to object-oriented programming. The first time you used streams you were using objects. In Chapter 4, you learned some concepts of object-oriented programming (OOP) and some important OOP terms when you began working with strings and the string class. Then, in Unit 3, you worked with template classes to create vector and matrix objects.

Now that you have experience declaring and interacting with classes, you are ready to learn more about some of the concepts behind object-oriented programming. Also in this chapter, you will have the opportunity to see how a class is actually created and to create you own classes.

10.1 Concepts of Object-Oriented Programming

Procedural Programming vs. Object-Oriented Programming

As the field of computer science has grown, different methods have been developed for programming computers. The first programming was accomplished by flipping switches on a control panel or feeding machine language instructions into a computer. Later, computer-programming languages that could be more easily understood were developed. To make programming easier, higher-level languages have continued to be developed.

Object-oriented programming (OOP) continues the trend toward higher-level programming languages. OOP, however, does more than that. Object-oriented programming changes the way a programmer uses data and functions.

The different methods used for writing programs are known as paradigms. A *paradigm* is a model or a set of rules that defines a way of programming. Two primary paradigms are used to program computers today: the procedural paradigm and the object-oriented paradigm.

Procedural Paradigm

You have used the procedural paradigm in writing your own programs in this book up to this point. The *procedural paradigm* focuses on the idea that all algorithms in a program are performed with functions and data that a programmer can see, understand, and change. In a program written procedurally, the focus is on the functions that will process the data. The programmer then devises ways to pass the required data to and from the functions, which do the processing. To successfully write procedural programs, the programmer must understand how data is stored and how the algorithms of the program work.

Even though your programs were written procedurally, you have been using classes that were developed using a different paradigm. When you learned about strings, you learned that strings are stored in character arrays. Working with character arrays requires you to know the technical details of the character array and the functions that manipulate the array. To avoid this technical detail, we chose to use a string class, which is an object-oriented character array.

Procedural programming has served programmers well for many years and will continue to do so for some time. However, computer scientists are always searching for a better way to develop software. By looking at the world around them, computer scientists discovered that the world consists of objects that perform work and interact with each other. When this concept is applied to programming computers, the result is a different paradigm: object-oriented programming.

Computer Concepts

There are many different programming paradigms in computer science. Some of the paradigms are procedural, functional, object-oriented, and logic. Most common languages such as C, FORTRAN, and standard PASCAL are procedural. C++, Smalltalk, and Java are well-known object-oriented languages. The functional paradigm includes languages such as LISP and Scheme. Finally, Prolog is a language in the logic paradigm.

Object-Oriented Paradigm

The *object-oriented paradigm* centers on the idea that all programs can be made up of separate entities called objects. A program built from these objects is called an object-oriented program. Each of the objects used to build the program has a specific responsibility or purpose. In a string object, for example, the string itself and all of the operations that can be performed with the string are part of the object. The string object can initialize itself, store a string provided to it, and perform other functions such as reporting the length of the string the object holds. In other words, instead of an object being directly manipulated by other parts of the program, an object manipulates itself. Building programs using the object-oriented paradigm is called *object-oriented programming* or OOP.

Communication among objects is similar to communication among people. You cannot look inside someone's head to see what he or she knows. You must ask questions and allow the person to provide a response. In OOP, data is transferred through messages that are exchanged among objects. The data in an object is not intended to be accessed directly by code that is outside of the object (see Figure 10-1). You have already used messages while working with the string, vector, and matrix classes. For example, rather than going into the object and finding out the length, you used a length method to "ask" the object its length. In effect, you sent a message and received a response.

FIGURE 10-1

To get data from an object, you must give messages to the object.
You cannot simply take the data from inside an object.

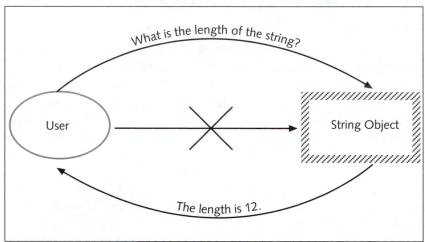

What is the length of the string?

User

String Object

The length is 12.

Communication among objects takes the form of messages because objects hide all of their data and internal operations. This "hiding" of data and code is known as *encapsulation*. By using encapsulation, objects can protect and guarantee the integrity of their data. In procedural programming, poorly written functions can often change important data, causing problems throughout the program. The threat of a poorly written function changing data is reduced when using the object-oriented paradigm.

There is more to object-oriented programming than the concepts and features mentioned in this text. The first step, however, is to visualize how a program can be implemented using objects, learn what is in an object, and understand how objects communicate with other parts of the program. Object-oriented programming in C++ does not take the place of what you have already learned. Instead, it extends the features of the language and gives you a new way to organize programs.

Computer Concepts

Messages can do more than simply initialize an object or return a length of a string or vector. A message can perform a high-level task such as sorting information in the object. A string object can even include a method to check the spelling of the text in the string.

The structures and data types you have been using are also used in object-oriented programs. In fact, what you have learned in previous chapters will provide the foundation you need to be successful as an object-oriented programmer.

Reusability, Containment, and Inheritance

You have already seen many advantages of using object-oriented programming. Three additional important advantages of the paradigm are reusability, containment, and inheritance.

Reusability

Among the greatest advantages that object-oriented programming offers is *reusability*. After an object is designed and coded into a class, that class can be reused in any program. This means that productivity may be increased because less code has to be written. In addition, because less code is written, fewer errors can occur. Although procedural code can be reused, object-oriented code is often easier to use, especially when using more advanced techniques of data handling.

For example, you have used the string, vector, and matrix classes in a number of programs. Best of all, you did not have to write them in the first place. You are reusing code written by other programmers. Suppose you had to write the functions of the matrix class into every program you wrote that requires a matrix. Because classes are reusable, matrix objects can be included whenever needed in your programs with little effort and with reliability.

Computer Concepts

The fact that classes are reusable does not mean that you are free to make use of any class for which you can acquire the code. Programming code is a form of intellectual property and belongs to its creator. Before using code you have not written in your programs, be sure that you have license or permission to do so.

Containment

One of the features of objects that make them so reusable is that objects can contain other objects and use them to implement another object. For example, suppose you want to create a class that defines a car. If you already have a wheel object that defines the properties of a wheel, your car object can use the wheel class to declare four wheel objects. This type of relationship among objects is called *containment* because the car object contains four wheel objects. The relationship is also referred to as a *has-a relationship* because a car has a wheel (four wheels, in this case).

The matrix class is a good example of containment. Although it is not necessary to know how the matrix object gets its job done, the matrix object is, in fact, a vector of vectors. So, because a matrix object declares multiple vector objects, you would say that the matrix object contains vector objects and there is a has-a relationship between the matrix and vector.

Inheritance

Inheritance is the ability of one object to inherit the properties of another object. For example, you might have a building class that defines the properties of a building. The building class could define attributes such as the dimensions of the building, the number of floors, and the types of materials used to construct the building. Suppose you have debugged and perfected your building class, but what you need is a house object. A house has all the attributes of a building as well as additional attributes such as number of bedrooms, number of bathrooms, and size of garage.

Rather than write a new class from scratch or modify the building class, you can create a house class that inherits the properties of the building and then extends those properties with properties that describe the house. The house object and the building object have what is called an *is-a relationship*, meaning the house is a building.

When one class inherits the properties of another, the class from which the properties are inherited is known as the parent class. The class that inherits the properties of another is the child class or derived class. In the previous example, the building class is the parent class and the house class is the child class. The building class can also be described as a base class upon which other classes are built.

An object created from the derived class can call a parent class's member functions as if they were members of the derived class. Users of the class do not need to know what members are implemented in each class. In fact, the users of the class do not need to know that the class is derived, as long as they know what members are available to them.

Inheritance can be multilevel. For example, a class called `garden_home` could inherit properties of the house class that inherits properties of the building class (see Figure 10-2). Multilevel inheritance is one of the features that makes the work done in an object-oriented program more reusable.

FIGURE 10-2
Inheritance can continue for multiple levels.

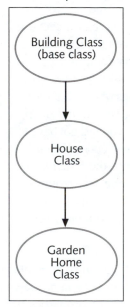

SECTION CHECKPOINT

1. What paradigm have you been using thus far to create programs?

2. What are the main differences between the procedural paradigm and the object-oriented paradigm?

3. What is a major advantage of encapsulation in a program?

4. How is the matrix class that was used in earlier chapters a good example of containment?

5. Think of an example of inheritance that uses everday objects outside the field of computers. Explain how the concept of inheritance works in your example.

VOCABULARY REVIEW

Define the following terms:

containment	is-a relationship	procedural paradigm
encapsulation	object-oriented paradigm	reusability
has-a relationship	object-oriented programming	
inheritance	paradigm	

10.2 The Circle Class

Using a Simple Circle Class

In previous chapters, you used a string class, a vector class, a matrix class, and stream classes. Internally, those classes are fairly complicated. In this section, you will use a class that defines a circle and allows you to include circle objects in your programs. This circle object is very simple. It allows you to declare a circle and define its radius. The object then reports the area of the circle. Through this simple example, you will see how encapsulation and messages make it possible for you to use the object without knowing how the data is stored in the object or how the algorithms are implemented. Later in the section, we'll look at how the circle class is written.

Classes

Recall that the definition for an object is known as a class. Our circle class will be named simply *circle*. The class *circle* tells the compiler how to create each object of type circle. You declare a circle object the same way you declared other objects. The following statement declares a circle named `my_circle`.

```
circle my_circle;
```

When the compiler encounters this declaration, it refers to the circle definition to find out how much memory to reserve for a circle object. The object is then created in memory and given the name `my_circle`. In the same way that many different variables of the same data type can be created, many different objects of the type circle can be created. Each different object of the type circle is independent of the other circle objects in the program. If you were to declare two circle objects, you would have two independent objects, which could be used to represent two distinct circles.

 Note

When multiple objects are declared from the same class, the code required to perform the operations (methods) is not duplicated in memory for each object. The data for each object is stored separately in memory, but all objects defined by the same class share the same code. Any exception to this is in template classes where objects of different data types are created.

1. Load the program **oop.cpp**. The program in Code List 10-1 appears.

2. If necessary, copy the **circle.h** file to the folder that contains **oop.cpp**.

3. Look at the program and see how the objects are declared and how messages are passed between the objects. Notice that there is no way of knowing how the circle objects store the radius or how they calculate area.

4. Run the program.

5. Leave the source code file open while you analyze the program in the paragraphs that follow.

 Computer Concepts

Another way to look at the relationship between a class and an object is to consider examples in the real world. If the definition of a human being were a class, then you and I are instances of that class. We are not the same person, but we both have the characteristics of the human class.

CODE LIST 10-1

```cpp
// oop.cpp
// This object-oriented program shows the use of simple
// objects which represent circles.

#include "circle.h"      // contains the circle class
#include <iostream.h>

int main()
{
 circle Circle_One;      // declare objects
 circle Circle_Two;      // of type circle
 double User_Radius;
 double Area;

 cout << "\nWhat is the radius of the first circle? ";
 cin  >> User_Radius;

 // send a message to Circle_One telling it to set its
 // radius to User_Radius
 Circle_One.SetRadius(User_Radius);

 cout << "\nWhat is the radius of the second circle? ";
 cin  >> User_Radius;

 // send a message to Circle_Two telling it to set its
 // radius to User_Radius
 Circle_Two.SetRadius(User_Radius);
```

CODE LIST 10-1 (continued)

```
    // send a message to Circle_One asking for its area
    Area = Circle_One.Area();

    cout.setf(ios::fixed);
    cout << "\nThe area of the first circle is " << Area << ".\n";

    // send a message to Circle_Two asking for its area
    Area = Circle_Two.Area();

    cout << "\nThe area of the second circle is " << Area << ".\n";

    return 0;
}
```

Writing a Program to Use the Circle Class

Let's analyze the source code you ran in the previous Step-by-Step exercise. After the beginning comments, there are two compiler directives, shown again in Code List 10-2.

CODE LIST 10-2

```
#include "circle.h"        // contains the circle class
#include <iostream.h>
```

The first compiler directive includes the header file **circle.h**. The **circle.h** header file contains the definition for the circle class. Without the class definition, the compiler would not know how to create a circle object, nor would it know what properties a circle object has. The next compiler directive includes the **iostream.h** header file so that the program can get input from the user and output data to the screen.

In the `main` function, the program declares two copies of the circle class, `Circle_One` and `Circle_Two` (see Code List 10-3). A variable to hold a radius and an area of a circle are also declared. The variables `User_Radius` and `Area` are used in your program and are not part of either object.

CODE LIST 10-3

```
int main()
{
    circle Circle_One;        // declare objects
    circle Circle_Two;        // of type circle
    double User_Radius;
    double Area;
```

The program then prompts the user for the radius of the first circle. After the program receives the user's response, it sends a message to `Circle_One` requesting that it set its radius to `User_Radius`, as shown in Code List 10-4.

```
    cout << "\nWhat is the radius of the first circle? ";
    cin  >> User_Radius;

    // send a message to Circle_One telling it to set its
    // radius to User_Radius
    Circle_One.SetRadius(User_Radius);
```

After the radius of `Circle_One` has been set to `User_Radius`, the program prompts the user for the radius of the second circle and sets the radius of `Circle_Two` using the same method that was used to set the radius of `Circle_One`.

Finally, the program sends a message to each of the circle objects and requests its area. The area of `Circle_One` is assigned to Area and then output to the screen. Then the area of the second circle is also retrieved and output to the screen (see Code List 10-5).

CODE LIST 10-5

```
    // send a message to Circle_One asking for its area
    Area = Circle_One.Area();

    cout.setf(ios::fixed);
    cout << "\nThe area of the first circle is " << Area << ".\n";

    // send a message to Circle_Two asking for its area
    Area = Circle_Two.Area();

    cout << "\nThe area of the second circle is " << Area << ".\n";

    return 0;
}
```

There are many different ways the radius could be stored in the object as well as different ways the area could be calculated. Is the size of the circle stored in the form of the radius or the diameter? How is the area calculated? You do not know the answers to these questions. To use the object, however, you do not need this information.

Designing and Implementing the Circle Class

You now have lots of experience using classes that have been created for you. At some point, however, you will need to design a class or modify an existing class. Implementing a class is not difficult, but it does involve some syntax that may be new to you.

Designing a Class

Designing a class requires you to think in an object-oriented way. For example, consider a typical telephone answering machine. It encapsulates the functions of an answering machine as well as the data (your incoming and outgoing messages). The buttons on the answering machine are the equivalent of messages. Pushing the Play button sends a message to the answering machine to play the stored messages. It is not hard to understand how an answering machine is an object that contains all the storage and functions it needs within itself.

To design a class, you must think of computer programs in the same way that you think of an answering machine or other objects around you. If you were to design the circle class you used in the previous section, you should first take into account what needs to be stored and what functions are necessary. In other words, you define the purpose of the object. The purpose will determine how an object is coded, what data it will hold, and how its operations will be implemented.

In the case of the circle, all that is required to define a circle is a radius. You then decide what functions the object needs to perform. For example, you may want the circle to report its area and circumference. The circle also needs to be able to set its radius.

A class should be designed with enough functions and data to perform its responsibilities—no more and no less. You've never seen an answering machine that can function as a stapler. Likewise, a class should not perform an unrelated task. You also do not need to store more data than is necessary. For example, since the radius is all that is necessary to define a circle, you shouldn't store both a radius and a diameter.

Object-oriented design (often abbreviated OOD) involves much more than the guidelines outlined here. For this chapter, the goal is just to get a taste of object-oriented design.

Implementing a Class

The best way to learn how to implement a class is to study the code of an implemented class. Code List 10-6 is the header file **circle.h** that was used in Step-by-Step 10.1. You have used header files before. However, you may not have opened one to see what's inside. A header file is a source code file that typically includes code or declarations of code that you intend to include in more than one program. Classes are normally defined in header files so that they may be reused.

CODE LIST 10-6

```
// circle.h

#ifndef _CIRCLE_H
#define _CIRCLE_H

const double PI=3.14159;

class circle
{
 public:
        // constructors
        circle();                  // default constructor
        circle(const circle &); // copy constructor

        // member functions
        void   SetRadius(double);
        double Area();

 private:
        // data
```

```
        double radius;
};

// default constructor
circle::circle()
{
  radius = 0.0;
}

// copy constructor
circle::circle(const circle & Object)
{
  radius = Object.radius;
}

// method to set the radius of the circle
void circle::SetRadius(double IncomingRadius)
{
  radius = IncomingRadius;
}

// method to find the area of the circle
double circle::Area()
{
 return(PI*radius*radius);
}

#endif
```

Before continuing, familiarize yourself with the code in Code List 10-6. In the following paragraphs, the implementation of the circle class will be broken down and examined.

COMPILER DIRECTIVES

At the beginning of the file are the compiler directives `#ifndef` and `#define`. These are used to prevent the class from being defined twice, which can create problems. The `#define` directive instructs the compiler to define a symbol and to remember that the symbol exists. The `#ifndef` directive checks the compiler's symbol table for a specified entry.

 Note

Header files normally contain declarations of variables, functions, and classes, but not the implementation of the functions and classes. This is the case with almost all header files that come with a C++ compiler. However, in some situations the functions and classes may also be implemented in the header file.

In this case, these compiler directives are used together to make sure that the circle class has not already been defined. The `#ifndef` directive checks for the existence of a symbol named _CIRCLE_H. If the entry is not found, the `#define` directive defines the symbol and the source code that follows defines the circle class. If the _CIRCLE_H symbol is already defined, it means that this header file has already been compiled and the definition of the circle class is skipped.

At the end of Code List 10-6 is the compiler directive `#endif`, which ends the original `#ifndef` directive. The `#ifndef` compiler directive works with the `#endif` directive to form an if structure similar to those you worked with in previous chapters. The `#ifndef` directive instructs the compiler to compile everything between the `#ifndef` and the `#endif` if the symbol is not defined.

CLASS DEFINITION

A class definition is made up of several different parts (see Code List 10-7). The definition begins with the keyword `class`, followed by the class name and an opening brace. The definition ends with a closing brace and a semicolon. Functions and variables that are prototyped and declared in a class definition are called ***members***.

 Note

If the semicolon after a class definition is omitted, the compiler will report several errors. Therefore, if multiple errors are encountered when compiling a class, check for the presence of the semicolon at the end of the class definition.

CODE LIST 10-7

```
class circle
{
 public:
        // constructors
        circle();                  // default constructor
        circle(const circle &); // copy constructor

        // member functions
        void    SetRadius(double);
        double Area();

 private:
        // data
        double radius;
};
```

After the opening brace is the keyword `public` followed by a colon. The `public` keyword tells the compiler to let the programmer using the class have direct access to all the variables and functions between the `public` and `private` keywords. Any variables and functions after the `private` keyword cannot be accessed from outside the object. The `private` keyword allows a circle object to protect its data. This data protection is known as ***information hiding***, which is an important benefit provided by encapsulation. By using information hiding, objects can protect the integrity of their data.

The constructor prototypes follow the `public` keyword (see Code List 10-8). ***Constructors*** tell the compiler how to create the object in memory and what the initial values of its data will be. Constructors are given the same name as the class.

CODE LIST 10-8

```
// constructors
circle();                  // default constructor
circle(const circle &); // copy constructor
```

The circle class has two constructors. The first constructor is known as the default constructor. The default constructor is used when the object is declared. The second constructor is known as the copy constructor. A copy constructor receives a reference to another object as an argument and is used when objects are passed to functions by value.

At this stage, constructors can be confusing. All you need to understand right now is that constructors allow you to declare objects. Classes often have multiple constructors to allow you to declare objects in different ways. For example, recall how the vector class allowed you to declare an empty vector, a vector of a specific length, or a vector of a specific length initialized to a value. Each of those different ways to declare a vector requires a separate constructor within the class.

After the constructors are the member function prototypes (see Code List 10-9). *Member functions* allow programmers using an object to send information to it and receive information from it. Member functions are the messages used for communication in object-oriented programming.

CODE LIST 10-9

```
// member functions
void    SetRadius(double);
double Area();
```

The circle object needs two member functions: one to set the radius and one to retrieve the area. Member function prototypes are written just like normal function prototypes with a return type, a name, and an argument list. Recall that it is not necessary for a prototype to include the names of the parameters, just the type. The implementation of the member functions follows the definition of the class.

The private keyword comes after the member function prototypes. The only data required for the circle object is the radius, so it is declared as a float with the identifier radius, as shown in Code List 10-10.

CODE LIST 10-10

```
private:
        // data
        double radius;
};
```

Because radius is after the private keyword, a programmer using a circle object cannot access the radius directly, so member functions must be used. After the radius variable, the definition of the circle class is closed with the closing brace and a semicolon.

IMPLEMENTING MEMBER FUNCTIONS

To implement a member function, you must use a special syntax. The function is implemented like a normal C++ function except that the class name and the *scope-resolution operator* (::) precede the function name. Constructors are slightly different from other member functions because they do not have any return type—not even void.

Constructor implementation in the circle class is very simple (see Code List 10-11). The default constructor sets the radius equal to zero. The copy constructor sets the radius equal to the passed object's radius.

CODE LIST 10-11

```
   // default constructor
   circle::circle()
   {
     radius = 0.0;
   }

   // copy constructor
   circle::circle(const circle & Object)
   {
     radius = Object.radius;
   }
```

The implementation of the other member functions is also simple. Code List 10-12 shows how the `SetRadius` function sets the radius equal to the value it is passed and the `Area` function calculates and returns the area of the circle.

CODE LIST 10-12

```
   // method to set the radius of the circle
   void circle::SetRadius(double IncomingRadius)
   {
     radius = IncomingRadius;
   }

   // method to find the area of the circle
   double circle::Area()
   {
    return(PI*radius*radius);
   }
```

STEP-BY-STEP ▷ 10.2

1. Open the **circle.h** header file.

2. Modify the class definition to include a member function that returns the radius of the circle.

The class definition should be modified to include the prototype for the `GetRadius` function as shown in Code List 10-13.

CODE LIST 10-13

```
class circle
{
 public:
        // constructors
        circle();                // default constructor
        circle(const circle &); // copy constructor
```

CODE LIST 10-13 (continued)

```
        // member functions
        void    SetRadius(double);
        double Area();
        double  GetRadius();

  private:
        // data
        double radius;
};
```

3. Add the function shown in Code List 10-14 to the end of the **circle.h** file, before the `#endif` line.

CODE LIST 10-14

```
double circle::GetRadius()
{
  return(radius);
}
```

4. Save **circle.h** and open **oop.cpp**.

5. Add the statement in Code List 10-15 below the line that reports the area of the first circle.

CODE LIST 10-15

```
cout << "The radius of the first circle is "
    << Circle_One.GetRadius() << ".\n";
```

6. Add the statement in Code List 10-16 below the line that reports the area of the second circle.

CODE LIST 10-16

```
cout << "The radius of the second circle is "
    << Circle_Two.GetRadius() << ".\n";
```

7. Compile and run the modified program.

8. Close the program.

SECTION CHECKPOINT

1. What happens in the compiler when it encounters a line of code like the following?
   ```
   circle my_circle;
   ```

2. Where are classes normally defined?

3. What function do the compiler directives `#ifndef` and `#define` serve?

4. How are constructors different from member functions?

5. What part of a class provides the messages used for communication in an object-oriented program?

VOCABULARY REVIEW

Define the following terms:

constructors	member functions	scope-resolution operator
information hiding	members	

Summary

In this chapter, you learned:

- A paradigm is a model or set of rules that define a way of programming.

- In the procedural paradigm, the functions and algorithms are the focus, with data viewed as something for the functions to manipulate.

- The object-oriented paradigm dictates that data should be placed inside of objects and that these objects should communicate with each other in the form of messages.

- Object-oriented programming (OOP) is the process of developing programs using the object-oriented paradigm.

- Reusability is a major benefit of object-oriented programming.

- Containment is the term used to describe an object that contains one or more other objects as members.

- Inheritance is the term used to describe an object that inherits properties from another object.

- The class from which an object inherits properties is called a parent class or base class. The class that inherits the properties is called a child class or derived class.

- Inheritance can be multilevel.

- Constructors tell the compiler how to create an object in memory and what the initial value of its data will be.

- Member functions provide a way for a programmer to pass data to and get data from an object.

CHAPTER 10 REVIEW QUESTIONS

TRUE/FALSE

Circle T if the statement is true or F if the statement is false.

T F **1.** A paradigm is a model or set of rules that define a way of programming.

T F **2.** The procedural paradigm involves sending messages.

T F **3.** Object-oriented programming reduces the problems caused by poorly written functions changing data that should not be changed.

T F **4.** Classes can be easily reused in multiple programs.

T F **5.** Containment creates an is-a relationship among objects.

T F **6.** Inheritance can be multilevel.

T F **7.** The circle class calculates the area of the circle.

T F 8. Functions and variables that are prototyped and declared in a class definition are called objects.

T F 9. Classes often have more than one constructor.

T F 10. Constructors have a void `return` type.

WRITTEN QUESTIONS

Write a brief answer to the following questions.

1. What are the two primary programming paradigms discussed in this chapter?

2. What paradigm centers on the idea that all programs can be made up of separate entities called objects?

3. Give an example of a class that you have reused in the chapters of this book.

4. What is a parent class?

5. When you write a program that includes string objects, are you using containment or inheritance?

6. Is a program that extends the properties of a class using containment or inheritance?

7. The circle class allows you to declare a circle. What data is provided by the programmer using the circle class?

8. Write the code necessary to declare two circle objects: `CircleA` and `CircleB`.

9. Why are classes normally defined in a header file separate from your main program?

10. What is the purpose of a constructor?

CHAPTER 10 PROJECTS

PROJECT 10-1

Write a program similar to **oop.cpp** that declares two circle objects. The program should set the radius of the first circle to 1.5 and then obtain the area of the first circle from the object. The program should then set the radius of the second circle to the area of the first circle. As output, the program should provide the area of both circles. Save the program as **oop2.cpp**.

PROJECT 10-2

Add a method to the circle class that returns the circumference of the circle. Modify **oop.cpp** to report the circumference of the circle.

PROJECT 10-3

Write a program named **bucktest.cpp** that declares a bucket object based on the class definition in **bucket.h**, which is provided for you. Open **bucket.h** to see the methods in the class. The program should perform the following operations:

1. Declare an object of type bucket.

2. Use the `SetGallonSize()` method to set the bucket size to 5.0 gallons.

3. Use the `FillBucket()` method to fill the bucket with 3.2 gallons of water.

4. Use the `GetWeight()` method to output the weight of the 3.2 gallons of water.

CRITICAL THINKING

ACTIVITY 10-1

Using the circle class definition as a model, create a file named **square.h** and implement a class that models a square and includes an `Area` method. Also write a program to test the square class. Name the test program **sqrtest.cpp**.

POINTERS, ENUM, AND STRUCTURES

A pointer is a variable or constant that holds a memory address. *Pointer* may be a new term to you, or you may have heard that pointers are difficult to understand. As with any new concept, however, once you become familiar with the principles and how to apply them you will see that pointers are not difficult. This chapter will cover the basics of pointers and give you a firm foundation that you will use in chapters to come.

You will also learn some ways to create your own data types. One of the methods allows you to create a type that can only contain certain values. Another method allows you to group data together into structures.

11.1 Pointer Basics

Refresh Your Memory about Memory

Each byte of a microcomputer's memory has a unique address. The address is just a number. Memory addresses start at zero and count up from there. Actually, the way memory is organized and the way addresses are assigned varies among computers. The important thing to know is that each byte is numbered in order. For example, memory location 221345 is next to memory location 221346.

Programming would be more difficult if you had to remember the addresses where you stored your data. Instead, the compiler lets you assign names to memory locations when you declare variables.

What Is a Pointer?

A *pointer* is a variable or constant that holds a memory address. You can think of a pointer as a variable or constant that *points* to another variable or data structure. You can create a pointer that points to any data type. For example, suppose you want a pointer that points to an integer. Figure 11-1 shows how the actual integer is stored, and how the pointer variable points to the integer.

In this example, the integer i (with value 3) is stored in two bytes of memory at address 216801. The pointer iptr points to the variable i. The pointer occupies four bytes of RAM. The pointer stores the value 216801, which is the memory location where the integer begins.

You may be wondering why anyone would want a pointer to an integer. At this level, pointers may seem "pointless." In later chapters, however, you will learn how to put the power of pointers to work for you when more advanced methods of handling data are discussed. In Chapter 12, for example, you will create a very flexible data structure called a linked list, which is a high-powered array. Creating a linked list requires lower level programming and makes extensive use of pointers. Later in this section you will see a simple program that makes use of pointers to create an efficient algorithm for working with two variables. But first we'll learn how to declare pointers and do some simple pointer operations.

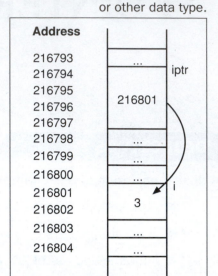

FIGURE 11-1
A pointer can point to an integer or other data type.

> **✓ Note**
>
> Pointer size varies among computers and operating systems. For our purposes, the size of pointers is unimportant.

Declaring Pointers

The code in Code List 11-1 shows how an integer and pointer like the one in Figure 11-1 is declared.

CODE LIST 11-1

```
int main()
{
 int i;       // declare an integer i
 int *iptr;   // declare a pointer to an integer

 iptr = &i;   // initialize the pointer to the address of i
 i = 3;       // initialize i to 3;
 return 0;
}
```

Working with pointers requires the use of two new operators: the ***dereferencing operator*** (*) and the ***address-of operator*** (&). Let's examine what is accomplished by the previous code.

The statement `int *iptr;` declares a pointer by preceding the variable name with a dereferencing operator (*). Notice this is the same symbol used to indicate multiplication; however, your compiler can tell the difference by the way it is used.

Notice that pointers have types just like other variables. The pointer type must match the type of data you intend to point to. In the previous example, an `int` pointer is declared to point to an `int` variable. The * before the variable name tells the compiler that we want to declare a pointer, rather than a regular variable. The variable `iptr` cannot hold just any value. It must hold the memory address of an integer. If you try to make a pointer point to a variable of a type other than the type of the pointer, you will get an error when you try to compile the program.

Like any other variable, a pointer begins with an indeterminate value and must be initialized to "point" to something. The statement `iptr = &i;` is what makes `iptr` point to `i`. Reading the statement as "iptr is assigned the address of i" helps the statement make sense. The address-of operator (&) returns the "address of" the variable rather than the variable's contents.

Just because you use pointers does not mean you have to concern yourself with exact memory locations. When you use pointers, you will assign an address to a pointer using the address-of operator (&). The exact address returned by the operator is of importance only to the computer. Let's write a simple program to declare and initialize a pointer.

S TEP-BY-STEP ▷ 11.1

1. Enter the program in Code List 11-2. Save the source code as **pointer.cpp**.

2. Compile and run the program to see that `i`, `j`, and `k` hold the values you expect. The variable `int_ptr` outputs a memory address to your screen when you print it. The address will probably print in a form called hexadecimal, which is a combination of numbers and letters. Learning the exact meaning of the address is of little importance right now: just realize that it is the address where the variable `i` is stored.

3. Leave the source code file on the screen for the next Step-by-Step exercise.

CODE LIST 11-2

```
#include <iostream.h> // necessary for cout command

int main()
{
  int i, j, k;    // declare three integers
  int *int_ptr;   // declare a pointer to an integer

  i = 1;
  j = 2;
  k = 3;
  int_ptr = &i;   // initialize the pointer to point to i

  cout << "i = " << i << '\n';
  cout << "j = " << j << '\n';
```

```
    cout << "k = " << k << '\n';
    cout << "int_ptr = " << int_ptr << '\n';
    return 0;
}
```

In Step-by-Step 11.1, you declared the pointer (int *int_ptr;) and initialized it in a different statement (int_ptr = &i;). Like other variables, you can initialize a pointer when you declare it. For example, the following statement could have been used in the program in Code List 11-2 to declare the pointer and initialize it in one statement.

```
    int *int_ptr = &i;
```

Note

A pointer can be named using any legal variable name. Some programmers use names that make it clear the variable is a pointer, such as ending the name with ptr or beginning the name with p_, but it is not necessary.

Using the * and & Operators

The dereferencing operator (*) is used for more than declaring pointers. In the following statement, the dereferencing operator tells the compiler to return the value in the variable being pointed to, rather than the address of the variable.

```
    result = *int_ptr;
```

The variable result is assigned the value of the integer pointed to by int_ptr.

S TEP-BY-STEP ▷ 11.2

1. Enter the lines of code in Code List 11-3 to the program you saved named **pointer.cpp**. The output statement with the &i does the same thing as outputting int_ptr, since int_ptr holds the address of i. Sending *int_ptr to the output stream prints the contents of the variable pointed to by int_ptr, rather than printing the pointer itself.

2. Compile and run to see the output of the new statements.

3. Enter the statements in Code List 11-4 at the end of the program.

4. Compile and run again. Because int_ptr now points to the integer j rather than i, the output statement prints the value of j, even though the exact statement (cout << "*int_ptr = " << *int_ptr << '\n';) printed the value of i just two statements back.

5. Enter the statements in Code List 11-5 at the end of the program.

6. Compile and run again. The pointer now points to the variable `k`, so `*int_ptr` returns the value of `k`, which is 3.

7. Save and close the source code file.

CODE LIST 11-3

```
cout << "&i = " << &i << '\n';
cout << "*int_ptr = " << *int_ptr << '\n';
```

CODE LIST 11-4

```
int_ptr = &j; // store the address of j to int_ptr
cout << "int_ptr = " << int_ptr << '\n';
cout << "*int_ptr = " << *int_ptr << '\n';
```

CODE LIST 11-5

```
int_ptr = &k; // store the address of k to int_ptr
cout << "int_ptr = " << int_ptr << '\n';
cout << "*int_ptr = " << *int_ptr << '\n';
```

Changing Values with *

The dereferencing operator allows you to do more than get the value in the variable to which the pointer is pointing. You can change the value of the variable to which the pointer points. For example, the following statement assigns the value 5 to the integer to which `int_ptr` points.

```
*int_ptr = 5;
```

You are probably now beginning to see why C++ is so powerful—and so dangerous. A statement like the previous one should be avoided because it fails to indicate the specific variable that is being changed. Although C++ programmers are given the freedom to work with memory in a rich variety of ways, pointers should be used only when they improve the program.

Consider the program in Code List 11-6. The program declares and initializes two floating-point numbers of type `double`. Using a do while loop, the program repeatedly selects the larger of the two numbers and divides it by 2. The loop ends when one of the variables becomes less than 1.

The program uses a pointer to provide an efficient solution. By setting a pointer to point to the larger of the two values, the larger value can be printed and divided by 2 by use of the pointer, rather than the variable itself. By using a pointer, the same code can be used no matter which variable is larger.

```
#include <iostream.h> // necessary for cout command

int main()
{
  double a, b;             // declare two floating-point numbers
  double *double_ptr;      // declare a pointer to a double

  a = 169.8;
  b = 237.5;

  do
   {
      cout << "The two numbers are " << a << " and " << b << endl;

      if (a >= b)
       {
         double_ptr = &a;
       }
      else
       {
         double_ptr = &b;
       }

      cout << "The largest of the two numbers is "
           << *double_ptr << endl;
      cout << *double_ptr;
      *double_ptr = *double_ptr / 2;
      cout << " divided by 2 is " << *double_ptr << endl;
   } while((a > 1.0) && (b > 1.0));
   return 0;
}
```

STEP-BY-STEP ▷ 11.3

1. Enter the program shown in Code List 11-6. Save the source code file as **thepoint.cpp**.

2. Study the source code closely before you run the program. Compile and run the program to see its output. The program divides the larger of the 2 values by 2 until one of the values becomes less than 1.

3. Close the source code file.

SECTION CHECKPOINT

1. What is stored in a pointer?

2. What symbol is used for the address-of operator?

3. Write a statement that declares a pointer to a variable of type double.

4. Write a statement that assigns the pointer you declared in question 3 to the address of a variable named **x**.

5. Now change the value of the variable **x** to 9.9 using the pointer you declared and the dereferencing operator.

VOCABULARY REVIEW

Define the following terms:

address-of operator   dereferencing operator   pointer

11.2 Using enum

The **enum** keyword (short for enumerated) is a C++ feature that is often overlooked. It allows you to create your own simple data types for special purposes in your program. For example, you could create a data type called `colors` that allows only the values red, green, blue, and yellow as data. In this section, you will learn how enum works and how you can use it in your programs.

How to Use enum

The enum keyword is easy to use. You simply create a type, give it a name, and tell the compiler what values your new data type will accept. Consider the following statement.

```
enum sizes {small, medium, large, jumbo};
```

The data type called `sizes` can have one of four values: small, medium, large, or jumbo. The next step is to declare a variable that uses `sizes` as a type. Let's declare two variables of the type `sizes`.

```
enum sizes drink_size, popcorn_size;
```

The variable `drink_size` and `popcorn_size` are of type `sizes` and can be assigned one of the four sizes defined in the `sizes` type.

1. Enter the program shown in Code List 11-7. Save the source code as **enumtest.cpp**.

2. Run the program to see the output. Close the source code file.

CODE LIST 11-7

```cpp
#include <iostream.h> // necessary for cout command

int main()
{
  enum sizes {small, medium, large, jumbo};
  sizes drink_size, popcorn_size;

  drink_size = large;
  popcorn_size = jumbo;

  if (drink_size == large)
   { cout << "You could have a jumbo for another quarter.\n"; }

  if ((popcorn_size == jumbo) && (drink_size != jumbo))
   { cout << "You need more drink to wash down a jumbo popcorn.\n"; }
  return 0;
}
```

How enum Works

Internally, the compiler assigns an integer to each of the items in an enum list. For example, the following statement does not print small, medium, large, or jumbo to the screen. It prints either 0, 1, 2, or 3.

```cpp
cout << drink_size << '\n';
```

 Warning

Attempting to print the value of an enumerated type results in an error on some compilers. Enumerated types are best used in expressions and switch structures, rather than directly for output.

By default, the compiler begins assigning integers with zero. For example, in the `sizes` type, small = 0, medium = 1, large = 2, and jumbo = 3. You can, however, choose your own values. For example, suppose you wanted to use an enumerated type to assign quantities. You could use a statement like the following to declare an enumerated type with the values 1, 2, 12, 48, and 144.

```cpp
enum quantity {Single=1, Dozen=12, Full_Case=48, Gross=144};
```

As another example, suppose you want to create a type called `month` that is made up of the months of the year. Because the months are commonly numbered 1 through 12, you decide to have the compiler assign those numbers to your list. The assignment in the first value of the list sets the beginning value for the items in the list, as in the following statement. January will be assigned the value 1, February the value 2, etc.

```
enum month {January=1, February, March, April, May, June, July,
            August, September, October, November, December};
```

You can use the fact that enum uses integers to your advantage. For example, a statement like the following can be used with the sizes type.

```
if (drink_size > medium)
  { cout << "This drink will not fit in your cup holder.\n"; }
```

Using typedef

Another C++ feature which is related to enum is **typedef**. You can use typedef to give a new name to an existing data type. For example, if you prefer to use the term *real* to declare a variable of type float, you can give the data type an alias of real with typedef.

```
typedef float real;
```

You should, of course, use typedef sparingly because you may confuse the reader of your code.

You can use typedef for more than just changing the names of data types to fit your liking. For example, recall from Chapter 2 that some C++ compilers include a Boolean data type and some compilers do not. You can use typedef and a couple of constants to create your own Boolean data type.

```
typedef int bool;
const int TRUE = 1;
const int FALSE = 0;
```

These three statements make it possible to declare variables of type bool and assign values to the variables using TRUE and FALSE.

```
bool acceptable;
acceptable = TRUE;
```

SECTION CHECKPOINT

1. Write a statement that declares an enum type called speed that allows the values stopped, slow, and fast.

2. Write a statement that declares a variable named rabbit of the type you declared in question 1.

3. Write a statement that assigns the value fast to the rabbit variable you declared above.

4. What does the compiler use internally to represent the values of an enum type?

5. What can be used to give a new name to an existing data type?

Define the following terms:

enum   typedef

11.3 Structures

Structure Basics

C++ structures allow variables to be grouped to form a new data type. The data elements in a structure are arranged in a manner that is similar to the way database programs arrange data.

In a database program, data is stored in records. For example, suppose you have a database of items sold by a mail-order company. Each item that the company sells is stored as a record in the database. Each record is made up of data called *fields*. Figure 11-2 shows a series of three records contained in a database. Notice that each record has identical field names (i.e., Item ID).

Note

Recall from Chapter 2 that any organized way of storing data in a computer is a data structure. The term *structure* used in this section refers to a specific data structure made by grouping other data structures. Do not confuse the term *structure* used in this section with the more generic term *data structure*.

C++ allows you to create a record by grouping the variables and arrays necessary for the fields into a single structure. The variables in the structure can be of mixed types. For example, in Figure 11-2, strings must be used for the item ID and the description, an integer type can be used to store the quantity on hand and reorder point, and a floating-point type is necessary for cost and retail price. Objects, such as a string object, can be included as part of a structure.

FIGURE 11-2

A record in a database is one completed set of fields.

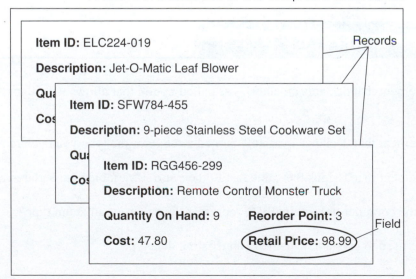

Declaring and Using Structures

A structure must be declared. Because a structure is a collection of data structures, a special syntax is used to access the individual variables of a structure.

Declaring a Structure

Code List 11-8 shows the declaration for the structure in our example.

CODE LIST 11-8

```
struct inventory_item
  {
    apstring item_ID;
    apstring description;
    int quantity_on_hand;
    int reorder_point;
    double cost;
    double retail_price;
  };
```

The `struct` keyword identifies the declaration as a structure. The identifier associated with the structure is `inventory_item`. The variables and objects in the structure are called members. The members of the structure are placed within braces. Within the braces, however, the variables and objects are declared using the syntax to which you are accustomed.

Once you have declared a structure, you must declare an identifier, called a ***structure variable***, that is of the structure's type. This may seem confusing, but what the `struct` keyword does is define a new data type. You can then create as many instances as you want of the new type. The following statement creates a structure variable of a structure named `todays_special` that is of type `inventory_item`.

```
inventory_item todays_special;
```

Computer Concepts

A structure has many similarities to a class. In fact, classes in C++ are an expanded version of the structure. In C++, structures are actually capable of performing the same basic features of a class. But because structures traditionally were used simply to group data, that is as far as we will take the use of structures in this book.

Accessing Members of a Structure

Accessing data in a structure is identical to accessing the members of an object. To access a member of the structure, use the name of the variable, the dot operator, and then the name of the member you need to access, as shown in Figure 11-3.

FIGURE 11-3

Accessing a member of a structure is identical to accessing a member of an object.

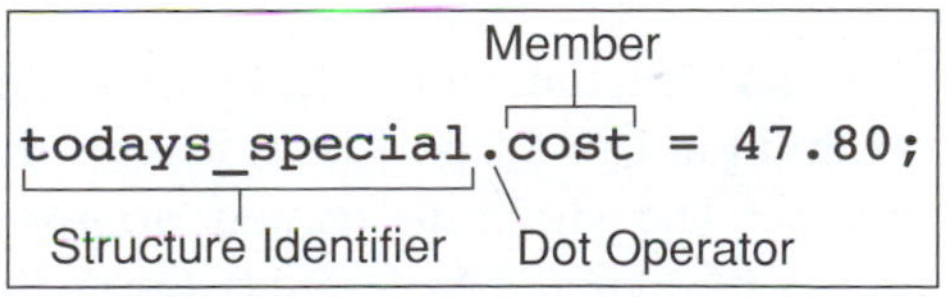

```
todays_special.cost = 47.80;
```
Member
Structure Identifier   Dot Operator

The code segment in Code List 11-9 declares a structure variable named `todays_special` of the type `inventory_item` and initializes each member of the structure.

CODE LIST 11-9

```
inventory_item todays_special;

todays_special.item_ID = "RGG456-299";
todays_special.description = "Remote Control Monster Truck";
todays_special.quantity_on_hand = 19;
todays_special.reorder_point = 3;
todays_special.cost = 47.80;
todays_special.retail_price = 98.99;
```

STEP-BY-STEP ▷ 11.5

1. Retrieve the source code file **struct.cpp**. A program appears that includes the declaration and initialization of the `todays_special` structure variable.

2. Enter the code in Code List 11-10 at the bottom of the program (before the closing brace, of course).

3. Compile and run the program to see the output from the structure.

4. Save the source code file and close.

CODE LIST 11-10

```
cout << "Today's Special\n";
cout << "      Item ID: " << todays_special.item_ID << endl;
cout << "  Description: " << todays_special.description << endl;
cout << "     Quantity: " << todays_special.quantity_on_hand << endl;
cout << "Regular Price: " << setprecision(2)
     << todays_special.retail_price << endl;
cout << "   Sale Price: " << todays_special.retail_price * 0.8
     << endl;
```

Nested Structures

A structure can include enumerated data types and even other structures as members. Consider the program in Code List 11-11. The program sets up a structure to be used to store vital data about blood donors. The structure named `donor_info` includes two enumerated data types (`blood_type` and `rh_factor`) and a structure (`blood_pressure`) among its members.

CODE LIST 11-11

```cpp
#include<iostream.h>

enum blood_type { unknown, A, B, AB, O };
enum rh_factor { negative, positive };
struct blood_pressure
    {
     int systolic;
     int diastolic;
    };

struct donor_info
    {
     blood_type type;
     rh_factor rh;
     blood_pressure bp;
     int heart_rate;
    };

int main()
{
   donor_info current_donor;

   current_donor.type = A;
   current_donor.rh = positive;
   current_donor.bp.systolic = 130;
   current_donor.bp.diastolic = 74;
   current_donor.heart_rate = 69;
   cout << "The donor's blood pressure is "
        << current_donor.bp.diastolic << " over "
        << current_donor.bp.systolic << ".\n";
   return 0;
}
```

The blood_type and rh_factor data are good candidates for an enumerated data type because only a few values are possible. Because blood pressure is actually two values, a structure is used to group the two values into one variable. When a structure appears within a structure the resulting data structure is called a *nested structure*.

Accessing the nested structure requires that two periods be used. As the statement in Figure 11-4 illustrates, initializing the blood pressure values requires that the first structure be accessed by name, then the structure variable within the first structure, and finally, the variable within the nested structure.

FIGURE 11-4

This assignment stores the value 130 in the systolic variable which is in the bp structure which is in the current_donor structure.

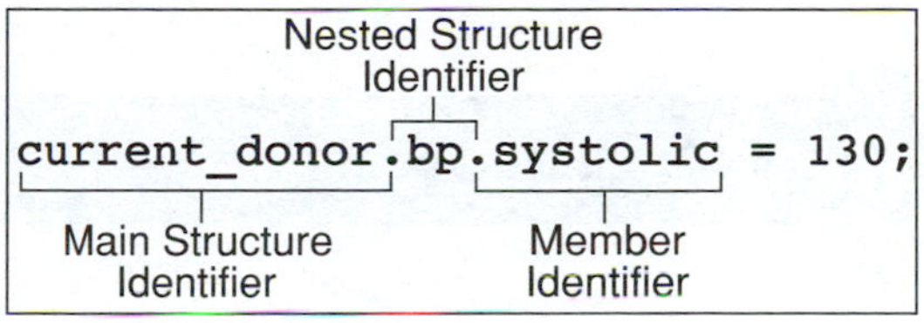

1. Enter the program shown in Code List 11-11. Save the source code as **donors.cpp**.

2. Compile and run the program. Save and close the source code.

It is easy to get locked into thinking about structures in terms of database applications. Structures, however, have many other applications. For example, some mathematical or graphical applications use coordinates such as (x,y) in calculations. You can use a structure like the one in Code List 11-12 to group the x and y into a structure that represents a graphical point.

CODE LIST 11-12

```
struct point
   {
    float x;
    float y;
   };
```

You might then want to use nested structures to create a data type that defines two points that, when connected, form a line, as shown in Code List 11-13.

CODE LIST 11-13

```
struct line
   {
    point p1;
    point p2;
   };
```

Structures can be passed as parameters, which can reduce the number of parameters that must be passed. For example, passing a structure variable of the line structure type can take the place of passing four coordinates (two x and two y values). In the following Step-by-Step exercise, you will run a program that passes a structure variable to calculate the slope of a line.

1. Open **Inslope.cpp**. A program appears that uses the previous structures to calculate the slope of a line.

2. Compile and run the program. Provide the points (1,2) and (2,5) as input and view the result.

3. Add the statements in Code List 11-14 after the declaration of the variable `m`.

4. Compile and run the program again to see the result of the new lines.

5. Save the source code and close.

CODE LIST 11-14

```
line horizontal_line;

horizontal_line.p1.x = 1;
horizontal_line.p1.y = 2;
horizontal_line.p2.x = 5;
horizontal_line.p2.y = 2;
m = slope(horizontal_line);
cout << "The slope of every horizontal line is " << m << endl;
```

SECTION CHECKPOINT

1. What is the purpose of a structure?

2. Write a declaration for a structure named `house` that is to be used to store records in a database of house descriptions for a real estate agent. The fields in the record should include address, square footage of the house, number of bedrooms, number of bathrooms, number of cars that can fit in the garage, and the listed price of the house.

3. Write a statement that declares a structure variable named `featured_home` using the structure declared in question 2.

4. Write a series of statements that initialize the structure variable declared in question 3. Do your best to initialize the structure variable with realistic values.

5. Write a statement that prints the information in the `featured_home` structure variable in the format of the following example, where 3-2-2 is the number of bedrooms, baths, and garage stalls respectively, and 1800 is the square footage.

   3918 Shonle Road 3-2-2   1800 $89,000

VOCABULARY REVIEW

Define the following terms:

fields   structure   structure variable
nested structure

Summary

In this chapter, you learned:

- Pointers are variables and constants that hold memory addresses.

- The dereferencing operator (*) is used to declare pointers and to access the value in the variable to which the pointer points.

- The address-of operator (&) returns the address of a variable, rather than the value in the variable.

- The enum keyword allows you to create custom data types. Internally, the values you include in your enum data types are stored as integers.

- Structures are very useful data structures that allow variables and objects to be grouped to form a new data type.

- Structures are very similar to classes.

- The variables within a structure are called members.

LESSON 11 REVIEW QUESTIONS

TRUE/FALSE

Circle T if the statement is true or F if the statement is false.

T F **1.** A pointer can point to any data type.

T F **2.** The code statement `int_ptr=&i;` causes the value of the variable `i` to be assigned to `int_ptr`.

T F **3.** By using the dereferencing operator, you can change the value of the variable the pointer points to.

T F **4.** The enum keyword allows you to create your own simple data types.

T F **5.** Each of the items in an enum list is stored internally in the computer as a float.

T F **6.** If your compiler does not support Boolean variables, you could create your own Boolean type by using typedef.

T F **7.** All of the data types within a structure must be the same.

T F **8.** You can access a member of a structure by using the structure name, the dot operator, and the member name.

T F **9.** It is possible to use nested structures in a C++ program.

T F **10.** Structures cannot be passed as parameters in C++.

WRITTEN QUESTIONS

Write a brief answer to the following questions.

1. What symbol is used for the address-of operator?

2. Where do you think that the dereferencing operator gets its name?

3. Why might a statement like `*int_ptr = 5;` be considered dangerous?

4. Explain in detail what the following statement actually does.

   ```
   *double_ptr = *double_ptr / 2;
   ```

5. Would the enum feature be useful for defining variables to hold a group of people's heights measured in inches? Why or why not?

6. Write a statement that declares an enum type called `temperature` that allows the values frigid, cold, cool, mild, warm, hot, and sizzling. Have the list begin with the value 1.

7. Is it a good idea to use the typedef statement to rename existing data types? Why or why not?

8. What is the term that describes the variables and objects in a structure?

9. Give an example of a situation that might use nested structures.

10. How is a structure like a database?

LESSON 11 PROJECTS

PROJECT 11-1

Write a program that declares two variables of type float and a single pointer of type float. First initialize the pointer to point to the first float variable. Use the dereferencing operator to initialize the variable to 1.25. Next point the pointer to the second float variable and use the pointer to initialize the variable to 2.5. Print the value of the first variable to the screen by accessing the variable directly. Print the second variable using the dereferencing operator. Save the source code file as **pointer2.cpp**.

PROJECT 11-2

Make a list of several different enumerated data types that could be useful in programs. For example, `enum TrueFalse {FALSE, TRUE}` or `enum Position {open, closed}`.

PROJECT 11-3

1. Open **struct.cpp** (the program you saved in Step-By-Step 11.5).

2. Add code to the end of the program that asks the user for the anticipated number of sales during the day the item is on special and the anticipated sales for the product if it were not on special.

3. Check the value entered against the quantity on hand to make sure that the anticipated orders can be filled. Warn the user if the quantity on hand is less than the anticipated sales.

4. Calculate the amount of income the product is anticipated to generate if the product is put on special and the amount of income the product is anticipated to generate if the product is not put on special.

5. Save the new source code as **struct2.cpp**. Compile and run the program. After testing the program, close the source code file.

PROJECT 11-4

Write a program that uses the point and line structures from Step-By-Step 11.7 to calculate the midpoint of a given line. Have the program ask the user for the points that define the line, then use the formula below to calculate the midpoint of the line and output the coordinates of the midpoint. Save the program as **midpoint.cpp**.

$$\frac{x_1 + x_2}{2} \ , \ \frac{y_1 + y_2}{2}$$

CRITICAL THINKING

ACTIVITY 11-1

On a coordinate plane, the length of a line connecting two points can be found using the following formula.

$$\sqrt{(x_2 - x_1)^2 + (y_2 - y_1)^2}$$

Extend the **lnslope.cpp** program you saved in Step-By-Step 11.7 to calculate the length of the line using the formula.

LINKED LISTS

OBJECTIVES

Upon completion of this chapter, you should be able to:

- Declare and initialize linked list nodes.

- Add nodes to the end of a linked list.

- Move through the nodes of a linked list.

- Dispose of a linked list.

- Insert and delete nodes into a linked list.

- Save a linked list to disk.

- Understand doubly-linked lists.

- Understand circularly-linked lists.

Estimated Time: 4 hours

VOCABULARY

allocating

circularly-linked list

deallocating

doubly-linked list

free

heap

linked list

node

null pointer

singly-linked list

structure pointer operator

traversing

Imagine you are participating in two scavenger hunts. The first scavenger hunt requires that you go to each house on a residential block to obtain a clue. Your search ends at the last house on the block when you discover the final clue.

The second scavenger hunt is different. You are given the address of a house that contains the first clue, but you have no other information. When you arrive at the first house and locate the clue, you are also given the address of the house that contains the second clue. At the second house you find a clue and another address. You are unaware of how many houses you must visit or their locations, but eventually you reach a house that has the last clue.

A vector object is like the first scavenger hunt. The data in a vector is lined up in a row like houses on a city block. In C++ programming, you can use a method like the second scavenger hunt to store data: the *linked list*. Like the houses in the second scavenger hunt, the data in a linked list may be at scattered addresses. Each piece of data in the linked list holds the address of the next piece of data.

Inserting a house into the first scavenger hunt is impossible. The block is already full of houses. If you want to insert a clue into the hunt, you would have to move all the clues from that house forward by one house in order to free up a house for the new clue. But in the second scavenger hunt, you can insert a clue by rerouting the clues to point to a new house that was not previously in the hunt.

In this chapter, you will learn how linked lists are created using C++, and how to use data once it is in a linked list.

12.1 Linked List Basics

Programming a linked list can be tricky. However, if you understand how a linked list works before you do the programming, you'll find the programming is not that difficult. In this section, you will learn how a linked list works.

Using a Linked List

Suppose you are developing a program that accepts the names and populations of the counties in a state and ranks them by population. Recall the analogy of the second scavenger hunt at the beginning of this chapter. Each clue to the puzzle was contained in a house, and each house contained the address of the next house. In a linked list, the data is contained in a structure called a **node**, and each node has a memory address.

Figure 12-1 is an illustration that may help you visualize a node for our program. The node is made up of three parts: the name of the county, the population of the county, and the address of the next node.

Each node in the linked list has this same structure. To create a list, all we have to do is link them together. Figure 12-2 shows a linked list with three counties entered. Let's examine the figure piece by piece.

At the top of Figure 12-2 you see an arrow pointing to the first node. This represents a pointer (called the head pointer) to the first node in the list. You must always have a pointer that points to the first node in the list. Without this pointer that gives the address of the first node, the whole list is lost, just like you need the address of the first house to begin the scavenger hunt.

The first node has data for the first county (name and population), and a pointer that provides the address of the next node. The second node also has data for a county and an address of a third node. The third node has zero address, known as a **null pointer**, to let your program know the end of the list has been reached.

In the next section you will implement the program just described that uses a linked list to store the names and populations of counties.

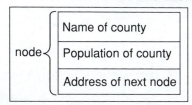

FIGURE 12-1
A linked list is a collection of nodes like this one.

node { Name of county / Population of county / Address of next node

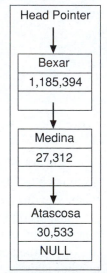

FIGURE 12-2
The nodes of a linked list are connected by pointers.

Head Pointer
↓
Bexar
1,185,394

Medina
27,312

Atascosa
30,533
NULL

Handling Memory with Dynamic Data

When you declare a variable or vector, the compiler reserves memory for your data and later frees that memory for use by other data. Linked lists are a form of data structure called dynamic data. When using a linked list, you must use special operators to reserve and free memory manually. You must also keep track of the location of your dynamic data using pointers.

MEMORY AND DATA

Dynamic data structures are stored in a portion of memory called the **heap**. Exactly where and what the heap is varies among operating systems, but basically the heap is the memory left over after your operating system and programs are loaded.

Reserving memory on the heap is called *allocating*. Returning reserved memory to the heap for use by other data is called *deallocating* or *freeing*. When memory is allocated, the operating system returns the address of the memory location where the data is stored. That address is stored to a pointer variable that you will use to access the data. Let's look at how memory is allocated and deallocated in C++.

THE NEW AND DELETE OPERATORS

The new operator allocates memory on the heap and the delete operator frees memory. The program in Code List 12-1 demonstrates some features of C++ that you will use when creating linked lists. We'll analyze the program listed in Code List 12-1 in the pages to come.

CODE LIST 12-1

```cpp
// allocate.cpp

#include<iostream.h>
#include"apstring.h"

struct chemical_element
  {
    apstring element_name;
    double atomic_weight;
  };

int main()
{
  chemical_element *my_ptr;        // Declare pointer to point to the
                                   // dynamically-allocated structure.
  my_ptr = new chemical_element;   // Allocate memory for structure.

  if(my_ptr != NULL)  // Check to make sure allocation was successful.
    {
      // Initialize members of the structure.
      my_ptr->element_name = "Nitrogen";
      my_ptr->atomic_weight = 14.0067;


      // Display members of the dynamically-allocated structure.
      cout << "Element Name: " << my_ptr->element_name << endl;
      cout << "Atomic Weight: " << my_ptr->atomic_weight << endl;

      delete my_ptr;  // Free memory used by the data.
    }
  else
    {
    cout << "Memory allocation was unsuccessful.\n";
    }
  return 0;
}
```

Examine Figure 12-3. The new operator is used to allocate the memory for the data. The new operator returns the address of the allocated memory and the program assigns the address to the pointer variable named my_ptr.

FIGURE 12-3
The new operator allocates memory on the heap.

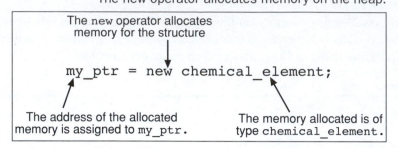

The new operator allocates
memory for the structure

my_ptr = new chemical_element;

The address of the allocated
memory is assigned to my_ptr.

The memory allocated is of
type chemical_element.

You should test the address returned by the new operator to make sure that the memory was successfully allocated. If an error occurs during allocation, the new operator returns a null pointer. The most common reason for unsuccessful allocation is insufficient free RAM to satisfy your request. The programs you will write in this course are unlikely to result in an allocation error, but you should get into the habit of checking the operation. In the program shown in Code List 12-1, the value of my_ptr is checked in an if statement, as shown in Code List 12-2.

Note

The structure pointer operator is actually two characters: the hyphen (-) and the greater-than symbol (>). Used together, they are interpreted as the structure pointer operator (->).

CODE LIST 12-2

```
my_ptr = new chemical_element; // Allocate memory for structure.

if(my_ptr != NULL)  //Check to make sure allocation was successful.
{
// successful allocation
}
else
{
cout << "Memory allocation was unsuccessful.\n";
}
```

As you saw in Figure 12-3, memory allocated by the new operator is associated with a data type. The data type allows the compiler to allocate the correct amount of memory. In addition, the data type makes it easier to use the allocated memory.

Individual members of a dynamically-allocated structure are accessed using the *structure pointer operator* (->). Examine the statements in Code List 12-4. Notice that the dot operator normally used to access members of a structure has been replaced by the structure pointer operator.

Computer Concepts

The structure pointer operator (->) is a shortcut provided to simplify the pointer syntax. The same result can be obtained by combining the dereferencing operator and dot operator. For example, my_ptr->element_name could be replaced by (*my_ptr).element_name.

CODE LIST 12-3

```
// Initialize members of the structure.
my_ptr->element_name = "Nitrogen";
my_ptr->atomic_weight = 14.0067;

// Display members of the dynamically-allocated structure.
cout << "Element Name: " << my_ptr->element_name << endl;
cout << "Atomic Weight: " << my_ptr->atomic_weight << endl;
```

Finally, the program frees (deallocates) the memory it allocated. Memory is deallocated with the `delete` operator, as shown in the following statement. When deallocating, only the `delete` operator and the name of the pointer are necessary.

```
delete my_ptr;  // Free memory used by the data.
```

STEP-BY-STEP ▷ 12.1

1. Retrieve the source code file **allocate.cpp**.

2. Compile and run the program.

3. Add a member of type int to the `chemical_element` structure. Name the new member `atomic_number`.

4. Initialize the atomic number of the Nitrogen element to 7, and add a statement to output the value.

5. Save the source code, compile, and run the program again.

6. Close the source code file.

SECTION CHECKPOINT

1. Define dynamic data structure.

2. Give an example of a static data structure.

3. What is the term for the structures that store data in a linked list?

4. What is the name of the portion of memory where dynamic data structures are stored?

5. What operators allow you to allocate and deallocate memory?

Define the following terms:

allocating	heap	null pointer
deallocating	linked list	structure pointer operator
free	node	

12.2 Linked Lists in C++

Now that you have seen how linked lists work in general, let's look at how linked lists are implemented in C++.

Declaring Nodes and Necessary Pointers

The declaration in Code List 12-4 looks like other structures you have used, except for the link to the next node.

CODE LIST 12-4

```
struct county_node          // node for linked list
   {
    apstring county_name;
    long population;
    county_node *next;       // link to next node
   };
```

Recall that in Chapter 11 you used the asterisk when declaring pointers, as in the following statement.

```
int *i_ptr;      // declares a pointer to an integer
```

The asterisk causes the compiler to declare a pointer named `i_ptr` that can be used to point to any integer. In our `county_node` structure, the last member is a pointer named `next`. The `next` pointer can hold the address of any node that is created using the `county_node` structure. In our case, the pointer will hold the address of the next node in the linked list.

The program will need two pointers in addition to the pointer in the `county_node` structure. Recall from Figure 12-2 that a pointer is necessary to point to the first node in the list. We will also need a pointer to keep track of the current node as we use the list. The following statements will declare two pointers for those purposes.

```
county_node *head_ptr;       // pointer to first node of linked list
county_node *current_ptr;    // pointer to current node
```

The two pointers declared in these statements must be initialized before they point to anything. The pointers will be initialized in the `main` function.

Initializing the Linked List with the First Node

The next step is to create a node, initialize it with data, and initialize your pointers. The `county_node` structure (shown again in Code List 12-5) creates a data type that will be used to create nodes. The actual nodes have yet to be created.

> **Note**
>
> Remember, a pointer is a variable and can point to any data of the pointer's data type. The pointer named `current_ptr` can point to any node in the linked list.

CODE LIST 12-5

```
//global structure definitions, variables, and constants

struct county_node          // node for linked list
    {
      apstring county_name;
      long population;
      county_node *next;      // link to next node
    };
county_node *head_ptr;       // pointer to first node of linked list
county_node *current_ptr;    // pointer to current node
```

Consider the `main` function in Code List 12-6. First, a string object and variable are declared to temporarily hold the name and population of a county. These local variables are used to hold the user's input before the node that will eventually hold the data is created.

CODE LIST 12-6

```
// beginning of main function
int main()
{
 apstring name;
 long popul;

 if(get_county_data(name, popul)) // prompt user for data for the node
    {
      head_ptr = new county_node; // initialize list head
      head_ptr->county_name = name;
      head_ptr->population = popul;
      head_ptr->next = NULL; // initialize next node pointer to NULL

      while(get_county_data(name, popul))
        {
         add_node(name, popul);
        }
```

```
        display_list();    // display the counties and populations
        delete_list();     // free the memory used by the linked list
    }
  return 0;
}
```

Notice that most of the `main` function is in an if structure. Within the parentheses of the if statement is a call to a function named `get_county_data`, which prompts the user for the name and population of a county. The name is returned in the `name` string object and the population is returned in the `popul` variable. The data in the string object and variable will be used to create the first node of the list.

As you'll see later, the if structure is there because the `get_county_data` function returns a value that lets us know if the user entered valid data that needs to be added to the linked list. For now, let's assume the data is valid and focus on the first four lines within the if structure.

The statements in Code List 12-7 are all that is necessary to create the first node.

CODE LIST 12-7

```
    head_ptr = new county_node; // initialize list head
    head_ptr->county_name = name;
    head_ptr->population = popul;
    head_ptr->next = NULL; // initialize next node pointer to NULL
```

As you learned earlier in the chapter, the first statement in the previous code segment allocates memory for the node we are creating and assigns the address of the node to the pointer named `head_ptr`. We don't know or care exactly where the node is located in memory. We do, however, want the address of the new node to be placed in `head_ptr` so that we can find the first node in our list. The next three statements use the pointer (`head_ptr`) to initialize the node with data. The pointer named `next` is assigned the value NULL because at this point it is the last (and only) node in the list. Remember, the last node in the list must always have a NULL value in the `next` pointer to signify the end of the list. NULL is a constant defined in the `iostream.h` header file. Use NULL whenever you need to assign a NULL value to a pointer.

As a preview of what is coming, let's quickly look at the remaining statements in the `main` function as shown in Code List 12-8. A while loop is used to continually ask the user for additional counties for the list. The name and population of each of the counties will be added to the linked list by the `add_node` function, which we will study later. When the user has entered all of the counties, the `display_list` function will display all of the nodes in the linked list, and the `delete_list` function will free the memory used by the linked list. You'll see how this is done later in this chapter.

CODE LIST 12-8

```
    while(get_county_data(name, popul))
     {
       add_node(name, popul);
     }
    display_list();    // display the counties and populations
    delete_list();     // free the memory used by the linked list
```

We have covered a lot of material so far. To take a short break from the reading, let's enter the parts of the program we have covered so far.

STEP-BY-STEP ▷ 12.2

1. Enter the code from Code List 12-9 into a blank editor screen. As you enter the source code, remind yourself of the purpose of each statement. If you come to a statement you don't yet understand, go back and read about it again. The function prototypes appear in the source code, although the contents of each function have yet to be covered. Go

ahead and enter their prototypes now. We'll add the actual functions in a later exercise.

2. The program is incomplete, so it will not yet run. Save the source code on your screen as **counties.cpp** and leave the file open for the next Step-by-Step exercise.

CODE LIST 12-9

```cpp
// counties.cpp
// Example of a dynamically-allocated linked list.

// include files
#include<iostream.h>
#include<iomanip.h>
#include"apstring.h"

// global structure definitions, variables, and constants

  struct county_node          // node for linked list
    {
      apstring county_name;
      long population;
      county_node *next;      // link to next node
    };

  county_node *head_ptr;       // pointer to head of linked list
  county_node *current_ptr;    // pointer to current node

// function prototypes
int get_county_data(apstring &name, long &popul);
void add_node(apstring &name, long popul);
void move_current_to_end();
void display_list();
void delete_list();

// beginning of main function
int main()
{
 apstring name;
 long popul;
```

```
if(get_county_data(name, popul)) // prompt user for data for the node
  {
    head_ptr = new county_node; // initialize list head
    head_ptr->county_name = name;
    head_ptr->population = popul;
    head_ptr->next = NULL; // initialize next node pointer to NULL

    while(get_county_data(name, popul))
     {
      add_node(name, popul);
     }
    display_list();  // display the counties and populations
    delete_list();   // free the memory used by the linked list
   }
 return 0;
}
```

Communicating with the User

Let's take a break from pointers and nodes for a while and add the part of the program that interacts with the user.

Our county population program is designed to work regardless of how many counties a particular state may have. That's why we are using a linked list to store the data. We must also give the user the flexibility to enter however many counties he or she needs to enter. In our design for this program, the user is repeatedly asked for a county name and population until the county name is left blank.

Let's look at the `get_county_data` function (shown in Code List 12-10) to see how it works.

CODE LIST 12-10

```
// Function that gets data from user.
int get_county_data(apstring &name, long &popul)
 {
  int keep_data = 1;

  cout << "Enter county name (Press Enter alone to stop): ";
  getline(cin, name);
  if(name != "")
   {
    cout << "Enter county population: ";
    cin >> popul;
    cin.ignore(80,'\n');
   }
  else
   {
    keep_data = 0;
   }
  return(keep_data);
 }
```

The function has a string object and a long integer as parameters. Because the string object and the long integer are passed by reference, the data will be passed back to the calling function.

The function returns the value of a local variable named `keep_data`. If, at the end of the function, the value in `keep_data` is 1, the data entered by the user is intended to be used. If the user presses the Enter key without entering a county name, `keep_data` becomes 0 and the calling function will ignore the data.

STEP-BY-STEP ▷ 12.3

1. Add the function shown in Code List 12-10 to the bottom of the program on your screen. The program still lacks the code necessary to run.

2. Save the source code and leave the file open for the next Step-by-Step exercise.

Adding a Node to the End of the List

The purpose of our program is to rank the counties of a state by population. Therefore, we must have the ability to add counties to the linked list. Adding a node to the end of the linked list is similar to creating the first node. First, you must create the new node that you want to add. After creating the node, you attach it to the list by changing the `next` pointer of the last node in the list to point to the newly created node. Figure 12-4 illustrates the process.

FIGURE 12-4

To add a node to the end of a linked list, first (a) create the new node and keep track of it using a temporary pointer. Next (b) attach the new node to the end of the list.

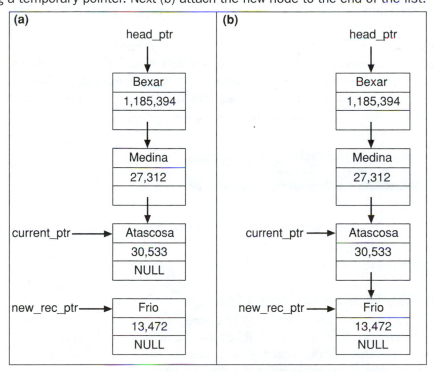

In the (a) portion of Figure 12-4, you see that a new node (Frio county) has been created. It has yet to become part of the list. The temporary pointer (`new_rec_ptr`) is keeping track of the address of the new node until it is safely attached to the list. In the (b) portion of the figure, the next pointer of the Atascosa county node has been changed from NULL to point to the new node.

Code List 12-11 shows the add_node function. Let's analyze the code to see how the new node is added.

```
// Function that adds a node to the end of the linked list.
void add_node(apstring &name, long popul)
{
 county_node *new_rec_ptr; // Declare local pointer for the new node.

 new_rec_ptr = new county_node; // Allocate memory for a new node and
                                // initialize pointer to point to it.

 new_rec_ptr->county_name = name;
 new_rec_ptr->population = popul;
 new_rec_ptr->next = NULL;  // Set next pointer of new node to NULL.

 move_current_to_end();     // Make sure current_ptr is at end of list.
 current_ptr->next = new_rec_ptr; // Place new node at end of the list.
}
```

First, a local pointer is declared (new_rec_ptr), which will be used to keep track of the new node until it is attached to the list. Next, memory is allocated for the new node, and its address is assigned to new_rec_ptr.

The next three statements are like the statements used to initialize the data in the first node. The data for the node is passed into the function as parameters. What happens next is what makes adding a node at the end of the list different from creating the first node.

The function move_current_to_end moves the pointer current_ptr to the end of the linked list. Later, you'll see how the move_current_to_end function works. For now, just understand that the function is called to make sure current_ptr is pointing to the last node in the list.

Finally, the next node pointer of the last node in the list is changed to point to the new node. At the end of the function, the new node is the last node in the list.

STEP-BY-STEP ▷ 12.4

1. Add the function in Code List 12-11 to the end of the source code on your screen. The program is still not ready to run.

2. Save the source code and leave the source code file open for the next Step-by-Step exercise.

Accessing the Nodes of the List

To be useful, the data in a linked list must be accessible. As you learned earlier in the chapter, the head pointer to the first node is the key to the linked list. The address of the second node in the list is contained in the first. The address of the third node is contained in the second, and so on. To get to a particular node in the list, start at the node pointed to by the head pointer and move through the list. The process of accessing (also called *visiting*) every node in the list is called *traversing* the list.

Let's look at the function that moves `current_ptr` to the end of the linked list. The function is executed before a new node is attached to make sure that the new node is being attached at the end of the list. The function simply moves through the list looking for the null pointer at the end of the list (see Code List 12-12). In other words, it traverses the list.

CODE LIST 12-12

```
// Function that moves current_ptr to end of the linked list.
void move_current_to_end()
{
 current_ptr = head_ptr;   // Move current_ptr to head of the list.

 while(current_ptr->next != NULL)
   {                        // Traverse list until NULL is reached.
    current_ptr = current_ptr->next;
   }
}
```

The function begins by setting `current_ptr` equal to `head_ptr`, which puts `current_ptr` at the beginning of the list. A while loop then moves `current_ptr` through the list until a node with the null pointer is reached, signaling the end of the list. Only one statement within the loop is necessary. In the statement, the address of the next node in the list is assigned to `current_ptr`.

Note

The statement `current_ptr = current_ptr->next;` may seem strange to you. Remember, however, that the right side of the equal sign is evaluated and then assigned to the variable on the left side. Therefore, even though `current_ptr` is on both sides of the equal sign, the statement is valid.

STEP-BY-STEP ▷ 12.5

1. Add the function in Code List 12-12 to the end of the source code on your screen. The program is nearly ready to run.

2. Save the source code and leave the source code file open for the next Step-by-Step exercise.

Displaying the List

To display the list, the same method of traversing the list is used (see Code List 12-13). This time, instead of just traversing the list to reach the end, the data in the list is displayed as `current_ptr` moves through the list.

```
// Function that displays entire linked list.
void display_list()
{
 current_ptr = head_ptr;      // Move current_ptr to head of list.
 cout << "County               ----------\n"; Population\n";
 cout << "----------
 do
  {
   cout.setf(ios::left);
   cout << setw(25) << current_ptr->county_name;
   cout.setf(ios::right);
   cout << setw(12) << current_ptr->population << endl;
   current_ptr = current_ptr->next; // point current_ptr to next node
  } while(current_ptr != NULL); // loop until end of list
 }
```

S TEP-BY-STEP ▷ 12.6

1. Add the function in Code List 12-13 to the end of the source code on your screen. There is only one more function to add before the program is ready to run.

2. Save the source code and leave the source code file open for the next Step-by-Step exercise.

Disposing of the List

The final step in using a linked list is to dispose of it properly when you are finished with it. Just as the new keyword reserved memory for our list, the delete keyword releases that memory to be used for other purposes.

To dispose of a linked list, you again must traverse the list (see Code List 12-14). This time, an additional pointer is necessary to prevent losing track of the list as nodes are being deleted.

 Note

When you declare variables, the compiler allocates and disposes of the variables at the appropriate time. In the case of a linked list, you must dispose of the memory manually because you allocated it manually.

CODE LIST 12-14

```
// Function that frees the memory used by the linked list.
void delete_list()
{
 county_node *temp_ptr;  // pointer used for temporary storage

 current_ptr = head_ptr;  // Move current_ptr to head of the list.

 do     // Traverse list
  {
```

CODE LIST 12-14 (continued)

```
    temp_ptr = current_ptr->next;    // Set temporary pointer to point
                                     // to the remainder of the list.
    delete current_ptr;    // Delete current
    current_ptr = temp_ptr;
  } while(temp_ptr != NULL);
}
```

On each iteration of the loop we set the temporary pointer (`temp_ptr`) to point to the node that follows the current node. It is then safe to delete the current node, because we have a pointer to the rest of the list. As soon as the current node is deleted, we copy the address in `temp_ptr` to `current_ptr` so that we can repeat the process to delete the next node. When the NULL at the end of the list is reached, the loop ends and the entire list has been deleted.

Note

In the next section, you will learn about saving the data in a linked list to disk before disposing of the list in RAM.

Dispose of a linked list only when you have completed the necessary processing of data in the list. The linked list exists only in RAM, and therefore is accessible only when your program is running. Depending on your operating system, however, the memory occupied by the list may not be automatically freed when your program terminates.

STEP-BY-STEP ▷ 12.7

1. Add the function shown in Code List 12-14 to the bottom of your program. Save the source code file.

2. Compile and run the program. If the program does not successfully compile and run, check the source code against the figures in this section for errors.

3. As input, let's enter the counties of New Hampshire. When entering the populations, enter the numbers without entering the commas.

County	Population
Belknap	49,216
Carroll	35,410
Cheshire	70,121
Coos	34,828
Grafton	74,929
Hillsborough	335,838
Merrimack	120,240
Rockingham	245,845
Strafford	104,233
Sullivan	38,592

4. After you have entered the last county, leave the next prompt for county name blank to signal the program that you have entered all the counties.

299

5. The program will print the counties back to the screen by traversing the linked list and delete the linked list.

6. Save any changes you have made to the source code file and close.

SECTION CHECKPOINT

1. What is the purpose of the head pointer?

2. What is purpose of the next pointer in a linked list node?

3. In the example in this section, what pointer moves through the linked list pointing to the current node?

4. What steps are involved when adding a node to the end of a linked list?

5. Why does disposing of a linked list require an additional pointer?

VOCABULARY REVIEW

Define the following terms:

traversing

12.3 Advanced Linked List Operations

The linked lists with which you have worked up to this point allowed nodes to be added to the end of the list only. In this section, you will learn how to insert a node anywhere in the list. You will also learn how to delete individual nodes from the list and how a linked list can be saved to disk.

Inserting Linked List Nodes

You may recall that the ultimate goal for the program that stores the names and populations of counties is to rank the counties by population. If the program were to insert the nodes in the proper position in the list as the information is entered, the final display would be ranked by population.

Let's consider what must occur for a node to be inserted in a linked list. Examine the linked list illustrated in Figure 12-5(a), which consists of four nodes. A new node, for Penobscot county, is to be inserted between Cumberland and Kennebec counties. For this to happen, the next pointer of the first node must be changed to point to the new node. In addition, the next pointer of the new node must be initialized to point to the remainder of the list, as shown in Figure 12-5(b).

FIGURE 12-5

Inserting a node in a linked list requires that pointers be redirected to include the new node.

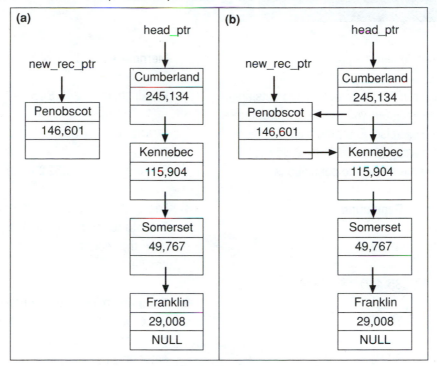

The process illustrated in Figure 12-5 is sufficient if the node is to be inserted in the middle of the list. There are times, however, when placing a new node in a proper sequence may mean adding it to the beginning or the end of the list. Figure 12-6 shows that a node may be inserted somewhere in the middle of a list, at the head of a list, or at the end of a list.

To insert at the head of the list, the new node's next pointer must point to the node that was first in the list. In addition, the head pointer must be changed to point to the new node.

You have experience with inserting at the end of the list. The next pointer of the node that used to be the end of the list is changed to point to the new node. When adding to the end of a linked list, remember to place a null pointer in the next pointer of the new node.

In the Step-by-Step exercise that follows, you will run a version of the county population program that ranks the counties by inserting them in the proper position as the counties are entered.

FIGURE 12-6

A node may be inserted in one of three ways.

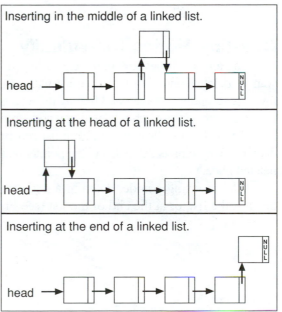

Inserting in the middle of a linked list.

Inserting at the head of a linked list.

Inserting at the end of a linked list.

1. Retrieve the file **insert.cpp**.

2. Compile and run the program. The prompts are just like the program you ran in the previous Step-by-Step exercise. Enter the following counties as input again. Remember to leave out the commas when entering the populations.

County	Population
Belknap	49,216
Carroll	35,410
Cheshire	70,121
Coos	34,828
Grafton	74,929
Hillsborough	335,838
Merrimack	120,240
Rockingham	245,845
Strafford	104,233
Sullivan	38,592

3. Leave the county prompt blank and press Enter to terminate input. The program will display the counties ranked from largest to smallest.

4. If you would like, run the program again using the counties of your own state. If your state has more counties than you wish to enter, enter only the counties in your area.

5. Close the source code file.

Deleting Nodes Individually

You already know how to traverse a linked list while deleting each node. Sometimes, however, you will want to delete a node from a linked list without disposing of the entire list. Deleting a node from a linked list involves rerouting a pointer and freeing the memory used by the node you are deleting. Figure 12-7 graphically illustrates the concept behind deleting a node from a linked list.

Figure 12-7(a) illustrates a linked list consisting of four nodes. In Figure 12-7(b), the node that holds the data for Stacy Finn is deleted, and the pointer that previously pointed to the deleted node is rerouted to skip the deleted node.

Like inserting a node, deleting a node from a linked list can occur in the middle of the list, at the head of the list, or at the end of the list (see Figure 12-8).

FIGURE 12-7

When a node is deleted from a linked list, the pointer from the previous node must be rerouted to skip the node that follows the deleted one.

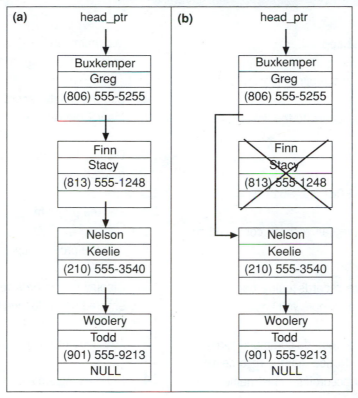

In the Step-by-Step exercise that follows, you will run a program that manages a database of your friends and their phone numbers. The first time the program is run, there are no records in the database. Each time the user chooses to add a record, a node is inserted into a linked list in alphabetical order, by last name. The user can display the records, search for a specific record, or delete a specific record. When the exit option is selected, the data in the linked list is saved to disk. The next time the program runs, the data in the disk file is loaded into the linked list.

FIGURE 12-8

The position of the node to be deleted dictates the method used to perform the deletion.

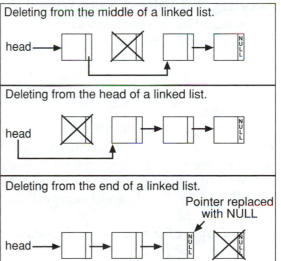

1. Retrieve **phonelst.cpp**.

2. Compile and run the program.

3. Add the following record to the linked list:

   Name: Mark Tittle

   Phone Number: (806) 555-8517

4. Choose the Display all records command to see the record.

5. Enter three more records using names and phone numbers of people you know.

6. Use the Display all records command again to view the records. Notice that the records were inserted in order according to last name.

7. Use the Search command to find one of the people in your list. You must enter the entire last name the way it appears in the list in order for the program to find the record.

8. Use the Delete record command to delete the Mark Tittle record.

9. Display the records again to see that it was deleted.

10. Exit the program.

11. Run the program again.

12. Display the records to see that the data you entered was reloaded from disk.

13. Add another record before exiting again.

14. Exit the program and close the source code file.

Saving a Linked List to a File

A linked list is a flexible way to store data in RAM. To save the data beyond the execution of your program, however, you must save the data from the linked list to a file. The program you ran in the previous exercise does just that.

Saving data from a linked list to a file requires that you traverse the list and save the data from each node to the file. A sequential-access data file is all that is necessary because the list will be traversed sequentially.

When you save a linked list to a file, you are saving only the data stored in the linked list. The pointers are not saved. Because memory usage and availability changes each time a program executes, the linked list must be rebuilt when the data is reloaded.

When data from a disk file is reloaded into a linked list, each node must be created and added to the list individually. The data will occupy different memory and, therefore, the pointers linking the nodes will be different.

You can see the source code required to save and load linked list data in the next case study.

Doubly- and Circularly-Linked Lists

Linked lists like the ones you have studied so far can be traversed in only one direction. Even if the node you need is only a few nodes back from the current node, you must start at the head of the list and traverse until you reach the desired node. This type of linked list is called a *singly-linked list.*

To improve the efficiency and usefulness of a linked list, you can link the nodes together in more elaborate ways: the doubly-linked list and the circularly-linked list.

Doubly-Linked List

In a *doubly-linked list* each node has a pointer linking it to the next node and the previous node, as shown in Figure 12-9. A doubly-linked list allows you to traverse a list in both directions and reverse the direction of traversal at any time.

FIGURE 12-9
A doubly-linked list uses an extra pointer on each node to allow traversal in both directions.

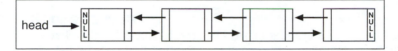

Each node has a pointer to the previous node, as well as a pointer to the next node. Because there are twice as many pointers, programming a doubly-linked list adds a new level of complexity. Each time a node is added or deleted, two pointers must be properly initialized to form links in both directions.

Suppose you wanted to expand the friends database to include the ability to browse through the records by choosing to move to the next or previous record. Without the doubly-linked list, moving to the previous record would require traversing from the head of the list.

The structure used for the nodes of the friends database linked list must be expanded to include a pointer to the previous node in the list, as shown in Code List 12-15.

CODE LIST 12-15

```
struct friend_node
{
 apstring last_name;
 apstring first_name;
 apstring phone_num;
 friend_node *next;
 friend_node *previous;
};
```

As mentioned previously, the change to a doubly-linked list requires that functions which add and delete nodes be modified to work with both pointers. In the Step-by-Step exercise that follows, you will compile the modified source code of the friends database program.

1. Retrieve **double.cpp**. An extended version of the friends database appears on your screen.

2. Compile and run the program to see the new browsing capabilities. Use commands 5 and 6 to move to the next and previous records in the database. If you attempt to browse past

the beginning or end of the list, the message FIRST RECORD or LAST RECORD will appear.

3. After you have experimented with the program, exit the program and close the source code file.

Circularly-Linked List

A *circularly-linked list* is like a singly-linked list, with one exception. Instead of the last node's next pointer having a null pointer, the last node points back to the first node, as shown in Figure 12-10.

FIGURE 12-10

The only difference between a standard linked list and a circularly-linked list is that the null pointer is replaced with a pointer to the first node on the list.

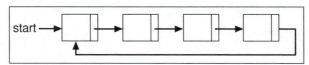

A circularly-linked list does not necessarily have a head pointer. Some circularly-linked lists have a pointer called "first" that points to one of the nodes as a starting point. Depending on your problem, however, you may keep a pointer that moves among the nodes rather than a stationary one.

Suppose you are representing a batting rotation for a baseball team. A circularly-linked list could be used to represent the batters in the rotation. As shown in Figure 12-11, a pointer could be maintained to point to the current batter.

FIGURE 12-11

A circularly-linked list could be used to represent a batting rotation.

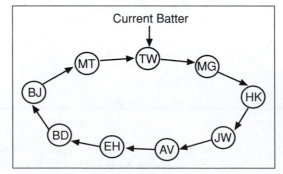

STEP-BY-STEP ▷ 12.11

1. Retrieve the file **batorder.cpp**. A program that implements the batting rotation linked list described previously appears on your screen.

2. Compile and run the program.

3. Enter nine players' names and then enter a blank player name to begin the rotation. You can enter players from a real team or make up names.

4. Press Enter until you have moved through the batting rotation at least twice.

5. When you have finished rotating through batters, press Q and Enter to quit the program.

6. Close the source code file.

SECTION CHECKPOINT

1. Identify the three ways a node can be inserted.

2. When does inserting a node involve changing the head pointer?

3. What is the term for the simple linked list that requires you to begin traversing at the head of the list and allows traversing in only one direction?

4. What type of linked list uses two pointers per node to allow traversal in two directions?

5. Of the two types of linked lists listed in questions 3 and 4, which uses more memory, assuming the data stored is identical?

VOCABULARY REVIEW

Define the following terms:

circularly-linked list   doubly-linked list   singularly-linked list

Summary

In this chapter, you learned:

■ In a linked list, data is contained in nodes. Each node contains a pointer to the next node in the list. The last node in the list has a null pointer.

■ Dynamic data structures are stored in a portion of memory called the heap. Reserving memory is called allocating. Freeing memory is called deallocating. The `new` operator allocates memory and the `delete` operator frees memory.

■ When accessing members of a structure with a pointer, the structure pointer operator (->) is used rather than the period (.).

■ To add a node to the end of a linked list, a new node is first created. After creating the node, you attach it to the list by changing the `next` pointer of the last node to the newly created node.

■ The process of moving through every node of a linked list is called traversing.

■ Each node of a linked list must be deleted when no longer needed.

■ Inserting a node in a linked list involves redirecting pointers to include the new node at the appropriate position in the list.

■ A node may be inserted at the head of the list, the middle of the list, or the end of the list.

■ Deleting an individual node from a linked list involves rerouting the pointers to bypass the removed node and deallocating the memory occupied by the node.

■ A node may be deleted at the head of the list, the middle of the list, or the end of the list.

■ A linked list may be saved to a file by traversing the list and saving the data to disk during the traversal. The pointers are not saved to disk because the linked list must be reallocated when the data is loaded again.

■ A doubly-linked list has pointers pointing in each direction. Each node has a pointer to the next and previous nodes.

■ In a circularly-linked list, the next pointer of the last node points back to the first node.

CHAPTER 12 REVIEW QUESTIONS

TRUE/FALSE

Circle T if the statement is true or F if the statement is false.

T F **1.** A linked list is an example of a static data structure.

T F **2.** In a linked list, data is contained in a structure called a node.

T F **3.** The `delete` operator allocates memory.

T F **4.** Individual members of a dynamically allocated structure are accessed using the structure pointer operator.

T F **5.** When adding a node to the end of a linked list, there is no need to worry about any null pointers that may have already been in the list.

T F **6.** To dispose of a linked list, you must traverse through it to delete it.

T F **7.** Inserting a node in a linked list requires that pointers be redirected to include the new one.

T F **8.** A node may only be inserted in one way.

T F **9.** A doubly-linked list can be traversed in two different directions.

T F **10.** A circularly-linked list does not have a null pointer.

WRITTEN QUESTIONS

Write a brief answer to the following questions.

1. What is the difference between a static data structure and a dynamic data structure?

2. What does the `new` operator do? What does the `delete` operator do?

3. What does the `new` operator return if there were errors during allocation?

4. How are individual members of a dynamically allocated structure accessed?

5. Why is it important to dispose of a linked list when you are finished using it?

6. Describe, with words only, the process of deleting a node from the end of a linked list.

7. Why are pointers not saved to disk when saving the data from a linked list?

8. What distinguishes a circularly-linked list from a standard singly-linked list?

9. Give an example, other than batting rotation, of when a circularly-linked list might be useful.

10. What type of linked list does not necessarily have a head pointer?

CHAPTER 12 PROJECTS

PROJECT 12-1

Write a program based on **hightemp.cpp**. However, instead of using an array for the temperatures, implement the program using a linked list. Save the program as **linktemp.cpp**.

PROJECT 12-2

Write a program that allows the user to enter a series of positive floating-point numbers. Store the numbers in a linked list. Allow the user to enter numbers until a negative number is entered. Do not include the negative number in the linked list. Next, traverse the list to total the numbers entered and count the number of nodes in the list. Use the count to average the numbers in the list. Report the total, number of nodes, and average to the screen. Save the program as **floatlst.cpp**.

CRITICAL THINKING

ACTIVITY 12-1

Write a program that creates a linked list from the following `patient_info` structure. The program should make a linked list of patients and store their vital signs. The program should allow the user to add donors to the linked list, inserting them in alphabetical order by last name, and print the donors' names to the screen. Save the program as **donorlst.cpp**.

```
struct blood_pressure
  {
   int systolic;
   int diastolic;
  };

struct patient_info
  {
   apstring last_name;
   apstring first_name;
   blood_pressure bp;
   int heart_rate;
   patient_info *next;
  };
```

Object-Oriented Programming and Linked Lists

REVIEW QUESTIONS

MATCHING

Write the letter of the description from Column 2 that best matches the term or phrase in Column 1.

Column 1	Column 2
____ 1. address-of operator	A. the structure that contains the data in a linked list or tree
____ 2. allocate	B. tells the compiler how to create an object in memory and what the initial values of its data will be
____ 3. circularly-linked list	C. the relationship between classes where one class contains another class
____ 4. constructors	D. a way of programming where data and operations are seen as existing together in objects that are similar to real world objects
____ 5. deallocate	E. the operator used to access individual members of a dynamically-allocated structure
____ 6. dereferencing operator	F. a variable inside a structure
____ 7. doubly-linked list	G. to reserve computer memory
____ 8. encapsulation	H. data structure that allows data to be stored in a list in which memory is assigned to the data as needed
____ 9. enum	I. to return memory to the heap for use by other data
____ 10. fields	J. can be used to give a new name to an existing data type
____ 11. has-a relationship	K. an operator that returns the "address of" the variable rather than the contents of the variable
____ 12. heap	L. a pointer variable with a value of zero
____ 13. inheritance	M. data items that make up a record
____ 14. is-a relationship	N. an operator for declaring pointers and for returning the value in a variable pointed to by a pointer
____ 15. linked list	O. the ability of one object to inherit the properties of another object
____ 16. members	P. a variable or constant that holds a memory address
____ 17. node	Q. a keyword that allows the creation of enumerated data types
	R. a way of programming that focuses on the idea that all algorithms in a program are performed with functions and data that a programmer can see, understand, and change
	S. a linked list in which the last node's next pointer points back to the first node

____ **18.** null pointer

____ **19.** object-oriented paradigm

____ **20.** pointer

____ **21.** procedural paradigm

____ **22.** scope-resolution operator

____ **23.** structure pointer operator

____ **24.** structures

____ **25.** traversing

____ **26.** typedef

T. the portion of memory in which dynamic data structures are stored

U. the operator that separates the class name and the function name in a member function

V. a linked list in which each node has a pointer linking it to the next node and the previous node

W. a data structure that allows variables to be grouped to form a new data type

X. the process of assessing every node in a list or tree

Y. the relationship where one object inherits characteristics from another class

Z. the hiding of data and code inside a class

WRITTEN QUESTIONS

Write a brief answer to the following questions.

1. Is a program that extends the properties of a class using containment or inheritance?

2. How does reusability improve productivity and reduce errors?

3. What does the dereferencing operator do?

4. Assuming that your compiler does not support Boolean data types, in what way could you use the `typedef` keyword to create Boolean types? Write the code that would implement Boolean data types using typedef.

5. How are individual members of a structure accessed?

6. Why are vectors and matrices considered flexible data structures?

7. Explain in your own words what the following line of code does.

```
my_ptr-> atomic_weight = 14.0067;
```

8. What denotes the last value in a singly-linked list?

9. Describe, with words only, the process of adding a node in the middle of a linked list.

10. Which type of linked list does a circularly-linked list most resemble, a singly-linked list or a doubly-linked list? Why?

PROJECT 4-1

1. Write a statement that uses the enum keyword to declare a data type called `movie_types` with possible values of western, sci_fi, romance, drama, and horror.

2. Write a statement to declare two variables named `video1` and `video2` based on the `movie_types` data type that you created in requirement 1.

3. Write the statement to assign the `video1` variable to the `movie_type` of western. Write a second statement to assign the `video2` variable to the `movie_type` of drama.

4. Write an if then statement that checks to see if the movie type is a western. If it is, print a message that tells the user that he or she can rent a second western for half price.

PROJECT 4-2

Write a program that accepts two points as input. Have the program calculate the equation for a line that is parallel to the line that the two points define. Call this program **parallel.cpp**.

PROJECT 4-3

Use the class you implemented in Activity 10-1 in Chapter 10 (**square.h** and **sqrtest.cpp**) as a starting point to create a rectangle class which models a rectangle and includes an `Area` method. The class should also include methods to set and retrieve the length and width properties of the object. Name the class file **rect.h** and the test program **recttest.cpp**.

PROJECT 4-4

Write a program that creates a linked list of historical events. The program should insert events in the proper order (by year) in the linked list as the user enters them. Provide a way to display the time line. Save this program as **timeline.cpp**.

ACTIVITY 4-1

1. Open your Web browser.

2. Use a Web search engine such as **www.yahoo.com** to locate information about object-oriented programming (OOP). Also search for OOA (object-oriented analysis) and OOD (object-oriented design).

3. After you see what your search finds, go to **http://www.programcpp.com/third.**

4. One the home page, click the link called **Internet Activities** and then go to the **Unit 4** link. On that page, you will find links to sites that provide information on object-oriented programming and design.

5. Write a paragraph or more describing something you learned while researching object-oriented programming and design on the Web.

PHONE DATABASE

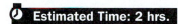

Overview

In this case study, you will analyze the phone number database program you compiled and ran in Chapter 12. The program is a complete, working program that manages a database of names and phone numbers. The program allows you to add, delete, and search for records. Also, the program allows you to display a list of the records. The records are loaded from a file into a linked list each time the program is run, and they are saved back to a file when the program exits.

A Look at the Entire Program

As C++ programs become more useful, they often become larger. It is not unusual for a C++ program to consist of thousands of lines of code. The program listed in Code List CSIV-1 is about 500 lines long. Familiarize yourself with the program. The comments throughout the program are designed to help you understand its operation.

CODE LIST CSIV-1

```cpp
// phonelst.cpp
// Phone Number Database
// By Todd Knowlton
// Complete linked list database program.

// compiler directives
#include<fstream.h>
#include<iostream.h>
#include<iomanip.h>
#include"apstring.h"

// global structures and variables
  struct friend_node
    {
      apstring last_name;
      apstring first_name;
      apstring phone_num;
      friend_node *next;
```

```
      };

   friend_node *head_ptr;
   friend_node *current_ptr;

// function prototypes
void handle_choice(int choice);
void add_record();
void insert_node(friend_node *new_rec_ptr);
friend_node *position_insertion_point(apstring &lastname);
void make_node_new_head(friend_node *new_rec_ptr);
void add_node_to_end(friend_node *new_rec_ptr);
void move_current_to_end();
void display_list();
void delete_record();
void delete_head_of_list();
void delete_end_of_list(friend_node *previous_ptr);
void delete_from_middle_of_list(friend_node *previous_ptr);
int verify_delete();
void delete_node(friend_node *previous_ptr);
void delete_list();
void search_by_lastname();
void write_list_to_file();
void load_list_from_file();

// main function
int main()
{
  int choice;

  head_ptr = NULL;        // Initialize head pointer to NULL.
  load_list_from_file(); // Load data from the disk file into linked list.
  do
   { // Display menu.
    cout << "\nFRIEND DATABASE\n";
    cout << "0 - Exit program\n";
    cout << "1 - Add record\n";
    cout << "2 - Display all records\n";
    cout << "3 - Search for friend by last name\n";
    cout << "4 - Delete record\n";
    cout << "Enter choice: ";
    cin >> choice;
    handle_choice(choice); // Call function to direct flow based on choice.
   } while(choice != 0);  // Repeat menu until user chooses to exit.
   return 0;
} // end of main function

// Function to direct program flow based on user's choice.
void handle_choice(int choice)
 {
```

```
    switch(choice) // choice is passed into the function by value.
     {
      case 0:  // If choice was to exit,
       write_list_to_file();  // save database to a file and
       if(head_ptr != NULL)   // delete the list from memory.
        {
         delete_list();
        }
       break;
      case 1:  // If choice was to add a record to the database,
       add_record();  // call function to add a record to the linked list.
       break;
      case 2:  // If choice was to display all records in the database,
       display_list(); // call function to display all records in
       break;           // the linked list.
      case 3:  // If choice was to search for a record in the database,
       search_by_lastname(); // call function to search for record by
       break;                 // last name.
      case 4:  // If choice was to delete a record in the database,
       delete_record(); // call a function that searches for record
       break;            // by last name and deletes it.
      default : // If any other (invalid) choice was entered,
       cout << "Invalid choice\n"; // display error message.
       break;
     }
 } // end of function handle_choice

// Function to add record to the linked list.
void add_record()
 {
  friend_node *new_rec_ptr; // Declare temporary pointer for the new node.

  new_rec_ptr = new friend_node; // Allocate memory for a new node and
                      // initialize pointer to point to it.
  if(new_rec_ptr != NULL) // If no error allocating memory, get data
   {                       // and insert node.
    // Get name and phone number from the user.
    cin.ignore(80,'\n');
    cout << "\nEnter a new record.\n";
    cout << "Last Name: ";
    getline(cin,new_rec_ptr->last_name);
    cout << "First Name: ";
    getline(cin,new_rec_ptr->first_name);
    cout << "Phone Number: ";
    getline(cin,new_rec_ptr->phone_num);

    insert_node(new_rec_ptr);
   }
  else  // If error occurred allocating memory, display warning
   {     // and do not create node.
    cout << "WARNING: Memory error. New record cannot be added.\n';
```

317

```
      }
   } // end of function add_record

// Function to insert new node into correct position in list.
void insert_node(friend_node *new_rec_ptr)
  {
   friend_node *before_ptr;
   friend_node *after_ptr;

   if(head_ptr == NULL)
     {                                  // If no nodes exist, make the node
      new_rec_ptr->next = NULL;    // the head.
      head_ptr = new_rec_ptr;
     }
   else
     {
      if(new_rec_ptr->last_name < head_ptr->last_name)
        {                                  // If new record comes before head,
         make_node_new_head(new_rec_ptr);  // make it the new head.
        }
      else                               // Else, determine where the new node
        {                                // should be inserted.
         current_ptr = position_insertion_point(new_rec_ptr->last_name);
         before_ptr = current_ptr;       // Use pointers to keep track of nodes
         after_ptr = current_ptr->next; // on each side of the insertion point.

         if(after_ptr == NULL) // If after_ptr is NULL, the node needs to be
           {                   // added to the end of the list.
            add_node_to_end(new_rec_ptr);
           }
         else                 // Else add the node between the nodes pointed to
           {                  // by before_ptr and after_ptr.
            before_ptr->next = new_rec_ptr;
            new_rec_ptr->next = after_ptr;
           }
        }
     }
   } // end of function insert_node

// Function that positions current_ptr at the node before the position
// where the new node should be inserted.
friend_node *position_insertion_point(apstring &lastname)
  {
   apstring temp_name;
   friend_node *temp_ptr;
```

```
 if(head_ptr->next != NULL) // If more than one node exists, search the
    {                       // list for the correct insertion point.
    current_ptr = head_ptr;
    temp_ptr = current_ptr->next;
    temp_name = temp_ptr->last_name;
    // Loop until the proper insertion point is located.
    while((lastname > temp_name) && (current_ptr->next !=NULL))
      {
      current_ptr = temp_ptr;

        // check to see if the current node is the last node
        if(current_ptr->next != NULL)
        {
        temp_ptr = current_ptr->next;
        temp_name = temp_ptr->last_name;
        }
      }
    }
  else  // If only one node exists in the list, current_ptr is the same
    {   // as head_ptr. New node will be added to the end of the list.
    current_ptr = head_ptr;
    }
  return(current_ptr);
 } // end of function position_insertion_point

// Function that makes the node pointed to by new_rec_ptr the new
// head of the linked list. It handles the special case of inserting at
// the front of the list.
void make_node_new_head(friend_node *new_rec_ptr)
 {
  friend_node *temp_ptr;  // temporary pointer to keep track of the head

  temp_ptr = head_ptr;  // Set temp_ptr to point at the current head.
  new_rec_ptr->next = temp_ptr; // Make new nodes next pointer point to
  head_ptr = new_rec_ptr;       // current head and make new node the head.
 } // end of function make_node_new_head

// Function that adds a node to the end of the linked list. It handles
// the special case of inserting at the end of the list.
void add_node_to_end(friend_node *new_rec_ptr)
 {
  new_rec_ptr->next = NULL;  // Set next node pointer of new node to NULL.

  move_current_to_end();       // Make sure current_ptr is at end of list.
  current_ptr->next = new_rec_ptr; // Place new node at the end of the list.
 } // end of function add_node_to_end

// Function that moves current_ptr to end of the linked list.
void move_current_to_end()
```

319

```
  {
   current_ptr = head_ptr;  // Move current_ptr to head of the list.

   while(current_ptr->next != NULL)
    {                          // Traverse list until NULL is reached.
     current_ptr = current_ptr->next;
    }
  } // end of function move_current_to_end

// Function that displays entire linked list.
void display_list()
 {
  apstring fullname;  // used to combine names into one array

  current_ptr = head_ptr;    // Move current_ptr to head of list.
  if(current_ptr != NULL)
   {
    cout << endl;
    cout << "Friend            Phone Number\n";
    cout << "------------------ ------\n";
    do
     {
      fullname = ""; // Clear fullname.
      fullname = fullname + current_ptr->last_name;  // Put last name, then a
      fullname = fullname + ", ";                    // comma, then the
      fullname = fullname + current_ptr->first_name; // first name into fullname.
      cout.setf(ios::left);
      cout << setw(36) << fullname;
      cout.unsetf(ios::left);
      cout.setf(ios::right);
      cout << setw(12) << current_ptr->phone_num << endl;
      current_ptr = current_ptr->next; // Set current_ptr to next node.
     } while(current_ptr != NULL); // Loop until end of list.
   }
  else  // If list is empty, display message.
   {
    cout << "\nNO RECORDS TO DISPLAY\n";
   }
 } // end of function display_list

// Function that searches linked list for the first occurrence of a given
// last name and displays the record to the screen.
void search_by_lastname()
 {
  apstring search_string;  // Character array for last name to search for.

  current_ptr = head_ptr;  // Move current_ptr to head of list
                           // to begin search.
  cin.ignore(80,'\n');
```

```
    cout << "\nEnter the last name for which you want to search: ";
    getline(cin,search_string);

    // Loop until search_string is found or end of list is reached.
    while((current_ptr != NULL) &&
          (current_ptr->last_name != search_string))
     {
      current_ptr = current_ptr->next;
     }

    if(current_ptr != NULL) // If current_ptr is not NULL, then match was
     {                      // found.
      cout << "\nRECORD FOUND\n";
      cout << current_ptr->first_name << ' '
           << current_ptr->last_name << endl;
      cout << current_ptr->phone_num << endl;
     }
    else
     {
      cout << "NO MATCH FOUND\n";
     }
   } // end of function search_by_lastname

// Function that deletes individual nodes from the linked list.
void delete_record()
 {
  apstring search_string;
  friend_node *previous_ptr;

  previous_ptr = NULL;      // Initialize previous_ptr to NULL.
  current_ptr = head_ptr;   // Move current_ptr to head of list
                            // to begin search.
  cin.ignore(80,'\n');
  cout << "\nEnter the last name of the friend you want to delete: ";
  getline(cin,search_string);

  // Loop to find matching record.
  while((current_ptr != NULL) &&
        (current_ptr->last_name != search_string))
   {
    previous_ptr = current_ptr;      // A pointer must be maintained that
    current_ptr = current_ptr->next; // points to the node before the node
   }                                 // to be deleted.

  if(current_ptr != NULL) // If current_ptr is not NULL, then match was
   {                      // found.
    cout << "\nRECORD FOUND\n";
    cout << current_ptr->first_name << ' '
         << current_ptr->last_name << endl;
    cout << current_ptr->phone_num << endl;
    if(verify_delete()) // Ask user if he/she wants to delete the record.
```

```
          {                                  // If user wants to delete the record,
           delete_node(previous_ptr);        // delete the node that follows the
           cout << "\nRECORD DELETED\n";     // one pointed to by previous_ptr.
          }
         else                                // Otherwise, do nothing.
          {
           cout << "\nRECORD NOT DELETED\n";
          }
       }
      else // If no match for the record found, display message.
       {
        cout << "\nNO MATCH FOUND. NO RECORD DELETED.\n";
       }
    } // end of function delete_record

// Function to ask user to verify intention to delete the node.
int verify_delete()
  {
    char YesNo;

    cout << "\nDo you wish to delete this record? (Y/N) ";
    cin >> YesNo;
    if((YesNo == 'Y') || (YesNo == 'y'))
      {
        return(1); // Return TRUE if user wants to delete.
      }
    else
      {
        return(0); // Return FALSE if user does not wants to delete.
      }
   } // end of function verify_delete

// Function that deletes node pointed to by current_ptr.
void delete_node(friend_node *previous_ptr)
  {

    if(current_ptr == head_ptr)   // If node to be deleted is the head of the
      {                           // list, call a special function that
        delete_head_of_list();    // deletes the first node in the list.
      }
    else
      {                                     // Otherwise:
        if(current_ptr->next == NULL)       // If node to be deleted is at the
          {                                 // end of the list, call a special
            delete_end_of_list(previous_ptr); // function to delete that node.
          }
        else                                // Otherwise:
          {                                           // Delete the node from the
            delete_from_middle_of_list(previous_ptr); // middle of the list using
```

```
        }                                      // a function that does that.
    }
  } // end of function delete_node

//Function that deletes the head of the list.
void delete_head_of_list()
  {
  current_ptr = head_ptr;  // Make current_ptr point to the head of the list.
  if(head_ptr->next != NULL)
    {                              // If more than one node is in the list,
     head_ptr = current_ptr->next; // make second node in list the new head.
    }
  else                              // Otherwise, just set head_ptr to NULL
    {                              // to signal that the list is empty.
     head_ptr = NULL;
    }
  delete current_ptr; // Deallocate memory used by the deleted node.
  } // end of function delete_head_of_list

// Function that deletes the last node of the linked list.
void delete_end_of_list(friend_node *previous_ptr)
  {
  delete current_ptr; // Deallocate memory used by the deleted node.
  previous_ptr->next = NULL; // Make node before deleted node the end of list.
  current_ptr = head_ptr; // Set current_ptr to head to give it a value.
  } // end of function delete_end_of_list

// Function that deletes a node from the middle of the list.
void delete_from_middle_of_list(friend_node *previous_ptr)
  {
  // Set pointers of the nodes before and after the node to be deleted to
  // skip the node that is to be deleted.
  previous_ptr->next = current_ptr->next;
  delete current_ptr; // Deallocate memory used by the deleted node.
  current_ptr = head_ptr; // Set current_ptr to head to give it a value.
  } // end of function delete_from_middle_of_list

// Function that frees the memory used by the linked list.
void delete_list()
  {
  friend_node *temp_ptr;  // pointer used for temporary storage

  current_ptr = head_ptr;  // Move current_ptr to head of the list.

  do     // Traverse list, deleting as we go.
    {
```

```
      temp_ptr = current_ptr->next;   // Set temporary pointer to point
                                      // to the remainder of the list.
   delete current_ptr;    // Delete current node.
   current_ptr = temp_ptr;    // Set current_ptr to next node after the
  } while(temp_ptr != NULL); // deleted one.
 } // end of function delete_list

// Function to write linked list data to the data file.
void write_list_to_file()
 {
  ofstream outfile;  // output file pointer

  outfile.open("FRIENDS.DAT",ios::out);  // Open file for output.

  if (outfile)  // If no error occurred while opening the file,
   {            // it is okay to write the data to the file.
    current_ptr = head_ptr;  // Set current_ptr to head of list.
    if(head_ptr != NULL)  // If the list is not empty, begin
     {                     // writing data to the file.
       do    // Traverse list until the end is reached.
        {
          // Write the nodes data to the file.
          outfile << current_ptr->last_name << endl;
          outfile << current_ptr->first_name << endl;
          outfile << current_ptr->phone_num << endl;
          current_ptr = current_ptr->next;  // Move current_ptr to next node.
        } while(current_ptr != NULL); // Loop until end of list is reached.
      }
    // The words END OF FILE are written to the end of the file to make it
    // easy to locate the end of the file when the data is read back in.
    outfile << "END OF FILE" << endl;
    outfile.close(); // Close the file.
   }
  else // If an error occurs while opening the file, display a message.
   {
    cout << "Error opening file.\n";
   }
 } // end of function write_list_to_file

// Function to load the linked list from the data file.
void load_list_from_file()
 {
  friend_node *new_rec_ptr;
  ifstream infile;  // input file pointer
  int end_loop = 0;

  infile.open("FRIENDS.DAT",ios::in);  // Open file for input.

  if (infile)  // If no error occurred while opening file
   {           // input the data from the file.
```

```
    do
    {
      new_rec_ptr = new friend_node; // Allocate memory for a node.
      if(new_rec_ptr != NULL) // Check for allocation error.
       {
         // Get the next last name from the file.
         getline(infile,new_rec_ptr->last_name);
         // If the end of the file has not yet been reached, get other data.
       if((new_rec_ptr->last_name != "" &&
         (new_rec_ptr->last_name != "END OF FILE"))
          {
            getline(infile,new_rec_ptr->first_name);
            getline(infile,new_rec_ptr->phone_num);
            insert_node(new_rec_ptr);
          }
         else // If end of file has been reached, delete the most recently
         {    // created node and set the flag that ends the loop.
           delete new_rec_ptr;
           end_loop = 1;
         }
       }
      else  // If a memory allocation error occurs, display a message and
      {     // set the flag that ends the loop.
        cout << "WARNING: Memory error. Load from disk was unsuccessful.\n";
        end_loop = 1;
      }
    } while(end_loop == 0); // Loop until the end_loop flag becomes TRUE.
    infile.close(); // Close the file.
  }
 else  // If error occurred opening file, display message.
 {
   cout << "No usable data file located. List is empty.\n";
 }
} // end of function load_list_from_file
```

We will analyze only selected portions of the program in this case study because of the program's large size. To refresh your memory as to the operation of the program, let's compile and run the program again.

1. Open **phonelst.cpp**. Compile and run the program.

2. Choose the option to display all records. If a data file exists from the last time the program was run, there may already be records in the database.

3. Enter three new records into the database. Use your friends' names or make up fictitious names.

4. Display all records again.

5. Use the `search` function to find one specific record in the database.

6. Use the `delete` function to delete one of the records in the database.

7. Exit the program and leave the source code open for the next Step-by-Step exercise.

Global Structures and Variables

As you learned in the previous chapters, nodes of a linked list are implemented as structures. The globally-defined structure in Code List CSIV-2 defines a node for the friends database. Two additional global variables are also necessary. The variable `head_ptr` keeps track of the head of the linked list, and `current_ptr` is used throughout the program to perform operations on the list. Any other variable you see used in a function is either declared locally or passed in as a parameter.

CODE LIST CSIV-2

```cpp
// global structures and variables
  struct friend_node
    {
    apstring last_name;
    apstring first_name;
    apstring phone_num;
    friend_node *next;
    };

  friend_node *head_ptr;
  friend_node *current_ptr;
```

The Main Function and Menu Processing

Refer back to the Code List CSIV-2 at the `main` and `handle_choice` functions. The `main` function begins by initializing the head pointer (`head_ptr`) to null to indicate that the list is empty. Next, the disk file that holds the friends database is loaded into the linked list. Later in this case study, we will analyze the functions that load and save the linked list.

The `main` function displays the menu and gets the user's choice. The choice is passed to a function named `handle_choice` that directs the flow of the program based on the user's menu choice. The menu and call to `handle_choice` are in a loop that continues until the user chooses to exit.

Adding Records to the Database

A major part of the program's code is dedicated to adding records to the database. Because the database is maintained in a linked list in RAM, the data must be placed in linked list nodes and inserted into the linked list. As an added feature, the nodes are inserted in last name order.

Examine the `add_record` function (shown again in Code List CSIV-3). First, a temporary pointer is declared to point to the new node until the node is properly inserted in the list.

Next, memory is allocated for the new node. Recall that in the previous chapters you learned that errors can occur when a program attempts to allocate memory. The `add_record` function uses an if statement to check for an error. If an error occurs, a message is displayed and the function ends without adding a record.

CODE LIST CSIV-3

```
// Function to add record to the linked list.
void add_record()
 {
  friend_node *new_rec_ptr; // Declare temporary pointer for the new node.

  new_rec_ptr = new friend_node; // Allocate memory for a new node and
                                 // initialize pointer to point to it.
  if(new_rec_ptr != NULL) // If no error allocating memory, get data
   {                      // and insert node.
    // Get name and phone number from the user.
    cin.ignore(80,'\n');
    cout << "\nEnter a new record.\n";
    cout << "Last Name: ";
    getline(cin,new_rec_ptr->last_name);
    cout << "First Name: ";
    getline(cin,new_rec_ptr->first_name);
    cout << "Phone Number: ";
    getline(cin,new_rec_ptr->phone_num);

    insert_node(new_rec_ptr);
   }
  else  // If error occurred allocating memory, display warning
   {    // and do not create node.
    cout << "WARNING: Memory error. New record cannot be added.\n";
   }
 } // end of function add_record
```

327

If no errors occur during memory allocation, the user is prompted for data for the record, and the pointer to the new record is passed to the `insert_node` function (shown again in Code List CSIV-4). The `insert_node` function determines where the node should be inserted. If the linked list is empty, then the new node becomes the head of the list. If the list is not empty, the function determines whether the node should be inserted before the current head, somewhere in the middle of the list, or at the end of the list.

CODE LIST CSIV-4

```
// Function to insert new node into correct position in list.
void insert_node(friend_node *new_rec_ptr)
 {
  friend_node *before_ptr;
  friend_node *after_ptr;

  if(head_ptr == NULL)
   {                                    // If no nodes exist, make the node
    new_rec_ptr->next = NULL;    // the head.
    head_ptr = new_rec_ptr;
   }
  else
   {
    if(new_rec_ptr->last_name < head_ptr->last_name)
     {                                    // If new record comes before head,
      make_node_new_head(new_rec_ptr);  // make it the new head.
     }
    else                                  // Else, determine where the new node
     {                                    // should be inserted.
      current_ptr = position_insertion_point(new_rec_ptr->last_name);
      before_ptr = current_ptr;        // Use pointers to keep track of nodes
      after_ptr = current_ptr->next; // on each side of the insertion point.

      if(after_ptr == NULL) // If after_ptr is NULL, the node needs to be
       {                      // added to the end of the list.
        add_node_to_end(new_rec_ptr);
       }
      else                  // Else add the node between the nodes pointed to
       {                      // by before_ptr and after_ptr.
        before_ptr->next = new_rec_ptr;
        new_rec_ptr->next = after_ptr;
       }
     }
   }
 } // end of function insert_node
```

The `position_insertion_point` function (shown again in Code List CSIV-5) returns a pointer to the node that precedes the insertion point for the new node. The syntax of a function that returns a pointer is slightly different than functions that return other data types. The data type is `friend_node`, and the dereferencing operator (*) precedes the name of the function. This syntax causes the compiler to return a pointer to a `friend_node` as a return value.

CODE LIST CSIV-5

```
// Function that positions current_ptr at the node before the position
// where the new node should be inserted.
friend_node *position_insertion_point(apstring &lastname)
 {
  apstring temp_name;
  friend_node *temp_ptr;

  if(head_ptr->next != NULL) // If more than one node exists, search the
    {                        // list for the correct insertion point.
    current_ptr = head_ptr;
    temp_ptr = current_ptr->next;
    temp_name = temp_ptr->last_name;
    // Loop until the proper insertion point is located.
    while((lastname > temp_name) && (current_ptr->next !=NULL))
      {
      current_ptr = temp_ptr;

      // check to see if the current node is the last node
      if(current_ptr->next != NULL)
        {
        temp_ptr = current_ptr->next;
        temp_name = temp_ptr->last_name;
        }
      }
    }
  else  // If only one node exists in the list, current_ptr is the same
    {   // as head_ptr. New node will be added to the end of the list.
    current_ptr = head_ptr;
    }
  return(current_ptr);
 } // end of function position_insertion_point
```

If the node is to be inserted in the middle of the list, the `insert_node` function handles the insertion itself. If the node must be inserted as the new head or at the end of the list, special functions (shown again in Code List CSIV-6) are called to perform those insertions.

329

```
// Function that makes the node pointed to by new_rec_ptr the new
// head of the linked list. It handles the special case of inserting at
// the front of the list.
void make_node_new_head(friend_node *new_rec_ptr)
 {
  friend_node *temp_ptr;   // temporary pointer to keep track of the head

  temp_ptr = head_ptr;   // Set temp_ptr to point at the current head.
  new_rec_ptr->next = temp_ptr; // Make new nodes next pointer point to
  head_ptr = new_rec_ptr;        // current head and make new node the head.
 } // end of function make_node_new_head

// Function that adds a node to the end of the linked list. It handles
// the special case of inserting at the end of the list.
void add_node_to_end(friend_node *new_rec_ptr)
 {
  new_rec_ptr->next = NULL;   // Set next node pointer of new node to NULL.

  move_current_to_end();         // Make sure current_ptr is at end of list.
  current_ptr->next = new_rec_ptr; // Place new node at the end of the list.
 } // end of function add_node_to_end

// Function that moves current_ptr to end of the linked list.
void move_current_to_end()
 {
  current_ptr = head_ptr;   // Move current_ptr to head of the list.

  while(current_ptr->next != NULL)
   {                                   // Traverse list until NULL is reached.
    current_ptr = current_ptr->next;
   }
 } // end of function move_current_to_end
```

Displaying a List of Records

The `display_list` function in this program creates a string made up of the friend's last name, a comma, and first name. This string is used to output the names in a consistently formatted fashion.

Searching the Database

The ability to search the database is provided by a straightforward function named `search_by_lastname`. The function prompts the user for a last name and searches the database for an exact match. The program could be extended to be more flexible. For example, the search might be more useful if it were not case sensitive.

Another limitation of the current program is that the search will not locate the second record of two records with the same last name.

Deleting Individual Records

Deleting individual records from a linked list requires a set of functions similar in complexity to the function that adds records. The delete_record function (shown again in Code List CSIV-7) prompts the user for a last name and searches for the record. This function has the same limitations as the search function.

CODE LIST CSIV-7

```cpp
// Function that deletes individual nodes from the linked list.
void delete_record()
 {
  apstring search_string;
  friend_node *previous_ptr;

  previous_ptr = NULL;     // Initialize previous_ptr to NULL.
  current_ptr = head_ptr;  // Move current_ptr to head of list
                           // to begin search.
  cin.ignore(80,'\n');
  cout << "\nEnter the last name of the friend you want to delete: ";
  getline(cin,search_string);

  // Loop to find matching record.
  while((current_ptr != NULL) &&
    (current_ptr->last_name != search_string))
   {
    previous_ptr = current_ptr;      // A pointer must be maintained that
    current_ptr = current_ptr->next; // points to the node before the node
   }                                 // to be deleted.

  if(current_ptr != NULL) // If current_ptr is not NULL, then match was
   {                      // found.
    cout << "\nRECORD FOUND\n";
    cout << current_ptr->first_name << ' '
         << current_ptr->last_name << endl;
    cout << current_ptr->phone_num << endl;
    if(verify_delete()) // Ask user if he/she wants to delete the record.
     {                                  // If user wants to delete the record,
      delete_node(previous_ptr);      // delete the node that follows the
      cout << "\nRECORD DELETED\n";   // one pointed to by previous_ptr.
     }
    else                                // Otherwise, do nothing.
     {
      cout << "\nRECORD NOT DELETED\n";
     }
   }
  else // If no match for the record found, display message.
```

331

```
      {
        cout << "\nNO MATCH FOUND. NO RECORD DELETED.\n";
      }
   } // end of function delete_record
```

While searching for the record to be deleted, the `delete_record` function maintains a pointer to two nodes: the node being compared and the previous node. The reason is because when the node to be deleted is located, the program must have a pointer to the nodes on both sides so that the pointers can be properly redirected around the deleted node.

If the search is successful, the user gets an opportunity to verify that the correct record was located before the actual deletion takes place. The `verify_ delete` function (shown in Code List CSIV-8) is called to ask the user for verification.

CODE LIST CSIV-8

```
// Function to ask user to verify intention to delete the node.
int verify_delete()
  {
   char YesNo;

   cout << "\nDo you wish to delete this record? (Y/N) ";
   cin >> YesNo;
   if((YesNo == 'Y') || (YesNo == 'y'))
     {
       return(1); // Return TRUE if user wants to delete.
     }
   else
     {
       return(0); // Return FALSE if user does not want to delete.
     }
  } // end of function verify_delete
```

If the user verifies that the node is to be deleted, the `delete_node` function (Code List CSIV-9) is called to decide the method required to delete the node. Like adding nodes, deleting nodes requires that different methods be applied depending on whether the node is at the head, in the middle, or at the end of the list.

CODE LIST CSIV-9

```
// Function that deletes node pointed to by current_ptr.
void delete_node(friend_node *previous_ptr)
  {

    if(current_ptr == head_ptr)  // If node to be deleted is the head of the
      {                          // list, call a special function that
```

CODE LIST CSIV-9 (continued)

```
        delete_head_of_list();      // deletes the first node in the list.
    }
  else
    {                               // Otherwise:
      if(current_ptr->next == NULL)         // If node to be deleted is at the
        {                                   // end of the list, call a special
          delete_end_of_list(previous_ptr); // function to delete that node.
        }
      else                          // Otherwise:
        {                                               // Delete the node from the
          delete_from_middle_of_list(previous_ptr);     // middle of the list using
        }                                               // a function that does that.
    }
} // end of function delete_node
```

If the node to be deleted is at the head of the list, the `delete_head_of_list` function (Code List CSIV-10) makes the second node in the list the new head. If the list contains only the one node, `head_ptr` is simply set to null to signal that the list is now empty. Either way, the memory allocated for the node is released by the `delete` operator.

CODE LIST CSIV-10

```
//Function that deletes the head of the list.
void delete_head_of_list()
  {
    current_ptr = head_ptr;  // Make current_ptr point to the head of the list.
    if(head_ptr->next != NULL)
      {                                 // If more than one node is in the list,
        head_ptr = current_ptr->next; // make second node in list the new head.
      }
    else                              // Otherwise, just set head_ptr to NULL
      {                               // to signal that the list is empty.
        head_ptr = NULL;
      }
    delete current_ptr; // Deallocate memory used by the deleted node.
  } // end of function delete_head_of_list
```

If the node to be deleted is at the end of the list, the `delete_end_of_list` function (Code List CSIV-11) frees the memory allocated to the node. Then it makes the next pointer of the second node from the end of the list null, which makes the list end there. Because `current_ptr` is a global variable, it should not be left pointing to a deleted node. To give it something to point to, `current_ptr` is set to point to the head of the list.

```
// Function that deletes the last node of the linked list.
void delete_end_of_list(friend_node *previous_ptr)
 {
   delete current_ptr; // Deallocate memory used by the deleted node.
   previous_ptr->next = NULL; // Make node before deleted node the end of list.
   current_ptr = head_ptr; // Set current_ptr to head to give it a value.
 } // end of function delete_end_of_list
```

Deleting from the middle of the list is also a simple task (see Code List CSIV-12). The next pointer of the node before the one being deleted is set to point to the node that follows the one being deleted. In other words, the pointers of the list are arranged to bypass the node being deleted. Then the memory is freed, and `current_ptr` is made to point to the head of the list so it will not point to a deleted node.

CODE LIST CSIV-12

```
// Function that deletes a node from the middle of the list.
void delete_from_middle_of_list(friend_node *previous_ptr)
 {
   // Set pointers of the nodes before and after the node to be deleted to
   // skip the node that is to be deleted.
   previous_ptr->next = current_ptr->next;
   delete current_ptr; // Deallocate memory used by the deleted node.
   current_ptr = head_ptr; // Set current_ptr to head to give it a value.
 } // end of function delete_from_middle_of_list
```

Saving and Retrieving the Data

The functions at the end of the program allow the data in the linked list to be saved to a disk file and reloaded the next time the program runs. Let's first look at the function that writes the data in the linked list to a file.

The function (shown in Code List CSIV-13) opens a file for output. If no errors occur, a do loop is used to traverse the list. As each node is visited, the data in the node is written to the data file, separated by end-of-line characters. When the last node's data has been written to disk, the string END OF FILE is written to the file. This string will be used to make detecting the end of the file easier when the data is read back in.

CODE LIST CSIV-13

```
// Function to write linked list data to the data file.
void write_list_to_file()
 {
  ofstream outfile;  // output file pointer

  outfile.open("FRIENDS.DAT",ios::out);  // Open file for output.

  if (outfile)  // If no error occurred while opening the file,
   {             // it is okay to write the data to the file.
    current_ptr = head_ptr;  // Set current_ptr to head of list.
    if(head_ptr != NULL)  // If the list is not empty, begin
     {                       // writing data to the file.
       do    // Traverse list until the end is reached.
        {
         // Write the nodes data to the file.
         outfile << current_ptr->last_name << endl;
         outfile << current_ptr->first_name << endl;
         outfile << current_ptr->phone_num << endl;
         current_ptr = current_ptr->next;  // Move current_ptr to next node.
        } while(current_ptr != NULL); // Loop until end of list is reached.
     }
    // The words END OF FILE are written to the end of the file to make it
    // easy to locate the end of the file when the data is read back in.
    outfile << "END OF FILE" << endl;
    outfile.close(); // Close the file.
   }
  else // If an error occurs while opening the file, display a message.
   {
    cout << "Error opening file.\n";
   }
 } // end of function write_list_to_file
```

STEP-BY-STEP ▷ CSIV.2

1. Run the program again. Enter two or three additional names into the database. Use names of your friends, celebrities, or make up fictitious names.

2. Exit the program to cause the data file to be written.

3. Open the **FRIENDS.DAT** data file. Notice that the format is a straightforward text format.

4. Leave the **FRIENDS.DAT** data file and the program's source code open for the next Step-by-Step exercise.

The function that reads the data from the file back into the linked list (shown in Code List CSIV-14) is slightly more complicated than the function that writes the data to the file. The reason is because the function that loads the data from disk must rebuild the linked list from scratch. The task is simplified, however, by reusing the functions that allow records to be added from user input.

CODE LIST CSIV-14

```
// Function to load the linked list from the data file.
void load_list_from_file()
{
  friend_node *new_rec_ptr;
  ifstream infile;  // input file pointer
  int end_loop = 0;

  infile.open("FRIENDS.DAT",ios::in);  // Open file for input.

  if (infile)  // If no error occurred while opening file
   {           // input the data from the file.
    do
     {
      new_rec_ptr = new friend_node; // Allocate memory for a node.
      if(new_rec_ptr != NULL) // Check for allocation error.
       {
         // Get the next last name from the file.
         getline(infile,new_rec_ptr->last_name);
         // If the end of the file has not yet been reached, get other data.
  if((new_rec_ptr->last_name != "") &&
     (new_rec_ptr->last_name != "END OF FILE"))
          {
            getline(infile,new_rec_ptr->first_name);
            getline(infile,new_rec_ptr->phone_num);
            insert_node(new_rec_ptr);
          }
         else // If end of file has been reached, delete the most recently
          {   // created node and set the flag that ends the loop.
           delete new_rec_ptr;
           end_loop = 1;
          }
       }
      else  // If a memory allocation error occurs, display a message and
       {    // set the flag that ends the loop.
        cout << "WARNING: Memory error. Load from disk was unsuccessful.\n";
        end_loop = 1;
       }
     } while(end_loop == 0); // Loop until the end_loop flag becomes TRUE.
    infile.close(); // Close the file.
   }
  else  // If error occurred opening file, display message.
   {
    cout << "No usable data file located. List is empty.\n";
   }
} // end of function load_list_from_file
```

First, the input file is opened. An if statement performs a check after the attempt to open to make sure the file was located and no errors occurred. Next, a loop allocates memory for each node and assigns data from the file to the nodes. The insert_node function is called to actually build the linked list. The loop ends when the END OF FILE string is encountered.

STEP-BY-STEP ▷ CSIV.3

1. In your text editor, position the cursor at the bottom of the **FRIENDS.DAT** file, before the END OF FILE string.

2. To demonstrate the flexibility of the data file, insert another name and phone number before the END OF FILE string. Enter Adams on one line, John on the next line, and 555-1234 on the next line. Be sure to leave the other records unchanged. Also be sure to leave the END OF FILE string on a line by itself at the bottom of the file.

3. Save and close **FRIENDS.DAT** and run the program again. Although the John Adams record was not entered into the file in proper order, the linked list will be created in order because the insert_node function is used to place the nodes in the list.

4. Direct the program to display records to verify that the John Adams record appears in the list.

5. Exit the program. Exiting the program will cause the data file to be rewritten with the data from RAM.

6. Open **FRIENDS.DAT** again to see that the John Adams record is now in its proper place in the file, sorted alphabetically.

7. Close **FRIENDS.DAT** and **phonelst.cpp**.

Modifying the Program

Here are some suggestions of ways you might modify the program.

1. Modify the program to allow the birthday of each friend to be included in addition to the other data. Use a string object to store dates of birth in the form MM/DD/YY. For example, someone born on July 10, 1980, would have his or her birthday entered as 07/10/80. Before you begin, analyze the code to determine all of the places the program will be affected by the added field. Also, delete the **FRIENDS.DAT** file the first time you run the modified program because it will not contain birthday information for the friends who are already in the database.

2. Rewrite the program to use the vector class rather than a linked list.

COMMON
DATA
STRUCTURES
AND
ALGORTHMS

UNIT 5

Upon completion of this chapter, you should be able to:

■ Understand stacks.

■ Understand the way stacks can be implemented.

■ Use a stack class.

■ Understand queues.

■ Understand how a queue can be implemented with a linked list.

■ Use a queue class.

■ Understand binary trees.

🕐 **Estimated Time: 2 hours**

ancestors

balance

binary tree

branch

branch nodes

children

dequeue

descendants

enqueue

first-in first-out (FIFO)

key

last-in first-out (LIFO)

leaf nodes

left child

levels

linear data structure

node

nonlinear data structure

nonterminal nodes

offspring

parent

pop

push

queue

right child

root

siblings

stack

subtree

terminal nodes

tree

The linked lists you have been studying are an important and useful data structure. In this chapter, you will learn three more data structures that are also important in computer science: the stack, the queue, and the binary tree.

13.1 Stacks

A *stack* is a data structure that allows items to be added and deleted from only one end. Imagine a stack of books on a table. It is impractical to add a book to the bottom of the stack. The easiest way to add a book to or take a book away from the stack is to work with only the top of the stack. A stack in a computer works the same way.

Special terms are used to describe putting items on and taking items off a stack. Adding an item to the stack is called *pushing*. Removing an item from the stack is called *popping*.

Figure 13-1 shows a stack of books to illustrate the stack operations push and pop. Figure 13-1(a) shows a math book being pushed onto the stack. In (b), the book is part of the stack. In (c), the book is popped off the stack. A stack is a *last-in first-out (LIFO)* structure, meaning the last item pushed on the stack is the first item popped off the stack.

FIGURE 13-1

Items are "pushed" onto a stack and "popped" off a stack.

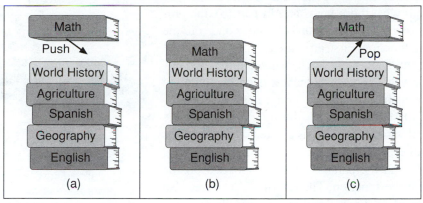

Math

Push

World History		Math			Math
Agriculture		World History		Pop	World History
Spanish		Agriculture			Agriculture
Geography		Spanish			Spanish
English		Geography			Geography
		English			English

(a)   (b)   (c)

Uses for a Stack

So what good is a stack? There are several good uses for a stack in programming. A stack is a good way to reverse the order of a list of items. A stack is also useful when evaluating expressions and when implementing many other algorithms. In the case study that follows this unit, you will see an example of how expressions are evaluated with the assistance of stacks.

Every time you run a C++ program, a stack is created. This stack is used to store local variables used by your functions. The stack also stores addresses that the program needs for proper execution. Figure 13-2 illustrates how a program's stack changes as the flow of logic (represented by the arrow) progresses.

FIGURE 13-2

A stack is used to aid in the execution of programs to store local variables.

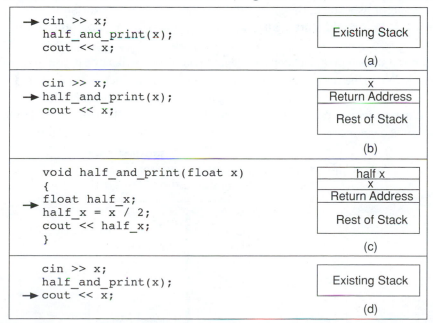

```
→ cin >> x;
  half_and_print(x);
  cout << x;
```
Existing Stack

(a)

```
  cin >> x;
→ half_and_print(x);
  cout << x;
```
| x |
| Return Address |
| Rest of Stack |

(b)

```
  void half_and_print(float x)
  {
→ float half_x;
  half_x = x / 2;
  cout << half_x;
  }
```
| half x |
| x |
| Return Address |
| Rest of Stack |

(c)

```
  cin >> x;
  half_and_print(x);
→ cout << x;
```
Existing Stack

(d)

Figure 13-2(a) shows a segment of code just prior to a call to a function. There are already items on the stack, but we are not concerned with what those items are. In part (b), the program prepares to make the jump to the code of the `half_and_print` function. First, an address is pushed onto the stack. Execution returns to this address when the function terminates. Next, the value of the argument x is pushed onto the stack to make it available to the `half_and_print` function.

Figure 13-2(c) shows the stack during execution of the function. The local variable `half_x` is created on the stack, as are all local variables. In part (d), the function has terminated. The local variable and the parameter x were popped off the stack at the end of the function. The return address was also popped off and used to direct the flow of logic back to the function that made the call. Therefore, the stack is back to the state it was in before the call to `half_and_print`.

Note

The description given here of how a stack is used during the execution of a program is generally followed by C++ compilers. Other languages may use different methods, and C++ compilers may vary slightly.

Note

You learned in Chapter 7 that local variables are lost when the function terminates. Seeing how those variables are stored on a stack will help you understand why.

Programming a Stack

A stack can be implemented in C++ using a vector or a linked list. Let's look at both methods of programming a stack.

Using a Vector as a Stack

A vector or array may be used to implement a stack. For example, assume you need a stack of floating point numbers. The following declaration creates the vector for a stack of up to 100 numbers.

```
apvector <float> my stack;
```

When using a vector as a stack, the stack starts at the top of the vector and works its way down, as shown in Figure 13-3. You could start with a vector of a set size, or you could allow the vector to be resized as the stack grows.

To use a vector as a stack, you must keep an integer variable (we will name it `top`) that holds the subscript of the top of the stack. When the stack is created, `top = 0` because the stack is empty. When an item is pushed onto the stack, `top` is incremented and the value being added to the stack is placed in the element indexed by the variable `top`. When an item is popped off the stack, the value in the element indexed by `top` is copied out of the vector and `top` is decremented. Decrementing `top` gives an index to the new top of the stack.

FIGURE 13-3

When implementing a stack using a vector or array, the stack begins at the top of the array.

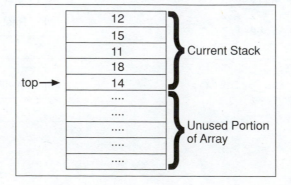

COMMON DATA STRUCTURES AND ALGORITHMS

Using a Linked List as a Stack

Because you have already worked with linked lists, you will easily understand how to use a linked list to implement a stack. A stack is simply a linked list that allows nodes to be added and deleted at only one end of the list. Figure 13-4 shows how the head pointer is called the top when using a linked list as a stack.

Rather than adding nodes to the end of the list, or allowing nodes to be inserted in the middle of the list, new nodes are attached to the head (or top) of the list. When an item is popped off the stack, the top pointer is moved to the second node in the list and the node that is being popped off the stack is deleted.

FIGURE 13-4
A stack can be implemented using a linked list.

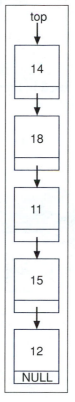

STEP-BY-STEP ▷ 13.1

1. Retrieve **namestak.cpp**. A program that implements a stack using a linked list appears.

2. Compile and run the program.

3. Choose option 1 from the menu of choices. Enter any name at the prompt.

4. Repeatedly select option 1 until you have entered four names onto the stack.

5. Choose option 3 from the menu of choices to display the names in the stack. Notice the last person's name entered appears at the top of the stack.

6. Choose option 2 to pop the top name off the stack and then display the stack again.

7. Push another name onto the stack and display the stack again.

8. Repeatedly pop the names off the stack until the stack is empty.

9. Quit the program.

10. Close the source code file.

Using a Stack Class

After running the program in Step-by-Step 13.1, you can see that the stack is a very useful data structure. However, programming a stack into a program can be very time consuming. To make using a stack easier, a template class could be programmed. Using a stack class that supports templates allows a programmer to create and use a stack of any data type anywhere in a program by simply declaring an instance of the stack class.

In Step-by-Step 13.2, you will run a program that uses a simple stack class. You have seen how a stack can be implemented using an array or a linked list. If you open the header file for the stack class used in Step-by-Step 13.2, you can see that this class is based on the vector class you used in Chapter 9. If you read further through the class definition you can see that there are methods for returning the object on the top of the stack, checking the status of the stack, and checking the length of the stack. Most importantly, the stack class has the standard stack operations, push and pop. The class also has a method for flushing the stack so that it contains no objects.

STEP-BY-STEP ▷ 13.2

1. Open **stackex.cpp**. The program uses the stack class defined in **apstack.h**.

2. Read through the source code and examine the way the stack class is used in the program.

3. Compile and run the program.

4. Run the program multiple times, if desired.

5. Close all source code files.

SECTION CHECKPOINT

1. LIFO is an acronym for what kind of structure?

2. What term refers to adding an item to a stack?

3. What term refers to removing an item from a stack?

4. Identify two common uses for a stack.

5. Where are new nodes inserted when a linked list is used as a stack?

VOCABULARY REVIEW

Define the following terms:

last-in-first-out (LIFO)   push   stack
pop

13.2 Queues

A *queue* (pronounced "Q") is another form of list. A queue allows additions at only one end (called the rear of the queue) and deletions at the opposite end (called the front of the queue). The best way to visualize a queue is to think of a line of people waiting for their turn, for example, a line waiting to get on a roller coaster. People are added to the back of the line, and people at the front of the line get on the roller coaster.

A queue is a *first-in first-out (FIFO)* structure. The first person in line is the first person who gets on the roller coaster.

Uses for a Queue

Queues are very common in computer software, including the operating system. The `cin` stream you have been using to get data from the keyboard is an example of a queue. As you press keys on the keyboard, the characters are placed in the queue. Your program pulls the characters out of the queue.

Computer networks use queues to line up processes to be performed. For example, five people on a computer network may need the printer at the same time. Since that is not possible, the operating system "queues" the documents to be printed and feeds them to the printer one at a time.

Implementing a Queue

A queue can be implemented using a linked list like the one in Figure 13-5. Instead of having a pointer to the head only, we have a pointer to the head and the tail. Two pointers are used so that we can add new nodes at the tail and remove nodes from the head.

Note

The terminology used to describe adding and removing items from a queue differs from stack terminology. Rather than push and pop, you *enqueue* to add an item to a queue and *dequeue* to remove an item from a queue.

FIGURE 13-5

A queue allows insertions at one end and deletions at the other.

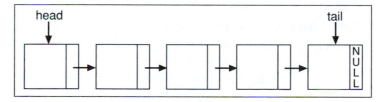

Let's assume we have a queue of characters. The statements in Code List 13-1 declare a node structure and the two necessary pointers.

```
struct queue_node
  {
    char ch;
    queue_node *next;
  };


queue_node *head_ptr;
queue_node *tail_ptr;
```

Inserting a node at the tail of the queue is accomplished with the statements shown in Code List 13-2. The statements assume that the new node already exists, and that it is pointed to by a pointer named new_node.

CODE LIST 13-2

```
tail_ptr->next = new_node;  // attach new node to the end of the list
new_node->next = NULL;      // make the new node's next pointer NULL
tail_ptr = new_node;        // move the tail pointer to the new node
```

Removing a node from the queue involves the other end of the list. As the statements in Code List 13-3 illustrate, the second item in the list becomes the new head as the first node is deleted. The statements use a pointer named temp_ptr to keep track of the node being removed until the memory is deallocated.

CODE LIST 13-3

```
temp_ptr = head_ptr;        // set temporary pointer to point to head
head_ptr = head_ptr->next;  // move head to the next node
delete temp_ptr;            // delete the old head of the list
```

The statements in Code List 13-3 show how to remove the node from the queue. Before removing the node, you will use the data stored in the node or copy the data to another data structure. For example, the queue discussed earlier that feeds documents to the printer would make sure the document had printed without error before removing the document from the queue.

S T E P - B Y - S T E P ▷ 13.3

1. Retrieve **namqueue.cpp**. A program appears that forms a queue of customers.

2. Compile and run the program.

3. Enter four customers in the queue.

4. Display the queue.

5. Take the next customer and redisplay the queue. Notice the first customer has been removed from the queue.

6. Take the next customer and redisplay the queue.

7. Add another customer to the queue and redisplay the queue.

8. Take customers from the queue until the queue is empty.

9. Quit the program.

10. Close the source code file.

Using a Queue Class

The header file **apqueue.h** contains a queue class definition that supports templates. Using a simple queue class like the one defined in **apqueue.h** allows a programmer to have all the benefits of using a queue without having to worry about how long it will take to program and test a new queue data structure for every program that could use a queue. After reading the **apqueue.h** header file you can see that this queue is based on the vector object you used in Chapter 9.

The queue class has member functions to return the object at the front of the queue, to check the status of the queue, and to check the total number of items in the queue. The methods that enqueue and dequeue items from the queue are the most important. Finally, the class has a method to empty the queue.

STEP-BY-STEP 13.4

1. Retrieve **queueex.cpp**. The program utilizes the queue class defined in **apqueue.h**.

2. Read through the file and see how the queue class is used. Notice how easy it is to use the queue class and how you do not have to

understand how the class is programmed in order to use it.

3. Compile and run the program.

4. Close all open source code files.

SECTION CHECKPOINT

1. A queue allows additions to which end of the queue?

2. A queue allows deletions from which end of the queue?

3. FIFO is an acronym for what kind of structure?

4. Identify a way your computer's operating system uses a queue.

5. Give a real-world example of a queue.

Define the following terms:

dequeue   first-in-first-out (FIFO)   queue
enqueue

13.3 Binary Trees

The data structures you have been using are called *linear data structures*, meaning the elements or nodes are arranged in a line. In this section, you will learn about a *nonlinear data structure* called a tree.

A *tree* is a data structure in which the nodes are in an arrangement that resembles branches of a tree. There are many kinds of trees and even more variations of those kinds. In this chapter, you will learn about a special kind of tree called a binary tree. A *binary tree*, like the one shown in Figure 13-6, can have only two branches from each node.

FIGURE 13-6

Each node of a binary tree contains a maximum of two branches.

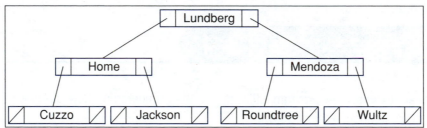

Why Trees?

The reason data is arranged in a binary tree is to allow it to be more easily and quickly searched. The data in the tree is ordered by a *key* value. The key might be a name or a number. In the example in Figure 13-6, the data is keyed by last names. At the top is the name Lundberg. All the names on the half of the tree to the left of Lundberg come before Lundberg alphabetically. All the names on the right half come after Lundberg. The same is true of any node on the tree. For example, Horne comes before Lundberg, so Horne is attached to the left of Lundberg. Jackson comes before Lundberg, but after Horne, so Jackson is attached to the right of Horne.

Because of this arrangement, any name on the tree can be reached with only a few comparisons. You will learn more about searching in the next chapter. For now, let's examine the characteristics of the tree itself.

Tree Terminology

The way trees are represented in diagrams is actually more of an upside-down tree, as shown in Figure 13-7. The top of the diagram is called the *root*. Every element in the tree is a *node*, just like every element of a linked list is a node. But a node can be classified in several different ways. A node has two links. A link may be NULL, or may have a *branch* to another node. Nodes that have branches are called *branch nodes* or *nonterminal nodes*. Nodes that do not have branches are called *leaf nodes* or *terminal nodes*.

Trees are described as having *levels*. The root is the only node at Level 0. The number of levels in a binary tree indicates the maximum number of comparisons necessary to find the desired data. For example, suppose the nodes in Figure 13-7 represent database records. In a search for the record labeled "P," the search would begin at the root ("K"). The search would progress to "R," then "N," and finally to "P." The worst case search would go only to level 3.

FIGURE 13-7
A tree and its nodes are described using special terminology.

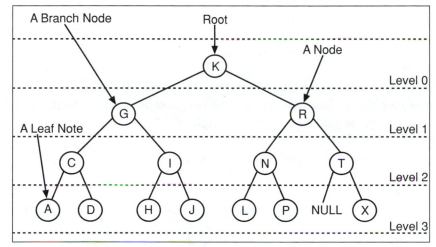

In a tree, nodes have parents, children, siblings, ancestors, and descendants. These relationships among nodes are like those in a family tree. A node's *parent* is the node above it to which it is linked. Every node except the root has a parent. For example, in Figure 13-7, the parent of node A is node C. The one or two nodes below a given node are its *children* (sometimes called *offspring*). Nodes H and J are children of node I. The children of a node are often referred to as the *left child* or *right child*. Node H is the left child of I, and J is the right child of I. Two nodes with the same parent (like H and J) are *siblings*.

Following all the links from a node back to the root give you the node's *ancestors*. All the nodes linked below a node are the node's *descendants*.

For purposes of discussion, trees are sometimes divided into *subtrees*. A subtree can be any node with branches extending below it. For example, the two nodes directly below the root form left and right subtrees.

Tree Shape and Efficiency

A tree is built by attaching nodes to the tree one at a time. Let's look at how a sorted binary tree of integer values grows. Assume that the tree is to be built using the following values in the order that the values appear.

7, 12, 9, 4, 15, 3, 11

Figure 13-8 illustrates the development of the tree by the first three nodes. The first value (7) becomes the root. The next value (12) is attached as the right child of the root, because 12 is greater than 7. The value 9 is also greater than 7, but it is less than 12. Therefore, it becomes the left child of the node containing 12.

FIGURE 13-8

A tree is built by attaching nodes one at a time. (a) The first node becomes the root. (b) The second node is greater than the root, so it is attached to the right of the root. (c) The third node is greater than the root (7), but less then 12, so it becomes the left child of the node containing 12.

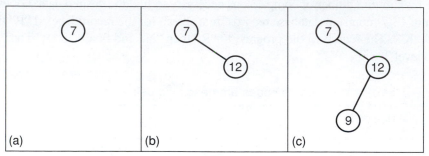

At this point, the tree looks more like a stick. But as Figure 13-9 shows, the addition of the next two nodes help the tree take shape. Because 4 is less than 7, a node is added to the left side of the root. Because 15 is the largest value yet, it attaches to the right of 12.

FIGURE 13-9

The two nodes added in this figure help the tree take shape.

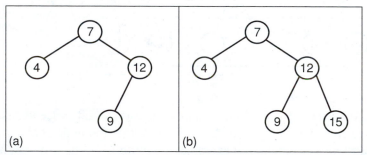

Figure 13-10 shows the addition of the last two values. The node containing the value 3 becomes the left child of 4. The value 11 is greater than 7, less than 12, and greater than 9. Therefore, it gets attached as the right child of 9.

FIGURE 13-10

The last value added to the tree requires the addition of a new level.

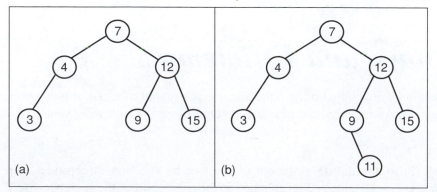

The tree in the preceding figure has only two nodes to the left of the root and twice that many on the right. The shape of the tree depends on the order the nodes are attached. In tree terminology, the arrangement of nodes is referred to as the *balance* of the tree.

A balanced tree allows more efficient access to the data in the tree. Figure 13-11 shows the same values that built the previous tree arranged in a perfectly balanced tree. The balanced tree has fewer levels, and therefore requires fewer comparisons to find any given node in the tree.

If the values being inserted into a tree structure are either in ascending or descending order, the result is just a list, as shown in Figure 13-12.

Having a balanced tree is important. An unbalanced tree lacks some of the efficiency that makes a tree desirable. Advanced programmers of trees use algorithms that detect an unbalanced tree and rearrange nodes to create a more balanced tree. Selecting a root that falls near the midpoint of the data is an important step in creating a balanced tree. For our purposes, understanding why a balanced tree is important is sufficient.

FIGURE 13-11

If the nodes had been inserted in the order 9, 12, 4, 7, 15, 3, 11, the tree would have been perfectly balanced.

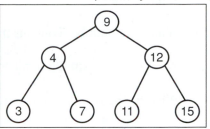

FIGURE 13-12

If the nodes attached to a tree are in ascending or descending order, the result is a linked list rather than a tree.

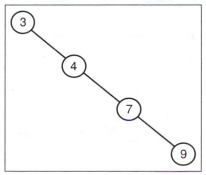

Deleting Nodes from a Tree

You have seen how nodes are attached to a tree. But how is the removal of a node accomplished? Actually, deleting from a binary tree can be complicated, depending on whether the node has children and how many children it has.

If the node to be deleted has no children (in other words, a leaf node), then the node can simply be removed, as shown in Figure 13-13.

If the node to be deleted has one child, the parent of the node to be deleted is connected to the child of the node to be deleted, as shown in Figure 13-14.

If the node to be deleted has two children, the process can become very complicated. Some implementations simply mark the node as deleted without physically removing it. This can be done by adding a Boolean data member to each node that indicates whether it is active or deleted.

Another method involves finding the node below which has the value closest to that of the deleted node and moving that value to the location of the node to be deleted. However, unless the node you move is a leaf, you must repeat the process to properly delete the node you moved.

FIGURE 13-13

Deleting a node that has no children requires no rearranging of the tree's nodes.

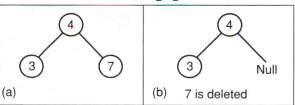

FIGURE 13-14

Deleting a node that has one child requires that the child of the deleted node be attached to the deleted node's parent.

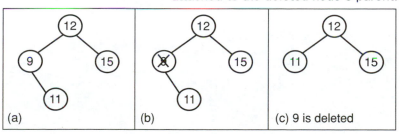

1. What is the term used to describe the node at the top of a tree?

2. What level number contains the node at the top of the tree?

3. What is the maximum number of nodes that can appear in level 2 of a binary tree?

4. What happens if nodes that are inserted in a tree are in ascending or descending order?

5. What is the disadvantage of an unbalanced tree?

VOCABULARY REVIEW

Define the following terms:

ancestors	leaf nodes	parent
balance	left child	right child
binary tree	levels	root
branch	linear data structure	siblings
branch node	node	subtree
children	nonlinear data structure	terminal nodes
descendants	nonterminal nodes	tree
key	offspring	

Summary

In this chapter, you learned:

- A stack is a data structure that allows items to be added and deleted from only one end. Adding an item to a stack is called pushing, and removing an item is called popping.

- A stack is a last-in first-out (LIFO) data structure.

- A stack can be implemented using an array or a linked list.

- A stack class that supports templates allows you to use the same class to implement a stack anytime you need one.

- A queue is a data structure that allows additions at one end and deletions at the other.

- A queue is a first-in first-out (FIFO) structure.

- A queue can be implemented using a linked list or a queue class.

- A tree is a nonlinear data structure in which nodes are arranged like branches of a tree.

- A binary tree has a maximum of two branches from each node. Special terms are used to describe the nodes of trees.

- The shape of a tree affects the tree's efficiency. A tree with unevenly distributed nodes is called unbalanced.

- Deleting nodes from a tree can be complicated depending on whether the node has children.

CHAPTER 13 REVIEW QUESTIONS

TRUE/FALSE

Circle T if the statement is true or F if the statement is false.

T F **1.** Data can be added to both ends of a stack.

T F **2.** Adding an item to a stack is known as pushing.

T F **3.** C++ programs use stacks to store local variables used by functions.

T F **4.** A stack is simply a linked list that allows nodes to be added and deleted at only one end of the list.

T F **5.** A queue is a LIFO structure.

T F **6.** Queues use two pointers to add new nodes at the tail and remove nodes from the head.

T F 7. A tree is an example of a nonlinear data structure.

T F 8. Every element in a tree is known as a node.

T F 9. An unbalanced tree accesses data more efficiently than a balanced treee.

T F 10. Deleting a node that has no children requires no rearranging of the tree's nodes.

WRITTEN QUESTIONS

Write a brief answer to the following questions.

1. What are two ways that a stack may be implemented in C++?

2. How is a stack like a linked list? How is a stack different from a linked list?

3. What is an advantage of using a stack class?

4. How might computer networks use queues?

5. What object serves as the basis for the apqueue class?

6. Why is a tree considered to be "nonlinear"?

7. What are nonterminal nodes?

8. What is the maximum number of nodes that could be located at level 8 of a binary tree?

9. Could a tree with 8 nodes ever be balanced? Why or why not?

10. Describe in words what happens if a node to be deleted has one child.

CHAPTER 13 PROJECTS

PROJECT 13-1

Write a program that uses the apstack class to reverse a string. The program should use subscript notation to individually access each character of the string, pushing them onto a stack of characters. When the end of the string is reached, do not push it on the stack. Instead, begin to build a new string with the characters as they are popped off the stack. The result will be a reversed string. Name this program **reverse.cpp**.

PROJECT 13-2

Write a program that queues jobs for a desktop publishing company. Implement the queue using the queue class. For each job, store the customer's name and a description of the job. The program should have a menu similar to the following.

```
0 - Exit
1 - Add incoming job to the queue
2 - Display the number of jobs in the queue
3 - Remove job from the queue
```

Save the program as **workq.cpp**.

PROJECT 13-3

Draw a tree built by inserting the numbers 29, 44, 17, 32, 11, 25, 50 in that order. Label the branch nodes and the leaf nodes, and answer the following questions about the tree.

1. Is the tree balanced?

2. What is the left child of the node containing the value 44?

3. List the ancestors of the node containing the value 25.

4. List the descendants of the node containing the value 17.

5. What values are in the root's right subtree?

6. What node is the sibling of the node containing the value 11?

CRITICAL THINKING

ACTIVITY 13-1

Extend **workq.cpp** from Project 13-2 to include a fourth menu option. The fourth option should allow the user to display the contents of the queue. Hint: Copy the queue to a backup queue and dequeue all jobs in the backup queue, displaying them to the screen.

14 RECURSION AND SEARCHING

OBJECTIVES

Upon completion of this chapter, you should be able to:

- Understand recursion.
- Understand sequential searching.
- Understand binary searching.
- Search binary trees.
- Traverse binary trees.
- Understand hashing.

⏱ **Estimated Time: 2 hours**

VOCABULARY

binary search

collision

division-remainder method

exit condition

hashing

hashing algorithm

in-order traversal

key

key field

postorder traversal

preorder traversal

recursion

sequential search

In this chapter, you will learn several important concepts, beginning with recursion. Recursion is a technique that allows functions to call themselves. Recursion can greatly simplify certain programming problems. You will also learn about four methods of searching for data. Each method of searching has its advantages and disadvantages. You will first look at a simple sequential search. Then you will see how an ordered array can be searched more efficiently using a binary search. You will also see how binary trees are searched, and learn about a search method called hashing.

14.1 Recursion

Recursion is a programming technique used to simplify many programming problems, such as searching, sorting, and solving mathematical problems. A function is said to be recursive if the function calls itself, either directly or indirectly.

At first, recursion may seem impossible. In this section, however, we will cover the concept of recursion step-by-step and show you that it is possible for a function to call itself. In fact, recursion is often the best way to solve a problem.

Why Recursion?

There are some problems that are greatly simplified by using recursion. However, anything that can be programmed using recursive functions can be programmed without recursion.

Think of recursion as another type of loop. A for loop, while loop, or do while loop repeats a block of code until a specified condition is met. A recursive function repeats a block of code by calling itself until a specified condition is met.

A Simple Example of Recursion

Let's look at a simple example of recursion. The program in Code List 14-1 shows how something normally done with a loop can be accomplished with recursion. This program prints the word *Hello* on the screen a specified number of times. In most cases, including this one, a loop is faster and more efficient than using recursion.

CODE LIST 14-1

```cpp
// recursiv.cpp
// A simple example of recursion.
// By Macneil Shonle

#include<iostream.h>  // necessary for stream I/O

// function prototype
void PrintHello(int How_Many_Times);

// main function
int main()
{
 int n;

 cout << "How many times do you want to print the message? ";
 cin >> n;
 PrintHello(n);

 return 0;
}

// recursive function
void PrintHello(int How_Many_Times)
{
 cout << "Recursive function begins with the parameter value "
     << How_Many_Times << ".\n";
 if(How_Many_Times > 0)   // If How_Many_Times is greater than zero,
  {                        // make another recursive call.
   cout << "Hello\n";
   PrintHello(How_Many_Times - 1); // Reduce How_Many_Times by one.
  }
 cout << "Recursive function with parameter value " << How_Many_Times
     << " ends.\n";
}
```

The program in Code List 14-1 calls the function `PrintHello` repeatedly, each time reducing the integer it passes as an argument by one. Eventually, the number passed reaches the value zero, and the recursion ends.

S TEP-BY-STEP ▷ 14.1

1. Retrieve the source code file named **recursiv.cpp**. A program similar to the one in Code List 14-1 appears. The version on your screen has added output statements to help you trace the path of the recursion.

2. Compile and run the program. If you have access to a debugger, step through the program to see the flow of logic as the recursive calls are made.

3. Provide the integer 5 as input.

4. Analyze the output to understand the flow of logic.

5. Close the source code file.

In the example that follows, you'll see how recursion can be used to calculate the factorial of a positive integer.

Using Recursion to Solve

Calculating the factorial of a positive integer can be accomplished with a simple recursive function. To calculate the factorial of a positive integer, the integer is multiplied by each integer less than the original integer until the integer 1 is reached. For example, the factorial of four is calculated as follows.

factorial of four = 4 * 3 * 2 * 1 = 24

Calculating the factorial of an integer can be done recursively. Consider the factorial of four. As shown in Figure 14-1, the factorial of four can be expressed as 4 times the factorial of three, the factorial of three can be expressed as 3 times the factorial of two, and so on.

FIGURE 14-1
Calculating a factorial is a problem that can be solved recursively.

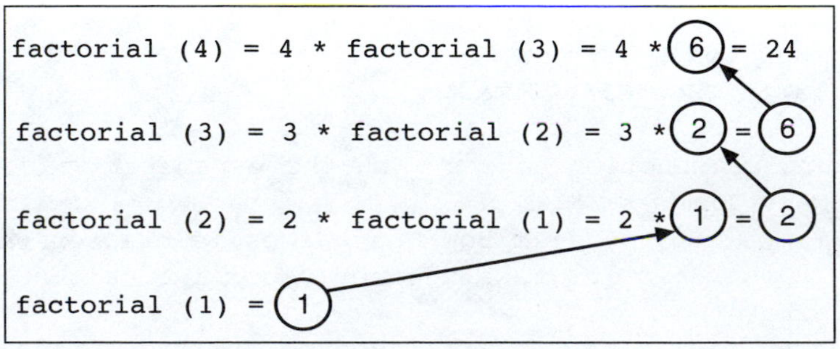

```
factorial (4) = 4 * factorial (3) = 4 * ( 6 ) = 24

factorial (3) = 3 * factorial (2) = 3 * ( 2 ) = ( 6 )

factorial (2) = 2 * factorial (1) = 2 * ( 1 ) = ( 2 )

factorial (1) = ( 1 )
```

WRITING A RECURSIVE FUNCTION

Code List 14-2 shows a complete program for calculating a factorial recursively. The user is asked for a nonnegative integer, and the program returns the factorial of the integer.

```
// factfind.cpp
// A program that calculates the factorial of an integer recursively.

#include<iostream.h>  // necessary for stream I/O

// function prototype
long factorial(long n);

int main()
{
 long n;        // number entered by user
 long result;   // result returned by factorial function

 cout << "Enter a nonnegative integer: ";
 cin >> n;
 if(n == 0) // If the integer is 0, print message and do no calculation.
   {
    cout << "By definition, the factorial of 0 is 1.\n";
   }
 else
   {
    if(n > 0) // If the integer is greater than zero, calculate
     {          // the factorial.
      result = factorial(n);  // Call the recursive function.
      cout << "The factorial of " << n << " is " << result << ".\n";
     }
    else    // If the integer is less than zero, entry is not valid.
     {
      cout << "Not a valid integer.\n";
     }
   }
 return 0;
}

// Recursive function that calculates factorial.
long factorial(long n)
{
 long fact;    // Local variable returned by function.

 if(n > 1)
   {           // If n is not one, make another recursive call.
    fact = n * factorial(n - 1);
   }
 else
   {           // Exit condition
    fact = 1; // If n is one, recursion stops and flow of logic
   }           // begins "backing out" of recursive calls.
 return(fact);  // Return fact to the next level of recursion.
}
```

Let's look at the factorial function. When the function is originally called, the number the user enters is passed in through the parameter n. If the value in n is not equal to 1, the following statement is executed.

```
fact = n * factorial(n - 1);
```

Let's analyze this statement piece by piece because it is the heart of the function. The variable named fact is local to the factorial function. The statement assigns the value of n * factorial(n - 1) to fact. The function is recursive because this statement includes a call to the function that is already being executed.

Note

Recall that truncation means that digits to the right of the decimal point are removed.

Each recursive call passes an integer that is one less than the previous call. Eventually, the integer 1 will be passed, which will end the recursion.

WHAT HAPPENS IN A RECURSIVE CALL?

To understand recursion, you must understand what happens when a recursive call takes place. Recall what you learned in Chapter 13 about the way a stack is used during the execution of a program. When a function is called, the address needed to return from the function is pushed on the stack, along with local variables and the values being passed to the function.

When a function "calls itself," the instructions of the function are used again. To the compiler, however, the function call is treated like any other function. Even though the same function's instructions are being used again, new values are pushed on the stack as if an entirely different function was called.

Eventually, a recursive function stops calling itself. When the flow of logic reaches the end of the last recursive call, the stack begins to shrink as each recursive call is exited in last-in first-out order.

THE EXIT CONDITION

A recursive algorithm must have an *exit condition*, sometimes called a base case or base clause. Each time the recursive function is called, the exit condition is tested. If the exit condition has yet to be met, statements are executed that result in another recursive call. In the factorial function in Code List 14-3, the value passed in as n is checked to determine if it is 1. As long as n is not 1, the recursion continues. When the number passed in is 1, the exit condition is met. Instead of making another recursive call, the value 1 is returned.

CODE LIST 14-3

```
// Recursive function that calculates factorial.
long factorial(long n)
{
 long fact;   // Local variable returned by function.

 if(n > 1)
   {          // If n is not one, make another recursive call.
    fact = n * factorial(n - 1);
   }
 else
   {          // Exit condition
    fact = 1; // If n is one, recursion stops and flow of logic
   }          // begins "backing out" of recursive calls.
 return(fact);  // Return fact to the next level of recursion.
}
```

As each of the separate occurrences of the factorial functions exit, the statement that made the recursive call is completed. In other words, n is multiplied by the value returned from the function that just exited. The local variable `fact` is assigned the result of the multiplication, and then the value of `fact` is returned to the previous recursive call. Figure 14-2 illustrates how the value returned by each recursive call completes the function that made the call.

FIGURE 14-2

As the recursive calls are exited, the value returned by each call is used to complete the calculation of the call that precedes it.

```
(a)

fact = 4 * factorial (3)

            3 * factorial (2)

                2 * factorial (1)

                            1 ◀——Exit condition
```

```
(b)

fact = 4 * factorial (3)

            3 * factorial (2)

                2 * 1 = 2
```

```
(c)

fact = 4 * factorial (3)

            3 * 2 = 6
```

```
(d)

fact = 4 * 6 = 24
```

S TEP-BY-STEP ▷ 14.2

1. Retrieve **factfind.cpp**. The program shown in Code List 14-2 appears.

2. Compile and run the program. Enter 4 as input.

3. Run the program again and enter 12 as input. Twelve is the largest number that the program can calculate due to the limits of the long integer.

4. Close the source code file.

1. What makes a program recursive?

2. What is the reason that recursive algorithms are used in programming?

3. What can happen if too many recursive calls occur?

4. What is the purpose of the exit condition?

5. At what point in a program that uses recursion does the stack have the most values on it?

VOCABULARY REVIEW

Define the following terms:

exit condition   recursion

14.2 Sequential and Binary Searching

When working with large data structures such as arrays, linked lists, and trees, it is often important to search for specific data. For example, a database of library books may need to be searched by subject or author. The item upon which the search is based is called the *key*, and the field being searched is the *key field*.

Computers are uniquely suited for searching large databases because computers can compare data very quickly. Even though a computer can search much more quickly than a human, searching a large database can require special techniques.

Two common methods of searching are the sequential search and the binary search.

Sequential Search

The simplest search is the sequential search. In a *sequential search*, each record in the database is compared in the order it appears until the desired record is found. The following vector of characters could be searched with a sequential search.

N H V E J Y C X S F P L

If you are searching for the character H or another character near the front of the vector, a sequential search finds the character quickly. To find the character L, however, requires that every character in the vector be compared. The more data that must be searched, the longer it may take to find the data that matches the key.

As you will see later in this section, there are methods of searching that are more efficient than sequential searches. When the amount of data to be searched is small, the simplicity of a sequential search may make it a good choice. The function in Code List 14-4 searches a vector for a given value (`search_num`) and returns the position of the value in the vector.

CODE LIST 14-4

```
// Sequential search function.
int sequential_search(apvector <int> x, int search_num)
{
 int index = 0;

 while((index < 100) && (search_num != x[index]))
  {  // Loop while the number is not found and while more elements remain.
   if(x[index] != search_num)
     {            // If current element is not the one for which we are
      index++; // searching, increment subscript index.
     }
  }
 return(index);
}
```

As you can see from Code List 14-4, a sequential search can be accomplished with a while loop. The loop continues until a match is found or the vector is completely searched.

Binary Search

If the vector that contains your data is in order based on the key field, you can use what you know about the list to locate the data more quickly. For example, suppose you are searching in the telephone book for a friend whose last name is Stence. You would not begin on page 1 and turn pages until you reach the page that lists Stence. You would probably open the phone book in the middle. You would judge from the page to which you have turned the direction you need to move from there and the number of pages you should skip. Eventually, you will narrow the search to the exact page.

You can search an ordered vector in a way similar to the way you search a phone book, using a **binary search**. To see how such a search is performed, consider the following vector of characters. (Note: The numbers below the characters represent subscripts of the vector.)

C	E	F	H	J	L	N	P	S	V	X	Y
0	1	2	3	4	5	6	7	8	9	10	11

Suppose we search the vector for the character N. First the middle is located by adding the vector subscript of the first character to the subscript of the last character and dividing by two: $(0 + 11) / 2 = 5$. The actual middle would be between elements 5 and 6. Integer division is used to arrive at element 5 as the middle.

Element 5 holds the character L, which comes before N. Therefore, we know that N exists in that portion of the vector to the right of L and we need to find the middle of that portion of the vector by using the formula $(6 + 11) / 2 = 8$.

Element 8 holds the character S, which comes after N, so we next find the middle of the portion of the vector to the right of L, but to the left of S using the formula $(6 + 7) / 2 = 6$.

Element 6 holds the character N, which is the character for which we are searching.

The function in Code List 14-5 performs a binary search on a vector of 100 integers.

```
// Binary search function
// Function accepts an array, a range of elements for the search,
// and the number for which we are searching.
void binary_search(apvector <int> x, int lowerbound, int upperbound, int
    search_num)
{
 int search_pos;
 int compare_count = 1; // Variable used to count the comparisons.

 // Calculate initial search position.
 search_pos = (lowerbound + upperbound) / 2;

 while((x[search_pos] != search_num) && (lowerbound <= upperbound))
   {
    compare_count++;
    if(x[search_pos] > search_num) // If the value in the search
     {                             // position is greater than the number
      upperbound = search_pos - 1; // for which we are searching, change
     }                             // upperbound to the search position
    else                           // minus one.
     {                             // Else, change lowerbound to search
      lowerbound = search_pos + 1; // position plus one.
     }
    search_pos = (lowerbound + upperbound) / 2;
   }
 if(lowerbound <= upperbound)
   {
    cout << "A binary search found the number in "
       << compare_count << " comparisons.\n";
   }
 else
   {
    cout << "Number not found by binary search after "
       << compare_count << " comparisons.\n";
   }
}
```

The `binary_search` function in Code List 14-5 uses the `lowerbound` and `upperbound` parameters in its search of the ordered vector. The variables `lowerbound` and `upperbound` are passed in as parameters so that the calling function can specify the range of the search. For example, if only 70 of the 100 elements in the vector are in use, there is no need to search the entire vector. In such a case, `lowerbound` would be 0 and `upperbound` 69.

With each iteration of the loop, `lowerbound` and `upperbound` close in on the value for which we are searching. If `lowerbound` ever becomes greater than `upperbound`, we know the value is not in the vector.

STEP-BY-STEP ▷ 14.3

1. Retrieve **search.cpp**. A program that performs a sequential and binary search appears. The program will need access to the data file named **numbers.dat**.

2. Compile and run the program. An ordered vector of 100 integers are loaded. The numbers are positive integers less than or equal to 350.

3. When prompted for the number for which you want to search, enter 350. The program will perform both a binary and sequential search, and report the number of comparisons required to locate the number. Because 350 is the last integer in the vector, the sequential search required 100 comparisons to locate the number. The binary search, however, required only 6 comparisons.

4. Run the program again. Enter 9, which is the first integer in the vector. The binary search requires 6 comparisons. The sequential search located the number in one comparison, because it was the first number in the vector.

5. Run the program again. Enter 21. None of the elements in the vector contain the integer 21. It takes the binary search 8 comparisons to determine that 21 is not in the array. The sequential search searches the entire vector before determining that the value is not in the vector. Note: In the case of an ordered vector, a sequential search could be programmed to stop searching once a value larger than the key is encountered.

6. Run the program additional times trying search values such as 39, 161, 252, and 260.

7. Close the source code file.

SECTION CHECKPOINT

1. When searching a data structure, what is the term for the item upon which the search is based?

2. Describe how a sequential search works.

3. In what case is a sequential search more efficient than a binary search?

4. In a binary search, what formula is used to locate the middle of a 100-element array?

5. Which type of search (sequential or binary) may be conducted without the array being ordered?

VOCABULARY REVIEW

Define the following terms:

binary search
key

key field

sequential search

14.3 Searching Binary Trees and Hashing

There are many methods of searching that are more advanced than the sequential and binary searches of the previous section. In this section you will learn about two advanced search techniques: searching a binary tree and hashing.

Searching Binary Trees

Searching a binary tree is similar to the binary search of a vector. Using a tree, however, gives added flexibility because the data is ordered as the tree is created.

In the previous chapter, you learned that the search of a binary tree begins at the root. The data stored at the root of the tree is compared to the key. If a match is not found, the search moves down the tree. If the key comes before the value in the root, the left subtree is searched. If the key comes after the value in the root, the right subtree is searched.

For example, consider the tree in Figure 14-3. To locate node H, the search would begin at the root. Because H comes before K, the node to the left of K (G) is compared next. H comes after G, so the search moves to the node to the right of G (I). Because H comes before I, the node to the left of I is compared. That is where H is found.

FIGURE 14-3
A binary search tree provides very efficient searching.

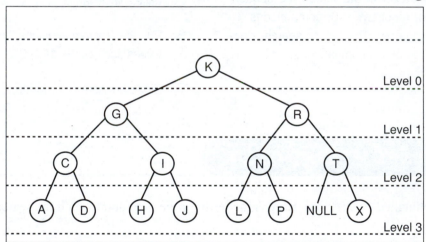

Each comparison of data ordered in a binary tree eliminates half of the remaining nodes. There are 14 nodes in the tree. After the first comparison, 7 of the nodes have been eliminated from the search. The second comparison eliminates 4 more, leaving only 3 possibilities.

The efficiency of a binary tree becomes evident as the number of nodes increases. A four-level tree such as the one in Figure 14-3 can have a maximum of 15 nodes. Each added level, however, can accommodate twice the nodes of the level above it. Table 14-1 shows how the maximum number of nodes increases geometrically.

TABLE 14-1

Number of Levels	Maximum Number of Nodes	Number of Levels	Maximum Number of Nodes
1	1	11	2,047
2	3	12	4,095
3	7	13	8,191
4	15	14	16,383
5	31	15	32,767
6	63	16	65,535
7	127	17	131,071
8	255	18	262,143
9	511	19	524,287
10	1,023	20	1,048,575

What is so greapt about the way the number of nodes increases so quickly with each level of a binary tree? It means that a binary tree is a very efficient way to search a large amount of data. As the table shows, a twenty-level tree could have more than one million nodes. That means that any one of more than a million items in the tree could be located in 20 comparisons or less.

Tree Traversals

Traversing a tree involves "visiting" every node in the tree. You have experience traversing a linked list. Traversing a tree is a bit more complicated because the nodes are not linear. Let's look at three ways to traverse trees: the in-order traversal, the preorder traversal, and the postorder traversal. For the discussion of these traversal methods, let's use the tree in Figure 14-4.

FIGURE 14-4
Traversing a tree involves visiting every node in the tree.

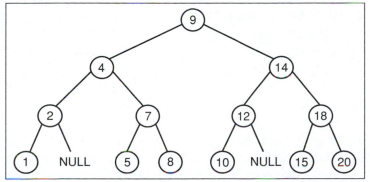

In-Order Traversals

An *in-order traversal* visits all the nodes of a tree in its sorted order. The first node visited is the lower-left node of the tree, because that's where the smallest value is found. The traversal works its way back up to the root, and then down the right subtree until the lower-right node is reached. The result of an in-order traversal on the tree in Figure 14-4 results in the nodes being visited in the following order.

1, 2, 4, 5, 7, 8, 9, 10, 12, 14, 15, 18, 20

Preorder Traversals

A *preorder traversal* visits the root first, then always goes as far left as it can before traversing to the right. Preorder traversals are useful when working with trees used to aid in evaluating mathematical expressions. The nodes of the tree in Figure 14-4 would be visited in the following order by a preorder traversal.

9, 4, 2, 1, 7, 5, 8, 14, 12, 10, 18, 15, 20

Postorder Traversals

A *postorder traversal* always visits the left node first, then the right node, and then the root. To visualize a postorder traversal, understand that the traversal begins at the node at the lower-left node of the tree, like an in-order traversal. The difference is that before a node is visited, every node below it has been visited from left to right. The last node to be visited is the root. Postorder traversals are also used with trees that aid in evaluating mathematical expressions. The nodes of the tree in Figure 14-4 would be visited in the following order by a postorder traversal.

1, 2, 5, 8, 7, 4, 10, 12, 15, 20, 18, 14, 9

S T E P - B Y - S T E P ▷ 14.4

1. Retrieve **tree.cpp**. The program that loads allows you to enter a list of names or other strings. The strings are placed in an ordered binary tree.

2. Compile and run the program. Enter at least 10 (but not more than 20) last names as input. Do not enter the names in alphabetical order. The tree will order the data as the tree is created. Enter a blank string to stop the input.

3. The program displays the last names in alphabetical order by doing an in-order traversal. Press Enter to continue.

4. The program displays the last names in preorder. Press Enter to continue.

5. The program displays the last names in postorder. Press Enter to continue.

6. Close the source code file.

Hashing

Suppose you are assigning seats to people as they enter an auditorium. The goal is to have the youngest people seated at the front of the auditorium, and the oldest people at the back. Your challenge is that you have no control over the order in which people will enter the auditorium. When the first people arrive, you must estimate the proper seating position for each person. When all the people are seated, you can find people of a given age by looking in a particular section of the auditorium.

COMMON DATA STRUCTURES AND ALGORITHMS

Hashing is a method similar to that which is sometimes used to arrange records in a data file. When using hashing, a specified field in the record is used as the key for the hash-coding. Computer hashing differs from the example of seating people in an auditorium because the key used in computer hashing must be unique to each record. In other words, no two records can have the same key. In a customer database, a customer number could be used as the key, since no two customers will share a customer number.

Hashing requires that a *hashing algorithm* be used to convert the key to a number that corresponds to the position of the record. Several different hashing algorithms are commonly used. Possibly the most common method is the *division-remainder method*, which involves dividing the key value by a prime or odd number and using the remainder of the division as the relative address for the record.

No hashing algorithm is perfect. You will almost certainly have situations where two key values produce the same result, called a *collision*. Collisions can be solved in a variety of ways. One way is to move forward in the file from the location of the collision until an available location is found. Another popular method involves applying a second hashing algorithm in the event of a collision.

Searching a file ordered by hashing follows a process similar to that which stored the data. The key for which you are searching is converted to a location in the file using the same hashing algorithm that stored the data.

SECTION CHECKPOINT

1. The search of a binary tree begins at what node?

2. What is the maximum number of nodes in a four-level tree?

3. What type of traversal visits the nodes in sorted order?

4. What type of traversal visits the root last?

5. What is the term that describes the situation in which a hashing algorithm places two records at the same position?

VOCABULARY REVIEW

Define the following terms:

collision	hashing algorithm	preorder traversal
division-remainder method	in-order traversal	
hashing	postorder traversal	

Summary

In this chapter, you learned:

■ Recursion is a programming technique in which a function calls itself. Recursion is used to simplify many programming problems.

■ A recursive function must have an exit condition that ends the recursive calls.

■ When searching for specific data in a data structure, the data for which you are searching is called the key. The field being searched is called the key field.

■ In a sequential search, each record in the database is compared in the order it appears until the desired record is found.

■ In a binary search, a sorted array is searched by starting in the middle and narrowing the search in a way similar to the way you search for a name in a telephone book.

■ Searching a binary tree is very efficient and has the added flexibility of a dynamic data structure.

■ Traversing a tree involves visiting every node in the tree. An in-order traversal visits the nodes in sorted order. A preorder traversal visits the root first, then the left node, then the right node. A postorder traversal visits the left node first, then the right node, then the root.

■ Hashing is a search method that processes the key through a hashing algorithm to find the position of the data in a file.

CHAPTER 14 REVIEW QUESTIONS

TRUE/FALSE

Circle T if the statement is true or F if the statement is false.

T F **1.** A recursive function calls itself.

T F **2.** Many programs can only be coded using recursion.

T F **3.** The exit condition stops recursion from continuing.

T F **4.** The item upon which a search is based is called the loop.

T F **5.** A sequential search finds an item in the middle of a list before it finds the first item in the list.

T F **6.** A binary search of a list starts in the middle of the list.

T F **7.** A binary search does not require an ordered list.

T F 8. Searching a tree is more flexible than searching a vector.

T F 9. A four-level binary tree can include a maximum of 16 nodes.

T F 10. An in-order traversal visits all nodes of a tree in its sorted order.

WRITTEN QUESTIONS

Write a brief answer to the following questions.

1. Why does the stack grow when a recursive call is made?

2. When the flow of logic reaches the end of the last recursive call, the stack begins to shrink as each recursive call is exited in what order?

3. What is another term used to describe the exit condition of a recursive function?

4. In what type of search is each record compared in the order it appears until the desired record is found?

5. At what element of a binary tree does a search begin?

6. What is the maximum number of nodes that can exist on a two-level binary tree?

7. What is the maximum number of nodes that can exist on a three-level binary tree?

8. What type of tree traversal visits the root first, then goes as far left as it can before traversing to the right?

9. What type of tree traversal visits the left node first, then the right node, and then the root?

10. In hashing, what converts the key to a number that corresponds to the position of the record?

CHAPTER 14 PROJECTS

PROJECT 14-1

Write a program that uses a recursive function to sum the even integers less than a given even integer. For example, if the integer 12 is provided as input, the program should calculate 10 + 8 + 6 + 4 + 2 = 30.

Test the user's input to make sure he or she has entered an even number using a statement like the following.

```
if(n % 2 == 0)  // if n modulo 2 is zero, then the number is even.
```

Save the source code as **evensum.cpp**.

PROJECT 14-2

Draw a binary tree created by adding the following nodes in the order that they appear.

45, 12, 15, 67, 8, 90, 53

Write the order in which the nodes of the tree would be visited by:

1. an in-order traversal

2. a preorder traversal

3. a postorder traversal

PROJECT 14-3

Modify **tree.cpp** to accept integers rather than strings.

CRITICAL THINKING

ACTIVITY 14-1

Modify **search.cpp** to load a file of 110 values of type double and perform the searches on the vector of doubles, rather than a vector of integers. The program should load the file named **numbers2.dat**. Name the new program **search2.cpp**.

SORTING

OBJECTIVES

Upon completion of this chapter, you should be able to:

- Understand the basics of sorting.
- Understand the selection sort.
- Understand the insertion sort.
- Understand the bubble sort.
- Understand the Shell sort.
- Understand the quick sort.
- Understand the merge sort.

🕐 **Estimated Time: 2 hours**

VOCABULARY

ascending order

bubble sort

descending order

divide and conquer approach

external sort

incremental approach

input size

insertion sort

key field

key value

merge sort

partitions

quicksort

selection sort

Shell sort

sorting

Many computer programs require that data be arranged in a certain order. Rearranging data in alphabetical or numerical order is called *sorting*. One use for sorting is alphabetizing a list of names. Most database programs can sort records by date, state, ZIP code, area code, or other fields that are contained in a record.

Sorting is sometimes necessary to prepare data for a search algorithm. Recall from Chapter 14 that the binary search of an array requires that the array be sorted. A sorting algorithm must be used if the array is unsorted.

As you might guess, there is more than one algorithm you can use to sort data. In this chapter, you will learn about six different sorting algorithms. As you will see, each of the algorithms has advantages and disadvantages.

15.1 Introduction to Sorting Algorithms

Some sorting algorithms described in this chapter are best for sorting linked lists or data files, but most are designed for sorting arrays. In most of our examples we will be sorting arrays of integers in the form of vectors, but it is possible to sort virtually any other data type in many different data structures. Before a sorting procedure can begin, the key field and input size must be defined. The key field is the field by which the data is sorted. In a simple vector of integers, every element is a *key field*. But if we were sorting an array of structures (like the one in Code List 15-1) by last name, then `last_name` would be the key field.

CODE LIST 15-1

```
struct friend_data
  {
    apstring last_name;        // <- key field
    apstring first_name;
    apstring phone_num;
  };
```

The value of the key field is known as the *key value*. The key value of `friend_data` is the string stored in `last_name`. If we were sorting a vector of integers such as the following, the numbers assigned to the array `nums` are all key values.

```
apvector <int> nums(5);
```

The number of elements in a list to be sorted is known as the *input size*, because the list itself is input to the sorting procedure. If we were sorting the array `nums`, the input size would be five, because there are five elements in the array.

Each sorting algorithm explained in this chapter was designed with one of two approaches in mind: either an incremental or divide and conquer approach. A sorting algorithm designed with an *incremental approach* is usually characterized by loops that pass through the list, one element at a time. The number of passes through the list varies by algorithm and input size. A sorting algorithm that uses a *divide and conquer approach* splits the original unsorted list into smaller sublists. The sublists are then repeatedly split into even smaller sublists. The smallest sublists are then sorted and combined with other small sorted lists. After all sublists are combined the result is a fully sorted list. Divide and conquer approaches often use recursion.

Linked lists, a file, and other data structures may be sorted as well. In this chapter, the term list will apply to the data structure we are sorting, regardless of its type. Generally, it is possible to sort a list only if all elements are of the same type.

Selection Sort

The *selection sort* uses an incremental approach to sort a list. The number of times the sort passes through the list depends on the size of the list. The algorithm makes one less pass than the number of items in the list (`input_size - 1`). During each pass, the unsorted element with the smallest or largest key value is moved to its proper position in the list. If the list is to be sorted in *ascending order*, meaning from smallest to largest, the largest key value is moved. If the list is to be sorted in *descending order*, meaning from largest to smallest, the smallest key value is moved.

If we are given the array {54, 39, 90, 18, 27, 63} to sort in descending order with a selection sort, the first thing we know is the input size will be 6. The sort itself begins by passing through the list and sending the element with the smallest value to the end of the array. Figure 15-1 shows the result of the first pass, step-by-step. Notice that a variable named `small` holds the smaller of the two numbers each time a comparison is made.

Each successive pass through the list is similar to the first pass, as the next smallest value is sorted, as shown in Figure 15-2.

A selection sort function is shown in Code List 15-2. Notice that the function `selection_sort` is composed of two loops. There is an inner loop that passes through the list and finds the next smallest value, and an outer loop that places that value into its proper position.

FIGURE 15-1
The smallest element of the list is found by looking at each item in the list. The smallest element is then exchanged with the last item.

(a)
{ 54, 39, 90, 18, 27, 63 }
small = 54

(b)
{ 54, 39, 90, 18, 27, 63 }
small = 39

(c)
{ 54, 39, 90, 18, 27, 63 }
small = 39

(d)
{ 54, 39, 90, 18, 27, 63 }
small = 18

(e)
{ 54, 39, 90, 18, 27, 63 }
small = 18

(f)
{ 54, 39, 90, 18, 27, 63 }
small = 18

(g)
{ 54, 39, 90, 63, 27, 18 }
18 is switched with 63

FIGURE 15-2
After each pass, the next smallest element is placed into its proper place in the list.

Initial list	{ 54, 39, 90, 18, 27, 63 }
After Pass 1:	{ 54, 39, 90, 63, 27, *18* }
After Pass 2:	{ 54, 39, 90, 63, *27, 18* }
After Pass 3:	{ 54, *63*, 90, *39, 27, 18* }
After Pass 4:	{ *90*, 63, *54, 39, 27, 18* }
After Pass 5:	{ 90, *63, 54, 39, 27, 18* }
After Pass 6:	{ *90, 63, 54, 39, 27, 18* }

CODE LIST 15-2

```
// Selection sort procedure. Sorts a vector of ints in descending order.
void selection_sort(apvector <int> &input_vector)
{
  int i, j;
  int small, temp;
  int input_size = input_vector.length();

  for (i = input_size - 1; i > 0; i--)
    {
    small = 0;  // Initialize small to first element.
```

```
      // Find the smallest element between the positions 1 and i.
      for (j = 1; j <= i; j++)
        {
          if (input_vector[j] < input_vector[small])
            {
              small = j;
            }
        }
      // Swap the smallest element found with element in position i.
      temp = input_vector[small];
      input_vector[small] = input_vector[i];
      input_vector[i] = temp;
    }
}
```

The selection sort is one of the easiest sorts to implement, but is among the least efficient. Selection sort provides no way to end a sort early even if it begins with an already sorted list.

S TEP-BY-STEP ▷ 15.1

1. Retrieve the file **selsort.cpp**.

2. Compile and run the program.

3. Change the initial values of the elements of the nums vector to {0, -31, 19, 104, 19}.

4. Compile and run the program again.

5. Change the declaration of nums to a length of 7 elements.

6. Initialize the two new elements of the vector to 73 and -4.

7. Compile and run the program again.

8. Save the modified version of the source code as **selsort2.cpp** and close.

Insurtion Sort

Like the selection sort, the *insertion sort* uses an incremental approach for sorting lists. Unlike the selection sort, however, the insertion sort passes through the list only once. The insertion sort works similar to the way you might organize a hand of cards. The unsorted cards begin face down on the table and are picked up one by one. As each new unsorted card is picked up, it is inserted into the correct place in your organized hand of cards. The insertion sort works by splitting the list into two sublists. The first sublist, which is always fully sorted, gets larger as the sort progresses. It can be thought of as the hand that holds the organized cards. The second sublist is unsorted and contains all the elements not yet inserted into the first sublist. The second sublist gets smaller as the first sublist gets larger. The second sublist is like the table from where cards are picked up.

Sorting the list {54, 39, 90, 18, 27, 63} in descending order with an insertion sort begins by separating it into the two sublists, as follows.

First sublist:	{54}
Second sublist:	{39, 90, 18, 27, 63}

Note that the first sublist is sorted, even though it contains only one element, which is the first element of the original list. The algorithm then begins stepping through the second sublist.

For the first step, the first element of the second sublist (39) is placed into its proper position (descending order) into the first sublist and is removed from the second sublist, as follows.

First sublist:	{54, 39}
Second sublist:	{90, 18, 27, 63}

Next, the first element of the second sublist, 90, is once again inserted into its proper position in the first sublist and removed from the second sublist.

First sublist:	{90, 54, 39}
Second sublist:	{18, 27, 63}

The insertion continues until the second sublist is empty, as shown in the following three insertions.

First sublist:	{90, 54, 39, 18}
Second sublist:	{27, 63}

First sublist:	{90, 54, 39, 27, 18}
Second sublist:	{63}

First sublist:	{90, 63, 54, 39, 27, 18}
Second sublist:	{}

Code List 15-3 shows an insertion sort function that sorts a vector of integers into descending order. The function maintains the two sublists within the same vector. Initially, the first element in the vector is considered a sorted list, although only one element exists in that list. With each iteration of the loop, the next value in the unsorted portion of the vector is placed in the proper position in the sorted portion of the vector.

CODE LIST 15-3

```
// Insertion sort function. Sorts a vector of ints in descending order.
void insertion_sort(apvector <int> &input_vector)
{
   int j, i, key;
   int input_size = input_vector.length();

   for (j = 1; j < input_size; j++)
     {
     key = input_vector[j];

     // Move all values smaller then key up one position.
     for (i = j - 1; (i >= 0) && (input_vector[i] < key); i--)
       {
        input_vector[i + 1] = input_vector[i];
       }
     input_vector[i + 1] = key;  // insert key into proper position
     }
}
```

Although an insertion sort is not an efficient sorting algorithm when used with large lists, it can be a very efficient way to sort small lists. If a list is partially or fully sorted to begin with, then the insertion sort can be very quick.

STEP-BY-STEP ▷ 15.2

1. Retrieve the file **inssort.cpp**.

2. Compile and run the program.

3. Change the length of nums to 8 elements.

4. Append the elements {35, -10, 35} to the vector nums.

5. Compile and run the program again.

6. Save the modified version of the source code as **inssort2.cpp** and close.

SECTION CHECKPOINT

1. What are the two approaches algorithms use when sorting?

2. Which of the two approaches that you identified in question 1 is used by a selection sort?

3. Which of the two approaches that you identified in question 1 is most likely to be implemented using recursion?

4. What kind of sort (ascending or descending) would rank salaries from lowest to highest?

5. Suppose the following two sublists are part of a descending insertion sort. After the next item in the second sublist is processed, how will the first sublist appear?
   First sublist: { 45 }
   Second sublist: { 33, 88, 23, 67 }

VOCABULARY REVIEW

Define the following terms:

ascending order	input size	key value
descending order	insertion sort	selection sort
divide and conquer approach	key field	sorting
incremental approach		

15.2 More Incremental Sorting Algorithms

The selection and insertion sorts you learned in the previous section are examples of incremental sorting algorithms. In this section, you will learn about two more incremental sorting algorithms: the bubble sort and the Shell sort.

Bubble Sort

The *bubble sort* gets its name because as elements are sorted they gradually rise to their proper positions, like bubbles rising in water. A bubble sort works by repeatedly comparing adjacent elements of a list, starting with the first and second elements, and swapping them if they are out of order. After the first and second items are compared, the second and third items are compared, and swapped if they are out of order. This continues until the end of the list is reached. When the end is reached, items one and two are compared again, and the process continues until all elements are in their proper positions.

Let's examine how an ascending order bubble sort of the following list of integers would occur, step-by-step.

{54, 39, 76, 56, 90, 46}

The bubble sort begins by comparing the first two elements, 54 and 39. Because the sort is to be done in ascending order, 54 and 39 are exchanged, because 54 is greater.

{39, 54, 76, 56, 90, 46} ← 39 exchanged with 54

Next, 54 is compared with 76. Since 54 is less than 76, it remains in the same position.

{39, 54, 76, 56, 90, 46} ← no exchange (54 < 76)

The following steps show what happens as the algorithm continues down the list until the first pass is complete.

{39, 54, 56, 76, 90, 46} ← 56 exchanged with 76
{39, 54, 56, 76, 90, 46} ← no exchange (76 < 90)
{39, 54, 56, 76, 46, 90} ← 46 exchanged with 90

The number 90 is now in its proper position, at the end of the list (because it is the greatest number).

During the second pass, the process starts again from the beginning of the list. This time, however, we do not need to go all the way to the very end, because the last item is already correctly sorted. The following steps make up the second pass.

{39, 54, 56, 76, 46, 90} ← no exchange (39 < 54)
{39, 54, 56, 76, 46, 90} ← no exchange (54 < 56)
{39, 54, 56, 76, 46, 90} ← no exchange (56 < 76)
{39, 54, 56, 46, 76, 90} ← 46 exchanged with 76

For this next pass, we do not need to do any comparisons with the last two elements, because they are both correctly sorted.

{39, 54, 56, 46, 76, 90} ← no exchange (39 < 54)
{39, 54, 56, 46, 76, 90} ← no exchange (54 < 56)
{39, 54, 46, 56, 76, 90} ← 46 exchanged with 56

In the next pass, the last three elements are skipped.

{39, 54, 46, 56, 76, 90} ← no exchange (39 < 54)
{39, 46, 54, 56, 76, 90} ← 46 exchanged with 54

In the final pass, the elements are finally sorted from lowest to highest.

{39, 46, 54, 56, 76, 90} ← no exchange (39 < 46)

The bubble sort provides a way to end a sort early, if the list is completely or partially sorted to begin with. Consider the following array.

{17, 75, 67, 54, 37, 29}

If we are to sort in descending order, notice that the first element, 17, is out of place but all other elements are already in the correct order. The following lines illustrate the steps of the first pass.

{75, 17, 67, 54, 37, 29} ← 75 exchanged with 17
{75, 67, 17, 54, 37, 29} ← 67 exchanged with 17
{75, 67, 54, 17, 37, 29} ← 54 exchanged with 17
{75, 67, 54, 37, 17, 29} ← 37 exchanged with 17
{75, 67, 54, 37, 29, 17} ← 29 exchanged with 17

We can see that the whole list is now completely sorted. The bubble sort function, however, is not yet finished. In the next pass, no exchanges take place, indicating that the list is sorted. A bubble sort algorithm should include provisions to terminate the bubble sort early when a pass is made without exchanges occurring.

The function in Code List 15-4 performs a bubble sort on a vector of integers. The variable named `flag` is set to zero before each pass. If an exchange occurs during the pass, `flag` is set to one, indicating that another pass is necessary. If `flag` remains zero, indicating to the algorithm that the list is completely sorted, the bubble sort ends.

CODE LIST 15-4

```
// Bubble sort function. Sorts a vector of ints in descending order.
void bubble_sort(apvector <int> &input_vector)
{
    int i, j, flag = 1;
    int temp;
    int input_size = input_vector.length();

    for(i = 1; (i <= input_size) && flag; i++)
      {
        flag = 0;
        for(j = 0; j < (input_size - i); j++)
          {
            if (input_vector[j + 1] > input_vector[j])
              {
                temp = input_vector[j + 1];
                input_vector[j + 1] = input_vector[j];
                input_vector[j] = temp;
                flag = 1;
              }
          }
      }
}
```

Although the bubble sort's level of performance is often below that of other sorts, it does provide a way to end early, which can speed up the sort in some instances.

S TEP-BY-STEP ▷ 15.3

1. Retrieve the file **bubsort.cpp**.

2. Compile and run the program.

3. Change the line:

What is the effect of the change?

4. Compile and run the program again.

5. Save the modified version of the source code as **bubsort2.cpp** and close the file.

```
if (input_vector[j + 1] > input_vector[j])
```

to

```
if (input_vector[j + 1] < input_vector[j])
```

Shell Sort

The ***Shell sort*** (named after its inventor, D. L. Shell) is similar to the bubble sort, but instead of adjacent elements repeatedly being compared, elements that are a certain distance away from each other (d positions away) are repeatedly compared. The value of d is initially half the input size and is halved after each pass through the list. Elements are compared and swapped, if necessary, as in a bubble sort.

In a Shell sort in descending order with the following list, d would initially equal (6 + 1) / 2 = 3.

> ✅ **Note**
>
> We use the equation
> d = (N + 1) / 2 so d is rounded up and never drops below 1. The value of d is 3 and not 3.5 because numbers after the decimal place in integer calculations are truncated.

{54, 39, 76, 56, 90, 46}

The first pass begins by comparing the first and fourth items (with values 54 and 56) because they are three positions away from each other:

{56, 39, 76, 54, 90, 46} ← 56 exchanged with 54

Next, the second and fifth items are compared:

{56, 90, 76, 54, 39, 46} ← 90 exchanged with 39

And the pass concludes with comparing the third and sixth items.

{56, 90, 76, 54, 39, 46} ← no exchange (76 > 46)

After each pass the value of d is halved (and rounded up), so for the second pass d equals (3 + 1) / 2 = 2. Because d now equals 2, during the second pass items two places away from each other are compared:

{76, 90, 56, 54, 39, 46} ← 76 exchanged with 56
{76, 90, 56, 54, 39, 46} ← no exchange (90 > 54)
{76, 90, 56, 54, 39, 46} ← no exchange (56 > 39)
{76, 90, 56, 54, 39, 46} ← no exchange (54 > 46)

For the next pass d is halved again, so it now equals 1.

{90, 76, 56, 54, 39, 46} ← 90 exchanged with 76
{90, 76, 56, 54, 39, 46} ← no exchange (76 > 56)
{90, 76, 56, 54, 39, 46} ← no exchange (56 > 54)
{90, 76, 56, 54, 39, 46} ← no exchange (54 > 39)
{90, 76, 56, 54, 46, 39} ← 46 exchanged with 39

We can clearly see that the list is now fully sorted. However, the Shell sort continues until d equals 1 and the pass occurs without an exchange.

The value of d cannot drop below 1, so it remains at 1 for the final pass.

{90, 76, 56, 54, 46, 39} ← no exchange (90 > 76)
{90, 76, 56, 54, 46, 39} ← no exchange (76 > 56)
{90, 76, 56, 54, 46, 39} ← no exchange (56 > 54)
{90, 76, 56, 54, 46, 39} ← no exchange (54 > 46)
{90, 76, 56, 54, 46, 39} ← no exchange (46 > 39)

The Shell sort is now finished because d equals 1 and the last pass occurred without an exchange.

Although similar to bubble sort in some ways, the Shell sort is generally more efficient than the bubble sort. Comparing values that are non-adjacent results in a more efficient algorithm than comparing adjacent values. The function in Code List 15-5 performs a Shell sort on an array of integers.

CODE LIST 15-5

```
// Shell sort function. Sorts a vector of ints in descending order.
void shell_sort(apvector <int> &input_vector)
{
   int flag = 1;
   int input_size = input_vector.length();
   int d = input_size;
   int i;
   int temp;

   while (flag || (d > 1))
    {
      flag = 0;
      d = (d + 1) / 2;
      for (i = 0; i < (input_size - d); i++)
        {
           if (input_vector[i + d] > input_vector[i])
            {
               // swap items at
               // positions i + d and i:

               temp = input_vector[i + d];
               input_vector[i + d] = input_vector[i];
               input_vector[i] = temp;
               flag = 1; // indicate that a swap has occurred
            }
        }
    }
}
```

1. What type of sort compares adjacent elements in an array?

2. Where does the bubble sort get its name?

3. In the bubble sort function, what is the purpose of the `flag` variable?

4. Is the Shell sort an incremental or divide and conquer sort?

5. How does a Shell sort differ from a bubble sort?

Define the following terms:

bubble sort   Shell sort

15.3 Divide and Conquer Sorting Algorithms

In this section, you will learn about two divide and conquer sorting algorithms: the quicksort and the merge sort.

Quicksort

The *quicksort* uses a divide and conquer algorithm and is known to be very efficient. It starts by breaking down the original list into two *partitions* (sections) based on the value of the first item in the list. Because the following example will sort in descending order, the first partition will contain all the elements with values greater than the first item. The second partition will contain elements with values less than or equal to the first element. The first element itself can end up in either partition.

The following array will be partitioned into two partitions.

{54, 39, 76, 56, 90, 46}

The first of the two partitions will contain all the elements greater than the first element (greater than 54), as shown.

1: {90, 56, 76}

The second partition will contain the remaining elements less than or equal to the first element (it happens to contain the first element also).

2: {39, 54, 46}

If the two partitions are concatenated into one new list we have:

{{90, 56, 76}, {39, 54, 46}}

Now the lists {90, 56, 76} and {39, 54, 46} must be sorted, and this is accomplished in exactly the same way as with the original list.

We now partition {90, 56, 76} into two new lists:

1: {90}

2: {56, 76}

The first new list contains the first element, 90. The second list contains 76 and 56 because they are both less than or equal to 90.

Concatenating those two new lists we get:

{{90}, {56, 76}}

When and only when an element is placed in a partition by itself is it considered to be correctly sorted. Putting all partitions back into the big list we get the following list.

{{{90}, {56, 76}}, {39, 54, 46}}

In the same manner as before, partitioning {56, 76} creates the following lists.

1: {76}

2: {56}

Placing those partitions back into the full list gives us the following list.

{{{90}, {{76}, {56}}}, {39, 54, 46}}

Partitioning {39, 54, 46} gives the following lists.

1: {46, 54}

2: {39}

Placing those partitions back into the full list give us the following list.

{{{90}, {{76}, {56}}}, {{46, 54}, {39}}}

Finally, partitioning {46, 54} gives the following lists.

1: {54}

2: {46}

The full list is as follows. Note that each element is in its own partition. That means the entire list is completely sorted.

{{{90}, {{76}, {56}}}, {{{54}, {46}}, {39}}}

The quicksort is recognized as being one of the most efficient sorting algorithms. Although with some data it is not always the most efficient, the average quicksort requires very few steps.

A quicksort can be implemented using recursion or a stack. In the exercise that follows, you will run a program that uses a recursive quicksort algorithm.

STEP-BY-STEP ▷ 15.4

1. Retrieve the file **quiksort.cpp**.

2. Compile and run the program.

3. Examine the functions `quicksort` and `partition` carefully.

4. Reverse the positions of the following two lines:

```
quicksort(input_vector, top, middle);
quicksort(input_vector, middle + 1, bottom);
```

5. Compile and run the program again. Did exchanging the two lines make a difference?

6. Save the modified version of the source code as **quick.cpp** and close it.

Merge Sort

Like quicksort, the *merge sort* is a divide and conquer algorithm. As shown in Figure 15-3, the merge sort begins by placing each element into its own individual list, thus dividing the original list into equal sized parts. The merge sort then combines every two small lists into one list. The lists are merged in a way so that the newly created lists are all sorted. Every two new lists are then merged into a new, sorted list. This continues until all smaller lists have been merged into a single list, which is completely sorted.

There are many different ways to implement the merge

FIGURE 15-3
This merge sort example successively combines groups of elements until a single sorted list is achieved.

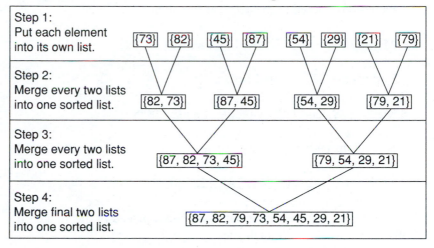

sort. The example we will present is to use it as an external sort. An *external sort* is designed specifically to sort data in a file. External sorts usually read only a portion of files into memory at one time. An external sort is helpful when sufficient internal memory is a concern and huge amounts of data must be sorted. Because an external sort loads only some data from a file into memory at one time it is capable of sorting very large quantities of data while using very little memory. The external merge sort in the following example loads only two elements into memory at once.

The merge sort function uses two files during the intermediate stages of sorting, which may be discarded after the sorting process. Our merge sort function begins its multiple passes, ultimately resulting in a list sorted in ascending order by distributing elements of the original file into the two scratch files. The initial file contains:

{38, 93, 48, 84, 79, 77, 28, 80}

Because the data being manipulated is in files, the number of items in the list may be unknown. To create two scratch files, alternate items are placed in each of the two files. In this case, the first, third, fifth, and seventh elements are placed in the first scratch file, and the second, fourth, sixth, and eighth elements are placed into the second scratch file.

First scratch file: {38}, {48}, {79}, {28}
Second scratch file: {93}, {84}, {77}, {80}

At this point, each element can be thought of as being in a different sublist.

Next, the sublists are copied back to the original file, beginning with the first elements of each scratch file ({38} and {93}). The elements are merged into the original file.

Merge {38} and {93} yielding the list {38, 93}

This new sublist {38, 93} is copied back to the original file. Because 38 is smaller, and we are sorting in ascending order, 38 is copied from the first scratch file to the original file first. Then 93 is copied from the second scratch file to the original file. Then the next two sublists are merged:

Merge {48} and {84} yielding the list {48, 84}

Here 48 is copied to the original file, then 84.

Merge {79} and {77} yielding the list {77, 79}

In this case 77 is copied before 79.

Merge {28} and {80} yielding the list {28, 80}

Now, at the end of the first pass, the original file contains all of the elements and looks like the following.

{{38, 93}, {48, 84}, {77, 79}, {28, 80}}

During the next pass, elements are again placed in the scratch files. This time, each newly created sublist is copied to the scratch files.

First scratch file: {38, 93}, {77, 79}
Second scratch file: {48, 84}, {28, 80}

The first sublists in each scratch file are now merged and copied back to the original file.

First, the sublists {38, 93} and {48, 84} are merged to form {38, 48, 84, 93}. Then {77, 79} and {28, 80} are merged to form {28, 77, 79, 80}. At this point, the merged file contains {38, 48, 84, 93, 28, 77, 79, 80}.

Next, the two new sublists are copied to the scratch files to form the following sublists.

First scratch file: {38, 48, 84, 93}
Second scratch file: {28, 77, 79, 80}

This time through, there is only one merge. The sublists {38, 48, 84, 93} and {28, 77, 79, 80} are merged to form {28, 38, 48, 77, 79, 80, 84, 93}, which is a sorted file.

Choosing a Sorting Algorithm

There are several factors to consider when choosing an appropriate sorting algorithm:

1. Will the data be sorted in RAM or on disk (internal or external sort)? Larger sets of data may have to be sorted on disk, in which case your algorithm options are limited to those designed to sort externally.

2. How much data is involved? If the amount of data to be sorted will always be fairly small, any convenient and easy to implement algorithm may be acceptable. It is not worth spending too much time choosing just the right algorithm if there is not much to gain in speed or performance.

3. How often will the sort be called? A small amount of data may sort so quickly that the algorithm you use seems unimportant. If the sort occurs regularly in the program, however, a more efficient algorithm may pay off.

4. In what condition is the data generally presented to the sorting algorithm? Some algorithms perform well on data which is highly "out of sorts," while others perform better on data that is partially or almost completely sorted.

Appendix K discusses how algorithms (including sorting algorithms) are analyzed.

SECTION CHECKPOINT

1. Which of the divide and conquer sort algorithms mentioned in this section is often used to sort data in a file?

2. What are two ways the quicksort can be implemented?

3. What type of sort breaks down the original list into two partitions as a first step?

4. What type of sort puts each element of the list into its own sublist as a first step?

5. What distinguishes an external sort from an internal sort?

VOCABULARY REVIEW

Define the following terms:

external sort   partitions   quicksort
merge sort

Summary

In this chapter, you learned:

- Arrays, linked lists, binary trees, or any other collection of homogeneous objects may be sorted.

- Before sorting a list, you must first choose the key field. Records or elements are sorted based upon the values contained in the key field.

- An incremental approach to sorting generally iterates through the elements of a list slowly putting elements in their proper positions.

- A divide and conquer approach to sorting repeatedly breaks the unsorted list down into smaller lists until each small list is sorted. Divide and conquer algorithms often use recursion.

- A selection sort uses an incremental approach to sort lists. After the first pass through the list, the element with the largest key value is sorted. After each successive pass, the next largest element is put in its proper position until all elements are sorted.

- An insertion sort uses an incremental approach and sorts elements the same way one might sort a hand of cards. The list is passed through only once and as each element is reached it is placed in its proper position in a sorted list.

- A bubble sort works incrementally by repeatedly comparing adjacent elements of an array, starting with the first and second elements, and swapping them if they are out of order.

- A Shell sort is similar to a bubble sort but instead of comparing adjacent elements it compares elements d positions away from each other. d initially is equal to half the length of the list and is halved after each iteration.

- A quicksort uses a divide and conquer approach and works by repeatedly breaking the list into partitions until each partition contains a single element.

- A merge sort merges small sorted lists into larger sorted lists. New lists are repeatedly merged until there is one large list.

- An external sort usually sorts files. External sorts load only a limited number of elements into memory at a time.

- When choosing an appropriate sorting algorithm, you should consider whether the data will be stored on disk or in RAM, how much data is involved, how often the sort will be called, and in what condition the data generally is presented to the sorting algorithm.

CHAPTER 15 REVIEW QUESTIONS

TRUE/FALSE

Circle T if the statement is true or F if the statement is false.

T F **1.** The key field is the field by which data is sorted.

T F **2.** The value of the key field is known as the input size.

T F **3.** A sort that uses a divide and conquer approach uses loops to pass through the list.

T F **4.** A sort with an incremental approach splits an original unsorted list into sublists.

T F **5.** The selection sort uses an incremental approach to sort a list.

T F **6.** An ascending order sort places the items in an order from largest to smallest.

T F **7.** The Shell sort is named after the shell game.

T F **8.** The quicksort uses a divide and conquer approach.

T F **9.** The bubble sort is one of the most efficient sorting algorithms.

T F **10.** An external sort is designed to sort data in a file.

WRITTEN QUESTIONS

Write a brief answer to the following questions.

1. What is the input size of a 10-element vector that is being sorted?

2. What kind of sort (ascending or descending) would sort people by age from oldest to youngest?

3. What approach does the insertion sort use (incremental or divide and conquer)?

4. In an insertion sort, the first sublist created contains how many elements?

5. What sort (selection or insertion) is most efficient when sorting a list which is partially sorted?

6. How does a bubble sort end a sort early when the list is completely sorted?

7. Why is a bubble sort efficient when only one item in the list is out of place?

8. Why is a Shell sort generally more efficient than a bubble sort?

9. A quicksort can be implemented using a stack or _____.

10. What are two factors to consider when choosing an appropriate algorithm?

CHAPTER 15 PROJECTS

PROJECT 15-1

Improve **selsort.cpp** by allowing the user to enter any five values they want for `nums`. Save the improved source code file as **selsort3.cpp**.

PROJECT 15-2

Rewrite the selection sort procedure (**selsort.cpp** or **selsort3.cpp**) to sort the vector of ints in ascending order. (Hint: Change the name of `small` to `large`. Other than that, you will only need to change a single operator.) Save the new source code file as **ascend.cpp**.

PROJECT 15-3

Modify the bubble sort program from Step-by-Step 15.3 to use a Shell sort function instead of a bubble sort. Save the new source code as **shellsrt.cpp**.

PROJECT 15-4

Write a program that reads 50 integers from a data file named **50ints.dat** and stores them in a vector. Use a quicksort to sort the integers in descending order. After sorting is complete, write the integers back to a file named **50sort.dat**. To test the program, create a text file named **50ints.dat** that includes 50 integers. Save the source code as **quick50.cpp**.

CRITICAL THINKING

ACTIVITY 15-1

Write a program that asks the user to enter eight strings. Place the eight strings into a vector named **unsorted**. Use getline to prompt the user for the strings.

Add three sort functions to the program using the following instructions. All three sort functions should sort the strings in ascending (alphabetical) order.

1. Declare a vector of strings named **bubblesorted**. Copy the contents of **unsorted** into **bubble-sorted** and pass **bubblesorted** to a bubble sort function that will sort the strings using a bubble sort. In the bubble sort function, insert two counter variables that will track the number of iterations of the inner and outer loops. After sorting the vector, report the number of iterations of the bubble sort loops to the screen.

2. Declare a vector of strings named **selectionsorted**. Copy the contents of **unsorted** into **selectionsorted** and pass **selectionsorted** to a selection sort function that will sort the string using a selection sort. Insert the counters in the inner and outer loops of the selection sort and report the results.

3. Declare a vector of strings named **insertionsorted**. Copy the contents of **unsorted** into **insertionsorted** and pass **insertionsorted** to an insertion sort function that will sort the string using an insertion sort. Enter the counter in the inner and outer loops of the insertion sort and report the results.

Run the program with a variety of inputs. Try an already sorted list. Also try a list in reverse order. Name your program **sorts.cpp**.

Common Data Structures and Algorithms

REVIEW QUESTIONS

MATCHING

Write the letter of the description from Column 2 that best matches the term or phrase in Column 1.

Column 1	Column 2
___ **1.** binary tree	**A.** to place in a queue
___ **2.** dequeue	**B.** used to convert a key to a file position
___ **3.** enqueue	**C.** the field upon which a search or sort is based
___ **4.** exit condition	**D.** a programming technique where a function calls itself
___ **5.** hashing algorithm	**E.** a tree structure that allows only two branches from each node
___ **6.** key field	**F.** to place an item on a stack
___ **7.** node	**G.** must be met to end recursion
___ **8.** pop	**H.** the structure that contains the data in a linked list or tree
___ **9.** push	**I.** to remove from a queue
___ **10.** recursion	**J.** to remove an item from a stack

WRITTEN QUESTIONS

Write a brief answer to the following questions.

1. What does knowing that a structure is LIFO tell you about the structure?

2. What does knowing that a structure is FIFO tell you about the structure?

3. In a queue, where do deletions occur?

4. In a tree, where is the root node?

5. What is the maximum number of nodes that can appear in level 3 of a binary tree?

6. Why is an exit condition required in a recursive function?

7. In what order does an in-order traversal visit the nodes of a tree?

8. Name the two approaches to sorting discussed in this unit.

9. How would an ascending sort rank a list of weights?

10. A bubble sort is what type of sort?

APPLICATIONS

APPLICATION 5-1

On paper, step through a selection sort of the following list: {2, 4, 9}. Sort the elements in descending order, and write out each step.

APPLICATION 5-2

On paper, step through a bubble sort of {4, 19, 8}. Sort in descending order, and write out each step.

APPLICATION 5-3

On paper, draw a diagram similar to Figure 15-3 that illustrates an ascending merge sort of the list {64, 79, 43, 85, 51, 27, 19, 77}.

APPLICATION 5-4

Rewrite the selection sort procedure (selsort.cpp or selsort3.cpp) to sort a vector of type double in ascending order. Save the new source code file as **sortdbl.cpp**.

INTERNET ACTIVITY

1. Open your Web browser and go to http://www.programcpp.com/third.

2. On the home page, click the link called Internet Activities and then go to the Unit 5 link.

3. On that page, you will find links to sites that provide information about sorting or that give visual demonstrations of sorts.

4. Visit the links provided to expand your knowledge of sorting.

OBJECT-ORIENTED PROGRAM DESIGN

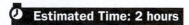 **Estimated Time: 2 hours**

Overview

This case study will guide you through the development of an object-oriented program. The program we will analyze in this case study is a simulated FM radio. The program consists of multiple objects comparable to the objects that make up a real radio. Our simulated radio will consist of a power switch, a volume knob, a tuning knob, an amplifier, a tuner, and a display. Each of these components will be implemented as objects in our program. The switches and knobs are simple objects. The amplifier, tuner, and display are more complicated objects, but their responsibilities are easily described and implemented.

Designing the Objects

To design each of the objects that make up the radio, you must decide what data and functions each object will contain. Next, you will determine what messages will be exchanged among the objects in order to make the objects function together.

Because the radio consists of several small objects, the bottom up design method will be used. Each of the objects will be created and tested before they are combined to make the radio. This approach is much like how you would work on objects in the real world. Each part must be completed before the parts can come together to form a final product.

We will begin by designing the basic objects of the radio: the toggle switch, knobs, amplifier, tuner, and display.

Toggle Switch

The radio has one switch to turn the power on and off. A switch's responsibility is to open or close a circuit. Therefore, the toggle switch object needs a member to store its current state and methods to toggle and report the current state of the switch.

Knobs

The radio object has two knobs, one for the volume and one for tuning in the desired station. A knob is a device that has a position between an upper and a lower bound. Because the bounds will change depending on how the object is being used, the upper and lower bounds will be set by the programmer who instantiates a knob object from the knob class.

For a knob object to perform its responsibilities, it needs a member that stores the knob's current position, its upper bound, and its lower bound. A knob object needs methods to turn it clockwise, turn it counterclockwise, and check its current position.

Amplifier

In an actual radio, the job of the amplifier is to power the speakers with the proper volume level. In our simulator, the amplifier has two properties. The amplifier can be on or off and it has an amplification level. The power switch will turn the amplifier on or off and the volume knob will set the amplifier's volume level.

The amplifier needs members that indicate whether it is on and what its amplification level is. The amplifier's methods will turn the device on and off, change the amplification level, and check the current amplification level.

Tuner

Much like the amplifier, the tuner has two properties: the state of being turned on or off and the frequency to which it is currently tuned. Therefore, it needs members that have the current power status and the current frequency. The tuner requires methods to turn the device on and off, set the frequency, and check the current frequency.

Display

Although the display on a typical radio is a complicated electronic object, its responsibility is very simple: displaying information. Like the amplifier and tuner, it can be on or off, so it needs members that indicate its current power status and the current message being displayed. In addition to methods needed to turn the device on and off, the object needs methods to set the current message and display the current message.

The Radio Object

The radio object will contain each of the objects previously discussed. All objects that are normally accessible by the user of a radio will be in the public section of the object. The amplifier, tuner, and display will be in the private section of the object. The radio object should not have any other members. However, it does need a method to display the status of all the components in the radio and a method to tell the radio to update all the components when a change has been made.

The Interface

The interface to the radio will be provided through a small program that displays a menu and allows the user to change a property of the radio or display the current status of the radio.

Coding and Testing the Objects

Now that all the objects have been designed, they must be coded and tested. Because the coding has been done for you in this case study, we will compile and run the program and then analyze it piece by piece.

STEP-BY-STEP ▷ CSV.1

1. Create a new project with your compiler and add the following files:

OORADIO.CPP	TUNER.H
RADIO.H	TUNER.CPP
RADIO.CPP	KNOB.H
AMP.H	KNOB.CPP
AMP.CPP	TSWITCH.H

DISPLAY.H	TSWITCH.CPP
DISPLAY.CPP	ON_OFF.H

2. Compile and run **OORADIO.CPP**. Notice the change in the display when the power is on versus when it is off.

3. Set the tuner and volume, then turn the power off. Without exiting the program, turn the power back on and check the tuner and volume settings.

4. Turn the power off and exit the program.

Toggle Switch

When designing the switch we determined that it needed a member to indicate its current state and methods to toggle its current state and to report its current state. The header file containing the class definition for a toggle switch object is shown in Code List CSV-1.

CODE LIST CSV-1

```
// TSWITCH.H
// Toggle switch class definition

#ifndef _TOGGLE_SWITCH_H
#define _TOGGLE_SWITCH_H

#include "on_off.h" // defines the constants ON and OFF

class ToggleSwitch
{
  public:
    ToggleSwitch(); // constructor
    ToggleSwitch(int StartingState); // constructor with init
    ToggleSwitch(ToggleSwitch & ts); // copy constructor

    void ChangeState();  // toggle the switch
    int  CurrentState(); // return current switch position

  private:
    int SwitchState; // stores the current switch position
};

#endif
```

The header file **ON_OFF.H** is included so that the constants ON and OFF will be defined. This header file is included in several of the classes in this case study. The source code for **ON_OFF.H** is shown in Code List CSV-2.

CODE LIST CSV-2

```
#ifndef _ON_OFF_H
#define _ON_OFF_H

const int OFF = 0;
const int ON  = 1;


#endif
```

The implementation of the toggle switch class (shown in Code List CSV-3) is also straightforward. It includes a standard constructor that initializes the switch to off. It also includes a constructor that allows you to set the original switch position.

CODE LIST CSV-3

```
// TSWITCH.CPP
// Toggle switch class implementation

#include "TSWITCH.H"

// Constructor
ToggleSwitch::ToggleSwitch()
:SwitchState(OFF)
{
}

// Constructor that allows you to specify the original
// state of the switch
ToggleSwitch::ToggleSwitch(int StartingState)
:SwitchState(StartingState)
{
}

// Copy constructor
ToggleSwitch::ToggleSwitch(ToggleSwitch & ts)
:SwitchState(ts.SwitchState)
{
}

// Method that toggles the position of the switch
void ToggleSwitch::ChangeState()
{
  SwitchState = !SwitchState;
}

// Method that returns the current state of the switch
int ToggleSwitch::CurrentState()
{
  return(SwitchState);
}
```

397

The method that toggles the position of the switch (shown again in Code List CSV-4) uses the logical not operator to efficiently change the state of the switch. If the switch is on, the not operation will change the state of the switch to off. If the switch is off, the not operation will change the state of the switch to on.

CODE LIST CSV-4

```
// Method that toggles the position of the switch
void ToggleSwitch::ChangeState()
{
    SwitchState = !SwitchState;
}
```

Knobs

The knob object has three members: one to hold the current position, one to hold the minimum position, and one to hold the maximum position. Following the design, the class has three methods: one to turn the knob clockwise, one to turn the knob counterclockwise, and one that returns the current position. The definition of the knob class is shown in Figure CSV-5.

CODE LIST CSV-5

```
// KNOB.H
// Knob class definition

#ifndef _KNOB_H
#define _KNOB_H

class Knob
{
  public:
    Knob(int UpperBound, int LowerBound); // constructor
    Knob(Knob & k);   // copy constructor

    void TurnClockwise();        // turn knob to the right
    void TurnCounterClockwise(); // turn knob to the left
    int  CurrentPosition();      // return current knob position

  private:
    int Current,  // current knob position
 Minimum,        // minimum allowed knob position
 Maximum;        // maximum allowed knob position
};

#endif
```

The constructor in the knob class requires that the minimum and maximum values be provided. The same knob class will be used to create knobs for the radio's volume control and the tuner (station selector). The implementation of the knob class is shown in Code List CSV-6.

CODE LIST CSV-6

```
// KNOB.CPP
// Knob class implementation

#include "knob.h"

// Constructor
Knob::Knob(int LowerBound, int UpperBound)
:Minimum(LowerBound), Maximum(UpperBound), Current(LowerBound)
{
}

// Copy constructor
Knob::Knob(Knob & k)
:Minimum(k.Minimum), Maximum(k.Maximum), Current(k.Current)
{
}

// Method that turns the knob clockwise by one notch unless
// the upper bound has been reached
void Knob::TurnClockwise()
{
  if(Current < Maximum)
    Current++;
}

// Method that turns the knob counterclockwise by one notch
// unless the lower bound has been reached
void Knob::TurnCounterClockwise()
{
  if(Current > Minimum)
    Current--;
}

// Method that returns the current knob position
int Knob::CurrentPosition()
{
  return(Current);
}
```

If an attempt is made to turn the knob beyond the minimum or maximum settings, the value does not change. Before the current setting is incremented or decremented in the object, the current position is checked against the bounds to make sure the knob has not reached the upper or lower bound.

399

Amplifier

The class definition for the amplifier is shown in Code List CSV-7.

CODE LIST CSV-7

```
// AMP.H
// Amplifier class definition

#ifndef _AMPLIFIER_H
#define _AMPLIFIER_H

#include "on_off.h" // defines the constants ON and OFF

class Amplifier
{
  public:
    Amplifier(); // constructor

    void On();                 // turn amplifier on
    void Off();                // turn amplifier off
    void Volume(int NewVolume); // set amplifier volume
    int  CurrentVolume();      // return current volume

  private:
    int power, // power status (on or off)
  volume;    // volume level
};

#endif
```

The class uses separate methods for turning the amplifier on and off. The third method sets the amplifier volume, and the `CurrentVolume` method returns the current volume of the amplifier. The implementation is shown in Code List CSV-8.

CODE LIST CSV-8

```
// AMP.CPP
// Amplifier class implementation

#include "amp.h"

// Constructor
Amplifier::Amplifier()
:power(OFF), volume(0)
{
}

// Method that turns on the amplifier
void Amplifier::On()
{
  power = ON;
```

CODE LIST CSV-8 (continued)

```
  }

  // Method that turns off the amplifier
  void Amplifier::Off()
  {
    power = OFF;
  }

  // Method that sets a new amplifier volume
  void Amplifier::Volume(int NewVolume)
  {
    if(power == ON)
      volume = NewVolume;
  }

  // Method that returns the current volume setting
  int Amplifier::CurrentVolume()
  {
    return(volume);
  }
```

The amplifier's constructor (shown again in Code List CSV-9) accepts no arguments. When instantiated, the amplifier is initialized as being off and having a volume setting of zero.

CODE LIST CSV-9

```
  // Constructor
  Amplifier::Amplifier()
  :power(OFF), volume(0)
  {
  }
```

Tuner

The tuner class is similar to the amplifier class. The amplifier can be on or off and can have a frequency (station dial position) passed to it. The class definition is shown in Code List CSV-10.

CODE LIST CSV-10

```
  // TUNER.H
  // Tuner class definition

  #ifndef _TUNER_H
  #define _TUNER_H

  #include "on_off.h"  // defines the constants ON and OFF
```

401

```
class Tuner
{
  public:
    Tuner();   // constructor

    void   On();   // turn tuner on
    void   Off(); // turn tuner off
    void   Frequency(double NewFrequency); // set tuner frequency
    double CurrentFrequency(); // return current tuner frequency

  private:
    int power;           // power status (on or off)
    double frequency; // stores tuner frequency
};

#endif
```

The implementation of the class is shown in Code List CSV-11.

CODE LIST CSV-11

```
// TUNER.CPP
// Tuner class implementation

#include "tuner.h"

// Constructor
Tuner::Tuner()
:power(OFF), frequency(0.0)
{
}

// Method to turn the tuner on
void Tuner::On()
{
  power = ON;
}

// Method to turn the tuner off
void Tuner::Off()
{
  power = OFF;
}

// Method to set the tuner to a new frequency
void Tuner::Frequency(double NewFrequency)
{
  if(power == ON)
    frequency = NewFrequency;
```

```
      }

      // Method to return the current frequency
      double Tuner::CurrentFrequency()
      {
        return(frequency);
      }
```

Display

The display on an actual radio constantly displays the station and other information as long as the radio is on. Because our radio is a simple simulation, the display class will display only the current frequency. The radio class will display the status of the other components of the radio. The class definition is shown in Code List CSV-12.

CODE LIST CSV-12

```
      // DISPLAY.H
      // Radio display class definition

      #ifndef _DISPLAY_H
      #define _DISPLAY_H

      #include <iostream.h>
      #include <iomanip.h>
      #include <string.h>
      #include "on_off.h"   // defines the constants ON and OFF

      class Display
      {
        public:
          Display();   // constructor

          void On();   // turn display on
          void Off(); // turn display off
          void FrequencyToDisplay(double value); // set message
          void DisplayMessage(ostream &); // display message

        private:
          int    power;       // power status (on or off)
          double MyValue;     // frequency value for display
      };

      #endif
```

The display class demonstrates how output streams can be passed to an object. Look at the implementation in Code List CSV-13. Notice how the `DisplayMessage` method allows you to pass an output stream, such as `cout`, to the function. The function outputs the frequency setting to whatever output stream is passed to the function. By making it possible to pass the output stream, the same object can be used to print to the screen or to an output file or other output device.

CODE LIST CSV-13

```cpp
// DISPLAY.CPP
// Display class implementation

#include "display.h"

// Constructor
Display::Display()
:power(OFF), MyValue(0.0)
{
}

// Method that turns on the radio's display
void Display::On()
{
  power = ON;
}

// Method that turns off the radio's display
void Display::Off()
{
  power = OFF;
}

// Method that creates the message for displaying the
// tuner frequency
void Display::FrequencyToDisplay(double value)
{
  MyValue = value;
}

// Method that displays the tuner frequency
void Display::DisplayMessage(ostream & out)
{
  out.setf(ios::fixed); // prevent E-notation
  out << setprecision(1) << MyValue << " MHz";
  out.unsetf(ios::fixed);
}
```

Radio Object

The radio object includes instances of all of the other classes we have analyzed in this case study. Therefore, the radio object is an example of containment. The radio object does not inherit the properties of the other objects. It does, however, contain instances of the other objects. For example, you cannot say that the radio is a knob, but the radio has a knob. The radio class definition is shown in Code List CSV-14.

CODE LIST CSV-14

```
// RADIO.H
// Radio class definition

#ifndef _RADIO_H
#define _RADIO_H

#include <iostream.h>
#include "on_off.h"   // defines the constants ON and OFF
#include "tswitch.h"  // toggle switch class
#include "knob.h"      // knob class
#include "amp.h"       // amplifier class
#include "tuner.h"     // tuner class
#include "display.h"  // display class


class Radio
{
  public:
    Radio(); // constructor

    void Update();   // updates the status of components
    void DisplayStatus(ostream &);   // displays radio status

    ToggleSwitch Power;   // power switch
    Knob Volume;           // volume knob
    Frequency;             // tuner knob

  private:
    Amplifier    MyAmp;       // amplifier
    Tuner        MyTuner;    // tuner
    Display      MyDisplay;  // radio display
};

#endif
```

Because the radio object contains all previously created objects, it needs to know what members and methods they have and how they work. Therefore, the header files for all objects used in the radio object must be included in the definition.

The radio object instantiates one toggle switch object to be the power switch, two knobs (one for volume and one for the channel), an amplifier object, a tuner object, and a display object. To keep the object simple, there are only two methods and one constructor. One method updates the components of the radio to match the knob and switch settings. The other method displays the status of the radio's components. The implementation of the radio class is shown in Code List CSV-15.

```
// RADIO.CPP
// Radio class implementation

#include "radio.h"

// Constructor for radio object
Radio::Radio()
:Power(OFF), Volume(1,10), Frequency(1,103)
{
}

// Method to update the status of the radio object
void Radio::Update()
{
  if(Power.CurrentState() == OFF)
  { // If power is off, make sure each component is off
    MyAmp.Off();
    MyTuner.Off();
    MyDisplay.Off();
  }
  else
  { // If power is on, make sure each component is on
    MyAmp.On();
    MyTuner.On();
    MyDisplay.On();

    // Set volume to the current volume knob position
    MyAmp.Volume(Volume.CurrentPosition());
    // Set frequency to the current tuner knob position
    MyTuner.Frequency( (Frequency.CurrentPosition() * 0.2) + 87.3 );
    // Set display message to reflect current frequency
    MyDisplay.FrequencyToDisplay( MyTuner.CurrentFrequency());
  }
}

// Method to display the current status of the radio
void Radio::DisplayStatus(ostream & out)
{
  Update(); // Execute Update method to ensure that all
            // components are operating at current knob settings.
  if(Power.CurrentState() == OFF)
  {                                  // If power is off,
    out << "Radio:" << endl    // display message indicating
        << "------"  << endl    // that the power is off.
        << "Power: OFF" << endl
        << endl;
  }
  else
  {
    out.setf(ios::fixed);      // If power is on,
    out << "Radio:" << endl    // display current settings.
```

CODE LIST CSV-15 (continued)

```
          << "------" << endl
          << "Power: ON" << endl
          << "Volume: " << MyAmp.CurrentVolume() << endl
          << "Frequency: " << setprecision(1) << MyTuner.CurrentFrequency()
          << endl << "Display: [ ";
        out.unsetf(ios::fixed);

        MyDisplay.DisplayMessage(cout);  // Activate the radio's display

        out << " ]" << endl << endl;
    }
}
```

The constructor for the radio class (shown again in Code List CSV-16) initializes the radio's power to off and sets the ranges for the volume and tuner knobs. The volume is a straightforward range of 1 to 10. The tuner knob allows a range of 1 to 103. These values do not directly relate to the frequency of FM radio stations. The FM stations range from approximately 87.5 to 107.9. A formula will be used to convert the knob position to a station in the acceptable range of stations.

CODE LIST CSV-16

```
// Constructor for radio object
Radio::Radio()
:Power(OFF), Volume(1,10), Frequency(1,103)
{
}
```

The Update method reacts based on the position of the power switch. If the power is off, the function makes sure that all the radio's components are off. If the power is on, the code shown again in Code List CSV-17 is executed.

CODE LIST CSV-17

```
    { // If power is on, make sure each component is on
      MyAmp.On();
      MyTuner.On();
      MyDisplay.On();

      // Set volume to the current volume knob position
      MyAmp.Volume(Volume.CurrentPosition());
      // Set frequency to the current tuner knob position
      MyTuner.Frequency( (Frequency.CurrentPosition() * 0.2) + 87.3 );
      // Set display message to reflect current frequency
      MyDisplay.FrequencyToDisplay( MyTuner.CurrentFrequency());
    }
}
```

407

First, the program makes sure that the amplifier, tuner, and display are turned on. Then statements are executed to set the amplifier, tuner, and display to the appropriate values. To set the tuner frequency, the knob setting is multiplied by 0.2 and added to 87.3. Because the knob ranges from 1 to 103, the resulting frequency range is 87.5 to 107.9, and the stations increment in steps of 0.2.

The `DisplayStatus` method also reacts based on the power switch position. If the power is off, a message to that effect is displayed. If the power is on, the status of each device is reported and the display object is activated to display the station.

The OORADIO Program

The **OORADIO.CPP** program (see Code List CSV-18) is a procedural program that makes use of the radio object. Recall that C++ is considered to be a hybrid language rather than a strictly object-oriented language. The **OORADIO.CPP** program instantiates a radio object, but defines no class itself. Notice also that **OORADIO.CPP** includes only `iostream.h` and `radio.h`. We do not have to include the classes that the radio object uses.

CODE LIST CSV-18

```
// OORADIO.CPP
// Object-Oriented Radio Case Study
// Written by Greg Buxkemper
//

#include <iostream.h>
#include "radio.h"

void DisplayMenu();

int main()
{
  int    MenuChoice;
  Radio MyRadio;     // instantiate radio object

  do{
      DisplayMenu();
      cout << "Choice: ";
      cin >> MenuChoice;
      cout << endl;

      switch(MenuChoice)
      {
       case 0 :  break;
       case 1 :  MyRadio.Power.ChangeState();
          break;
       case 2 :  MyRadio.Volume.TurnClockwise();
          break;
       case 3 :  MyRadio.Volume.TurnCounterClockwise();
          break;
       case 4 :  MyRadio.Frequency.TurnClockwise();
          break;
       case 5 :  MyRadio.Frequency.TurnCounterClockwise();
          break;
       case 6 :  MyRadio.DisplayStatus(cout);
```

CODE LIST CSV-18 (continued)

```
                cout << endl;
                break;
            default:  cout << "Choice is not valid." << endl;
                break;
        }
    }while(MenuChoice != 0);

  return 0;
}


void DisplayMenu()
{
  cout << " 0 - Quit" << endl
        << " 1 - Toggle Power Switch" << endl
        << " 2 - Turn Volume Knob Up" << endl
        << " 3 - Turn Volume Knob Down" << endl
        << " 4 - Turn Frequency Knob Up" << endl
        << " 5 - Turn Frequency Knob Down" << endl
        << " 6 - View Radio Information" << endl;
}
```

The program iterates until the user chooses to quit the program. A simple menu gives the user the options for operating the radio, and then appropriate messages are sent to the radio object to handle the user's requests.

Modifying the Program

Here are some suggestions for modifying or extending the program.

1. Add error checking to the amplifier and tuner. Currently, the knobs and the radio object set the limits as to what the amplifier and tuner will accept as values. A better approach may be to allow the amplifier and tuner to set their own limits to ensure that the user of the amplifier and tuner objects does not misuse the objects.

2. Add the ability to have preset stations. You may want to allow the user to program the letters A, B, and C to change frequency to preset stations. You may even want to save the preset station information to a file to preserve it for the next time the program is run.

3. Add a graphical user interface. If the system on which you are programming allows you to create graphical user interfaces, you may want to put a "pretty face" on the program. You could also change the program to automatically update the display each time a control is accessed.

APPENDIX A

INTRODUCTION TO COMPUTERS AND THE INTERNET

The History of Computers

People have almost always looked for tools to aid in calculations. The human hand was probably the first tool used to help people count. And although the fingers are still used as counting tools, devices have been invented to make the job easier and to keep people from taking off their shoes when counting to twenty. Calculating tools evolved from manually-operated devices, to more complex mechanical devices, to electro-mechanical devices, and finally to electronic computers.

MANUALLY-OPERATED DEVICES

The abacus, shown in Figure A-1, may have existed as early as the third century A.D. However, the Chinese perfected it in the 12th century.

FIGURE A-1
The abacus is a manually-operated device used to aid in counting. The abacus is still in use in some parts of the world.

MECHANICAL DEVICES

In 1642, Blaise Pascal designed the first gear-driven counting machine. He was eighteen years old at the time. Blaise designed the machine in an attempt to make his father's work as a tax collector easier. The machine could add and subtract by using a series of interlocking wheels and gears. The wheels were marked with the numbers 0 through 9, and there was a wheel for the ones, tens, hundreds, and so on. Pascal named the machine the Pascaline, and he developed more than 50 versions of it. The principle behind the Pascaline was used in adding machines for the next 300 years.

In the early 1670s, the German mathematician Gottfried Wilhelm Leibniz invented a mechanical calculator that improved greatly on Pascal's design. Leibniz's calculator employed a crank on the side that simplified the repetitive operations necessary to multiply and divide.

In 1834, an English mathematician named Charles Babbage proposed the construction of an "Analytical Engine." Babbage's design was unique and could be characterized as the first general-purpose programmable computer.

If Babbage's Analytical Engine had been built, it would have included the use of punched cards to feed instructions to the machine. It also would have had the capability to calculate and store numbers. Punched cards and the capability to calculate and store numbers became standard features of many computers to follow.

ELECTRO-MECHANICAL DEVICES

Do you believe that necessity is the mother of invention? Well, if it had not been for a need that the United States Census Bureau had, the world of computing might have developed quite differently.

Tabulating the 1880 census took seven and a half years. The United States Census Bureau became convinced that a better way to tabulate the census had to be found. An employee of the census office in Washington D.C., named Herman Hollerith, spent the 1880s working on a machine that would tabulate census figures using punched cards. Hollerith had perfected his machine by 1890—and just in time. By 1890, the population of the U.S. had grown by 25% since 1880, to over 62 million people. Hollerith's machine performed a simple count of the population in only six weeks and full statistical analysis in two and a half years.

Hollerith's invention allowed him to start a company called the Tabulating Machine Company, which sold his machines to others. That company eventually became the International Business Machines Corporation (IBM).

Hollerith's machine was an electro-mechanical device that used gears and wheels and other mechanical parts, but was powered by electricity.

In 1944, IBM built the Mark I. The machine used a combination of electrical signals and mechanical gears to quickly add and subtract large numbers. The machine was 51 feet long and 8 feet high, and included almost 500 miles of wires. The Mark I was the most elaborate electro-mechanical computer ever built.

The era of electronic computers was about to dawn.

ELECTRONIC COMPUTERS

In 1946, the Electronic Numerical Integrator and Computer (ENIAC) was developed by John William Mauchly and John Presper Eckert. ENIAC was one of the first computers without mechanical parts.

Instead of mechanical switches and gears, ENIAC used electronic switching devices called vacuum tubes. Figure A-2 shows a row of vacuum tubes. Vacuum tubes made ENIAC about 1000 times faster than the Mark I.

The vacuum tube began the era of electronic computers.

By the late 1950s, the transistor began to replace the vacuum tube in computers (see Figure A-3). Transistors accomplish the same work as vacuum tubes, but are smaller and faster. The transistor also proved to be more reliable than vacuum tubes, which had to be replaced often.

FIGURE A-3
Transistors were a faster, smaller, and more reliable alternative to the vacuum tube.

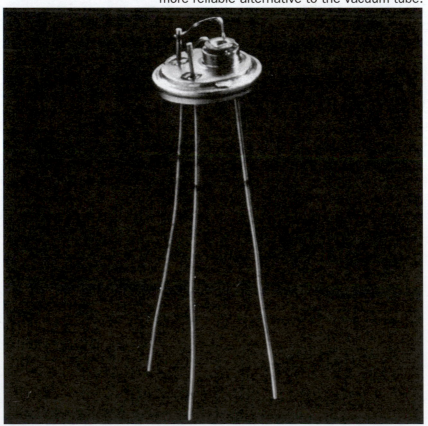

In the 1960s the integrated circuit, commonly called a chip, was developed. An integrated circuit is a thin slice of photo-sensitive silicon, usually smaller than a dime, upon which microscopic circuits have been inscribed. The first integrated circuits usually performed only one function, such as adding. But in the 1970s, designers began to put multiple functions on a single chip. Soon, nearly all of the main functions of a computer were placed on a single chip. This new invention was called the microprocessor, shown in Figure A-4.

FIGURE A-4
The microprocessor is the device that put computers within reach of small businesses and individuals.

A revolution began as manufacturers started building complete computer systems that had microprocessors at their core. The first microcomputers became available in the 1970s.

Since the 1970s, microcomputers have evolved more rapidly than ever. Each new model does more and costs less than the one before. The timeline below shows some of the major events in microcomputers from 1975 to the early 1990s. You may not recognize many of the items on the timeline. That is because most of them quickly became history. The timeline is intended to show you how rapidly the industry has evolved since the 1970s. The computers you are using today will probably become obsolete as quickly as the computers in this timeline.

1971   ■ The first microprocessor (the Intel 4004)

1975   ■ The first real microcomputer (the Altair 8800)

1976   ■ Apple I appears and Apple Computer is founded

1977   ■ Apple II

1978   ■ Epson introduces the first affordable dot-matrix printer

1979   ■ Intel 8088 microprocessor (later used in the first IBM PC)

        ■ Motorola 68000 microprocessor (later used in the first Macintosh)

1980	■ Apple III
1981	■ IBM PC
	■ Hayes Smartmodem 300
1982	■ Intel 80286 microprocessor
1983	■ Apple IIe
	■ IBM PC/XT
1984	■ Macintosh
	■ Apple IIc
	■ IBM AT
	■ Motorola 68020 microprocessor
1985	■ Commodore Amiga 1000
1986	■ Intel 80386 microprocessor
	■ Motorola 68030 microprocessor
1987	■ IBM PS/2
1989	■ Intel 80486 microprocessor
1990	■ Motorola 68040 microprocessor
1993	■ Intel Pentium microprocessor
	■ PowerPC 601 microprocessor
1995	■ PowerPC 603 microprocessor
1997	■ Intel Pentium II microprocessor
	■ PowerPC G3 microprocessor
1999	■ Intel Pentium III microprocessor
	■ PowerPC G4 microprocessor
2000	■ Intel Pentium 4 microprocessor

Computers Today

Today computers are everywhere. Both large and small businesses use computers for everything from word processing and bookkeeping to desktop publishing. Computers are used at home for personal finance, correspondence, education, entertainment, and more. Because computers have become inexpensive to make, they have also become a part of many products we buy. Special-purpose computers are usually made to carry out a specific task, whereas other computers are made to be programmed for a variety of tasks.

COMPUTERS FOR SPECIFIC PURPOSES

Computers can now be found in our wristwatches, cameras, televisions, and VCRs. In automobiles, computers control fuel injection and the spark plugs. Computers monitor everything from fuel efficiency to the comfort of the passengers. Computers tell automatic transmissions when to shift gears. Computers can also help you quickly change from one radio station to another.

Specific-purpose computers can be used for little else other than what they are designed to accomplish. For example, the computer in a camera calculates the settings and exposure time required for a perfect photograph, but it can't help you with your math homework. The computer in your VCR will remember to record your favorite show Tuesday night at 8 PM, but it can't remind you that you have a project due tomorrow.

GENERAL-PURPOSE COMPUTERS

The kind of machine most people think of when they hear the term computer looks something like Figure A-5. What makes this computer system so popular is that it can perform a wide variety of tasks. Computers like the one in Figure A-5 are general-purpose computers and can be programmed to perform many different tasks. General-purpose computers can balance checkbooks, perform calculations, schedule events, help you write letters, store important information, and (of course) play great games. Try to do all that with the computer in your car's transmission.

FIGURE A-5
A typical workstation includes a monitor, keyboard, mouse, and system unit.

SYSTEM COMPONENTS

The equipment that makes up a computer is called hardware. Each piece of hardware is involved in one of four tasks: input, output, processing, or storage.

INPUT AND OUTPUT

All computers, whether on your wrist or on your desk, interact with someone or something. Interaction involves getting information and giving a response. In a computer, this interaction is called input and output. For example, input could be a user entering customer names and addresses into a database program. An example of output would be the printing of mailing labels from a database.

A desktop computer interacts primarily with people. A typical desktop computer interacts using a keyboard, a mouse, speakers, a monitor, and a printer. Some desktop computers may also have other input and output devices, such as a microphone or modem. A modem, which is a device that allows interaction to occur between computers over the telephone, is capable of both input and output.

The keyboard, mouse, and microphone are input devices. The computer uses these devices to get information and instructions from the person using the computer (the user). The computer gives information back to the user via output devices, such as the monitor, printer, and speakers.

You may not have thought about speakers as an output device, but they have become an important way for the computer to give information to the user. Early computers were incapable of sophisticated sound output. They could only beep. Now multimedia computers speak, play music, and have sound cards that add realism to games.

When you think of computer input and output, you may think of data going in and answers coming out. For example, a program might receive the temperature in Fahrenheit as input and then convert it to provide the temperature in Celsius as output. But even a game has input and output. The keys you strike, or the movement of a mouse or joystick, is the input. The image on the monitor and sound through the speakers is the output.

PROCESSING AND STORAGE

At the heart of the computer, the inputs are processed and stored, and output is created. This is accomplished using a variety of devices such as a microprocessor, RAM, ROM, a bus, and disk drives. In the next section, you will learn more about these devices and how they work together.

NETWORKS AND THE INTERNET

Individual computers, working alone, can accomplish very sophisticated tasks. However, when groups of computers work together, expanded opportunities present themselves. Connecting computers together is called networking. Networks are groups of computers that are connected by some communications link that allows them to share data or hardware resources. For example, two or more computers in an office or school can be networked so that hard drive space or printers can be shared. A network can also reach around the world. Every day, computers communicate with each other over phone lines (using modems), over special wires, or even using satellites.

Networks allow computer users to send electronic mail (e-mail) to other computer users in the same building or on the other side of the planet. Networks allow programs and data to be shared quickly and efficiently.

The Internet is a network of networks. Because the Internet is world-wide, it allows information, e-mail, messages, and files to be exchanged by anyone in the world whose computer has access to the Internet. Today there are many ways to obtain an Internet connection. The traditional modem dialing up over a standard analog phone line is becoming less common as broadband connections are available in several varieties.

1. What manually-operated calculating device existed prior to the 12th century A.D.?

2. List two mechanical calculating devices.

3. What is the name of the most elaborate electro-mechanical computer ever built?

4. What type of computers replaced electro-mechanical computers?

5. What device replaced the vacuum tube?

6. What device integrated nearly all of the main functions of a computer on a single chip?

7. During what decade did the first microcomputers become available?

8. List two devices used for input in a general-purpose computer.

9. List three devices that can provide output from a general-purpose computer.

10. List two devices involved in either processing or storage in a general-purpose computer.

APPENDIX B

ASCII TABLE

ASCII Character	Decimal	Hexadecimal	Binary
NUL	0	00	000 0000
SOH	1	01	000 0001
STX	2	02	000 0010
ETX	3	03	000 0011
EOT	4	04	000 0100
ENQ	5	05	000 0101
ACK	6	06	000 0110
BEL	7	07	000 0111
BS	8	08	000 1000
HT	9	09	000 1001
LF	10	0A	000 1010
VT	11	0B	000 1011
FF	12	0C	000 1100
CR	13	0D	000 1101
SO	14	0E	000 1110
SI	15	0F	000 1111
DLE	16	10	001 0000
DC1	17	11	001 0001
DC2	18	12	001 0010
DC3	19	13	001 0011
DC4	20	14	001 0100
NAK	21	15	001 0101

ASCII Character	Decimal	Hexadecimal	Binary
SYN	22	16	001 0110
ETB	23	17	001 0111
CAN	24	18	001 1000
EM	25	19	001 1001
SUB	26	1A	001 1010
ESC	27	1B	001 1011
FS	28	1C	001 1100
GS	29	1D	001 1101
RS	30	1E	001 1110
US	31	1F	001 1111
space	32	20	010 0000
!	33	21	010 0001
"	34	22	010 0010
#	35	23	010 0011
$	36	24	010 0100
%	37	25	010 0101
&	38	26	010 0110
'	39	27	010 0111
(	40	28	010 1000
)	41	29	010 1001
*	42	2A	010 1010
+	43	2B	010 1011
,	44	2C	010 1100
-	45	2D	010 1101
.	46	2E	010 1110
/	47	2F	010 1111
0	48	30	011 0000

ASCII Character	Decimal	Hexadecimal	Binary
1	49	31	011 0001
2	50	32	011 0010
3	51	33	011 0011
4	52	34	011 0100
5	53	35	011 0101
6	54	36	011 0110
7	55	37	011 0111
8	56	38	011 1000
9	57	39	011 1001
:	58	3A	011 1010
;	59	3B	011 1011
<	60	3C	011 1100
=	61	3D	011 1101
>	62	3E	011 1110
?	63	3F	011 1111
@	64	40	100 0000
A	65	41	100 0001
B	66	42	100 0010
C	67	43	100 0011
D	68	44	100 0100
E	69	45	100 0101
F	70	46	100 0110
G	71	47	100 0111
H	72	48	100 1000
I	73	49	100 1001
J	74	4A	100 1010

ASCII Character	Decimal	Hexadecimal	Binary
K	75	4B	100 1011
L	76	4C	100 1100
M	77	4D	100 1101
N	78	4E	100 1110
O	79	4F	100 1111
P	80	50	101 0000
Q	81	51	101 0001
R	82	52	101 0010
S	83	53	101 0011
T	84	54	101 0100
U	85	55	101 0101
V	86	56	101 0110
W	87	57	101 0111
X	88	58	101 1000
Y	89	59	101 1001
Z	90	5A	101 1010
[	91	5B	101 1011
\	92	5C	101 1100
]	93	5D	101 1101
^	94	5E	101 1110
_	95	5F	101 1111
`	96	60	110 0000
a	97	61	110 0001
b	98	62	110 0010
c	99	63	110 0011
d	100	64	110 0100

ASCII Character	Decimal	Hexadecimal	Binary
e	101	65	110 0101
f	102	66	110 0110
g	103	67	110 0111
h	104	68	110 1000
i	105	69	110 1001
j	106	6A	110 1010
k	107	6B	110 1011
l	108	6C	110 1100
m	109	6D	110 1101
n	110	6E	110 1110
o	111	6F	110 1111
p	112	70	111 0000
q	113	71	111 0001
r	114	72	111 0010
s	115	73	111 0011
t	116	74	111 0100
u	117	75	111 0101
v	118	76	111 0110
w	119	77	111 0111
x	120	78	111 1000
y	121	79	111 1001
z	122	7A	111 1010
{	123	7B	111 1011
		124	7C	111 1100
}	125	7D	111 1101
~	126	7E	111 1110
DEL	127	7F	111 1111

THE BINARY NUMBER SYSTEM

Overview

Data is a computer representation of something that exists in the real world. For example, data can be values such as money, measurements, quantities, or a high score. Data can also be alphabetic, such as names and addresses or a business letter.

In a computer, all data is represented by numbers, and the numbers are represented electronically in the computer. To understand how electrical signals become numbers, let's begin by looking at a simple electric circuit that everyone is familiar with: a switch controlling a light bulb.

From Circuits to Numbers

When you think of an electric circuit, you probably think of it being either on or off; for example, a light bulb is turned on and off by a switch. The light bulb can exist in two conditions: on or off. In technical terms, the light bulb has two states.

Imagine you had two light bulbs on two switches. With two light bulbs there are four possible states, as shown in Figure C-1. You could assign a number to each of the states and represent the numbers 0 through 3.

FIGURE C-1
There are four light combinations possible with two light bulbs.

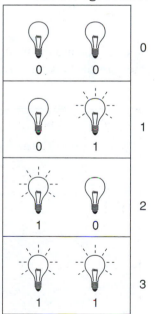

You can't do much using only the numbers 0 through 3, but if more circuits are added, the number of states increases. For example, Figure C-2 shows how three circuits can represent the numbers 0 through 7 because there are eight possible states.

FIGURE C-2
There are eight light combinations possible with three light bulbs.

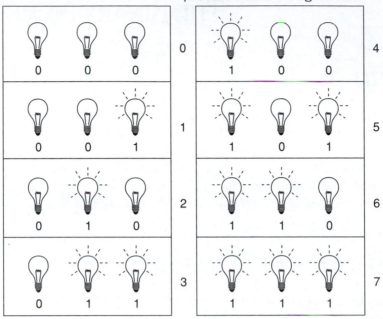

If you are the mathematical type, you may have noticed that the number of states is determined by the formula 2^n where n is the number of circuits (see Table C-1).

TABLE C-1

Number of Circuits	Number of States	Numbers That Can Be Represented
1	$2^1 = 2$	0,1
2	$2^2 = 4$	0..3
3	$2^3 = 8$	0..7
4	$2^4 = 16$	0..15
5	$2^5 = 32$	0..31
6	$2^6 = 64$	0..63
7	$2^7 = 128$	0..127
8	$2^8 = 256$	0..255

Now, instead of lights, think about circuits in the computer. A single circuit in a computer is like a single light; it can be on or off. A special number system, called the binary number system, is used to represent numbers with groups of these circuits. In the binary number system each binary digit, called a bit for short, is either a 0 or a 1. As shown in Figure C-3, circuits that are off are defined as 0, and circuits that are on are defined as 1. Binary digits (bits) are combined into groups of eight bits called bytes.

FIGURE C-3

In the computer, signals that are off are defined as 0 and signals that are on are defined as 1.

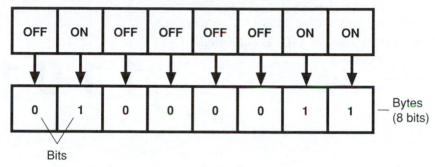

If a byte is made up of eight bits, then there are 256 possible combinations of those eight bits representing the numbers 0 through 255 (see Table C-1). Even though 255 is not a small number, it is definitely not the largest number you will ever use. So to represent larger numbers, computers group bytes together.

Binary vs. Decimal

The binary number system may seem strange to you because you count using the decimal number system, which uses the digits 0 through 9. Counting in the decimal number system comes very naturally to you because you learned it from a very young age. But someone invented the decimal number system just like someone invented the binary number system. The decimal number system is based on tens because you have ten fingers on your hands. The binary number system is based on twos because of the circuits in a computer. Both systems, however, can be used to represent the same values.

In the decimal number system, each digit of a number represents a power of 10. That is why the decimal number system is also called the base 10 number system. Consider the number 3208, for example. When you read that number, you automatically understand it to mean three thousands, two hundreds, no tens, and eight ones. Represented mathematically, you could say $(3 \times 1000) + (2 \times 100) + (0 \times 10) + (8 \times 1) = 3208$, as shown in Figure C-4.

FIGURE C-4

Each digit of the decimal number 3208 represents a power of 10.

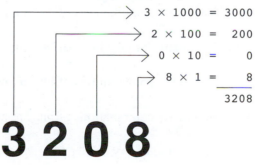

In the binary number system, each digit represents a power of 2, like you saw in Table C-1. Working with powers of 2 is not as natural to you as working with powers of 10. But with a little practice you will see that base 2 numbers are not so mysterious. Consider the binary number 1101. Even though the number is four digits long, its value is nowhere near a thousand. The powers of 2 are 1, 2, 4, 8, 16, 32, and so on. So for this number, its decimal equivalent is $(1 \times 8) + (1 \times 4) + (0 \times 2) + (1 \times 1) = 13$, as shown in Figure C-5. So the binary number 1101 is equivalent to 13 in the decimal number system.

FIGURE C-5

Each digit of the binary number 1101 represents a power of 2, so conversion to the decimal system is easy.

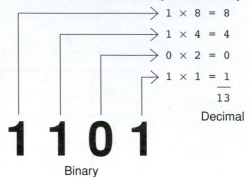

Decimal Points and Binary Points

You have used decimal points for a long time. Did you know there is a binary point? A decimal point divides the ones place and the tenths place, or 10^0 from 10^{-1}. There is an equivalent in the binary number system called the binary point. It divides the 2^0 place from the 2^{-1} place.

With a binary point, it is possible to have binary numbers like 100.1, which in decimal is 4.5. Can you convert the binary number 10.01 to decimal? If you got 2.25 as the answer, you are correct. Try converting the binary number 11.001001 to decimal.

REVIEW QUESTIONS

1. How many bits are in a byte?

2. How many combinations of bits are possible with three bits?

3. How many combinations of bits are possible with four bits?

4. How many combinations of bits are possible with five bits?

5. How many combinations of bits are possible with six bits?

6. Convert the binary number 1010 to decimal.

7. Convert the binary number 10001 to decimal.

8. Convert the binary number 101111 to decimal.

9. Convert the binary number 11111111 to decimal.

APPENDIX D

THE PROGRAMMING PROCESS

Overview

Programmers are always tempted to immediately begin writing code to solve a problem. There is a better way. Sure, if you are writing a program to print your name on the screen a million times you might get by with just sitting down and keying in a program. But most programs are more complicated, and therefore a more structured and disciplined approach to programming is necessary.

Although there are different approaches used by different programmers, most good programmers follow five basic steps when developing programs:

1. Define the problem.

2. Develop an algorithm.

3. Code the program.

4. Test and debug the program.

5. Document and maintain the program.

Defining the Problem

Defining the problem to be solved requires an understanding of what the program is to accomplish.

For example, a program that calculates interest on a loan is fairly easy to define. Start by identifying the inputs and outputs. As input, the program needs the loan amount, the interest rate, and the number of months that the money is to be borrowed. A specific known formula can be applied to the data, and the amount of interest is the output.

Many programs are more difficult to define. Suppose you are defining a game program that involves characters in a maze. In your definition, the abilities of each character must be defined. In addition, the maze and how the characters interact with the maze and each other must also be defined. The list goes on and on.

Imagine how much there is to define before writing a program to handle airline reservations for a world-wide airline or the software that controls the launch of the space shuttle. Before any part of the program is written, the programmer must know exactly what the goal is.

Defining the problem does not take into consideration how the program will do the job, just what the job is. Exactly how a program accomplishes its work is addressed in the second step of the process.

Developing an Algorithm

The second step in the programming process is to develop an algorithm. An *algorithm* is a set of sequential instructions that are followed to solve a problem. Algorithms have been commonly used for years. A recipe for baking a cake, instructions for assembling a bicycle, and directions to a shopping mall are all examples of algorithms. The directions to a mall, shown in Figure D-1, are a set of steps that you execute sequentially.

FIGURE D-1
This algorithm leads you to a shopping mall.

Drive south on University Avenue to 50th Street.
Turn right (west) on 50th.
Drive west on 50th to Slide Road.
Turn left (south) on Slide Road.
Drive south on Slide Road until you see the mall entrance on your right.

Some algorithms involve decisions that change the course of action or cause parts of the algorithm to be repeated. Consider the algorithm for parking the car once you reach the mall. A more complicated algorithm is best illustrated with symbols in a flowchart as shown in Figure D-2.

FIGURE D-2
Some steps in an algorithm may be repeated many times.

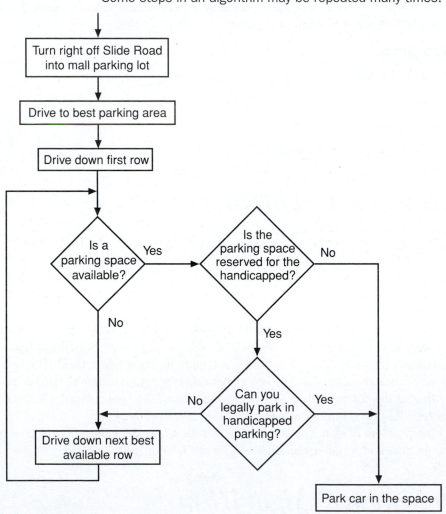

Programming a computer requires that you create an algorithm. The instructions the program gives the computer must tell the computer exactly what steps to do and in what order to do them. The computer executes each instruction sequentially, except when an instruction causes the flow of logic to jump to another part of the program.

When first developing an algorithm, you should avoid the temptation of initially writing in a programming language. A better method is to use pseudocode. *Pseudocode* expresses an algorithm in everyday English, rather than in a programming language. Pseudocode makes it possible for you to describe the instructions to be executed by the program. The precise choice of words and punctuation, however, is less important. Figure D-3 is an example of pseudocode for a mathematical program that prompts the user for an integer (a whole number without any decimal places) and squares it.

FIGURE D-3

Pseudocode allows you to develop an algorithm without being concerned about the commands and punctuation of a programming language.

```
declare j and k as integers
prompt user for j
l = j * k
print l
```

Depending on the complexity of your program, developing algorithms can be a quick process or the most time-consuming part of developing your program. Later you will learn methods programmers use to break down complex problems into manageable parts.

Coding the Program

An algorithm's pseudocode is next translated into program code. Most of this book teaches you the commands and structures you need to translate algorithms into actual programs.

Errors can be made during coding that can prevent the program from successfully compiling and linking. So part of the coding step involves resolving errors that prevent the program from running.

A common error is called a syntax error. A *syntax error* occurs when you key a command or some other part of the program incorrectly. Computers must be told exactly what to do. If someone leaves you a note that says "Lock the back dore before you leave," you will be able to figure out what the instruction means. However, when the computer recognizes a syntax error, the programmer is notified immediately. Everything has to be just right or the computer will not accept it.

There are other errors that the computer may detect when compiling. Most of them are easily resolved. When all of those errors are resolved, the program will compile, link, and be ready to run. Even if a program runs, it may still fail to do its job correctly. That is where the next step of the programming process comes in.

Testing and Debugging

Testing and debugging is an important step that is too often ignored. Programs typically fail to operate 100% correctly the first time they are compiled or interpreted. Logic errors and other hidden problems called bugs must be located. Software must be tested and "debugged" to make sure the output is correct and reliable.

 Did You Know?

Back when computers used vacuum tubes, the heat and light generated by the tubes sometimes attracted bugs such as moths. The bugs sometimes caused short circuits, resulting in the need to "debug" the computer.

One way to test a program is to provide input for which the results are known. For example, a program that converts meters to feet can be easily tested by giving the program input values for which you know the output. Carefully select a wide variety of inputs. Use values that are larger or smaller than those which are typical. Use zero and negative numbers as inputs when allowable.

You should also test every part of a program. Make sure you provide input that tests every line of your code. Test each part of the program repeatedly to make sure that consistent results are obtained.

A type of error that can cause your program to stop running (or crash) is called a run-time error. A *run-time error* occurs when a program gives the computer an instruction that it is incapable of executing. A run-time error may lead to a program "crash." For example, if your program tries to divide a number by zero, a run-time error will occur on most systems. A run-time error could also occur if the system runs out of memory while your program is running.

You will experience lots of bugs and errors as a programmer. They are a part of every programmer's day. Even the best programmers spend lots of time testing and debugging. Throughout this book you will be warned of possible pitfalls and bugs so that you can avoid as many as possible. However, the best way to learn how to avoid bugs is to experience them.

Documenting and Maintaining the Program

This fifth step applies mostly to programs used in the real world. But since you may someday write such programs, you should be aware of this step as well. Programmers must document their work so that they and other programmers can make changes or updates later. Documentation may also have to be written for the program's users.

You should document your programs while you are programming and avoid saving the task for last. The time to write documentation for a program is while you are programming. By the time you finish the programming, you may have already forgotten some of what you did.

You may also be less likely to write proper documentation once a program is complete. You may think your time is better spent on another project. However, you will be pleased to have the documentation when it is needed.

Documentation in the Program

Documentation that is included in the program itself is very important. Virtually all programming languages allow comments to be included in the source code. The comments are ignored by the interpreter or the compiler. Therefore, the programmer can include notes and explanations that will make the program easier for people to read. You will learn how to use comments in your source code in this book.

Documentation Outside of the Program

Many times a program is complex enough that documents should be written that explain how the programming problem was solved. This documentation might be diagrams, flowcharts, or descriptions.

Documentation for the User

You have probably already been exposed to user documentation. Programs that are to be used by more than a few people usually include user documentation that explains the functions of the software.

Program Maintenance

Maintenance is an important part of the programming process. Most programs are written to help with a task. As the task changes, the program must also change. Users are likely to request that additions and changes be made to the program. Maintaining a program is an important part of the process because it keeps the programmer's work up to date and in use.

During the maintenance phase of the programming process, bugs may be found that were not uncovered during the testing and debugging phase. It is also possible that better ways to accomplish a task in the program may be discovered. It is important to understand that the steps of the programming process may be repeated in order to refine or repair an existing program.

REVIEW QUESTIONS

1. List the five basic steps in the programming process.

2. Give an example of an algorithm used in everyday life.

3. Define the term *bug* as it relates to programming.

4. What is the purpose of documentation inside a program?

5. Write an algorithm that gives directions from one location to another. Choose a starting point (your home, for example), and give detailed, step-by-step directions that will lead anyone who might be reading the algorithm to the correct destination.

6. Draw a flowchart that describes the steps you follow when you get up in the morning and get ready for your day. Include as many details as you want, including things such as hitting the snooze button on your alarm clock, brushing your teeth, and eating breakfast.

APPENDIX E

ORDER OF OPERATIONS

In Chapter 3, you learned about the order of operations for the math operators. The following chart is a more complete table of the order of operators of all types. The operators shown in each group (divided by a line) have the same precedence level. The group with the highest precedence appears at the top of the table. Under the *Associativity* heading, you can see whether the operators are evaluated from right to left or left to right. If the operator you are looking for does not appear in the table, check your compiler's documentation for a complete list. Note: Some of the operators in this table were not covered in this book. They are included for completeness.

Group	Symbol	Description	Associativity
Scope Resolution	::	scope-resolution operator	Left to right
Structure Operators	-> .	structure pointer operator dot operator	Left to right
Unary Operators	! + – & * ++ – – (*typecast*) sizeof new delete	logical negation unary plus unary minus address of dereferencing increment operator decrement operator typecasting sizeof operator memory allocation memory deallocation	Right to left
Multiplicative Operators	* / %	multiplication divide modulus	Left to right
Additive Operators	+ –	addition minus	Left to right
Relational Operators	< <= > >=	less than less than or equal to greater than greater than or equal to	Left to right
Equality	== !=	equal to not equal to	Left to right

(continued)

Group	Symbol	Description	Associativity
Logical AND	&&	logical AND	Left to right
Logical OR	||	logical OR	Left to right
Assignment	= *= /= %= += –=	assignment operator compound assign product compound assign quotient compound assign remainder compound assign sum compound assign difference	Right to left

APPENDIX F

THE BOOL DATA TYPE

The bool data type (discussed in Chapter 2) was not originally in the C++ language. Before the bool data type, programmers used integers for all true and false values. As you learned, false is represented by 0 and true is represented by 1.

Some older C++ compilers do not support the bool data type. If your compiler is among those compilers, there is an easy fix. On the data disk for this book is a file named **bool.h**. The contents of the file are shown below. If your compiler does not automatically support the bool data type, simply include **bool.h** in your program and an equivalent data type will be defined for you.

```
#ifndef _BOOL_H
#define _BOOL_H

typedef int bool;
const int FALSE = 0;
const int TRUE = 1;

#endif
```

The string class requires the bool data type. The **apstring.h** file includes the following statement.

```
//#include "bool.h"
```

By default, the `#include "bool.h"` statement is commented out of the string class. However, if your compiler does not support the bool data type, simply remove the slashes and the **bool.h** file will be included.

USING A DEBUGGER WHEN PROGRAMMING

What Is a Debugger?

A debugger is a program that helps programmers find errors in their programs. In many cases, a debugger is integrated into the compiler's programming environment to make it easy to use.

Debuggers offer many features that allow a programmer to see what is going on inside a running program. In this appendix, we'll concentrate on three of the most useful features: stepping through instructions, setting breakpoints, and watching variables.

Stepping Through Instructions

One of the most useful features of a debugger, especially for beginning programmers, is the ability to step through the lines of a program individually and see the effect each line has on the operation of the program. With this feature, the programmer can see the actual source code and control when the program executes the next line of code.

Stepping through instructions lets a programmer see things that otherwise would be difficult to verify, such as verifying that code within if structures is getting executed or watching the flow of logic through loops and function calls.

Setting Breakpoints

Another useful feature of a debugger is the ability to set a breakpoint. Setting a breakpoint is like putting a stop sign somewhere in your program. For example, if you are having trouble debugging a certain function, you can set a breakpoint that stops the program from executing at the point where that function is called. Once the program is stopped by the breakpoint, you can step through the instructions within that function to get a closer look at the problem area.

Watching Variables

Watching variables is particularly useful. While stepping through a program, you can select variables for which you would like to display their value as the program runs. The displayed values are updated each time you step through an instruction. As a result, you can see the value of a variable at any point in the program's execution.

APPENDIX H

NUMERICAL APPROXIMATIONS

Some mathematical problems require that an approximation be made because an exact answer cannot be found. Sometimes a result which is close to being correct is close enough. There are many methods of solving by approximation. In this appendix, we will look at two such methods: the bisection method of finding zeros of a function, and the Monte Carlo technique of using random data to find a nonrandom result.

Bisection Method

If you are using a computer, the bisection method is probably the fastest and most exact approach for finding where a continuous function $f(x)$ is equal to zero. The technique relies on the fact that an interval $x_1 \leq x < x_2$ has been found such that:

$$f(x_1) \leq 0 \leq f(x_2)$$

The method finds the root by continuously cutting the size of the interval in half. (See Figure H-1). This is accomplished by evaluating the function:

$$f\left(\frac{x_1 + x_2}{2}\right)$$

FIGURE H-1
The bisection method of finding the zeros of functions.

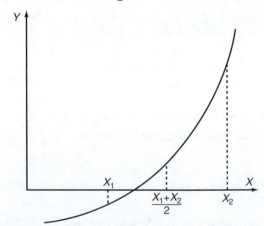

The above function is evaluated, and if it does not equal zero, the signs are compared. If the sign of $f(x_1)$ is different from that of the midpoint formula, the midpoint becomes the second endpoint. Meaning, $0.5 \, (x_1 + x_2)$ takes the place of x_2. This method effectively cuts the interval in half. This process is repeated until the root is found. The more times the interval is split in half, the more exact the root will be.

Monte Carlo Technique

The Monte Carlo technique relies on the generation of completely random numbers with a wide distribution. The best example as to how this technique works is finding the area of an oddly-shaped object. For example, suppose the area of the object in Figure H-2 needs to be found. We know the area of the square which contains the object. We can use the Monte Carlo technique to find the area of the oddly-shaped object.

FIGURE H-2
The Monte Carlo technique.

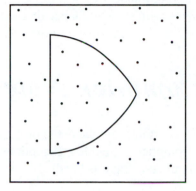

The Monte Carlo technique begins by choosing *n* random points within the square that contains the oddly-shaped object. These points are to be evenly distributed and completely random. Therefore, some of the points will fall inside the oddly-shaped object, and some will fall outside the object.

Let M represent the object for which you want to find the area. Let *N* be the number of points that are randomly distributed within the square and *F* be the number of points that fall in *M*. If the points are well distributed and completely random, the area of *M* can be found by taking the ratio *F/N*. In Figure H-2, 50 points were generated. Of those 50, 13 are inside *M*. This ratio is 13/50 or 26%. Therefore, the area of *M* is approximately 26% of the total area of the square.

Until the invention of the computer, this technique was not widely used because determining many random numbers is very time consuming. With the aid of a computer, however, determining random numbers is simplified. The more points that are used to determine the ratio, the more accurate the approximation.

APPENDIX I

C++ COMPILERS

Choosing, installing, and learning to use a C++ compiler may be the most difficult part of this course. This appendix will provide you with some guidance that will hopefully make the process easier. Additional information can be found at *http://www.programcpp.com/third*.

General C++ Compiler Notes

- Because C++ was written to be a portable language, the programs in this book can be run on DOS, Windows, Unix, or Macintosh compilers with a few exceptions. Minor inconsistencies may appear, especially in the way input and output is handled.

- Working with data files often exposes minor variations in the way C++ compilers handle input and output. Test data file input and output with your compiler before allowing students to begin that lesson.

- Use the most recent version of the compiler software your computer can run. Some older C++ compilers do not support the latest features of the language. For example, some older compilers do not support template classes, making it impossible to use the vector and matrix classes.

- Verify whether your compiler includes the bool data type. See Appendix F for more information about the bool data type.

- Most C++ compilers have a feature to group source code files into a project or workspace. When you begin to use classes, you will have to know how to create a project and add the required files to the project.

- Learning to use your compiler's debugger can be a powerful teaching tool. See Appendix G for more information about how to use a debugger.

- C++ has only basic screen formatting capabilities. Most compilers do not even include a Clear Screen command. The Web site mentioned above will have some pointers for you. As a general rule, however, you should not expect to be able to create intricately formatted output using standard C++ features.

- With some compilers, especially when running under Microsoft Windows, you may experience a situation where the output of your program appears in a window and disappears almost immediately. If your compiler does not have a built-in feature to pause the output, you can include an additional input statement at the end of your program to cause execution to pause. Examples are available on the Web site mentioned above.

- Sending output to a printer also varies among compilers and among operating systems. Examples are available on the Web site mentioned above.

- The Web site of the company that developed the compiler you are using is a good resource. Links to the major compiler developers are available at the Web address above.

APPENDIX J

AP CLASS QUICK REFERENCES

This appendix contains quick references for the five AP Classes, along with simple code examples.

String Class Quick Reference

Purpose: The string class provides easy-to-use, safe strings for your programs.

Required Header File

```
#include "apstring.h"
```

To Instanciate a String Object

```
apstring MyString1;                    // instanciate empty string object
apstring MyString2("Hello, World!");   // initialize while instanciating
```

To Obtain the Length of a String

```
length = MyString2.length();
```

To Find First Occurrence of One String within Another

The statement below returns the character position of the first occurrence of the string Wor in the MyString2 object and stores it in the variable named location. If the string is not found, the function returns –1.

```
location = MyString2.find("Wor");
```

To Find First Occurrence of a Character within the String

The statement below returns the character position of the first occurrence of the character W in the MyString2 object and stores it in the variable named location. If the string is not found, the function returns –1.

```
location = MyString2.find('W');
```

To Return a Substring of Characters from the String

The substr function allows you to specify a starting position and the number of characters you wish to copy from the string. The substring is returned as a string and can be assigned to another string object. In the example below, five characters are copied from MyString2, beginning at position zero. The new string of five characters is assigned to the MyString1 object.

```
MyString1 = MyString2.substr(0, 5);
```

Assigning Values to Strings

You can assign the contents of one string to another.

```
MyString1 = MyString2;
```

You can assign a string literal to a string object.

```
MyString1 = "string literal";
```

You can assign a character literal to a string object.

```
MyString1 = 'A';
```

Indexing Characters in a String Object

You can set the characters of the string individually.

```
MyString1[0] = 'B';
```

You can retrieve the characters of the string individually.

```
ch = MyString1[0];
```

String Object I/O

You can display the contents of a string object using cout.

```
cout << MyString1 << endl;
```

You can prompt for a string using cin, but no spaces or tabs are allowed.

```
cout << "Please enter a string ( no spaces or tabs please ): ";
cin  >> MyString1;
```

You can prompt for a string using a function called `getline`. The `getline` function accepts spaces and tabs.

```
cout << "Please enter another string ( spaces and tabs are ok ): ";
getline(cin, MyString1);
```

Comparing Strings

You can use the standard relational operators to compare string objects.

```
YesNo = (MyString1 == MyString2);   // equal to
YesNo = (MyString1 != MyString2);   // not equal to
YesNo = (MyString1 <  MyString2);   // less than
YesNo = (MyString1 <= MyString2);   // less than or equal to
YesNo = (MyString1 >  MyString2);   // greater than
YesNo = (MyString1 >= MyString2);   // greater than or equal to
```

String Concatenation

String concatenation is most flexible when you use the compound operator. You can concatenate a string object, a string literal, a character variable, or a character literal to the string.

```
MyString1 += MyString2;
MyString1 += "string literal";
MyString1 += ch;
MyString1 += 'A';
```

Using the + operator, you can add two string objects together, or add a character on either end of the string.

```
MyString3 = MyString1 + MyString2;
MyString1 = 'A' + MyString2;
MyString1 = MyString2 + 'Z';
```

Vector Class Quick Reference

Purpose: The vector class provides easy-to-use, safe one-dimensional arrays for your programs.

Required Header File

```
#include "apvector.h"
```

To Instanciate a Vector Object

Because the vector class is a template class, you must specify a data type when declaring the vector object.

```
apvector <int> MyVector;          // instanciate empty vector object
```

You can declare a vector and specify the number of elements the vector should contain.

```
apvector <int> MyVector(100);     // a vector with 100 elements
```

You can instanciate a vector and specify the size and a value with which to initialize each element. In the example below, `MyVector` is initialized with 100 elements, each holding the value 1.

```
apvector <int> MyVector(100,1); // vector with 100 elements set to 1
```

To Obtain the Length of a Vector

You can determine the number of elements in the vector using the `length` function.

```
length = MyVector.length();
```

To Resize a Vector

You can specify a new size for the vector using the resize function. Keep in mind that shortening the vector can result in lost data.

```
MyVector.resize(50);
```

Indexing Elements in a Vector

You can set the elements of the vector individually.

```
MyVector[5] = 3;
```

You can retrieve the elements of the vector individually.

```
value = MyVector[10];
```

Assigning One Vector to Another

You can assign the contents of one vector to another. The vector receiving the contents of the other is resized.

```
MyVector1 = MyVector2;
```

Matrix Class Quick Reference

Purpose: The matrix class provides easy-to-use, safe two-dimensional arrays for your programs.

Required Header File

```
#include "apmatrix.h"
```

To Instanciate a Matrix Object

Because the matrix class is a template class, you must specify a data type when declaring the matrix object.

```
apmatrix <float> MyFloatMatrix;  // instanciate a matrix with size 0 x 0
```

You can declare a matrix and specify the size in rows and columns. The example below declares a matrix with 3 rows and 2 columns.

```
apmatrix <char> CharMatrix(3,2);
```

You can declare a matrix and specify the size and a value with which to initialize each element. In the example below, MyMatrix is initialized with 4 rows and 3 columns, each holding the value 0.

```
apmatrix <int> MyMatrix(4,3,0);
```

To Obtain the Size of a Matrix

You can determine the number of rows in the matrix using the numrows function.

```
rows = MyMatrix.numrows();
```

You can determine the number of columns in the matrix using the numcols function.

```
columns = MyMatrix.numcols();
```

To Resize a Matrix

You can specify a new size for the matrix using the `resize` function. Keep in mind that resizing the matrix can result in lost data. The example below resizes the matrix to have 5 rows and 7 columns.

```
MyMatrix.resize(5,7);
```

Indexing Elements in a Matrix

You can set the elements of the matrix individually. The example below sets the element in the first row of the second column to 3.

```
MyMatrix[1][2] = 3;
```

You can retrieve the elements of the matrix individually. The example below retrieves the value of the element in the third row of the second column.

```
value = MyMatrix[3][2];
```

Assigning One Matrix to Another

You can assign the contents of one matrix to another. The matrix receiving the contents of the other is resized.

```
MyMatrix1 = MyMatrix2;
```

Stack Class Quick Reference

Purpose: The stack class provides an easy-to-use, last-in first-out data structure for your programs.

Required Header File

```
#include "apstack.h"
```

To Instanciate a Stack Object

Because the stack class is a template class, you must specify a data type when instanciating the stack object.

```
apstack <float> MyStack;  // instanciate a stack of floating-point values
```

To Push an Item on the Stack

You can push an item on the stack using the `push` function.

```
MyStack.push(value);
```

To Pop an Item Off the Stack

You can pop an item off the stack using the `pop` function.

```
MyStack.pop(value);
```

To Get the Value of the Top Element without Popping

You can get a copy of the item at the top of the stack without removing it from the stack using the top function.

```
value = MyStack.top();
```

To Determine If the Stack Is Empty

You can determine whether the stack is currently empty using the isEmpty function.

```
empty = MyStack.isEmpty();
```

To Obtain the Size of the Stack

You can determine the number of elements in the stack using the length function.

```
size = MyStack.length();
```

To Empty the Stack

You can empty the stack using the makeEmpty function.

```
MyStack.makeEmpty();
```

Assigning One Stack to Another

You can assign the contents of one stack to another. The overloaded operator can be used to copy a stack.

```
MyStack1 = MyStack2;
```

Queue Class Quick Reference

Purpose: The queue class provides an easy-to-use, first-in first-out data structure for your programs.

Required Header File

```
#include "apqueue.h"
```

To Instanciate a Queue Object

Because the queue class is a template class, you must specify a data type when instanciating the queue object.

```
apqueue <float> MyQueue;   // instanciate a queue of floating-point values
```

To Place an Item in the Queue

You can place an item in the queue using the enqueue function.

```
MyQueue.enqueue(value);
```

To Remove an Item from the Queue

You can remove an item from the queue using the dequeue function.

```
MyQueue.dequeue(value);
```

To Get the Value at the Front of the Queue without Removing It

You can get a copy of the item at the front of the queue without removing it from the queue using the front function.

```
value = MyQueue.front();
```

To Determine Whether the Queue Is Empty

You can determine whether the queue is currently empty using the isEmpty function. The isEmpty function returns a value of type bool.

```
empty = MyQueue.isEmpty();
```

To Obtain the Size of the Queue

You can determine the number of elements in the queue using the length function.

```
size = MyQueue.length();
```

To Empty the Queue

You can empty the queue using the makeEmpty function.

```
MyQueue.makeEmpty();
```

Assigning One Queue to Another

You can assign the contents of one queue to another. The overloaded operator can be used to copy a queue.

```
MyQueue1 = MyQueue2;
```

APPENDIX K

ANALYSIS OF ALGORITHMS

How Algorithms Are Analyzed

The efficiency and speed of algorithms can be mathematically analyzed to help programmers design and implement programs. Analysis can show which algorithms are best for particular applications. For example, a programmer may want to know which sorting algorithm is best to use before writing a sorting function for a database program.

Algorithms can be analyzed for both execution time and memory space. When computer memory was very expensive, it was more important to find algorithms that used little memory space. Today, computer memory is relatively inexpensive, so programmers usually focus on finding the fastest algorithms.

The standard method of algorithm time analysis involves finding out how many steps an algorithm needs to complete. The more steps needed, the more time the algorithm takes to execute. Analysis is not always easy because many algorithms use different numbers of steps each time they are executed. Some sorting algorithms require fewer steps if the list being sorting is fully or partially sorted to begin with. The size of the input usually affects execution time more than any other factor. In fact, in algorithm time analysis, the primary concern is finding out how changes in input size affect performance.

For the purposes of our analysis, only the worst case will be taken into consideration. The worst case is when the input data for an algorithm is in the worst possible state. For example, the worst case for many ascending sorting functions is when data starts out in descending order. We focus on the worst case because it is often fairly close to the average case.

At times, it is interesting to discover the average case and the best case. However, the average case and best case do not guarantee anything about performance. By knowing the worst case, you have a guarantee that the algorithm cannot get any slower than the worst case.

Big-O Notation

A common way to refer to the running time of an algorithm is with big-O notation. A big-O equation shows how the input size effects an algorithm's running time in the worst case. For example, the big-O running time for the bubble sort is $O(n^2)$. This equation tells us that the running time grows quadratically relative to the input size. This means that when the input size for a bubble sort function doubles, the running time will quadruple (be about four times as long). If an algorithm's big-O running time is $O(1)$, then the running time is the same regardless of the input size. Some very slow algorithms have a big-O running time of $O(2^n)$, which means the running time grows exponentially relative to the input size.

ANALYZING THE SEQUENTIAL SEARCH

Consider the sequential search function shown in Figure K-1. If the value in `key` is found in the array, then 1 is returned, otherwise 0 is returned. To the right of each line of code is a comment giving the number of times the statement is executed in the worst case (the worst case for the sequential search is when `key` is not found at all).

FIGURE K-1

This sequential search function can be analyzed easily.

```
int sequential_search(int array[], int array_length, int key)
{
    int i;
    for ( i = 0;              // 1 time
          i < array_length;   // array_length + 1 times
          i++)                // array_length times
    {
          if (array[i] == key) // array_length times
                return 1;      // 0 times
    }
    return 0;                  // 1 time
}
```

If the array length is represented by the variable n, the total number of steps in the worst case is $(1) + (n + 1) + (n) + (n) + (0) + (1)$. Simplified, the number of steps is $3n + 3$. Because we are analyzing the sequential search algorithm in general and not any particular implementation, we can ignore the specific constants and rewrite the equation as $k_1 n + k_2$. The constants referred to as k_1 and k_2 can change depending on how the sequential search algorithm is coded, so we are not concerned with their values.

The big-O notation for the sequential search running time is $O(n)$. The constants k_1 and k_2 do not need to be written because they are implicitly part of big-O notation. The particular value $O(n)$ indicates that the running time grows linearly relative to the input size. If the input size for the sequential search doubles, the running time will also double.

ANALYZING THE BINARY SEARCH

The binary search function shown in Figure K-2 is longer than the sequential search function, but it can search much more quickly through sorted arrays. The sequential search is more versatile because it can search through any array, regardless of the order of the elements. The binary search requires the input array to be sorted, but can operate much quicker because of its divide and conquer strategy.

The total number of steps in the worst case of the binary search function is $(1) + (\log_2 n + 1) + (\log_2 n) + (\log_2 n) / 2 + (\log_2 n) / 2 + (\log_2 n) + (1) + (0) + (1)$. Simplified, the number of steps is $4 (\log_2 n) + 4$. Ignoring the specific values of the constants, this can be rewritten as $k_1 (\log_2 n) + k_2$.

In big-O notation, the running time for the binary search is $O(\log_2 n)$. The term $\log_2 n$ is used because the number of steps grows logarithmically. The binary search works by repeatedly halving the list until the element is found or the entire list is eliminated. If we were to search through an array with 16 elements, then the search would cut the list to 8, 4, 2, then finally 1 element. That means that there are 4 iterations total (the list is cut in half during each iteration). When n is 16, $\log_2 n$ equals 4 (and $2^4 = 16$), which shows that the number of iterations grows logarithmically relative to the input size. If we had 64 elements to search through, the list would be cut to 32, 16, 8, 4, 2, and 1 element after each of 6 iterations. This is shown by the equations $\log_2 64 = 6$ and $2^6 = 64$.

The binary search algorithm is efficient when searching a sorted array.

```
int binary_search(int array[], int lowerbound, intupperbound, int key)
{
    int search_pos;

    search_pos = (lowerbound + upperbound) / 2;        // 1 time

    while((array[search_pos] != key)
          && (lowerbound <= upperbound)                // log₂n + 1 times
    {
            if (array[search_pos] > key)               // log₂n times
                upperbound = search_pos - 1;           // (log₂n) / 2times
            else
                lowerbound = search_pos + 1;           // (log₂n) / 2times

            search_pos = (lowerbound + upperbound) / 2; // log₂n times
    }
    if (lowerbound <= upperbound)                      // 1 time
            return 1;                                  // 0 times
    else
            return 0;                                  // 1 time

}
```

It is easy to see the efficiency difference between sequential and binary searches for different input sizes. When the input size n is 4, the binary search is only twice as fast as the sequential search. When n is 256, the binary search is 32 times faster. Remember that this only applies to sorted lists, because the binary search is unable to search through unsorted lists.

Search Algorithm	Big-O	$n = 4$	$n = 16$	$n = 256$
Sequential	$O(n)$	4	16	256
Binary	$O(\log_2 n)$	2	4	8

ANALYZING SORTING ALGORITHMS

The following table summarizes the big-O running times of some common sorting algorithms. Incremental comparison-based sorting algorithms usually run in $O(n^2)$ time, while divide-and-conquer sorting algorithms usually have an $O(n \log_2 n)$ running time. Different implementations of these algorithms may yield different big-O running times.

Sorting Algorithm	Big-O	$n = 4$	$n = 128$
Selection	$O(n^2)$	16	16,384
Insertion	$O(n^2)$	16	16,384
Bubble	$O(n^2)$	16	16,384
Shell	$O(n^2)$	16	16,384
Quick	$O(n \log_2 n)$	8	896
Merge	$O(n \log_2 n)$	8	896

GLOSSARY

++ operator A C++ operator that increments an integer.

-- operator A C++ operator that decrements an integer.

A

Address-of operator An operator that returns the "address of" the variable rather than the contents of the variable.

Algorithm A set of sequential instructions that are followed to solve a problem.

Allocate To reserve computer memory.

American Standard Code for Information Interchange (ASCII) A code most computers use to assign a number to each character. The numbers are used to represent the characters internally.

Ancestors A node's ancestors are the nodes that link it to the root.

Appending The process of adding data to the end of an existing file.

Argument Data passed to a function.

Arithmetic operators Operators that perform math operations such as addition, subtraction, multiplication, and division.

Array A group of variables of the same data type that appear together in the computer's memory.

Ascending order Arranged from A to Z or smallest to largest.

Assembly language A programming language that uses letters and numbers to represent machine-language instructions.

Assignment operator An operator (=) that changes the value of the variable to the left of the operator.

Automatic variable A variable declared within a function that is accessible only within that function (a *local* variable).

B

Balance The arrangement of nodes in a tree.

Binary search A search that works by starting in the middle and narrowing the search in a way similar to the way you search for a name in a phone book.

Binary tree A tree structure that allows only two branches from each node.

Boolean variable A variable that can have only two possible variables: true or false.

Bottom-up design A program design method that involves beginning at the bottom of the VTOC (Visual Table of Contents) and working up.

Braces Special characters used to mark the beginning and ending of blocks of code.

Branch A link from one node in a tree to another.

Branch nodes Nodes on a tree that have branches (also called *nonterminal* nodes).

Bubble sort An incremental sort that repeatedly compares adjacent elements of an array, starting with the first and second elements, and swapping them if they are out of order.

C

Case sensitive A characteristic of the C++ language that provides for the interpretation of uppercase and lowercase letters differently.

Characters The letters and symbols available for use by a computer.

Children The one or two nodes below a given node (also called *offspring*).

Circularly-linked list A linked list in which the last node's next pointer points back to the first node.

Close The final step of using a data file.

Collision In hashing, the condition where two key values produce the same result.

Comments Remarks in a program that are ignored by the compiler.

Compiler A program that translates a high-level language into machine language, then saves the machine language so that the instructions do not have to be translated each time the program is run.

Compiler directive Commands for the compiler, which are needed to effectively compile the program.

Concatenation Adding one string onto the end of another string.

Console I/O Using the screen and keyboard for input and output (I/O is an abbreviation of input/output).

Constant Stores data that remains the same throughout a program's execution.

Constructors Tell the compiler how to create an object in memory and what the initial values of its data will be.

Containment The term used to describe a has-a relationship among classes.

Control expression An expression that provides for a decision to be made in an if statement or to end a loop.

D

Data type A specification that defines the type of data that can be stored in a variable or constant.

Deallocating Returning memory to the heap for use by other data.

Declaring Indicating to the compiler what type of variable you want and its name or identifier.

Decrementing Subtracting 1 from a variable.

Dequeue To remove from a queue.

Dereferencing operator An operator for declaring pointers and returning the value in a variable pointed to by a pointer.

Descendants The nodes linked below a node in a tree.

Descending order Arranged from Z to A or largest to smallest.

Divide and conquer approach A sorting method that repeatedly breaks the unsorted list down into smaller lists until each small list is sorted.

Division-remainder method A hashing algorithm that involves dividing the key value by a prime or odd number and using the remainder of the division as the relative address for the second.

do while loop An iteration structure that repeats a statement or group of statements as long as a control expression is true at the end of the loop.

Dot operator The operator used to access the members of a structure.

Doubly-linked list A linked list in which each node has a pointer linking it to the next node and the previous node.

E

"E" notation *See* Exponential notation.

Elements Variables in an array.

Encapsulation The "hiding" of data and code inside an object.

Enqueue To place in a queue.

enum A keyword that allows the creation of enumerated data types.

End-of-line character *See* New line character

Executable file The output of a linker that can be executed without the need for an interpreter.

Exit condition The condition which must be met to end recursive calls.

Exponential notation A method of representing very large and very small numbers (also called *scientific notation*).

Expression A math statement made up of terms, operators, and functions.

External sort A sort that sorts data in a file, rather than in RAM.

External variable A variable declared before the main function which is accessible by any function (global variable).

Extraction operator The operator that outputs data to a stream.

F

Field width The width of a formatting field when using the I/O manipulators.

Fields Data items that make up a record.

File streams Objects that provide a data path to a file.

First-in first-out (FIFO) A data structure in which the first data put into the structure is the first data to be taken out.

Floating-point number A number that includes a decimal point.

Flowchart A diagram made up of symbols used to illustrate an algorithm.

for loop An iteration structure that repeats one or more statements a specified number of times.

Free To return memory to the heap for use by other data.

Function A block of code that carries out a specific task.

Fuzzy logic A logic system that allows for true, false, and variations in between.

G

Global variable A variable declared before the main function and accessible by any function.

Graphical user interface (GUI) A system for interacting with the computer user through pictures or icons.

H

has-a relationship The relationship between classes where one class contains another class.

Hashing A search method that processes the key through a hashing algorithm to find the position of the data in a file.

Hashing algorithm An algorithm used when hashing to convert the key to a number that corresponds to the position of the record.

Header file A file that serves as a link between the program code and standard C++ code that is needed to make the program run.

Heap The portion of memory in which dynamic data structures are stored.

High-level language A programming language in which instructions do not necessarily correspond with the instruction set of the microprocessor.

I

I/O manipulators A set of format options available in C++ that may be placed directly in the output statement.

Identifier Names given to variables and constants.

if structure A programming structure that executes code if certain conditions are met.

if/else structure A programming structure that executes one block of code if certain conditions are met and another block of code if the same conditions are not met.

Incremental approach A sorting algorithm characterized by loops that pass through a list, one element at a time.

Incrementing Adding 1 to a variable.

Infinite loop An iteration structure in which iterations continue indefinitely.

Information hiding Data protection that is an important benefit of encapsulation.

Inheritance The ability of one object to inherit the properties of another object.

Initialize To assign a value to a variable.

In-order traversal A tree traversal that visits all the nodes of a tree in their sorted order.

Input size The number of elements in a list to be sorted.

Input stream A stream used to receive input.

Insertion operator The operator that gets data from a stream and puts it into a variable.

Insertion sort An incremental sort in which the elements are arranged in a similar manner to a hand of cards.

Instance The data for one object which has been created in memory that has the behaviors defined by the class.

Integer A whole number.

Interpreter A program that translates the source code of a high-level language into machine language.

is-a relationship The relationship where one object inherits characteristics from another class.

Iteration A single loop or pass through a group of statements.

Iteration structures Programming structures that repeat a group of statements one or more times (loops).

K

Key The value by which the data in a tree is sorted or searched or data in a data structure is searched.

Key field The field upon which a search algorithm or the sorting of data is based.

Key value The value in a key field.

Keywords Words that cannot be used as identifiers because they are part of the C++ language.

L

Last-in first-out (LIFO) A data structure in which the last data in is the first data out.

Leaf nodes Nodes of a tree that do not have branches (also called *terminal nodes*).

Left child The node attached to the left of the node above.

Levels A way of identifying the depth of a tree.

Library functions Functions that come with your compiler.

Linear data structure A data structure in which the elements of nodes are arranged in a line.

Linked list A data structure that allows data to be stored in a list in which memory is assigned to your data as it is needed.

Linker A program that links object files created by a compiler into an executable program.

Literals Hard-coded values.

Local variable A variable declared within a function which is accessible only within that function.

Logical operators Operators that allow *and*, *or*, and *not* to be implemented as part of logical expressions.

Loop A programming structure that repeats a group of statements one or more times.

Lowercase The non-capital (small) letters of the alphabet.

Low-level language A programming language in which each instruction corresponds to one or only a few microprocessor instructions.

M

Machine language The programming language (made up of ones and zeros) that a microprocessor understands.

main function The function where every C++ program begins.

Member functions Allow programmers using an object to send information to an object and receive information from an object.

Members The functions and variables in a class definition.

Menu A set of options presented to the user of a program.

Merge sort An algorithm that repeatedly merges smaller sorted lists into larger ones.

Message In object-oriented programming, the method used to transfer data.

Method Code inside an object that is necessary to perform the operations on the object.

Modulus operator The operator that provides integer division.

N

Nested loop A loop within a loop.

Nested structure A structure within a structure.

New line character The end-of-line character.

Node The structure that contains the data in a linked list or tree.

Nonlinear data structure A data structure in which the elements or nodes do not appear in a line (a *tree*).

Nonterminal nodes Nodes on a tree that have branches (also called *branch nodes*).

Null pointer A pointer variable with a value of zero.

O

Object code The machine-language code produced by a compiler.

Object file The file produced by a compiler that contains machine language code.

Object-oriented paradigm A way of programming where data and operations are seen as existing together in objects that are similar to objects in the real world.

Object-oriented programming Building programs using the object-oriented paradigm.

Offspring The one or two nodes below a given node (also called *children*).

One-way selection structure A selection structure in which the decision is whether to go "one way" or just bypass the code in the if structure.

Open The operation that associates a physical disk file with a file pointer so that data in the file may be accessed.

Operating system The program in charge of the fundamental system operations.

Order of operations The rules governing the order in which operations (such as math operations) are performed.

Overflow The condition where an integer becomes too large for its data type.

P

Paradigm A model or set of rules that defines a way of programming.

Parallel vectors Two or more vectors that are indexed with the same variable.

Parameter The variable that receives the value or any other identifier in the parentheses of the function declaration.

Parent The node above a given node to which the given node is linked.

Partitions Sections used in some sorting algorithms.

Pass To send an argument to a function.

Passing by reference A method of passing variables in which any changes made to the variables are passed back to the calling function.

Passing by value A method of passing variables in which a copy of the value in the variable is given to the function for it to use.

Pointer A variable or constant that holds a memory address.

Pop To remove an item from a stack.

Postorder traversal A tree traversal that visits the left node first, then the right node, then the root.

Preorder traversal A tree traversal that visits the root first, then the left node, then the right node.

Procedural paradigm A way of programming that focuses on the idea that all algorithms in a program are performed with functions and data that a programmer can see, understand, and change.

Programming language A language that provides a way to program computers using instructions that can be understood by computers and people.

Promotion The condition in which the data type of one variable is temporarily converted to match the data type of another variable so that a math operation can be performed using the mixed data type.

Prototype A statement that defines the function for the compiler.

Push To add an item to a stack.

Q

Queue A data structure that allows additions at only one end (called the rear of the queue) and deletions at the opposite end (called the front of the queue).

Quicksort A sorting algorithm that uses a divide and conquer approach and works by repeatedly breaking the list into partitions until each partition contains a single element.

Quotient Quantity that results when one number is divided by another.

R

Random-access file A data file that allows you to move directly to any data in the file.

Recursion A programming technique in which a function calls itself.

Relational operators Operators used to make comparisons.

Remainder Quantity remaining when one number does not divide evenly into another.

Reusability Using an object again after it has been coded and tested.

Right child The node attached to the right of the node above.

Root The node at the top of a tree from which all nodes in the tree descend.

S

Scope The availability of a variable to functions.

Scope-resolution operator The operator that separates the class name and the function name in a member function.

Selection sort A sorting algorithm that uses an incremental approach. After the first pass through the list, the element with the largest key value is sorted. After each successive pass, the next largest element is put in its proper position until all elements are sorted.

Selection structures Structures that allow for logical decisions in C++ programs.

Sequence structures Structures that execute statements one after another without changing the flow of a program.

Sequential search A search technique in which each record in the database is compared in the order it appears until the desired record is found.

Sequential-access file A file with which you must start at the beginning and search each record to find the one you want.

Shell sort A sorting algorithm that compares elements **d** positions away from each other. **d** initially is equal to half the length of the list and is halved after each iteration.

Short-circuit evaluation A feature of C++ that allows the program to stop evaluating an expression as soon as the outcome of the expression is known.

Siblings Two nodes with the same parent.

Singly-linked list A linked list in which the pointers link the nodes in only one direction.

Sorting The process of arranging the items in a data structure in a specified order.

Source code A program in the form of a high-level language.

Special character A character that extends the normal alphanumeric characters.

Stack A data structure that allows items to be added and deleted from only one end.

Standard input device The default input device, usually the keyboard.

Standard output device The default output device, usually the screen.

Statement Line of C++ code. Statements end with a semicolon.

Stream Data flowing from one place to another.

Stream operation modes A mode that specifies the way you want to access the file.

String A group of characters put together to make one or more words.

String class An object-oriented class that allows strings to be included in programs.

String object An object for storing and processing strings.

Structure A C++ data structure that allows variables to be grouped to form a new data type.

Structure pointer operator The operator (->) used to access individual members of a dynamically-allocated structure.

Structure variable A variable that is a member of a structure.

Subscript An index value that accesses an element of an array.

Subtree Any node with branches extending below it.

Switch structure A selection structure capable of handling multiple options.

T

Template class A class that can be used with any data type.

Terminal nodes Nodes of a tree that do not have branches (also called *leaf nodes*).

Top-down design A program design method in which the general organization and flow of the program is decided before the details are coded.

Truncate To drop the digits to the right of the decimal point, without rounding the value.

Truth tables Diagrams that show the result of logical operations.

Two-way selection structure A selection structure in which one block of code is executed if the control expression is true and another block is executed if the control expression is false.

Typecast operator An operator that forces the data type of a variable to change.

Typecasting Changing the data type of a variable using a typecast operator.

U

Underflow The condition that occurs when a value becomes too small for a variable to hold accurately.

Uppercase The capital letters of the alphabet.

V

Variable Holds data that can change while the program is running.

Vector A one-dimensional array of any data type.

W

while loop An iteration structure that repeats a statement or group of statements as long as a control expression is true.

INDEX

W

Z